Pre-publication REVIEWS, COMMENTARIES, EVALUATIONS . . .

"This timely text argues that exposure to traumatic events can both precipitate and exacerbate many common childhood disorders and manifest in adolescence in a variety of conduct problems. Without taking a proper trauma history and directly addressing the effects of such trauma, most contemporary therapy approaches are doomed to fail. Children and adolescents deserve effective, evidence-based interventions, and this text blends findings from motivational interviewing, trauma-focused cognitive-behavior therapy, and EMDR in a practical, sensitive, and client-acceptable way.

The text results from many years of creative clinical work with children and adolescents. The active style developed with children is replicated in the workshops devised for therapist, and the text can be used as a basis for peer-group learning. It is strongly recommended for all child mental health therapists who are truly dedicated to making a difference to the lives of young people."

—William Yule, PhD, FBPsS
Professor of Applied Child Psychology, Institute of Psychiatry, King's College, London;
Consultant Clinical Psychologist, South London and Maudsley NHS Trust

"The *Child Trauma Handbook* is a practical guide to trauma-informed therapy with children and teens and the families who care for them (who may be traumatized themselves). Written to accompany training on the topic, all practitioners will find this book easy to read and apply immediately."

—Charles Figley, PhD
Director, Florida State University Traumatology Institute

"This is a fascinating book on how to respectfully approach and treat traumatized children. But it is so much more; it shows how to build on underlying health and strengths in both children and their caretakers. It is a well of clinical wisdom presented in a user-friendly step-by-step frame. It is an empowering book!"

—Atle Dyregrov, PhD
Founder, Center for Crisis Psychology, Bergen, Norway

"The past three decades have seen dramatic changes in our understanding of child development and our conceptual and methodological tools for dealing with childhood problems. One of the most important of these changes is our growing appreciation for the central role played by trauma in the lives of troubled kids. Dr. Greenwald's *Child Trauma Handbook* is a major contribution to these efforts. In language that is clear and accessible to a wide range of clinician-practitioners, he has translated research and theory into comprehensible and pragmatic tactics for recognizing and dealing with the developmental consequences of trauma in the lives of children. He exposes the gaps in traditional therapeutic approaches as well as in 'common sense' when it comes to an effective response to child trauma. His approach is respectful, both toward the child client and the adults in that child's life. Grounded in his understanding of the research on trauma and his clinical experience, he offers up a powerful learning experience for the reader."

—James Garbarino, PhD
E. L. Vincent Professor of Human Development, Cornell University

NOTES FOR PROFESSIONAL LIBRARIANS AND LIBRARY USERS

This is an original book title published by The Haworth Maltreatment and Trauma Press® and The Haworth Reference Press™, imprints of The Haworth Press, Inc. Unless otherwise noted in specific chapters with attribution, materials in this book have not been previously published elsewhere in any format or language.

CONSERVATION AND PRESERVATION NOTES

All books published by The Haworth Press, Inc. and its imprints are printed on certified pH neutral, acid-free book grade paper. This paper meets the minimum requirements of American National Standard for Information Sciences-Permanence of Paper for Printed Material, ANSI Z39.48-1984.

Child Trauma Handbook

A Guide for Helping Trauma-Exposed Children and Adolescents

Child Trauma Handbook
A Guide for Helping Trauma-Exposed Children and Adolescents

Ricky Greenwald, PsyD

The Haworth Maltreatment and Trauma Press®
The Haworth Reference Press™
Imprints of The Haworth Press, Inc.
New York • London • Oxford

For more information on this book or to order, visit
http://www.haworthpress.com/store/product.asp?sku=5506

or call 1-800-HAWORTH (800-429-6784) in the United States and Canada
or (607) 722-5857 outside the United States and Canada

or contact orders@HaworthPress.com

Published by

The Haworth Maltreatment and Trauma Press® and The Haworth Reference Press™, imprints of The Haworth Press, Inc., 10 Alice Street, Binghamton, NY 13904-1580.

PUBLISHER'S NOTE
Identities and circumstances of individuals discussed in this book have been changed to protect confidentiality.

AUTHOR'S NOTE
The author gives permission for forms and exercises to be copied and used freely by the reader in his or her practice setting.

Cover design by Jennifer M. Gaska.

TR: 8.9.05

Library of Congress Cataloging-in-Publication Data

Greenwald, Ricky.
Child trauma handbook : a guide for helping trauma-exposed children and adolescents / Ricky Greenwald.
p. cm.
Includes bibliographical references and index.
ISBN-13: 978-0-7890-2793-1 (pbk. : alk. paper)
ISBN-10: 0-7890-2793-3 (pbk. : alk. paper)
1. Psychic trauma in children—Treatment—Handbooks, manuals, etc. 2. Psychic trauma in adolescence—Treatment—Handbooks, manuals, etc. 3. Post-traumatic stress disorder in children—Treatment—Handbooks, manuals, etc. 4. Post-traumatic stress disorder in adolescence—Treatment—Handbooks, manuals, etc. I. Title.
[DNLM: 1. Stress Disorders, Post-Traumatic—therapy—Adolescent. 2. Stress Disorders, Post-Traumatic—therapy—Child. WM 170 G816c 2005]

RJ506.P66G74 2005
618.92'8521—dc22

2005001042

CONTENTS

ABOUT THE AUTHOR

Ricky Greenwald, PsyD, is the founder and Executive Director of the Child Trauma Institute. He was previously Assistant Clinical Professor of Psychiatry and Director of Training for the child trauma program at Mount Sinai School of Medicine in New York City. Dr. Greenwald is the author of numerous professional articles as well as several books, including *EMDR in Child & Adolescent Psychotherapy* (1999) and *Trauma and Juvenile Delinquency* (Haworth, 2002). His work has been translated into over a dozen languages. Dr. Greenwald, a clinical psychologist, has been working with children, adolescents, and their families since 1985.

Acknowledgments

I first acknowledge those who have taught me, mentored me, and invested in my professional development as a therapist and child trauma specialist. In chronological order: Tod Rossi, Deborah Roose, Cheryl Keen, Larry Allman, Jim Bibb, Claude Chemtob, and Nancy Smyth. Thanks to each of you for your friendship and guidance. You may not be able to tell, but something I learned from each of you is in here.

Thanks to Karen Johnston, who was such a strong source of personal support while this book was being developed and written. Thanks also to Hannah Greenwald, who provided encouragement and food in the final stretch.

Thanks to Esther Giller of the Sidran Institute. She approached me with the idea for this book—it's changed by now, of course!—and told me that I was the person to write it. If not for Esther's initiative, this book would probably not have been written.

Thanks also to the following individuals, who each reviewed a draft of the book and provided helpful feedback: Margaret Blaustein, Cristina Casanova, Susan Etkind, Denise Houston, Rebecca Hubbard, Nancy Knudsen, Naomi Kramer, Noemi Levi, Veronica Picone Matuk, Karen Nash, Angela O'Rawe, Lori Rockmore, Bart Rubin, Oliver Schubbe, and Beth Venart.

Thanks of course to all of the kids and families I've worked with over the years. Gotta learn somehow! I hope you've gotten as much out of it as I have.

Finally, thanks to my supervisees and to those who attended the workshops, seminars, and training programs on which this book is based. All those detailed evaluations I asked you to complete really did make a difference.

Introduction

Many sincere, hardworking people out there really care about kids. I hope you're one of them.

A great deal of knowledge has been developed about kids who have been exposed to trauma and/or loss—knowledge about what kids experience, how they can heal, and how to help them do it. These methods have been tested and proven effective. Unfortunately, most of this knowledge has been the province of specialists. The problem is, those specialists don't have your job.

The purpose of this book is to get this information to you, because you're the one who needs it to better help the kids you work with. I hope you will gain depth, specific skills, and grounding in your understanding of what to do with your kids, how to do it, when to do it, and why.

This book was designed as the text for a five-day course for mental health professionals, as well as for a two-day course for others who work with kids, including paraprofessionals, child care workers, foster parents, and others. Although the book can stand alone, you would get much more from the supervised practice of a live training experience. If you are on your own, I suggest that you act as if you're in a workshop and actually practice the exercises, ideally with one or more colleagues who are going through the book with you.

The book is based on programs I gave for widely divergent groups: open workshops attended by mental health professionals from around the world; weekly seminars for child psychiatry residents at Mount Sinai School of Medicine in New York City; workshops for school-based mental health professionals working for the New York City Department of Education after September 11; a course for undergraduate students at Hampshire College (Amherst, Massachusetts); and workshops for professional and direct care staff at Queen's Medical Center (Honolulu, Hawaii) Pediatric Department, Covenant Children's Home and Family Services (Princeton, Illinois), and Edgewood Children's Center (St. Louis, Missouri). On each occasion I asked for detailed feedback, and here's what I learned:

- All helping professionals want and need the big picture, even if they are not going to be personally responsible for each of the steps in treatment.
- When it comes to practical skills, people appreciate being given scripts for what to say and do. The next step is to actually use the scripts. This helps in the learning.
- Many participants already have considerable knowledge and skill. This training program/book does not negate that. Rather, it empowers individuals to use their skills more effectively, by providing a user-friendly model for knowing when to do what.
- This model applies to most distressed kids, even when trauma or loss is not identified as the presenting issue.
- This training program really works. Over and over I have seen people take this material and use it. Problem behaviors go down; grades go up. Kids get better. Not all of them, of course, but it seems to improve the odds.

I have also been working with colleagues to conduct research on this approach to training people in child/adolescent trauma treatment. So far, we have found the following:

- Following completion of the training, participants reported feeling better about their work and reported improved trauma treatment knowledge and competency (Greenwald, Stamm, Larsen, & Griffel, 2003).
- Following completion of a certain module of the training, participants reported feeling reduced distress when imagining themselves in a challenging work-related situation (Greenwald, Johnston, & Smyth, 2004).
- This finding has now been replicated and extended. We have gathered new data that shows that, following completion of a certain module of training, mental health professionals feel more caring and empathy when imagining a challenging acting-out client, and feel more comfort and confidence in their role as this client's therapist (Greenwald, Greenwald, & Smyth, 2005).
- By two months after a related training and consultation in an adolescent residential treatment facility, the monthly incident count (including assault, property destruction, and running away) decreased by at least 50 percent in every category, on all five units, compared to any of the six months prior to the training (Greenwald, 2003).

The model and methods seem to apply across class, ethnicity, culture, and language. Small glitches do occur when it comes to translation. People do sometimes tell me, "I had to change the script in one place to make it fit for the kids I work with." But they also consistently say, "This is working with my kids." In my mind, this is two kinds of good news. First, these comments suggest that these therapists have the sense and the skills to adapt the material to the culture of the kids and families with whom they're working. I don't teach this adaptability, but it's important to do it! Second, the comments suggest that the phase model of trauma-informed treatment, with emphases on safety, relationship, and empowerment, can be effective with trauma-exposed kids in any setting. I have already fielded requests to help start treatment and/or training centers based on this model in locations as diverse as Bangladesh, Burundi, California, Guatemala, India, Israel, and Northern Ireland.

HOW TRAUMA-INFORMED TREATMENT IS DIFFERENT

To do trauma-informed therapy well, it helps to already be a good therapist. Many of the skills and interventions are the same. Trauma-informed treatment is distinguished in part by the way standard interventions are informed by, and organized around, trauma theory. When we understand the way that past trauma may contribute to present-day problems, the treatment model guides us to specific strategies, specific ways of using our clinical skills, and sequencing our repertoire of interventions.

For example, parent training for consistent discipline is widely used in the treatment of children with disruptive behavior, typically with a learning theory rationale so that parents are taught to punish or disregard unwanted behaviors and reinforce wanted ones. In trauma-informed treatment, parent training is also used, with essentially the same techniques and rationale. However, additional rationale is also provided. The parent is told that the child's problem behavior is related to feeling unsafe and upset because of past trauma and that the acting-out behavior is a way of seeking external (parental) control, such discipline being interpreted by the child as reassurance that the parent is strong, in charge, and able to protect the child. Therefore, the parent can be an agent of healing by doing special things to help the child feel safe and secure. Thus, rather than implying that the "untrained" parent was the cause of the child's behavior problems (a risk in other treatment approaches), the parent is told that the child has a wound, entailing a special need that the parent can address. This rationale leads to increased sympathy for the child and to an active healing role for the parent. Both of these enhance the attachment that may have been disrupted not only by the trauma but by the child's rejection-inviting behavior problems.

Furthermore, this theory-driven treatment approach systematically utilizes parent training at a specific point in the course of treatment, in preparation for later treatment tasks. Other standard interventions are similarly incorporated, being implemented at specified points and using trauma-related rationale, to further the goals of the trauma treatment.

Finally, the "stance" of the therapist is authoritative and directive while also being collaborative, respectful, and, within certain limits, permissive, taking into account the special needs of the traumatized child. This differs from other therapy models in a variety of ways, for example:

- A psychiatrist might conduct an evaluation by reviewing a comprehensive list of possible symptoms, making a diagnosis, and then saying, "I can help you with your problem." This is based on the medical model of determining the diagnosis and offering treatment, with the implication that the "patient" is ill and the powerful doctor can effect a cure. The trauma therapist will not ask about the list of problems until first learning about the client and family's strengths. Then, after making a diagnosis, he or she will say, "I can help you help yourself." This conveys the belief that the client may be wounded but has underlying health and strength that can be enhanced and utilized for recovery, setting the stage for later strength-building treatment activities.
- A psychodynamic therapist might ask open-ended questions, be willing to sit with silences, and refuse to grant requests for judgment-laden opinions. The trauma therapist recognizes that each of these practices can tend to increase the child's anxiety in ways that are counterproductive for trauma treatment. The trauma therapist will help the child to feel successful by offering a menu of types of appropriate responses rather than allow the child to sit in silence, feel like a failure, or act out with a "don't know–don't care" attitude. The trauma therapist will provide frequent feedback and impressions so that the child does not have to wonder—and be afraid of—what the therapist might be thinking.
- A humanistic (or psychodynamic) therapist might encourage the child to disclose the details of the trauma memory and express related thoughts and feelings. A good session is characterized by the child's "opening up." The trauma therapist will actively prevent such opening up until the child has completed the preparatory tasks and is likely to be able to manage and contain the experience. Furthermore, the trauma therapist will make efforts to help the child "close down" and regain composure before ending the session, to assist with containment and self-control.
- A play (or art, psychodynamic, or humanistic) therapist might wait for the child to initiate disclosure and/or discussion of the trauma memory, on the principle that the child will bring it up when he or she is "ready." The trauma therapist will make the goal of trauma resolution explicit in the treatment contract and will lead the child to engage in a number of activities with the explicit goal of helping the child become ready to face the trauma. Later in treatment, the trauma therapist will help the child face the trauma in manageable doses. Even so, the child always retains the prerogative to stop; the trauma therapist is directive but not coercive.
- A cognitive-behavioral therapist might develop a functional/behavioral diagnosis and then offer a task-oriented treatment plan to help the child manage or overcome the symptoms. If the diagnosis is trauma related, the symptom-management activities may be followed by activities specific to desensitizing the trauma memory. The trauma therapist will do all of this too, but will first work on developing a supportive and empowering relationship, as well as mobilizing parents and others to engage in specific behaviors to support the child's recovery.

These therapy approaches were just presented in their traditional "pure" formats for the sake of contrast, whereas in practice many therapists integrate elements from a variety of therapy approaches. Indeed, the trauma therapy approach represents one such integration. Specific to the trauma therapy approach are the rationale and the theory-driven system, including a sequence of interventions that are borrowed from a variety of traditions. One workshop participant described this approach as "cognitive-behavioral with a relationship base and family systems interventions."

As you progress through the book learning the stages of trauma-informed treatment, many interventions will be familiar, but some may seem novel or even counterintuitive. For example, many therapists feel some initial discomfort with asking the child directly, as early as the second session, to disclose trauma/loss history. Many of the same therapists feel even more discomfort with asking the child not to disclose too much detail at that time, for those children who seem to be trying to tell the whole story on the spot. There are good reasons (that I'll explain along the way) for sticking to the trauma-informed treatment approach. So please keep your mind open and give it a try. Most therapists have reported that even interventions which they initially balked at worked out well with their clients. Remember, the goal is not merely to practice a favorite technique but to help the kids. Learning something new can be awkward at first, but that's what this book is for.

You'll be learning, step by step, a phase model of trauma treatment. That means that treatment tasks are done in a specific order for a specific reason. Don't let this step-by-step approach fool you. In real life, kids don't always go in order! In our work we are constantly reassessing, to figure out if our clients are still where we thought they were last week or even five minutes ago. Even so, having the phase model as a framework will help you know what to do at any given moment, providing that you are able to determine where your client is (within the phase model) in that moment.

HOW TO USE THE BOOK

This book is designed to teach you understanding, self-care practices, and intervention skills in a systematic way. The chapters are in their present order for a reason: each builds on what came before. Here's how I hope you'll use the book.

Mental Health Professionals

Those providing regular psychotherapy or counseling sessions to kids should read the whole book in order. The first five sections will take you through theory, therapeutic relationship, self-care, and the entire course of treatment. Section VI, "24/7," is focused on milieu treatment, so you may not be using skills from this section in your daily work. Still, you should be very familiar with the material in that section so that you can help parents, teachers, child care workers, youth counselors, and others to do their jobs as effectively as possible.

Others Who Work with Kids

These individuals, including child care workers/line staff, counselors, paraprofessionals, case workers, court personnel, shelter workers, and parents, should definitely read Section I and Section VI. Section I will help you understand the kids you work with, and will also explain the healing relationship, as well as self-care issues and skills for those who work with kids. Section I also provides an overview of how child trauma treatment helps kids recover from trauma and get their lives back on track, one step at a time. The more you understand about what the child's therapist is doing, the better you can work as a team. Section VI, "24/7," is focused on what to do with kids whom you are working or living with. It will help you understand how to create a safe and supportive environment; how to provide compassionate, effective discipline; how to motivate kids to try their hardest; and what to say to them when tricky situations arise. You might choose to read the rest of the book as well; it will give you more detail on what goes on during the therapy meetings.

Most chapters include at least one experiential exercise. If you came to learn skills, these exercises are a chance to try them out in a format carefully structured to help you learn. These exercises generally work best when you do them with others; many of the exercises that are focused on practicing an intervention can only be done with others. If you are going through the book on your own, you'll be able to do some of the exercises by yourself. Still, for the best learning, you should make an effort to try the interventions with kids or colleagues.

Some of the exercises involve using worksheets or forms. If you don't want to write in the book, take the trouble to make a good copy of the worksheets or forms. These forms have been used, and refined, with hundreds of workshop participants. Using the given format will help you to do well.

For easier reading, I have avoided cluttering the text with citations except where absolutely necessary. Still, it's important that you understand that the theories and methods taught in this book are solidly grounded in the scientific literature and that you know where to find this literature if you want to pursue it. At the end of each book section I've included a brief annotated bibliography. This provides the primary sources—or sometimes the classic sources—for the main topics covered in that section. The goal is not to provide an exhaustive literature review but only to give what I believe are the best examples of the sources of interest.

We still have not found a good pronoun that refers to both boys and girls. I just don't want to say "it" when I really mean "he or she"! So I've done my best to alternate pronouns, because the material in this book applies equally to both genders.

Finally, a comment about our professional community: Those of us who care about kids share both sadness and hope. It's important, for ourselves and for the kids, that the hope is paramount; it sustains us and allows us to persevere. So how can we keep hope alive and thriving? One way is to become more effective in our work, so that we achieve better results and have more reason to hope. This book can be one of your strategies. Another way is to share—the sadness, the hope, and the sense of mission—with one another. The sharing, the connection we have with one another, also sustains us and allows us to persevere.

You are here, and I take this as a gift. Thank you for joining me, for allowing me to share with you. I hope that your experience with this book will help you to become more effective and to find opportunities to share and connect with your colleagues as well.

SECTION I: UNDERSTANDING TRAUMA—A FRAMEWORK FOR ORGANIZING EXISTING SKILLS

To talk about helping trauma-exposed kids, we start with the basics: What is trauma? How does exposure to trauma affect kids? How can kids recover, heal, even grow, through dealing with their traumatic experiences? What does it take to be a person who can help kids through this process?

Section I lays the foundation for how to approach understanding and helping trauma-exposed kids. Perhaps some of the material in this section—and throughout the book—will be familiar to you. I hope you'll be learning new things here too, but the more you already know, the better. The goal here is to provide a framework, a systematic approach, through which you can use both existing and new skills. The trauma-informed treatment approach does not replace the activities and interventions you're already doing. Rather, it helps you to organize and sequence them for maximum effectiveness.

Chapter 1

Understanding Trauma

WHY TRAUMA MATTERS

If you are working with kids, chances are that you are trying to help them do better in some way: get in less trouble, do better at school, feel less angry or sad, not hurt people. So why not just focus on the problem? Why should we care about trauma?

Following is a partial listing of the kinds of problems kids might have that are potentially trauma related:

- Disruptive behaviors
- Poor frustration tolerance
- Depression
- Anxiety
- Poor concentration
- Loss of interest in activities/goals
- "Don't care" attitude
- Anger
- Fighting
- School absences
- Substance abuse
- Criminal behaviors
- Noncompliance with medical treatment
- Suicidal behaviors

This is not to suggest that trauma is the only reason kids have problems. But trauma can find the child's weak spot. Trauma is a powerful stressor that can either cause new problems or make existing problems worse. If we try to help kids but don't take trauma into account, we risk ignoring a driving force behind the problems. We risk being less effective.

A USEFUL DEFINITION OF TRAUMA

Trauma was previously defined as a horrific event "beyond the scope of normal human experience" (American Psychiatric Association, 1980). To qualify as traumatic, an event should be subjectively perceived as threatening to a person's life or physical integrity, and should include a sense of helplessness along with fear, horror, or disgust. Such events might include being in a car accident, house fire, or natural disaster; being raped; or being assaulted. Through research we have learned to identify a wider range of events as being possibly traumatic—for example, witnessing a parent or sibling being beaten; being diagnosed with a life-threatening illness.

The bad news is that traumatic events are not beyond the scope of normal human experience. Although not every child will be exposed to one or more traumatic events, most will. This is not just true for kids growing up in high-crime urban areas. Even our (presumably) best-protected kids experience trauma. For example, a study of second-year college students (modal age of nineteen) found that 84 percent had experienced at least one major trauma (Vrana & Lauterbach, 1994). Among disadvantaged urban populations, very few escape exposure to major trauma events (see Greenwald, 2002b). Trauma during childhood and adolescence is now so common as to be normative. When working with a child or adolescent with any kind of problem, we can't afford to assume that trauma is not a factor.

Although the focus here is on trauma, it is important to note that other adverse life events can have a traumalike impact on kids. For example, a child's response to a significant loss can be virtually identical to a posttraumatic response, except that following loss, hyperarousal may not be present (Pynoos, 1990). Indeed, the research on adjustment disorder shows that many children do not adjust to or recover from a range of adverse events (Newcorn & Strain, 1992) but maintain some symptoms indefinitely.

When working with a distressed child, we do not ask if the event qualifies as a trauma before offering help. We will offer essentially the same treatment regardless of whether the source of the distress is an earthquake, a sexual assault, or a death in the family. In this book, the term *trauma* is intended to apply to major trauma as well as loss and other adverse life events, as long as the event has had a traumalike impact on the child.

WHAT MAKES AN EVENT TRAUMATIC?

Not every upsetting event is so intense and overwhelming that it is experienced as traumatic. The biggest factor pushing an event into the traumatic range is, not surprisingly, how bad it is. Several factors determine the severity of the exposure to trauma:

- The nature of the event itself
- Direct experience versus witnessing versus hearing about it or seeing it on TV
- Personal impact versus impact on a known person versus impact on a stranger
- After-event impact (e.g., lifestyle disruption)

Severity of the Event

Some events are clearly worse than others. For example, an open-hand spanking is not as bad as being whipped with a belt, which is not as bad as being beaten to the point of broken bones. In most cases, once the event has been described, its severity is readily apparent. However, children with special vulnerabilities may experience certain insults especially severely. For example, being punched in the arm will hurt a child who has hemophilia more than it will hurt a child who does not have this condition. Also, how the event is perceived contributes to its severity. For example, a child who does not understand the danger she was in may not experience a nearly fatal near-miss event as traumatic.

Proximity of the Experience

The more directly the child is involved in the event, the higher the risk of posttraumatic stress symptoms. For example, in a school shooting, children witnessing the event had the most severe symptoms, followed by children nearby who heard the shots but did not see the event, followed by children farther away who neither saw nor heard (Pynoos et al., 1987). However, even distant exposure can have impact, especially when children can personally relate or feel directly affected in some way. For example, younger children who saw the World Trade Center towers collapse on television, and who saw this multiple times, were exposed repeatedly to this event because they did not understand that it was only the same event being replayed. They thought that many buildings had been hit and were coming down, and they felt more vulnerable.

Personal Impact

Something that happens to the child or to someone he cares about is likely to have a greater impact than something that happens to a stranger. Children take it very personally when a parent or sibling is victimized or hurt. On the other hand, it is important not to underestimate the impact that an apparently distant event can have on a child.

- A ten-year-old boy's classmate drowned during a school outing. He did not even like the drowned girl, but felt guilty that he had not been friendlier toward her and irrationally blamed himself for her death.
- A five-year-old boy looked out the window and saw a neighborhood man getting beaten up. After that he was afraid to go outside; he feared someone might beat him up too.
- A nine-year-old girl's best friend's father died of cancer. She became obsessed with the fear that her own parents might have cancer.

After-Event Impact

This is a critical element of severity of exposure that is often overlooked. Imagine that two identical bombs are dropped. One explodes and makes a crater in the ground. The other explodes somewhere else and also makes a similar crater in the ground, but then some nearby buildings collapse into the second crater. Although both bombs had the same strength, the second bomb has had more impact and thus can be considered more severe. Life experiences can be like this too. A traumatic event is more than just the single terrible moment.

- A fourteen-year-old girl was in a car accident. After the crash, she did not know for a few minutes whether her aunt (the driver) was dead or alive. In the hospital, she had to wait by herself in a small room for almost an hour. The attendants cut off and discarded the bloody jacket she had been wearing in order to tend to her wounds; her boyfriend had given her this jacket and she treasured it. She was left with a scar on her lower arm and felt that she could no longer wear short-sleeved shirts or bathing suits.
- A four-year-old boy's father died in a work-related accident. His mother became depressed and withdrawn. Spring came around and the boy's father was not there to teach him how to catch a baseball. He'd already received a baseball glove for Christmas. Father's Day came. His birthday. His first day of school. (This could go on indefinitely, as major losses can have fresh impact at every developmental milestone.)
- An eleven-year-old girl lost an uncle in the World Trade Center disaster. Even a month later, her parents were upset all the time and couldn't seem to talk about anything else. Also, her school wasn't any good anymore; everyone there was angry now because hundreds of kids from some other school were all crammed in there too, until they could go back to their own school again.

In other words, it's not just the event itself but the circumstances surrounding and following the event that may make it traumatic rather than merely upsetting. Personality, social support, and other factors (discussed later in this chapter) also help to determine whether a child can handle an event or will be overwhelmed.

THE "TRAUMA WALL"

A popular saying is that "What doesn't kill you makes you stronger," or, less colloquially, that we grow from adversity. Although this certainly can be true, it is not always the case. Sometimes what doesn't kill you may still hurt you or cause damage. So how does this work—why does it go one way rather than the other?

Here a food analogy is helpful. Usually, we chew food, swallow it, and digest it. It becomes part of our nutrition, something we can grow from. Ideally, we do something similar with an upsetting experience. Kübler-Ross (1969) described a similar process in the stages of processing grief.

For example, let's say your dog dies. Maybe you don't think about it or process it every minute of the day, but now and then you do think about it, remember different aspects: how frisky she was when you first got her, how she liked to have her belly scratched, how badly you feel about having let her out the day she got hit by a car. You remember, you talk to others, you take a walk, you write, you cry, you laugh. Little by little—or bite by bite—the hurt becomes smaller as more gets processed, integrated, "digested." When an upsetting experience is digested, it becomes your nutrition, something you grow from. Then it becomes part of long-term memory, part of the past. It is not as fresh or upsetting anymore. Along with the emotional processing, we have organized the elements of the experience into a coherent story, including a perspective that allows us to move on. For example, you might say to yourself, "Well, she loved to play outside. I guess there was always the risk of an accident, but she would have been miserable tied up," and "She was a great dog. I'll always love her."

However, sometimes upsetting experiences do not get processed in this ideal way. Sometimes it's just too much to face, to take bites out of. Maybe the event was too upsetting and overwhelming; maybe you try to talk about it and are punished for that (perhaps by parents getting upset or peers teasing); maybe just when you are ready to take a bite out of this upsetting memory, another one comes along. It can be so difficult to face this upsetting memory, to tolerate it, that many people try to push it aside, push it behind a wall. That brings quick relief, so the strategy is experienced as helpful. Unfortunately, it provides only a temporary solution.

Back to the food metaphor: Imagine that you have eaten some food that is bad for you or poisonous. Ideally you will be able to get rid of it somehow. Maybe you'll be shaky or sick for a little while, but it'll be gone from your system. Unfortunately, with an upsetting experience, you can't just reject it and flush it down the toilet. The only way out is to go through—through the memory processing system into long-term memory. Until the memory is processed, or digested, it stays behind the wall.

Although the wall may provide some relief, this system has problems. First, the memory stays fresh and keeps its power indefinitely, until it is digested. I have worked with people months, years, and even decades after the trauma, and the quality of the undigested memory is the same. When asked to concentrate on the memory, they say things like, "It's so vivid it's like it just happened yesterday," or, even more telling, "I'm there."

Also, although the memory retains its freshness and power, it is still behind the wall, so we can't get at it with the rest of our psychological resources the way we can with processed memories. This means that the memory, or parts of the memory, can negatively influence us and we may feel helpless to stop it. For example, many rape victims will say, "I *know* in my head that it wasn't my fault, that I didn't do anything wrong, that I didn't deserve that. But I can't help *feeling* ashamed, dirty, to blame." In other words, the healthy part that knows better can't manage to influence the powerful beliefs and feelings that are shielded behind the wall.

Furthermore, the memories stored behind the wall are not content to stay there. They are always waiting for a chance to come out, go through the system to be digested, and become part of the past. It is as if the memory is seeing its chance and saying, "Me too! Can I finally be treated like a normal memory and get processed already?" When this happens, we say that the memory was "triggered" or activated by a reminder, something thematically related. Another way of explaining this is that the stuff piled up behind the wall is like a "sore spot," and when some kind of reminder hits that sore spot, the reaction is stronger than others might expect. This is because the person is not just reacting to what's happening right now; the old stuff is kicking in, too.

- Most of us who drive are at least a little nervous about driving. This is reasonable and inspires us to put on our seat belts and watch out for bad drivers. However, we are still able to enjoy conversations with our passengers, listen to the radio, and think about where we are going. Now think about the woman who experienced a car accident because she couldn't stop on a snowy road. Afterward, whenever she got into the driver's seat, she had the usual amount of nervousness, plus all the extra fear from behind the wall. You've probably seen people like her on the road, clutching the wheel and gritting their teeth as if they are expecting an accident to occur at any second. On rainy or snowy days, so much of the fear piled on that she could not manage to drive herself to work.
- Most of us, when accidentally bumped in the hallway, will be slightly irritated, perhaps make a comment, but forget about it five minutes later. Now think about the twelve-year-old boy who has been routinely physically abused at home. Behind the wall is piled-up fear of being attacked, a sense of helplessness, and rage. When he is bumped in the hallway, the "sore spot" reaction from the stuff piled up behind the wall is so strong that he believes he is being attacked. Naturally, being angry and not wanting to feel helpless anymore, he defends himself. When he is sent to the assistant principal's office for "punching a peer with no provocation," he insists that the other kid started it.

Note that it is not necessary to be aware that an unprocessed memory is being triggered for it to be happening. Sometimes the person will be acutely aware of it, as unwanted images from the memory itself come back. For example, one thirteen-year-old girl said, "Every time my boyfriend tries to kiss me, I freak out. I see the face of that guy who messed with me when I was little." However, often the person is unaware of the impact of the behind-the-wall memory and just subjectively experiences a strong reaction to the present situation. For example, a sixth-grade boy who has experienced several events involving helplessness may give up too quickly when he does not immediately grasp how to do his math homework. He may say, "It's too hard—I can't do it" when he probably could do it with a little effort—if he weren't overwhelmed by the "sore spot" helplessness from behind the wall.

We all understand this phenomenon. We understand that people have their wounds, their sensitive areas, their sore spots. We say, "Don't mention John around her, unless you want her to start crying," or "Don't joke like that with him—he'll go ballistic." What we mean is that there are unprocessed memories piled up behind the wall that can get triggered by thematically related events in the present. We understand that people can be more reactive than the current situation warrants when they are hit on their sore spot. This is one of the consequences of carrying trauma memories that are not fully processed.

RESILIENCY AND VULNERABILITY

Beyond the objective severity of the event itself, several factors contribute to determining whether a given upsetting experience is ultimately processed or pushed behind the wall.

Social Support

The choice to face and digest an upsetting event versus pushing it behind the wall occurs in a social context. Children may not want to talk about upsetting thoughts and feelings around their peers for fear of being rejected and isolated. At home, kids may not want to worry their parents or other family members. When a parent says, "Don't talk about that. It'll only upset you!" the child learns, "Wow—this is so bad and scary that even Mom/Dad can't handle it!" So unless kids are in an accepting and supportive environment, they may be getting messages that do not provide support for talking about the trauma and that discourage processing.

Temperament

Pain threshold is a familiar concept that can be applied to emotional pain as well. People are unique in the ways they experience events. The same event with the same severity will bother one person more than another. Extending an earlier analogy, two identical bombs might make different size craters for each person. Furthermore, even if the same size bomb is making the same size crater for two people, it might bother one person more than the other. For example, on a 0–10 scale of severity of emotional upset, two kids might each report the same event as being a 6. However, one child might experience that 6 as no big deal, and the other might find it intolerable. Obviously, the more difficulty a child has with tolerating pain, the more tempted that child will be to push the memory behind the wall.

New and/or Repeated Insult/Wound

Suppose a child has experienced a minor everyday type of upsetting event, such as a peer insult or a school-related frustration. She is on track to digest it and is just getting ready to take a bite when some new stressor comes along, and then another, and another, and another. Eventually so many of these small events pile up that the pile is experienced as "too much" and pushed behind the wall. This pileup of minor events commonly occurs in kids who have an untreated learning disability or attention deficit/hyperactivity disorder (ADHD); kids who are bullied; and kids who are subject to emotional abuse.

You might have noticed that we just expanded our definition of trauma. If it's behind the wall, it counts. If it's behind the wall, it's creating sore spot reactivity, whether the sore spot comes from one big event or a hundred smaller ones.

Attachment Status

Some preliminary research suggests that attachment status can, to some extent, predict the child's preferred coping style. This also makes sense. How do you become someone with a secure attachment? You do this by having a "good-enough mother" (Winnicott, 1965). This parent figure actually doesn't need to be a mother, but he or she does need to be good enough! When you have a good-enough mother, you learn, through repeated experiences over time, that if you're cold, soon you'll get warm again; if you're hungry, soon you'll get fed; and if you get so angry that you want to kill, your mother will survive and so will you; she will not retaliate or reject you. In other words, in the process of developing a secure attachment, kids learn that although they may not like to feel bad, they can handle it and things will come out okay.

When securely attached kids have to deal with a trauma memory, they have an experience base and coping style that favors facing it and getting through it. Incidentally, kids with secure attachment are also more likely to have good social support, because they are probably still in the family in which the attachment was formed, and because they are more capable of forming other supportive relationships.

On the other hand, how do you form anxious, insecure, or disorganized attachment? You do so by having a (subjectively experienced) not-good-enough mother, or a good-enough-sometimes-but-not-other-times mother. Kids with problematic attachments have learned, through repeated experiences over time, that feeling bad can be disastrous and overwhelming. If you are cold, you might get warm, or you might stay cold and miserable. If you are hungry, you might get fed, or you might just get hungrier. If you get so angry that you want to kill, you might get rejected or attacked. In other words, in the process of developing a problematic attachment, kids learn that feeling bad is a danger sign, to be avoided if possible. When such kids have to deal with a trauma memory, they have an experience base and coping style that favors trying to push it out of the way, to get rid of the threat.

The more severely problematic type of attachment status is known as failed attachment or reactive attachment disorder. Unattached kids may experience trauma in a qualitatively different way than other kids do; they also have some unique ways of responding to various interventions. The treatment of kids with the most severe attachment problems is beyond the scope of this book. The treatment approach presented in this book is still necessary in their treatment, but it is not sufficient; an additional specialized treatment component is needed.

Safety and Attachment

There are also other consequences of traumatization. In Erikson's (1963) developmental theory, the first stage of development is trust versus mistrust. With a good-enough mother, the infant learns through repeated experience that he or she will be taken care of, that the world is a safe place. Trauma can alter that perspective, reverse that lesson.

We have understood this since the beginning of the modern era of trauma study. In the World War I literature on post-traumatic stress disorder (PTSD, which was called "shell shock" then), it was reported that soldiers under bomb attack would frequently call out either for God or their mothers. What is the significance of this? The first promise was being broken: "The world is no longer a safe place. I am not being taken care of. Mother, God, you lied to me."

Attachment and safety are inherently related, and when children feel unsafe they seek the comfort and protection of their primary attachment figures. The toddler at the zoo is not frightened by the tiger; he is safe with his mommy. However, trauma can disrupt attachment, in part because the attachment figures have, by definition, failed to protect and an unimaginably bad thing happened.

Some kids may react to this trauma-related attachment challenge by withdrawing, whereas others may seek out new attachment figures who are perceived as more likely to protect. For example, although there are practical reasons for affiliating with street gangs, the explanations kids offer are revealing: "We watch each other's backs," and "This is my family."

SURVIVAL ORIENTATION

When children are exposed to trauma, they learn that parents and others cannot be relied upon for protection; they learn that bad things can happen. They then make a profound shift in their worldviews, in their orientations to daily living. Instead of focusing on normal concerns and activities, the primary focus becomes keeping the bad thing (or other bad things) from happening again. When we say someone has "lost her childhood," this is what we mean. The child exchanges the healthy (if irrational or naive) optimism for a survival orientation.

POSTTRAUMATIC SYMPTOMS

Many posttraumatic stress symptoms can be understood from the perspective of the sore-spot reactivity, plus the survival orientation.

Reexperiencing

Reexperiencing, one of the primary posttraumatic symptoms, refers to instances in which the memory itself recurs or intrudes into awareness. The child might complain that he thinks of the memory "all the time" or that it comes to mind at random moments, without warning. However, on analysis, it turns out that such intrusions generally occur when they have been triggered by something in the present. Most people find these intrusions disturbing and disruptive. Flashbacks are an extreme and relatively rare reexperiencing symptom; nightmares and waking memories are much more common.

Avoidance

Avoidance, another of the primary posttraumatic symptoms, relates to both the sore-spot reactivity and to the survival orientation, the wish to keep any more bad things from happening. For example, a traumatized child might avoid walking down a certain street where she had been hit by a car, both to avoid a recurrence of the accident and to avoid being reminded of the memory. Avoidance can have significant impact on many areas of life:

- A fourteen-year-old boy, whose best friend had abandoned him during a street fight, says, "I don't have friends, only associates. Friends let you down." He is avoiding the possibility of being let down again by not trusting anyone anymore.
- A fifteen-year-old girl with exposure to multiple traumas is not doing much in the way of schoolwork, and she is having unprotected sex. She says, "What does it matter? Nothing's going to work out for me anyway. Why bother making the effort?" She is avoiding the possibility of feeling disappointed again by not getting her hopes up, not feeling optimistic, not setting goals for herself (the technical term for this is *pessimistic future*).
- A nine-year-old boy, who had been hit by a car while on his bicycle, has quit his baseball team. He says, "I just don't feel like going anymore." In fact, he's not going anywhere except school and home, because he doesn't feel safe anywhere else. He's learned that bad things can happen out in the world, and he doesn't want any more bad things to happen to him.

Hyperarousal and Hypervigilance

Hyperarousal and hypervigilance are also common outcomes of traumatization. Many children are in a constant state of alert, on the lookout for possible signs of danger. When kids are primed to expect the worst, they can be jumpy when startled or threatened. The problem is, when you think you're a nail, everything looks like a hammer. So many kids will interpret neutral or ambiguous social cues as being threatening (the technical term for this is *hostile attribution bias;* see Dodge & Coie, 1987). For example, a boy may notice a peer looking his way and assume that the peer is showing disrespect and trying to start a fight. Of course, this kind of assumption leads to problems!

Numbness

Many traumatized kids find themselves "numb" or unable to feel certain (or most) emotions. This may be a "freeze" response to being overwhelmed or it may be a special kind of avoidance. Some kids will say, for example, "I can't let myself feel anything or I'll feel everything; it'll all come back. And that's too much," or, "I'm afraid that if I start crying, I'll never stop." The numbness solution is to block it all out.

Substance Abuse and Other Avoidance Strategies

Many traumatized kids are unable to effect that numbness and so seek activities that will help them "forget about" the memory or related affect. For example, some kids become thrill seekers, troublemakers, or workaholics to stay busy and distracted with attention-compelling activities. Many youth turn to substance abuse to keep the trauma memories away, if only for a while. One nineteen-year-old boy who had been brutally assaulted by peers said, "I think about it every night. It keeps me awake for hours. I have to catch a buzz [smoke marijuana] to get myself to sleep."

Affect Dysregulation

The technical term for sore-spot reactivity is *affect dysregulation.* We should not use this term in front of our clients, but it's important to understand it. Breaking it down, *affect* is emotion, and *dysregulation* means unregulated, out of control, or volatile. Emotions may become out of control when traumatized kids react very strongly to minor stressors because they are already sensitized. This in-the-moment reaction, perhaps of anger, fear, sadness, shame, or helplessness, can

be very intense and uncomfortable, even intolerable. The fear of these reactions drives many of the avoidance behaviors.

Also, kids who react very strongly to minor stressors are at a high risk of impulsive acting out behavior (van der Kolk et al., 1996). The impulsive acting out provides quick relief from the intolerable feeling, but often leads to other problems. It is likely that unprocessed trauma plays a significant role in the acting-out problems of many kids with oppositional/defiant and conduct disorders (Ford, 2002; Greenwald, 2002b).

Posttraumatic Symptoms over Time

Unfortunately, kids don't just "get over" their traumatization. The memory (and associated symptoms) doesn't just fade away with time. It stays fresh as long as it's behind the wall. It stays fresh until it's digested. But what does it take for digestion to be possible? What needs to happen?

Going back to the food analogy. Suppose you've just had a nice lunch and you're back at work. Someone bursts into your office and announces that there's a bomb scare in the building, so you have to rush out and go somewhere else. Meanwhile, your nervous system is shifting from parasympathetic to sympathetic, and the blood is going away from the stomach to supply the brain, arms, and legs. This allows you to escape and survive. Twenty minutes later you hear an announcement that the whole thing was a hoax—there's no bomb. You go back to work and gradually your nervous system shifts back to parasympathetic. The blood goes back to your stomach, and you can proceed with digestion.

This return to relaxation does not happen with posttraumatic stress symptoms because they are self-perpetuating. The need for survival mode is repeatedly reinforced, with no shift to safety and relaxation, no opportunity for digestion:

- A young girl who had been assaulted on a certain street walks the long way home from school to avoid going down that street. She may say to herself every day that she does this, "Phew! I escaped another assault."
- A girl who was raped by the babysitter—who is now in jail—is bullied by her big brother in minor ways on a daily basis. She learns, over and over again, that males who are bigger and more powerful than she is can have their way with her. Her "psychological truth" is that she is in constant danger.
- A previously victimized teenaged boy believes that he is being stared at by a peer and interprets this as a hostile affront. If he
  —quickly leaves the situation, he may say to himself, "Phew! I got away! I'm glad I've stayed so alert."
  —challenges the peer, who then backs down, he may say to himself, "I defended myself well."
  —challenges the peer, who responds by fighting, he may say to himself, "I was right: he was hostile."

Regardless of specific outcome, these posttraumatic symptoms serve to reinforce the perception that the world is still dangerous. Every avoidant behavior—such as walking the long way around—only provides relief from fear, and reinforces the perceived need for avoidance. The defensive-intent aggressive behaviors also are self-reinforcing: by forcing the other's withdrawal or hostility, the need for the defensiveness is confirmed. Since traumatized kids tend to be hypervigilant and to overinterpret neutral cues, these types of situations may occur frequently. As long as kids remain in survival mode, they do not feel safe and are not prepared to relax or to digest their trauma memories.

Posttraumatic stress symptoms can also make it more difficult for kids to handle new challenges in a healthy way. A new upsetting experience may be hard enough to manage already. However, when this new experience triggers trauma-related reactivity from something that's already behind the wall, the reaction to the new experience can be much stronger than is apparently warranted. This extra-strong reaction can make it even more difficult to manage the new experience effectively, and the child is more likely to push the memory behind the wall rather than attempt to digest it. Thus, previously traumatized kids are at a higher risk for being overwhelmed, and traumatized, by new upsetting experiences.

The more trauma memories (and associated thoughts and feelings) are piled up behind the wall, the more likely this "trauma burden" (Greenwald, 1997) will affect the child's daily life. A single memory might be well contained, at least until the child is faced with a very closely related reminder. For example, after an initial period of adjustment, children of divorce tend to look and act like other kids, with no special problems—at least until they get old enough to attempt their own intimate/romantic relationships (Wallerstein, Corbin, & Lewis, 1988). Because kids can be good at containing or hiding their distress, many parents come to believe that the child has "gotten over" the trauma.

As unprocessed trauma accumulates behind the wall, two things happen. First, the strength of the reactivity to a current stressor is likely to be greater, so others are more likely to notice that the child is overreacting to things. Second, the child is more likely to overgeneralize and practice a wider avoidance. This is because humans are good at recognizing patterns and can use this ability to avoid repeating the same mistake. However, a traumatized child's interest in avoiding further trauma can be so powerful that she may take avoidance to an extreme.

Following is an example of how avoidance might be generalized from a specific identified high-risk situation to other less high-risk situations:

- I won't be alone in a room with Uncle Matt anymore. He messed with me last time.
- Uncle Matt has a beard—that must be it. I guess I can't trust men with beards.
- I can't trust men.
- I can't trust.

Pessimistic future can develop in a similar way:

- Wow—something bad happened. I didn't know that could happen.
- Something bad might happen again. I'd better be careful.
- I know bad things are going to happen.
- Only bad things will happen, and good things will turn bad, so why get my hopes up?

In summary, posttraumatic stress symptoms can persist indefinitely and can lead kids to react very strongly to minor stressors. In fact, sometimes others don't see any stressor at all, because we don't know what might be a trauma reminder to the child. When the triggers are not apparent to others, we are prone to forming opinions about the child's behavior that are not based on understanding. For example, we may be likely to assume that a child is gratuitously aggressive when, from his point of view, he is only defending himself.

A NOTE ON EXERCISES/ACTIVITIES IN THIS BOOK

The exercises and activities are included because they are likely to help you to learn the material. People tend to learn best when engaging personal experience is part of the lesson. Because this book is focused on trauma, the experiential component sometimes focuses on trauma as well. Participation in such experiences might hurt your feelings or at least bring up hurt feelings that were otherwise dormant. In live workshops, most people find that they can handle this and they are glad they participated. However, occasional exceptions do occur.

Although in general the value of the learning will outweigh the potential for discomfort, it will be up to you to make that determination for yourself at each instance. You will want to consider not only the value of the lesson but the possible impact of participation on your emotional status and functioning, in light of your current situation/surroundings and your plans for later in the day. You always have several options:

- Participate fully in the activity.
- Participate until you determine that your distress level is as high as you are willing to allow it to go; then stop.
- Participate but carefully select the content (e.g., which memory to focus on) to avoid an unwanted level of distress.
- Decline to participate.

Bear in mind that sometimes you get more than you bargained for. If you choose to participate and then find that it is too much for you, it is important to take care of yourself and make sure that you're okay. Here are some suggestions in this regard:

- Do the deep breathing or another of the calming exercises that are presented at various points in the book.
- Use any of your usual coping skills/methods as long as they are constructive (e.g., thinking of something else, taking a walk, listening to music, etc.).
- Discuss your concerns with the workshop leader if you are attending a workshop.

- Discuss your concerns with a trusted family member, friend, colleague, or supervisor.
- Discuss your concerns with a mental health professional.

EXERCISE: FLOAT-BACK

The main purpose of this exercise is to see how trauma-related triggers may be active in your own life. When you see how a principle applies to you, you can use your experience to better understand others. Another purpose of the exercise is to directly experience an activity that you might ask a client to do. For this exercise, you'll need a pencil or pen and paper.

Float-Back

1. Think of a situation that happened within the past couple of days in which you were somehow distressed: upset, mad, worried, hurt, sad, frustrated, etc. It doesn't have to be anything major. The first thing that pops into your head is probably the right one.
2. On a scale of 0–10, 0 is no bad feeling at all, 10 is the worst a feeling could possibly be. Concentrate on the worst part of the recent event. Notice the picture in your mind, what you are saying to yourself, and what you are feeling. On a scale of 0–10, how bad is the feeling *right now* as you are concentrating on it? (Not how bad it was then.) Write that number down.
3. Now as you are concentrating on this recent memory, again notice the image, what you are saying to yourself, what you are feeling, where you feel this in your body. Now try to make the feeling even more intense.
4. Let your mind float back in time, maybe a long way back, to when you first learned to feel this way. If something pops into your head, maybe that's it.
5. Now on a scale of 0–10, with 10 being the worst the feeling could be, how bad is the feeling from the old memory *right now* as you are concentrating on it? (Not how bad it was then.) Write that number down.

Deep Breathing

Because I asked you to think about something that might be upsetting, now I will ask you to do a deep-breathing exercise that might help you to feel better, to relax again. You might not need this, but please do it anyway for the experience. You will be taking a very deep, slow breath in, to a count of three, then hold for three, then breathe out slowly to a count of three. Ready?

Breathe in 1, 2, 3; hold 1, 2, 3; out slow 1, 2, 3. Again, breathe in 1, 2, 3; hold 1, 2, 3; out slow 1, 2, 3.

This time, when you breathe out, look for any bad stuff—tension in your body, upsetting thoughts or pictures—and when you breathe out, imagine the air coming from that place and the bad stuff going out with the exhale. Ready?

Breathe in 1, 2, 3; hold 1, 2, 3; breathe out the bad stuff, 1, 2, 3. Once more, breathe in 1, 2, 3; hold 1, 2, 3; breathe out the bad, 1, 2, 3.

Discussion Questions

How many (in a group, raise hands) had a higher number—a worse feeling—for the old memory than for the recent one? (Normally about three-fourths of the group will raise hands here.) What might this mean?

- What was once significant may maintain its influence, even over a long time period.
- Do you think that, for you, your reaction to the current event was at least in part due to hitting the sore spot from the old one?

How many (in a group, raise hands) had a higher number—a worse feeling—for the recent memory than for the old one? (Normally about one-fourth of the group will raise hands here.) What might this mean?

- Perhaps the recent event was actually a major trauma, although the odds are against this.
- What's fresh may feel more relevant than something that happened a long time ago.
- Will kids believe you when you say that the recent event is not relevant?

The trick here is that both answers are the right answer, and with kids we must somehow address both the past and the present if we are going to be helpful.

A twelve-year-old boy had been doing pretty well until his mother died suddenly, when he was seven. Since then, he has done worse in school, had a short temper, and gotten into a lot of fights. You are absolutely sure that his problems are directly related to the death of his mother (and you're right). But when you bring this up, he storms at you, "Everybody wants to talk about my mother all the time! I'm sick of talking about my mother! That's not what's bothering me! My problem is that my teacher picks on me. I'm the one that gets in trouble even though the other kid started it!"

If you insist on talking with him about his mother, what will probably happen? He will feel disrespected. He is trying to tell you what is important to him and you are ignoring him. He will then discount you and become uncooperative. This is especially tempting for him because then he can avoid talking about his mother! And you lose your chance to be of service.

But if you do it his way and talk only about the problem of the day, what will probably happen? He will feel respected, he will work with you, and he might even learn a few problem-solving or other coping skills. But the core problem will remain because the source of his reactivity never gets addressed. He might go from one counselor to the next for years and never solve his problem.

So what do we do about this? How do we address the past as well as the present? I'll tell you later! This is the part of the book in which we try to understand what's going on with traumatized kids. Later on step-by-step guidance is available for what to do and how to help them. In the next chapter we take the first step, by learning how to analyze a presenting problem to take into account both past and present-day contributing factors.

Chapter 2

The Structure of Trauma Treatment

An understanding of traumatized kids' experience is a good first step. However, to know what to do about it, we must also understand exactly how the child's posttraumatic stress symptoms might relate to the current presenting problem. The next step will be to use that understanding to determine a course of action.

MEANING OF BEHAVIOR

Just about half of all child/adolescent mental health referrals are for problem behaviors (Kazdin, 1987), so problem behavior is a good example to use for the present focus on understanding the child's presenting problem. However, the same principles will apply to kids' presenting problems and symptoms more widely, whether or not problem behaviors are part of the picture. Based on this discussion, following is a summary of the possible role of trauma in problem behaviors:

- Kids learn from experience. Trauma can be an intense experience that teaches powerful, long-lasting lessons. These lessons—or negative beliefs about the self and the world—are protected behind the wall and may not be amenable to rational intervention.
- Unprocessed trauma creates a pileup of unprocessed feelings, possibly including shame, guilt, anger, fear, hurt, helplessness, and sadness.
- Thematically related reminders of the trauma may trigger a heightened response, or overreaction, to the present situation. This happens when the new stressor hits the sore spot; then the negative beliefs and the piled-up feelings kick in.
- When a child is experiencing an intense reaction which includes a distorted interpretation of what is happening and which feels intolerable, the child is at high risk of impulsively acting out.

In sum, problem behaviors may be set in motion by present-day minor stressors that trigger a trauma-related overreaction. How often are kids' problem behaviors related to their overreaction to a trauma-related trigger? How do we figure this out for a given child? What kind of information do we need?

Following are the suggested steps (again, details on how to accomplish these steps are provided later):

1. Get a good trauma/loss history.
2. What would someone learn from this (trauma/loss) experience? What negative beliefs might the child develop?
3. What kinds of feelings might be piled up behind the wall?
4. Learn details about the context in which the problem behavior occurs. What is the apparent precipitating event? In what way might that be a trauma-related trigger?

5. What is the problem behavior? How does it relate to the trigger? Why has this problem behavior become the child's solution to this situation? Does it serve to make the child feel safer or better in some way? Does it get rid of the bad feelings?

When we meet a child, often we are only told what "the problem" is. We need to know more. We need to know what the problem means to the child, how it serves the child's needs. To become proficient at conducting a trauma-informed "meaning of behavior" analysis, it is useful to practice by breaking down the analysis into these steps.

Provided in this chapter is a Meaning of Behavior Worksheet for you to use in practicing these steps. Make photocopies of the worksheet to have on hand for your own future use. Shortly you'll have the opportunity to practice completing the worksheet using some case examples. Following is an illustration of how this might be done.

Meaning of Behavior Worksheet Example

Casey

Casey is an eight-year-old boy who is referred for frequent fighting in school and in his neighborhood. He has a history of witnessing domestic violence—seeing his father push his mother and hit her—and has tried unsuccessfully to protect his mother from his father. Casey tells you that he does not pick fights but only defends himself when other kids gang up on him and call him names.

Here is an abbreviated example of how you might fill out the worksheet:

1. *Trauma/loss event:* Saw father push and hit mother.
2. *Lesson learned (negative belief):* I am powerless.
3. *Piled-up feelings:* Anger, fear, shame.
4. *Trigger situation: Theme:* feeling threatened or attacked; *example:* being teased by other kids.
5. *Problem behavior:* Fighting.

Here is the story (the explanation) you might tell. Notice that the order of events in the story is the same as the order of steps on the worksheet.

1. There were times that Casey saw his father hurting his mother. Casey tried to stop it from happening, but he couldn't. He was too small.
2. Kids learn from experience. Kids who have had this kind of experience often learn to believe that they are powerless, that they can't protect themselves or those they love, that they are not good enough.
3. Also, when something like this happens, kids often have very strong feelings, like being afraid that someone will get hurt, being mad, and being ashamed that they can't stop it from happening. These feelings can be so big that they just pile up inside and leave a big sore spot.
4. Now, no one likes to be teased; it bothers everyone at least a little. But when Casey is teased, I can't help but wonder if it might be hitting that sore spot from the old thoughts and feelings that are piled up inside. Then his reaction is much stronger than other people think it should be. Then the bad feelings might be so strong that he can't stand it, and he has to get rid of them somehow.
5. So his solution is to attack the kids who are teasing him. When he hits them, this gets rid of the bad feelings. It gets out his anger. Also, he doesn't feel powerless anymore; he feels like he is able to protect himself.

Here are some tips on how to complete each of the sections on the form:

1. Trauma/loss events. Include any specific past events that might be stuck behind the wall and contributing to the current sore spot reactivity. These must be actual events, specific moments in time when specific incidents occurred. List the actual event (saw father push mother), not a label for the event (witness domestic violence). If you believe that the trauma actually consists of many small events, still be specific (told she was stupid by father many times) rather than general (emotional abuse). Note that even if the recent trigger situation was traumatic, it does not go here on the form.

2. Negative beliefs. Ask yourself: What kinds of lessons would a child tend to learn from those kinds of events? What would the negative beliefs be? The concept of negative beliefs is a bit complicated but worth getting right. Two kinds of beliefs come into play here. The first is about "who I am" and can be expressed as a negative self-statement such as "I am a bad person," "I am not safe," or "I'm not good enough." This is the type of negative belief that we use in Step 2 of this worksheet. The other is a belief about cause and effect, what works in the world, such as "If I am stubborn, I'll get my way," or "If I fight, I'll feel big and powerful instead of small and helpless." This type of belief comes from modeling as well as direct experience—what is reinforced. This type of belief is what informs the child's choice of a "solution" or problem behavior and is considered (but not necessarily spelled out) in Step 5 of the worksheet.

3. Piled-up feelings. Ask yourself: What kinds of feelings might kids tend to have with those kinds of events, along with those negative beliefs? Most people find this step fairly straightforward. Watch out for one thing, however: In everyday talk we often confuse the language of thoughts and feelings. For example, someone might say, "Boy, do I feel stupid!" Technically, though, the negative beliefs might be "I am stupid" and "I'm inadequate," whereas the piled-up feelings might be shame, frustration, and anger. Try to keep beliefs and emotions in their proper sections.

4. Trigger situation. This section has two parts. First we need a *theme.* What kinds of things hit the sore spot and set this kid off? How would these situations be characterized? What do they have in common? Then we need *specific examples,* typically recent and/or common specific instances that the child can easily recall which represent the theme in action. An example is specific when it includes time, place, and action.

5. Problem behavior(s). These should really be called solution behaviors. They are used habitually because the child has learned that they solve the problem; they make the trigger situation's intolerable feelings go away. Again we are looking for very specific behaviors (not generalizations or labels), what the child actually does to manage the trigger situations.

EXERCISE: MEANING OF BEHAVIOR

The following are some vignettes that you can practice with. In a group, talk together at each step before individuals write in their worksheets. For each vignette, complete the worksheet in order, starting at the first step (trauma/loss), filling in as many items as you can, then moving on to the next step. It is okay to fill in things that you can guess may be true, even if they are not specified in the vignette; use your experience and judgment here. Of course, we won't be sure about these things, but they are worth noting and then exploring with the child and family.

You may find yourself tempted to simply tell the story and give the explanation, without doing all of the steps. My experience as a trainer is that if you yield to this temptation, you'll be doing what you already know instead of trying something new; and you won't learn as much. I encourage you to go step by step. Just fill out the form. Telling the story will be addressed in a later chapter.

A sample response is included for the first vignette, but the point is to try it out for yourself and then use the sample response to check your work. If you are confused by a discrepancy, check back to the tips for completing each of the sections.

Damian

Damian is a thirteen-year-old boy who has a history of witnessing domestic violence as well as direct physical abuse, until his parents divorced when he was seven. His mother reports that he is respectful to her and helps out with the younger children when he is at home. He is a friendly, outgoing boy who seems to be popular with both boys and girls. However, his gregariousness has been escalating into verbal aggression: teasing peers, rudeness with teachers. The current referral follows an incident in which he physically intimidated a small female teacher by "getting in her face" without actually touching her or verbally threatening harm. You learn from Damian that (1) he did not intend to hurt her and (2) she asked for it, i.e., she criticized him for not knowing an answer and made him feel stupid in front of the class.

Jody

Jody is a seven-year-old girl, previously high functioning, who began wetting her bed and having nightmares following the anniversary of the World Trade Center attack. Her house burned down three years ago (she was not home at the time). She has also been picking on her younger sister more recently. The event precipitating the referral was a crying jag at school that occurred after a teacher asked Jody why she hadn't completed a quiz.

Michael

Michael is a ten-year-old boy who was diagnosed with ADHD at age nine after two years of school-related problems including impulsive/disruptive behavior, interpersonal conflicts, and poor work habits. Medication at age nine seemed to help at first, but after a few good weeks, his school performance deteriorated again. Trauma/loss history includes a minor auto accident at age five and the death of an uncle at age six.

Jessie

Jessie is a fourteen-year-old girl who was recently arrested for harassing peers (swearing at them, threatening, and throwing rocks) along with other girls. This precipitated the referral. She claimed that the harassed peers started it, were telling lies about her and her friends, and were threatening them as well. She was molested between age six and seven by her mother's live-in boyfriend. When this was discovered, her mother kicked the boyfriend out of the house.

Exercise Follow-Up

Note that although the examples in the vignettes focused on active problem behavior, the same trauma-informed model can be applied to kids with emotional problems such as depression and anxiety. These kids also may overreact to trauma-related triggers, leading to increased symptoms. Again, this does not mean that trauma is the only cause of any problem. However, when the trauma component is recognized, a more complete understanding of the problem is possible.

Many people comment that they have not looked at "presenting problem" behaviors in quite this way before. It is one thing to be aware that a child has been traumatized and that this might somehow relate to her problems; it is another to show exactly how the trauma and related issues might drive the problem, step by step.

When you understand a problem from this perspective, many more options are available for addressing it. For example, with the vignette of Casey, if we look only at the problem behavior, we are likely to punish him for hitting. We are also likely to conclude that he needs better "anger

Meaning of Behavior Worksheet

1. Trauma/loss event (all events):

2. Negative beliefs (negative self-statements):

3. Piled-up feelings:

4. Trigger situation (what sets off the reactivity):

   Theme:

   Example(s):

5. Problem behavior(s):

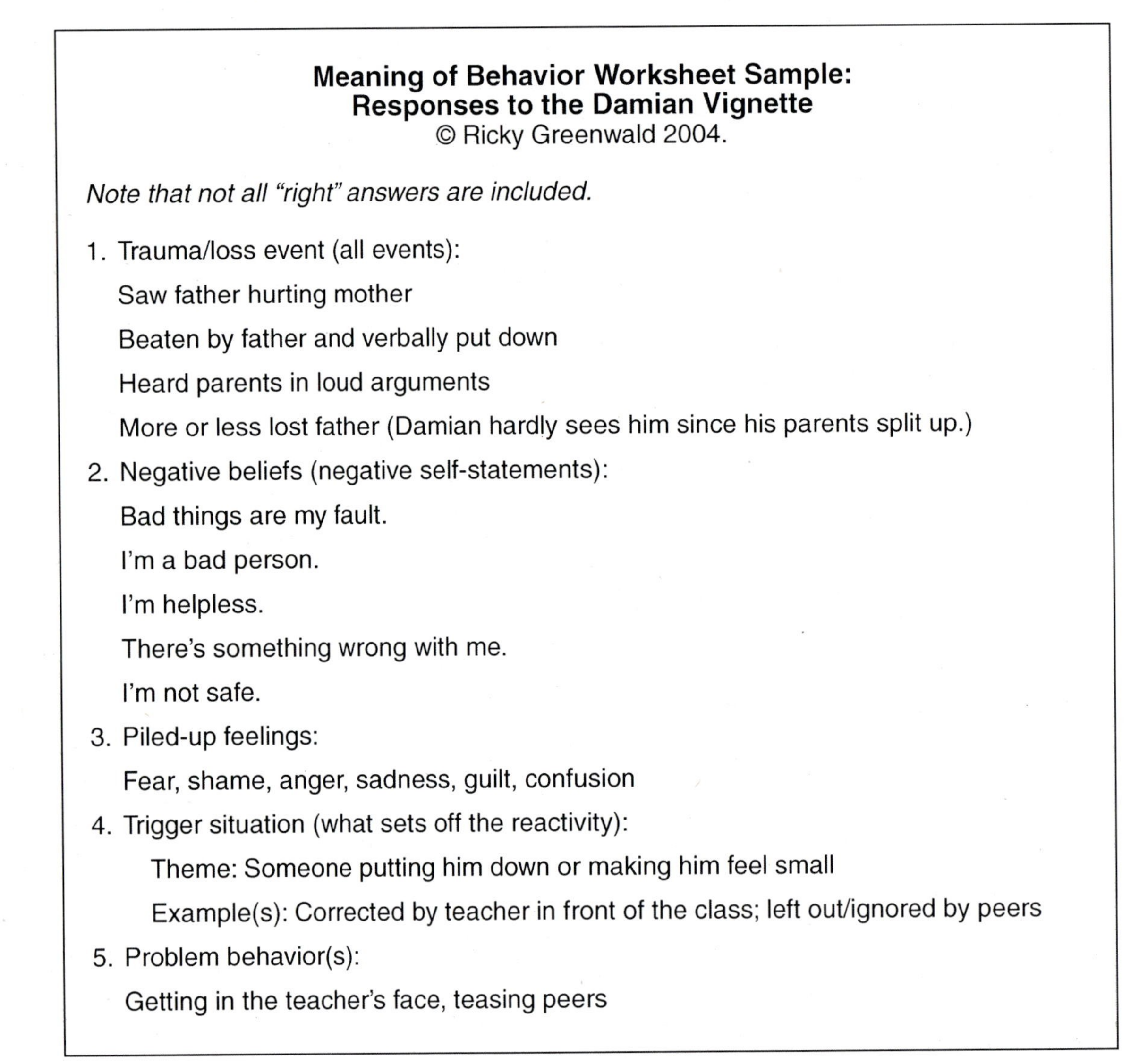

Meaning of Behavior Worksheet Sample:
Responses to the Damian Vignette

Note that not all "right" answers are included.

1. Trauma/loss event (all events):

   Saw father hurting mother

   Beaten by father and verbally put down

   Heard parents in loud arguments

   More or less lost father (Damian hardly sees him since his parents split up.)

2. Negative beliefs (negative self-statements):

   Bad things are my fault.

   I'm a bad person.

   I'm helpless.

   There's something wrong with me.

   I'm not safe.

3. Piled-up feelings:

   Fear, shame, anger, sadness, guilt, confusion

4. Trigger situation (what sets off the reactivity):

   Theme: Someone putting him down or making him feel small

   Example(s): Corrected by teacher in front of the class; left out/ignored by peers

5. Problem behavior(s):

   Getting in the teacher's face, teasing peers

management" or self-control skills, or perhaps better social skills so that he can make friends with kids who tease him. However, from his perspective, he doesn't need better self-control skills. He was controlling himself just fine: he was defending himself.

Once we develop a fuller understanding of why he hits the kids who tease him, there are more angles to work with, more possible solutions. Cover up the next paragraph so you can't read it. Done? Okay. Now, based on this fuller understanding, what other interventions can you suggest?

We will probably still punish him because we don't want to condone his hitting. We might still help him develop better self-control skills as part of a broader approach. We might also help him distinguish between being teased and being physically attacked. We might help him recognize when he is overreacting because of trauma-related triggers and how to calm himself down. We might intervene in his environment to help him feel safer and less vulnerable to attack. Finally, we might help him face the trauma memories and work through them or "digest" them so that less junk is piled up behind the wall. Then he is less likely to overreact in these situations, and it will be easier for him to handle it in a better way.

Many people comment that you must know a lot about a child to be able to complete the Meaning of Behavior Worksheet. That's true. You are generally told about the presenting problem up front. Then you must find out about the trauma history and the context of the problem behaviors. It takes a lot of time and effort to learn these things. In many work settings, it's difficult to find the time to get this information.

But if you can't fill out the Meaning of Behaviors form, maybe you don't really know enough about what's going on, about why the child is acting out. If you don't understand what's behind it, how can you be effective when you try to help?

This argues against the casual catch-as-catch-can "pep talk," "check-in," or "crisis response" approaches to counseling that are common in settings such as schools, where counselors are overburdened. The casual approach may be helpful for kids who need only the occasional support, encouragement, and advice of a friendly adult. However, for many kids with persistent problems, casual counseling is unlikely to get to the root of the problem. In many cases, the casual approach may offer little more than a few feel-good minutes for the child.

It is worth the investment of finding out what the problem really is so that you can respond in a way that has a better chance of making a difference. Once you understand, once you can complete the Meaning of Behavior form, you are in a better position to offer a systematic approach to trauma-informed treatment that is targeted to the individual child's needs.

SELECTING A TRAUMA TREATMENT STRUCTURE

The mental health field has been strongly influenced by physicians and psychiatrists, who have advocated for the medical model of diagnosis and treatment. In the medical model, the doctor determines what's wrong and, based on the diagnosis, prescribes the designated treatment. The medical model is ideal for broken bones, diseases that respond to a particular medicine, and many other medical conditions. In many instances, the correct diagnosis does lead to the correct treatment, which leads in turn to cure. Another benefit of the medical model is the placebo effect, in which the fact that treatment is being offered can itself be beneficial, regardless of the independent medical effect of the treatment. To perhaps oversimplify, the placebo effect reflects the psychological impact of being treated by someone with a doctor's authority and power.

However, when treating someone for posttraumatic stress-related problems, the medical model is not appropriate. Traumatized people already feel helpless and damaged; that's part of the problem. What happens when a helping professional takes an authoritarian role with a traumatized person and says, "I know your diagnosis and I will cure you"? The traumatized person feels damaged, controlled, small, and helpless. This only reinforces the problem. It doesn't solve it.

Trauma treatment requires a different attitude on the part of the helping professional. An empowerment model is needed that can allow and encourage the child to take initiative, to actively participate in each stage of the treatment, to recover from the trauma, and to grow from it. In fact, quite a bit of research has been conducted on which types of interventions help traumatized kids the most. I've organized these interventions into a systematic approach which I call the fairy tale model of trauma treatment. In this model, the fairy tale is used (loosely) as an analogy, with elements of the story representing treatment components. First we need the story.

The Fairy Tale

Once upon a time there was a small kingdom, about the size of a small town. Things were pretty regular there. People did their jobs; kids went to school. Some people went to church or temple and some didn't. Some people would go to a friend's house on the weekend, get together for a barbecue, play games, or have a party. Most people got along, but not everyone. And that's how things were: pretty regular.

Until one day . . .

The dragon came. One day the dragon ate a cow right out of a farmer's pasture. Another day the dragon ate a dog right out of someone's front yard. People got pretty scared! The parents told their kids that they weren't allowed to go outside anymore. The thing is, kids aren't very good at not going outside. So the parents stayed home to guard their kids, to keep them safe from the dragon.

Soon no one was going to school anymore, and not so many people were going to work, either. Everyone was so afraid of the dragon that they mostly just stayed inside their houses. And people started wondering, "How come our kingdom has a dragon, anyway? The other kingdoms don't have one." No one knew why, but they wanted to know, so they started making guesses. One group of people blamed another group of people; that group of people blamed some others . . . and pretty soon, everyone was blaming someone and they were all mad at each other.

It didn't take long until this kingdom got a bad reputation. People from the other kingdoms, well, they didn't know about the dragon, but they sure knew what was going on. They would say, "That kingdom's messed up. The people don't go to work, the kids don't go to school, nobody gets along, they're all mad at one another. All they do is stay inside all the time. They're messed up."

And that's how things were. Until one day . . .

A knight in shining armor came along. Well, he wasn't really a knight, and he didn't have any armor. He was just some guy who happened to be passing through. But the people in the town saw something in him.

"You!" they said. "You can slay the dragon; you're just the one to do it!"

The guy said, "No, sorry, I'm not a dragon slayer. You have the wrong guy. I've been walking a long way. I'm looking for this certain princess I'm in love with. But I don't know what kingdom she lives in." He pulled a picture out and showed it around. "Have you seen this princess? Do you know where I can find her?"

The people said, "Yes, she's our princess. She lives here. And what a coincidence: she really wants to get married—to whoever slays the dragon!"

When the guy heard this, he said, "Well, in that case, I'm your man. Take me to your dragon!"

So they took him to the dark place where the dragon was sleeping. The guy saw the dragon and said, "Whoa, this is a bad idea! I can't handle this dragon! No way! It's huge; it looks really strong. It's covered with scales—it breathes fire. Let's just forget the whole thing!"

The people said, "No, you can do it. We know you can! You can work out, do exercises, build yourself up. We'll help. We'll get you a personal trainer. And remember the princess!"

The guy said, "Oh yeah, the princess!" He was in love with this princess and he really wanted to marry her. "Okay, I don't know about this, but I'll give it a try and see how it goes."

So they gave him a personal trainer and took him to the schoolyard to start on his exercises. But he couldn't stay focused! Every time he got started on some exercise, he would suddenly stop and look all around. He was afraid the dragon would get him while he was out there, exposed. So he wasn't making any progress. This clearly was not working.

So they took him to a clearing at the edge of the forest where there were high trees on one side. Then they worked to build a high fence around the rest of the clearing. Everybody pitched in: cutting lumber, putting it up, securing it, cooking for the workers. . . . Even the little kids helped by bringing water to people, carrying messages, doing whatever they could. It wasn't long until they had a high fence around the rest of the clearing. Then the guy could concentrate on his exercises.

Things went better after that. Every day he worked hard with his personal trainer: he did push-ups, sit-ups, lifted weights, ran laps, did all kinds of exercises. Every day the trainer added a pound or two to the various weights. Every day the guy became a little stronger, a little faster, a little more agile. Eventually they got an athletic teenager to dress up in a dragon costume, and they did role-plays so the guy could practice his dragon-fighting moves.

Finally, the day came: he was ready. He went to the dark place where the dragon was, faced the dragon, fought it, and slew it.

He did marry the princess, but things didn't just go back to the same old way that the kingdom used to be.

For one thing, they now had a hero in their midst. People from the other kingdoms were saying, "That kingdom has a dragon slayer. I wish ours had one." And everyone in the kingdom felt proud, walked a little taller; they knew they'd all helped out and been a part of it.

But they were still asking each other, "How come our kingdom had a dragon, anyway? I wonder if we'll get another one?" They still didn't know. They were worried about this, and they really wanted to know. So they hired a consultant.

The consultant took a good look around. Then she called everyone together for a big meeting to tell them her findings. "You have two problems here. First of all, you throw all your garbage in the dump. It's this huge pile of garbage that stinks for miles around. That smell attracts dragons." So they decided that everyone would put their garbage in a compost pile in their own yard. No big smell to attract dragons, and compost is good for the gardens anyway.

The consultant also told them, "Here's your other problem. On the edge of the kingdom where the farms are, there are all these low fields. It's flat, flat, flat for miles! Dragons are lazy, and this place, it's just too easy for a dragon to cruise right in." So they decided to plant clusters of apple trees here and there in the fields. They liked apples anyway, and this way it wouldn't be such smooth sailing for any dragon that was wandering by.

Well, it didn't take long before they had so many apples that they didn't know what to do with them. So every year in the fall, they had a big apple festival, and people would come from all the kingdoms for miles around. There were all kinds of contests for the tastiest apples, the biggest apples, the best apple pies. They also had plenty of food, games, and music—everything a festival should have.

The highlight of the festival, on the Saturday night—the event that everyone would go to—was the dragon-slaying contest. Of course, they didn't have a real dragon, so whoever had won the year before got to play the dragon. All year long, teenagers from all the kingdoms were practicing, training, hoping that they'd be the one to win the big contest at the next year's festival. Not only was this great fun, but if another dragon ever did show up, they would be ready!

Then, they did live happily ever after—more or less. The end.

THE FAIRY TALE MODEL OF TRAUMA-INFORMED CHILD TREATMENT

The fairy tale was presented as the metaphorical basis of a model for an effective, comprehensive approach to trauma-informed child treatment. Each step in treatment is illustrated by the corresponding portion of the fairy tale. Here are the steps:

1. *Evaluation*—This includes the history of trauma/loss, strengths/successes, and circumstances in which the problem symptoms/behaviors occur.
2. *Motivational interviewing/goal setting*—It takes a lot of work, persistence, and courage to overcome trauma-related problems. Kids are not likely to commit to this unless we can help them identify their own goals—what they want for themselves—and understand how doing these treatment activities can help them to achieve their goals. This is the motivational component; most kids won't do all this work just because someone else says they should.

   In the fairy tale, without the princess, nothing would happen. With the princess in the picture, it's still a daunting task, but the guy says, "I guess I'll give it a try and see how it goes."
3. *Trauma-informed case formulation and psychoeducation*—Based on the evaluation, we communicate our understanding to our clients. The core of the case formulation is the Meaning of Behavior form. It is important to convey our findings in a sympathetic way that focuses not on blame but on deeper understanding. This opens the door to possible solutions.

   In the fairy tale, that kingdom just seemed "messed up" from the outside. If you knew about the dragon, what people were doing was still unfortunate, but at least it made sense.

   It is also important to focus on the child's strengths and resources, also an integral component of the case formulation. These become the foundation for success in treatment.

In the fairy tale, some guy came along who eventually became the dragon slayer. In real life, the client is his or her own knight in shining armor and becomes the dragon slayer himself or herself. We need hard facts so that when we say to the client, "You—you're the one who can do it," we have good reasons for believing this.

Remember that it takes a kingdom to slay a dragon. The guy in the story didn't do it by himself. So part of the evaluation is to learn about the resources available in the kingdom, or the family and community.

4. *Treatment contracting*—The treatment contracting involves coming to an agreement to pursue specific activities in service of the client's goals, in light of the strengths and challenges highlighted in the case formulation. The treatment plan typically includes doing activities to become more safe and stable, gain better self-control skills and emotional strength, and face and work through the trauma memories.

   In other words, create a safe fenced-in area, get stronger, build up skills, and slay the dragon.

5. *Case management and parent training for safety and other needs*—It is very difficult to focus on building up strength and skills when an ongoing threat exists. If we want to help kids to get over their trauma memories, we must first make sure that the trauma is not ongoing. We also must ensure, to the best of our ability, that their basic needs are being met. Otherwise, they will be too distracted by survival to focus on trauma recovery. We often work with parents and other caregivers to help them provide a more consistent and supportive environment, for example, by becoming more consistent in their discipline style. This helps kids feel more safe and secure so they can relax and concentrate on their tasks.

   In the fairy tale, the people had to find a safe place and build a fence around it so the guy could focus on his personal training tasks.

6. *Self-management skills training*—This training contributes to physical and psychological safety as well as improved affect regulation. We often train kids in various self-management and self-control skills. This also enhances their sense of safety and security, because the more they are able to control themselves, the better they are treated by others and the more supportive their environment becomes. At the same time, kids become more competent and confident, as well as emotionally stronger, and are able to handle progressively greater challenges.

   Once the fence is up, the guy can work with the personal trainer to become stronger and faster, and (in role-plays) practice fighting the dragon. It takes more than strength and skill to slay a dragon. If you're going to fight a dragon, you'd better be able to take a punch or two.

7. *Trauma resolution*—Remember the digestion metaphor? Digestion cannot happen while we are in survival mode. We need to feel safe and relaxed first. That's partly what all that preparation was about. Then it's a matter of facing the memory, taking a bite at a time, chewing it up—even if it tastes bad!—and digesting it. In treatment, this typically involves thinking and talking about it over and over again in a structured, systematic way.

   The guy in the fairy tale faced the dragon, fought it, and slew it. Actually, in treatment we'll probably start with a snake or two, and then a baby dragon or two before we go for the big one. Remember, we're the personal trainers here! We want to build on successes, not overwhelm our clients.

8. *Consolidation of gains*—Once the trauma is resolved, or digested, the other problems may melt away, but sometimes they don't. The child may have some bad habits or be missing some skills. Now that the trauma is no longer driving the problem, the child is in a position to respond positively to other interventions, to solve remaining problems, and to get firmly on a better track toward his goals.

   Now that the dragon is out of the way, the guy can marry the princess.

9. *Relapse prevention and harm reduction*—It's not enough just to recover from the trauma and get on a better track in life. Better to also learn from this experience and take measures to prevent a trauma recurrence. This is the time to work with the child and others in her life to identify potential risks and take specific actions to mitigate those risks. This makes other bad things less likely to happen in the future.

   Stop using that dump; compost instead, so that dragons are not attracted by the stink. Plant clusters of apple trees to make it harder for dragons to just cruise in.

   Since you can't guarantee that trauma will never recur, this is also the time to anticipate a possible recurrence and to make specific plans to recognize that and to minimize the damage.

   And if a dragon should ever come again, be ready with a bunch of teenagers who have been in training as dragon fighters.

The Fairy Tale Model of Trauma Treatment

Stage of treatment	Corresponding element of the fairy tale
Evaluation including Strengths/resources Trauma/loss history	I see your strengths; you're the one who can slay the dragon. We need to know about the dragon to make sense of the problems.
Motivational interviewing, goal setting	Without the princess, nothing will happen.
Trauma-informed case formulation and psychoeducation	Identify the strengths/resources as reason to hope for a chance of success. Take the dragon into account; then the problems make sense.
Trauma-relevant treatment contracting	Recommend fence-around, personal training to get stronger, and slay the dragon.
Case management for safety and other needs; parent training for safety and security	Build the fence around so you're not worried about being attacked at any moment. Then you can concentrate on your tasks.
Self-management skills training for physical and psychological safety as well as improved affect regulation	The personal training approach to build skill and strength.
Trauma resolution	Slay the dragon.
Relapse prevention and harm reduction	Compost instead of using the dump, to stop attracting dragons; stands of apple trees so it's harder for dragons to come along. Teens training for the dragon-slaying contest, so if another one does come along, we'll be ready.

Chapter 3

The Trauma-Informed Therapeutic Relationship

CHILD TRAUMA TREATMENT—BASIC PRINCIPLES

Each of the steps in treatment is made up of a number of specific interventions. These steps will be taught in detail in the following chapters. For now, I wish to introduce a few key principles that pervade the child trauma treatment approach. These principles are intentionally introduced in this chapter because relationships are created with attitudes and actions. By following these principles, the therapist can help the child feel safe enough and trust the therapist enough that she will be willing to engage in the necessary treatment activities.

It's important to recognize that you do not have to be a therapist to create a therapeutic or healing relationship with a child. Parents, counselors, teachers, coaches, direct care workers, case managers, and others are all in a position to help a child heal. The quality of your relationship is the vehicle for the healing. This is because when kids feel safe, respected, and cared for, they are more likely to "let you in" and benefit from what you have to offer. So please read this chapter with your own work in mind.

Safety First

The traumatized child's primary concern is safety. Kids feel safe when they know what to expect and what to do—when they feel that things are under control.

- Therapists can do many things to help kids feel safe in therapy. For example, at the beginning of the first session, the therapist can introduce "the rules" including the schedule for meeting, the purpose/goals of meeting, conditions of confidentiality, and what is expected of the child in sessions.
- Case managers can do many things to help kids feel safe, even when kids must be placed or moved. Case managers can tell kids what is going to happen, when it will happen, what the child is supposed to do, and specifically how the child will maintain important relationships after the move (e.g., "There will be supervised visits with your mom every Thursday after school"). Case managers can make life disruptions feel more under control, for example, by helping kids keep and carry their personal belongings from one placement to the next.
- Parents, teachers, and direct care workers can help make kids feel safe by preventing violence, by maintaining a daily routine, and by enforcing their rules consistently. If the adult enforces rules inconsistently, the child does not know what to expect—and when the rule finally is enforced, it's often done out of anger and the enforcement may be overly harsh and frightening. When the adult enforces the rule at the first violation, the consequence can be small and reasonable, and the adult is more likely to be calm and supportive.

Safety Last

When we are working our way through the treatment steps in the fairy tale model, we are asking our clients to face progressively greater emotional challenges. For example, as early as the second meeting, we are asking the child to tell us about the worst things that ever happened to him. Most children habitually avoid talking about such events because it upsets them. So after they answer our questions, get upset, and then the session ends, what then?

In many circles, child therapists have a bad reputation because this issue is managed poorly. Many therapists are trained to believe that their job is to help the child to "open up"—to express feelings, work on issues—whether through talk, art, or play. This opening up activates the trauma memory, which upsets the child. Then the session is over and she is sent on her way. Many teachers have complained, "It's bad enough that she gets taken out of my class—my class is important; she comes to school to learn—but then when she comes back after a meeting with the counselor, she's all upset. She can't concentrate. She's a mess!" Similarly, many parents have complained that the child is "a mess" in one way or another for some period after therapy.

Although some therapists believe that this is just the inevitable fallout that comes from doing therapy, these therapists are wrong. They are not trained in trauma treatment. Remember, as do the rest of us, kids learn from experience. What do kids learn from the experience of being a mess after their therapy session? They learn that bad things happen if they open up with you. One fourteen-year-old boy said, "Last time, after I left here, I was still heated. I ended up getting into a fight and I got in trouble. I don't want to talk about that [upsetting personal] stuff anymore."

When kids and their caregivers regularly experience bad outcomes from therapy sessions, it gives therapy (and the therapist) a bad reputation. Parents, teachers, and other adults feel that therapy is an imposition, a disruption to the day. They see it as harming rather than helping the child. So the adults are more likely to terminate the child's therapy or at least not support it as actively as the therapist would prefer. Also, the kids in this situation are likely to become more resistant and more reserved. Why trust the therapist who keeps setting you up for problems? Why open up if it only gets you upset and gets you in trouble?

The wise trauma therapist minimizes the risk of bad outcomes to sessions by using the following strategies:

- Carefully control what is discussed in a session so that the challenge (level of distress) is consistent with what the child can be expected to tolerate/handle. Using the personal trainer metaphor, if a client lifted fifteen pounds last meeting, don't give her fifty pounds this time. Give her fifteen again, or maybe eighteen or twenty if you think she's ready. With this approach, the child experiences repeated successes with progressively greater challenges, and is unlikely to become overwhelmed.
- Use the "cognitive-affective-cognitive sandwich." Make the sandwich by surrounding the emotional/expressive component of your session with more structured components grounded in rational thinking. For example, you might start out by reminding the child of the reason he is going to talk about the hard thing, how this relates to his goals. In the middle you do work with the emotion, at whatever level the child is ready to handle. The emotional component is finished with calming activities so that the level of upset/arousal is diminished. Then you move back to the cognitive, perhaps by discussing what was learned, perhaps by reorienting to what's next in the child's day. This helps the child to contain the emotion and to regain composure. Although there is no guarantee, therapists who make a practice of using the sandwich tend to have far fewer problems with their kids being a mess later on.
  —One example of this sandwich approach is the Float-Back exercise in Chapter 1. Remember what happened? First was the cognitive piece, about how kids are affected by

trauma and why it's worthwhile for you to feel bad, briefly, to gain insight into this dynamic. Then the emotional piece, where you explored your own upsetting memories, the recent one and one from the past. This part was finished with the calming activity—in this case, deep breathing. Then back to the cognitive, with a discussion about what this might mean for kids and what to do about it.

Safety in Between

No matter how carefully we follow the fairy tale model, no matter how well we plan, surprises always occur. We are working with humans! So it's important to continually monitor how your clients are doing and what is going on with them. Frequently, when things are not going according to plan, it's because the child no longer feels safe. If we are paying attention, we can catch this and address it.

- A fifteen-year-old girl has been doing well in treatment, and is ready for trauma resolution. The therapist prepares her for this, and they plan to start on it at the next meeting. Then for the next two meetings something comes up and the girl cancels at the last minute. The therapist telephones her and asks her to please come to the next scheduled meeting and tells her that the plan to talk about the trauma is off for now. When the girl arrives at the next meeting, she eventually explains that she does not feel ready to talk about the trauma yet and was afraid to come to sessions for that reason.
- An eleven-year-old girl has been very cooperative in treatment for the first four sessions with her school guidance counselor. Today she seems angry, refuses to answer questions in any detail, and keeps looking at her watch. The counselor asks her if she is in a hurry today. The girl says, "Yes, my group is presenting our project at ten o'clock and I'm supposed to be there!" The counselor thanks the girl for saying that, and they agree to reschedule their meeting so the girl can leave now and meet her classroom obligation.
- A six-year-old boy appears to be engaged in his rather new treatment and to like his therapist. However, when the therapist asks about the worst things that ever happened (the trauma/loss history), the boy clams up. The therapist switches to play with stuffed animals, and points out one small animal who wants to tell about the bad thing that happened, but is afraid to. After some discussion, the boy suggests that the animal is afraid that if it tells, its parents will get in trouble.
- A ten-year-old boy has been working well in treatment and has completed several sessions of trauma resolution work. However, in this session, he refuses to talk about the memory that is already partly resolved. The therapist is stumped and is unable to get a decent explanation from the boy. Later, the therapist mentions to the boy's mother that he seemed different today and did not accomplish as much as usual. The mother reports that she had blown up at her son a couple of days earlier and threatened to send him to live with his father if he didn't get a better attitude.

In each of these cases, some pressing concern prevented the child from moving forward according to the therapist's plan. If the therapist just barges ahead, the child's concern is not addressed. The child might then feel disrespected and/or pressured, and take protective action.

On the other hand, when the therapist notices when things are not going smoothly and shows respect and concern, the child learns that the therapist cares and wants what is best for the child. In general, the more the therapist can do to help the child feel safe and supported, the more work the child will be able to accomplish in therapy. Our goal is to create a "fenced-in" safe area in the room, in the therapy relationship itself.

Security Is Love

Therapists, like parents, can convey love and caring for the child by helping the child feel secure. The more the child knows what will happen in therapy and what to expect, the more secure and cared for he or she will feel. The therapist can do many more things to help the therapy situation be predictable and supportive for the child, including the following:

- Keep your promises. Be ready and start the session on time. (If you can't do this reliably, don't make the promise.)
- Start each session the same way. Routines are reassuring. The starting routine can be as simple as a check-in. For example, many therapists start by saying, "Tell me something good and something bad that happened since last time we met." In addition to the value of having a routine, this is also a good way to find out what's happening in the child's life. Often this material can be used in support of the treatment plan. For example, if the child reports having handled a peer confrontation poorly, this event can be used for practicing self-control skills.
- End each session the same way. Establish routines for putting toys or materials away, talking about what's next in the child's day, or asking the child to say something he or she liked and something he or she didn't like about the meeting. Again, part of the value is the fact of the routine, and part of the value is helping the child to gain closure on the session, regain composure, and be ready for what's next in his day.

Success

Remember the princess? The entire therapy enterprise is to serve the child's goals. In the trauma treatment approach, we may be part of the kingdom (providing safety and support); we are also the personal trainer. As the personal trainer, our job is to help the child make progress toward winning the princess. Remember, nothing succeeds like success. So one of our primary strategies is to help kids build a track record of success by achieving smaller goals one step at a time. This track record helps build confidence that the next steps will also be worthwhile and successful and nurtures hope that the larger goals can be attained.

WHAT IT TAKES TO BE A PERSON WHO HELPS TRAUMATIZED KIDS

If you've made it this far, you've got a pretty good understanding of what it means to be a traumatized child, and you have a good overview of the steps involved in treatment. However, it takes more than understanding and skills to be able to help traumatized kids. It takes a certain kind of person. It takes someone who cares enough to make the effort to understand, learn, and use the skills. It takes someone who cares enough, and who is strong and resilient enough, to persevere through the child's sometimes painful steps toward healing. It takes someone who can help children feel that they are with a person who cares about them and will care for them; they are in a safe place with a fence around it.

Being a person who is able to help traumatized kids is a big deal; it's not to be taken lightly. It entails a specific set of interpersonal skills and practices as well as self-care skills and practices. Not everyone can do this, and not everyone would choose to. There are inherent challenges and even risks or occupational hazards.

Having what it takes to do this work is not a categorical trait, such as being nice enough or smart enough. It's more about being able to come through for kids in certain ways, to maintain certain kinds of awareness, to self-monitor, and to use the information you obtain in constructive ways. It's also about taking good enough care of yourself (see Chapter 4) that you are able to focus on kids' needs when you're on the job.

THE THERAPEUTIC RELATIONSHIP

Special problems are inherent in trying to help traumatized kids. Each of the following makes it particularly challenging to form a therapeutic relationship with such a child, and to get the child to do anything productive:

- Traumatized kids by definition have had their primary attachment disrupted (the promise of safety having been broken) and they are cautious about trusting others and about forming relationships.
- Traumatized kids have been profoundly disappointed, and they are reluctant to be hopeful. They are afraid to hope because they don't want to be disappointed again. They are afraid to invest in therapy because that implies hope and invites disappointment.
- They are skeptical about the possibility that anything good will happen. Why work toward a goal that's "not gonna work out anyway"?
- Some of the trauma therapy activities involve talking about upsetting events. Traumatized kids often have poor affect tolerance and are uncomfortable with distress. It feels like "too much." They don't want to talk about it.

Traumatized kids have special needs from you in terms of how you behave toward them and how you relate to them. You need to be the person who helps kids feel safe and secure, to understand themselves and how to be successful in overcoming their problems. What kind of person would be able to help kids in this way? What would such a person be doing? How can you address the child's fears to the point that he or she is willing to trust you, invest in therapy, and do the work?

THE RICH *RELATIONSHIP MODEL*

The RICH model—Respect, Information, Connection, Hope—is one approach to therapeutic relationship that is well suited to trauma treatment (Saakvitne, Gamble, Pearlman, & Lev, 2000). It is an empowerment approach that encompasses the therapist's attitude and also implies specific behaviors that contribute to a safe, supportive, and therapeutic environment.

Note that although the focus here is on how to treat kids, the same principles can apply for how to treat parents, teachers, and co-workers. When we treat one another this way, we all feel safer, more supported, and more related/connected. This allows us to feel better, to work well together, and to focus more effectively on helping the kids.

Respect

This aspect encourages individual attention and respect for each child: "I can treat you like a person, not a number or a problem. I can treat you the way I would want (my own child) to be treated."

Many kids who are referred for treatment have learned to feel that something is wrong with them—that they are a problem. They may have experience with overburdened workers who cannot devote adequate attention to individual children, who are burned out and just not very nice, or who take out their own sense of frustration and helplessness on the kids they are supposed to help. Many kids have been treated impersonally or have been treated as if they are a problem. Actually, these kids often *are* a problem! They may behave in ways that elicit anger, frustration, and rejection from their parents, teachers, and others. That's why they are being sent for help. When the helper responds in the same way that others have responded, it doesn't help. It just adds to the problem and reinforces it.

When the helper treats the child with respect, this may break a pattern and open the door for something different to happen—perhaps something good. Treating a child with respect means listening as well as talking; respecting the child's autonomy and right to make his or her own choices (of course, choices have consequences); telling the truth; keeping promises; and seriously addressing the child's own concerns. Specific ways of doing these things will be detailed throughout the book. When children feel respected, they are more likely to respond positively.

Information

This aspect encourages honesty and creativity in providing children with information: "This is what you need to know to understand the situation."

When we tell kids what will happen and what to expect from us, they feel respected and safe. They know what's going on. They know what's coming. When we tell kids what we expect from them and how to do it, then they know what to do and have a better chance of being successful in their work with us. Being successful feels good, and *is* good, for all of us.

Another kind of information is particularly meaningful to traumatized kids. Many times, kids who have developed symptoms following a trauma or loss don't really understand what has happened to them or why they are not the way they used to be. Many such kids believe that they are bad, crazy, or damaged in some way. They may have been told, repeatedly, that they are "messed up" by people who didn't know about the dragon. We can tell the story a different way, using the fairy tale model, to explain that their symptoms are a reasonable (if unfortunate) response to the bad things that happened.

When we can help kids (and others) see themselves as hurt instead of bad, they have more empathy for themselves. Also, they understand, finally, what's been happening to them. Many kids have said, "No one's ever explained this to me before." This is often accompanied by considerable relief. The therapist also gains a certain credibility and status that can be helpful in the treatment contracting phase. If the therapist does have a map of this territory, maybe that map shows the way out, too.

Connection

This aspect encourages creating an emotional bond with the child: "I can imagine what it might feel like to be you. I'm here with you now."

This is perhaps both the simplest and most complicated aspect of the therapeutic relationship. You can have all the understanding and techniques in the world, but if kids feel that you don't care about them, they will not work with you. Kids understand that people who don't care about them may not have their best interests in mind and cannot be trusted.

When you care about a child, to some extent you open your heart. You form a relationship. A caring adult with good boundaries and a focus on the child's needs may create a unique and healing relationship for the child. Many traumatized kids have been victimized by people who were expected to care for them. For such children, your relationship might serve as a more positive model of an adult-child relationship. This paves the way for other successful relationships in the future.

Even kids whose parents have been appropriately protective and supportive will often withdraw from their attachment relationships to some extent following trauma. For these kids, the therapy relationship can serve as a step toward trusting adults again and reestablishing the primary attachment relationships.

Connection is also important in trauma therapy because we will eventually ask the kids we work with to face their pain. Of course, often the reason they need our help is because they can't stand to face their pain, but instead choose the quick-relief behaviors that others call a problem. Yet somehow the emotional support provided by the therapist can help. When a young child skins a knee and it must be washed, she may cry but will tolerate the washing if it is her mother doing it. Even as adults, when a friend or loved one is in some kind of pain, we offer a shoulder, an ear, a hug. Connection helps kids to tolerate their pain while they are learning to deal with it in healthier ways.

Many ways to convey caring to a child are detailed throughout the book. They might include actions to show respect and help the child feel safe; keeping the therapeutic frame (e.g., being on time, avoiding undue focus on the therapist, avoiding sexual contact), and focusing on the child's own interests and concerns. Empathy is a key means of showing caring; this involves being able to feel what the child feels while also maintaining the adult's sense of responsibility and objectivity. The caring adult (therapist or otherwise) feels and shows concern for the child's welfare, and expresses pleasure in his growth and achievements.

Risks are also inherent in opening your heart to a child. To care about the child and feel what he feels is to open yourself to his pain and to your own pain. This can be very difficult to manage, and will be discussed in more detail in Chapter 4.

Hope

This aspect focuses on providing experiences that will lead the child to develop a more positive outlook. "This process can lead to good outcomes."

For kids to engage in the hard work of treatment, there must be some sense of possibility that the work will be worthwhile. There must be hope for things to get better. The therapist can help the child develop hope in three ways:

1. As the relationship develops, the child may learn to trust more, by experimenting with trust and being rewarded. As the child comes to feel that the therapy relationship is successful, he may develop hope that other interpersonal relationships can work in the future.
2. When the therapist offers a case formulation that helps the child understand herself, and feel understood for perhaps the first time, the child is likely to take the therapist very seriously. When the therapist then explains that certain treatment activities are likely to help, the child may become hopeful. After all, the therapist seems to know.
3. As the child, step-by-step, makes progress through the treatment program, he is building a track record of progressively more substantial achievements. Each time the child takes another step forward, he becomes more confident and more hopeful that he can heal more fully and achieve his goals.

EXERCISE: WHO HELPED YOU AND HOW?

1. Think back to your own childhood/adolescence. Think of one person who stands out who really helped you in some way—someone who made a positive difference in your life, in your development. Maybe this person helped you overcome a problem, get a better attitude, feel better about yourself, or try to succeed at something. This person might be a therapist, a teacher, a coach, a relative, or someone else. Write down who the person was and what impact the person had on your development.
2. Now think about what actions this person took that made him or her have such a positive influence on you. Write down what the person did that made such a difference.
3. Now write down, for each of the following categories, a specific thing this person did that pertains to that category. In what ways were this person's actions consistent with the RICH model? In what ways were the person's actions inconsistent with the model?

Respect: ______________________________

____

Information: ______________________________

Connection: ______________________________

____

Hope: ______________________________

____

Share if in a group.

Discussion Questions

1. What did you notice by doing this?
2. What do you learn from this?
3. What qualities/behaviors seem to be most essential to helping a child?

The essence of this relationship approach is to come from the heart, to find some way of loving each child we work with. Considerable research indicates that the nonspecific components of therapy—empathy and positive regard—make a substantial contribution to the client's progress. However, just having and emanating the positive feeling is not enough. Many well-meaning therapists truly care for the children they work with but do not help them recover from trauma.

The rabbi at my grandmother's grave said, "Love is taking responsibility." The rabbi meant that my grandmother did more than merely say "I love you." She showed her love by putting food on the table and ensuring that her kids had clean clothes to wear to school. Therapists ought to care enough to take responsibility too: to learn what it takes to help children heal and to offer this to the kids they work with. It takes specific actions to recover from trauma. It is the therapist's job not merely to care, but to do something about it. The therapist's trauma-informed interventions help build the therapeutic relationship and convey the therapist's caring, while also helping the child take the actions essential to healing.

In other words, the therapeutic relationship is fundamental to the child's healing. However, a repertoire of specific practices, skills, and interventions is integral not only to the child's healing but to the development of the therapeutic relationship itself. Throughout this book, the technique and relationship aspects of the trauma treatment approach will be intertwined.

Chapter 4

Taking Care of Yourself

Mental health professionals and others who work with kids have a special interest in self-care. In every field from surgery to farming, it's important to keep the tools and equipment in good working order. For those who work with kids, our person is the primary tool. We use ourselves to form therapeutic relationships and to provide understanding, emotional support, and guidance. We use ourselves to bear witness, to share the burden of the child's pain. It is essential to keep this tool—ourselves—in good condition. If we can't handle it, how can we help the kids to do so?

Kids learn from experience. Many kids have learned that it's not okay to talk about the bad things that happened: "If I talk about it, people get upset: parents get sad or angry, other kids tease, people change the subject. It's better not to talk about it." When you encourage the child to talk about it, what will she learn from you? That depends on how you react. Hopefully, the child will learn that it's okay to talk about it, that you can handle it and won't freak out, fall apart, or reject her.

An eight-year-old boy was in his second session of treatment with a new therapist, after having been in weekly therapy with someone else for two years following a major trauma. The new therapist, wanting to know how much had already been accomplished, asked, "So how much did you talk about [the trauma] with your other therapist?" The boy replied, "Oh, we never brought it up. [The other therapist] wasn't ready yet." (As far as I know, this is a true story. It was told to me by the person who is the new therapist in the story.)

If we are impaired, we bring less to a relationship. When we are preoccupied with our own concerns, we are unlikely to "show up" at 100 percent capacity. We have less energy. When our own needs are unmet, we may have a hard time staying focused on what the kids need. Kids will pick up on this. They will feel less respected and less important to us. They will feel less secure and more likely to act out with us, to test us. When we are not at our best, we are at a higher risk of falling into traps instead of being helpful.

If we try to help others at our own expense, we cannot sustain this. Many extremely dedicated professionals correctly recognize that a great deal urgently needs to be done. It can be tempting to try to do it all or at least to routinely work to exhaustion. We may feel that we are saving lives, or something close to that, and that this justifies pushing ourselves. Although this kind of perception regarding the value and urgency of the work may be accurate, it does not mean that we have to destroy ourselves doing it.

Working to exhaustion is the pony express model. The pony express was an early mail delivery system in the United States (1860-1861). Because speed of delivery was highly valued, the strategy was to ride a horse to its limit. Then a new horse would pick up where the other left off, while the exhausted horse would be rested and cared for. If you are not part of a tag team—if no one is available to take over your job for you when you get tired and need a month off—you must pace yourself, otherwise you'll wear yourself out and nothing will be left for the kids you care so much about.

To care for ourselves properly, it is important to understand the challenges. What is the impact of doing what we do? How does it affect us?

EXERCISE: HOW HAS WORKING WITH TRAUMATIZED KIDS AFFECTED YOU?

Write down how working with traumatized/hurt kids has affected you in each of the following categories (from Saakvitne et al., 2000):

- Beliefs about the world
- Spiritual beliefs
- Sense of self, groundedness, emotional stability
- Sense of personal safety or family's safety
- Trust of yourself or others
- The way you judge people
- Sense of control
- Ability to be alone, to be with others
- Relationship to your body

If you are working with a group, once everyone is finished please feel free to share something that you wrote down. However, please also feel free *not* to share. It is important for people to feel that it is okay to either talk or be silent.

Then in a group discussion or on your own, answer these questions:

- What surprised you about your own responses?
- What surprised you about others' responses?
- Did you notice any common themes?
- Did you notice areas of divergence?

Following are some examples shared by others:

- "I used to always be heartbroken to see children being mistreated in public places. You know, like some mother slapping her kid and saying, 'Shut up or I'll really give you something to cry about.' After a few years in this field, I started to notice how *good* I felt when I was around kids who are being treated well. I used to just take that for granted. Now it really strikes me, makes my day better."
- "When my girlfriend's little daughter climbed on my lap, I kind of froze. I know I'm not a child abuser, but I've been exposed to so much of it I actually felt as if I was doing something bad with her. I had to catch myself, tell myself that this was normal, friendly physical contact and it was okay."
- "I've seen too much, the things people can do to each other. I've developed a cop's-eye view of the world. I am so ready to assume the worst about people I barely know."
- "I've learned that I often underestimate people. I can't tell you how many times these really pathetic-looking parents surprised me and came through for their kids, in one way or another. I think I've learned to have more respect. Even when people don't look so good, I've learned that maybe they really are trying, doing their best. And that when I give them the tools, maybe they can do even better. So I guess I don't just write people off the way I used to."
- "I lost my faith in God."
- "Working in this field has made me rely more on my faith, become a more spiritual person."

Clearly, this work has potential for personal impact. Just as self-care is particularly important for those who work with kids because the self is the primary tool, so is the self also at particular risk—especially when working with hurt children.

Why should working with hurt kids have so much impact? More specifically, why is there so much potential for negative impact? The following are some reasons why we may be particularly vulnerable:

- We are exposed to horrible stories of things that happened to kids we care about.
- When we do good work, we are empathetic. We open our hearts.
- We feel responsible for these kids' well-being.
- We feel angry and helpless about what happened.
- We may also feel angry and helpless about what is continuing to happen.
- The stories we hear might remind us of our own stories.

In many ways, working with traumatized children can be similar to exposing ourselves to a traumatic experience. Many mental health professionals and others who work with traumatized kids suffer from what has been called "secondary traumatic stress syndrome" or "vicarious traumatization." When we are exposed to someone else's trauma story and situation, we can be traumatized from that; it can hurt us. We are then vulnerable to developing symptoms ourselves.

EXERCISE: YOUR MOST UPSETTING CASE

Think about the most disturbing or upsetting case that you have had. Write down what aspect caused you the most distress. In a group, share this if you wish to. In a group, what do you notice about differences and/or common themes?

What Gets to Us?

Just as not every upsetting experience is traumatic, not every session with a traumatized child causes vicarious traumatization. Therapists tend to agree that certain key features of a case can make it especially difficult to handle: caring about the child, feeling helpless, and getting triggered by the child's story or behavior.

Caring

Many who work with children attempt to shield themselves from risk by trying to avoid caring. If you don't care, it doesn't have to hurt so much. Unfortunately, if you don't care, by definition you cannot do good work because children will not trust you or engage with you. If you do care, then what hurts the child has a better chance of hurting you too.

Feeling Helpless

The child with the most horrific story can be a "great case" if the therapist is able to be helpful. When therapists are asked to describe their most disturbing/distressing case, they typically tell about one in which the therapist, for whatever reason, is powerless to help or to make anything better. It is difficult to tolerate being helpless when a child you care about is hurting.

Getting Triggered

Just as children can experience some minor stressor as a trigger (a reminder of past trauma) and then overreact on that account, so too can therapists. We have sore spots too! Sometimes it is the child's trauma story that serves as a reminder of the therapist's own trauma history. Sometimes it is the child's behavior or situation that makes the therapist feel angry, frustrated, rejected, or helpless; and it is this feeling that serves as the therapist's trigger. When triggered, the therapist is at a higher risk of overreaction, of experiencing these strong feelings as intolerable.

In any of these situations (or a combination of them), the risk of vicarious traumatization is heightened, but it is still not automatic. It depends on how the therapist handles it. Vicarious traumatization occurs when the challenging/upsetting material is not processed but gets stuck somehow, maybe even pushed behind the wall.

When this happens, the therapist may be in trouble and some of those symptoms and problems might show up. Therapists may react inappropriately to certain kids, with the therapist's own distress interfering with a therapeutic focus on the child's experience and needs. The therapist may become preoccupied, sad, withdrawn, stressed, or irritable, possibly impacting the therapist's personal life as well. The therapist may develop a more impersonal style on the job to try to avoid further hurt or trauma-related triggers. The therapist may become cynical, exhausted, burned out.

EXERCISE: HOW DO YOU KNOW WHEN IT'S HAPPENED TO YOU?

Think of a time when you were hurt in some way by your work. Write down

1. what happened,
2. what your symptoms were,
3. how you noticed what was wrong, and
4. what you did about it.

In a group, share this if you wish to. In a group, what do you notice about differences and/or common themes?

Working with hurt kids is an occupational hazard. To do good work, we open our hearts. Thus we risk being hurt ourselves.

Think about the phrase *occupational hazard*. What comes to mind? In many other fields, the occupational hazards are recognized and addressed. On a construction site, people are required to wear hard hats. In a hospital, used needles are safely sequestered. Airplane crews are required to rest after a certain number of hours. What do we do to protect ourselves? What can we do?

EXERCISE: SELF-CARE CHECK-IN

Write down your answers to the following questions.
When is the last time that you . . .

- got what you consider a good night's sleep?
- spent quality time with a friend?
- did your favorite kind of exercise?
- had time to yourself when you didn't have to take care of others?
- put food into your body that you consider nutritious?

- spent quality time with your romantic partner or a family member?
- left work on time or early, even though there was more to do?
- took time for a meal without doing something else at the same time?
- talked to a supportive colleague about challenges in your work?
- did something you really enjoy doing when you have the time?

Follow-Up Questions

What did you notice about what you just did?
What did you learn about yourself?
What did you learn about your life situation?
How does that feel?
What are you saying to yourself about this now?

Self-Care Strategies

Each of us can do a number of things to minimize the impact of our occupational hazard. Not surprisingly, some of these are the same things that we might recommend to a stressed-out parent or friend. These self-care approaches are likely to keep us more healthy, balanced, and able to handle whatever comes our way:

1. *Nutrition.* It's easy to believe that you're too busy for lunch so you just grab a candy bar or bag of chips on the fly. However, this does not take care of you. It will only add stress and wear you down. Remember that you are the only pony doing your job. Treat yourself as you would treat your only pony, one who must be good for the long haul. Drink enough water. Eat foods that really nourish you.
2. *Exercise.* The typical obstacles to exercise are time, convenience, depression, and fatigue. However, you probably know from experience that regular exercise will help you feel better, less fatigued, more alert, and thus make better use of your time. Exercise gives more than it takes; it improves health and promotes longevity. If some obstacle prevents you from getting regular exercise, it is worth your while to find a way to overcome the obstacle.
3. *Sleep.* Those who don't get enough sleep incur a chronic burden of stress related to sleep deprivation. This can lead to health problems, bad moods, and underfunctioning. Typical obstacles to sleep are time and worry. Again, it's worth addressing these; would you rather have good excuses or good health?
4. *Substance avoidance.* When people feel stressed or upset, it is tempting to want to push the bad feelings out of the way, behind the wall. One of the more popular ways to do this is by drinking alcoholic beverages or using other so-called recreational drugs. The problem with this strategy is that pushing it out of the way only provides short-term relief but does not solve the problem—and substance use can bring new problems. If you find yourself stressed and tempted to increase your normal level of substance use, you would probably be better off finding a more productive way of dealing with the stress.
5. *Stress management.* What works for you? Many options are available for coping with stress, whether you do this as a daily routine or only when you notice that you are feeling stressed. Many people benefit from activities such as exercise, competitive sports, meditation, yoga, listening to music, reading, taking a bath, taking a walk, dancing, doing artwork, or even cleaning the house. It is important to figure out what works for you, and do it.
6. *Social support.* People with good social support networks tend to feel more positively about their life situation and to handle stress and challenges more effectively. It is impor-

tant to have people in your life who you can talk to, who can help you when you need it, who you can do things with, and feel close to.
7. *Time away/refreshing activities.* Everyone needs a break or a respite. Isn't this what you would tell a parent or a friend? If it's good advice for them, it's good advice for you. What do you enjoy doing? What's a good change of pace for you? If you build this into your life on a regular basis, it will help you to feel fresher and more content.

Many of us are in jobs in which it is literally impossible to get everything done or even to get all the important tasks done. We may feel that kids' well-being and even their lives are on the line, and we may be right about this. The temptations to engage in long work hours and heroic self-neglect can be powerful. This is why it's so important to step back and make conscious decisions about how we operate. It's fine to be dedicated to helping children and their families, but it's not fine to do this in an unsustainable way that hurts you and your family—and possibly the kids you're trying to help as well.

The self-care decision can involve real sacrifices. You might find yourself taking a break during the day to go to the bathroom, to call home, or to have a real lunch. You might find yourself leaving work at a reasonable time, even though there's more to do. You might find that you are doing less than you used to, which can be difficult to accept. It's important to understand the alternative.

Those who fail to take care of themselves are at high risk of developing stress-related problems such as underperformance, job burnout, health problems, bad moods, and damaged personal relationships. Most people with this understanding choose to do only what they can on the job, not what they wish they could do. With this choice, you have a better chance of being able to do good work tomorrow as well as today.

Which self-care practices are you currently using on a regular basis?

EXERCISE: SELF-CARE PLANS

This excercise can be done individually or in pairs. If you're in a pair, ask your partner each of the following questions, and don't quit until you get answers that are both realistic and very specific. Then switch to do the same exercise in the other role. If you're by yourself, it's more difficult to be hard on yourself and not let yourself squirm out of being specific. Do your best.

Questions

- What one self-care practice do you feel that you should be doing, and that, realistically, you can actually do?
- What's your next step? Start small, with one realistic example of the desired behavior.
- How will you do it? What day, what time, what place, what action?
- What are the obstacles? What could keep you from doing it?
- How will you handle this to keep yourself on track?

Discussion

Will you be able to find out if your partner followed through? Make a specific plan (you know, date, time, place, action—the whole thing!) for checking in. If you're doing this alone, put your plan in an envelope that you will open the day after you were to have done your planned action.

Special Self-Care Issues for Trauma Therapists

The self-care strategies just described can apply to anyone. There are also some self-care strategies that are specific to those who work with traumatized kids (or adults, for that matter). These relate directly to the challenges inherent in hearing about what has happened to the kids and to interacting with them and experiencing some of their problem behaviors firsthand. How is the mental health professional expected to avoid being traumatized by the kids' stories or being triggered by the frustration and helplessness that may be a natural response to the kids' problem behaviors?

This issue is often referred to as countertransference—the therapist's personal/emotional reaction to the client—and is considered perhaps the greatest challenge to doing good work. This is potentially an issue in any type of treatment, but when the treatment focus is trauma, the content can be particularly challenging for the therapist. Although having an emotional response to clients is unavoidable, ideally we use this to learn more about our clients. It becomes a problem when our emotional response takes over; then we are focused primarily on our own feelings and are at risk of acting out. Here are some of the more common counter-transference reactions to working with traumatized kids:

- Playing the rescuer
- Helping the client to avoid the painful material
- Being angry at the parent(s)
- Disliking the client
- Disconnecting: becoming bored, distracted, distant, disengaged

Several strategies together comprise an overall approach to this challenge. These are not mere techniques that can be mastered with an hour's practice. Rather, this approach represents a major commitment to personal development, self-awareness, self-care, and responsibility/integrity in relationships. How many times has someone said to you, "I don't see how you can do the work you do!"? Many people are not willing to make such a commitment, to be able to manage the pain and the challenges and remain effective. But this is what it takes.

Self-Care

The self-care strategies previously described help us be at our best. Then when our own trauma-related triggers come up while we are working with kids, we will have the best chance of handling this the way we would like to.

Personal Therapy

If we can't go to certain places within ourselves, how can we take a child there? To help the child work through his trauma, we should have worked through ours—or at least be working on it and know our way around. Then when the child tells his story, we will have a better chance of being able to focus on how he is doing and what he needs. Otherwise we risk being distracted and even overwhelmed by our own emotions or memories when they are triggered. Also, a therapist who has been a therapy client usually has a deeper understanding of the process.

Self-Monitoring

Self-awareness and self-monitoring allow the therapist to notice emotional reactions and to consider them, rather than merely acting out. Clinical supervision is essential to developing this skill; we may not be automatically good at seeing our own blind places, at seeing ways that we, not the client, might be the problem. When we are able to notice that we are feeling angry, frustrated, helpless, or rejected, we have a chance to reflect on this and make a decision rather than just acting on impulse.

- What does this mean about the client? Is she feeling helpless too? Is this how others usually feel when they are with her? I wonder if they do what I feel like doing? What would be a more helpful response right now?
- Also, what does this mean about me? Why is it always these sullen, silent kids who make me so mad? Do I have a sore spot that he is finding? How can I figure this out and take care of it?
- What's going on here? Am I really being hurtful the way she says I am? Or is she just reenacting her trauma, assuming that everyone victimizes her? Is it her or me? How can I sort it out?

More Supervision, More Therapy

What? Again? Just when we think we're in pretty good shape, some client comes along who surprises us. We find ourselves having a problematic emotional reaction and we know that we are not doing our best work with this client. The first step is to discuss the situation with a supervisor (senior therapists who no longer require weekly supervision often arrange for mutual peer supervision on a regular basis). Sometimes this consultation is sufficient for the therapist to get a better understanding of the situation and to then manage it effectively. Other times, the therapist may conclude that further personal therapy is needed to become less reactive and more capable of handling this particular type of challenge.

Self-care helps us to be at our best. Self-monitoring helps us take our own emotional responses as useful information, rather than allowing our emotions to take us over, lead us to acting out. Following are a few additional strategies we can use to keep our heads above water so that we can keep doing the work we care about.

Don't Be Helpless

Remember that feeling helpless can really get to us. This may seem like simplistic advice, but it is offered in all seriousness. Following are several ways to reduce the sense of helplessness that many helpers can feel:

- *Improve your skills.* The better you are at what you do, the more effective you will be, and the better your results are likely to be, on average. Part of this strategy is not merely to get better at some skill or another, but to get better at the skills that are most likely to make a difference for your clients. There is a myth that all therapy styles/approaches are equal, and that therapists can resonably and responsibily choose according to personal preference. In fact, considerable research exists on various approaches to trauma treatment. It is clear that some approaches are more equal than others! Our job is not merely to learn techniques that seem interesting, but to help our kids. The fact that you are here is an indication that this is one of your strategies.
- *Improve your work environment.* As you develop a more sophisticated understanding of your own needs and the needs of the kids you are helping, you may become aware of systemic problems in your work setting. For example, if the staff are being frequently assaulted, they are unlikely to feel safe enough to be able to concentrate on the kids' needs. Or if your kids and their families are being given a new worker every time they get to a new

phase of your program, their repeated experiences of disrupted relationships may detract from the benefits that any given worker may be attempting to offer. To the extent that you can educate and advocate for improvements in your work setting, these factors can then support rather than undermine your work. Other strategies may include reporting unethical practices and encouraging others in your setting to obtain trauma-related training.

- *Compensate for your work environment.* You may work in a setting that falls short of ideal when it comes to supporting the self-care and supervision needs of its staff. You can find creative ways of making sure that you get what you need. This might involve self-discipline for taking lunch breaks or leaving work at a reasonable time. It might involve developing a professional peer support group on your own, on or off the clock. It might involve obtaining supervision on your own (or with co-workers), if you are not receiving what you consider adequate supervision otherwise. Self-care is important both for you and your job, whatever it takes to do it.
- *Work where you belong.* This applies to the work setting itself, as well as the type of work and clientele. Does your workplace support your ability to do work that you feel good about, or are you constantly undersupported, undermined, and sabotaged? Will success with this type of person/problem make you feel successful? Is your personality and life situation suited to the work? There is enough work to go around! So we might as well find the kind of work that is right for us. We will be happier doing it and in the long run will have more to offer.

A case manager stayed in an "impossible" job for many years because she kept telling herself that the client families needed her there. However, she was always frustrated and stressed because her caseload was far too large to be able to do good work with anyone. Finally, when the stress threatened her marriage, she found another job that had more reasonable demands.

One woman moved from direct clinical service to administration when she adopted two children; she said that her kids took all of "that kind of emotional energy" and that she needed a little more emotional distance in her workday.

One man left a good job working with mentally retarded kids. He said, "My co-workers love it here; it's a good place, and the kids are making real progress. But for me, it's no good. I can't get past the fact that no matter how hard I work, they'll always be mentally retarded."

Rationalize

It is easy enough to beat ourselves up over every failure, because we care and we want to help every child, not just some of them or even most of them. But it's not fair to hold ourselves up to unrealistic standards. This only exposes us to unreasonable self-criticism, which is destructive.

We usually think of rationalizing as a bad thing, a defense mechanism, a way to avoid. But coming up with a fresh rationale, another way of looking at something, can also be constructive. Especially when it's a more accurate perspective than the way we have been thinking. It works better to be rational and fair, even with ourselves.

Sometimes when it is hard to get a perspective on our own situation, it can be helpful to imagine that the situation belongs to someone else. Probably you would say one or more of the following to a friend or colleague who, despite good effort, was unable to help a certain child:

- You did your best.
- Can't win 'em all.
- Look at your success rate. Do you expect perfection?
- The child knows you tried. That counts for something.
- You don't know what impact you may have had on that child, in the long run. Maybe you planted a seed.

Many of us work in such challenging circumstances that progress is often slow and uncertain, and "success" is relatively rare. As you learn to apply the model and the interventions in this book, your success rate might improve. Even so, more discouraging circumstances require more sophisticated rationalizations, to allow us to maintain our morale while continuing to fight the good fight.

- A clinician working with juvenile delinquents said, "The literature says that I'll be lucky to help maybe one out of ten of these kids. If I can help two or three out of ten, I'm beating the odds! Then I think I must be doing something right."
- A caseworker responsible for a large caseload of abused and neglected children said, "If I think about all the kids I can't save, it gets depressing. But when I think about giving up, I don't think the next person in my job would care as much as I do or try as hard. Realistically, I think I'm probably helping more kids than someone else would."

Process/Express the Feelings

Sometimes we absorb the pain of our clients and then carry it around with us. Sometimes we have our own feelings of sorrow, anger, or helplessness that stay with us long after the session is over. Then we may feel as if we are "taking our work home" with us, in a way that is unwelcome but difficult to shake. It is important to identify and then do something with these feelings so they don't just stay stuck inside and color the rest of our day or week. Many methods are available for processing or expressing these feelings, such as exercise, competitive sports, dancing, walking, writing, doing artwork, or talking to someone. Figure out what works best for you, and then do it.

Buddy System

Mental health professionals have a unique, somewhat priestlike role. Others bring their pain and suffering to the mental health professional, who is expected to absorb it, assist in its management and digestion, and keep the whole thing a secret. In some systems (e.g., schools, disaster response), the mental health professional may serve in this role not only for the child/family clients, but for the other staff members. Where does all this pain and suffering go? Who counsels the counselor?

We cannot unburden ourselves on our clients, nor on our nonclinician co-workers—this would compromise our role and our ability to do good work. Although some of us may discuss an occasional case (disguised, of course) with a significant other, in general we want to avoid this, too. We don't want to make a habit out of dumping the horrors of the day on our spouse. To do this would be to inflict secondary trauma, and to what purpose? War veterans and police officers tend to have a similar reticence about polluting their family environment with "war stories."

Fortunately, we can turn to one another. Professional peer support can be invaluable in many ways. When we meet regularly with professional peers, we can do the following:

- Obtain and provide consultation on challenging cases.
- Teach one another new ideas and skills we have learned at workshops or from books.
- Offer support and alternative perspectives to colleagues who are having difficulty with a client, co-worker, or boss.
- Identify and express work-related thoughts and feelings that might otherwise stay stuck inside us and do harm.
- Identify and problem solve systemic problems that undermine the clinical work.
- Discuss self-care strategies.
- Hold one another accountable to actually use the self-care strategies on a regular basis.

In short, the buddy system is what makes everything else work. We don't always have the distance or perspective to help ourselves, but we can help one another to learn, stay focused, self-monitor, solve problems, and maintain good habits.

In some work settings, once you have your professional license you may be told that "you don't need supervision anymore." This is wrong. We all need a regular opportunity to meet with professional peers to discuss our work in depth. Even after you are more experienced and don't require a senior supervisor, you can still benefit from peer supervision. Work settings that don't allot time and space for supervision (individual or peer-group) are being penny-wise and pound-foolish. They are likely to pay many times over in lower quality of work, worse morale, and higher turnover.

The buddy system—professional peer support—is the hard hat of our profession. If your work setting does not provide you with an opportunity for regular peer support, then it has failed

to address your occupational hazard. This is irresponsible. However, the failure is often the result of ignorance rather than bad intent, and so may be responsive to education. If you are unable to obtain this essential support within your workplace, as a responsible professional you are still obliged to build it into your professional life. You owe it to your clients, your family, and yourself.

Connecting with One Another

We get something else from interacting with professional peers: the interaction itself. When we connect with one another, we are not alone in our work. We interact with others who know what we know, who do what we do, who care about what we care about. We can communicate with one another in a special way because of these shared experiences and understandings.

EXERCISE: PEER SUPPORT

Write down your answers to each of the following questions:

1. Do you have any regular meeting/interaction with your professional peers? Describe it. Does it serve you?
2. When and where do you have a chance to learn new skills that can help you be more effective?
3. When and where do you have a chance to freely discuss issues (including systems and interventions as well as emotions) that come up in your work with kids?
4. When and where do you have a chance to feel a sense of camaraderie or closeness with your professional peers?
5. What would it take to develop a peer support system in your workplace? How, specifically, might you go about accomplishing this?
6. What would it take to develop a peer support system independently? How, specifically, might you go about accomplishing this?

For many of us, the work to help hurt kids is more than a job; it's a calling. And although it may be a noble calling, at times it can make us feel lonely, frustrated, and profoundly sad. It can be a great comfort to share this sadness with others who also share our commitment and our mission to help hurt kids. Of course, we do more than share sadness; we also share hope. This sharing of knowledge, skills, support, sadness, and hope might take place in our work setting, in our peer supervision group, and in professional conferences and meetings. We are enriched by being part of this community; it can sustain us.

Self-care is an ongoing obligation of the helping professional working with traumatized kids, and for many of us, an ongoing challenge. The challenge increases at times of stress, whether that stress is related to our personal lives, work settings, or what is going on within the treatment of a particular child. At times of stress it may be very difficult to focus on caring for ourselves, yet that's when it's most important that our "tools of the trade" are in good condition. As we progress through this training/book, self-monitoring and self-care issues will be raised on a regular basis. At each phase of treatment, we should check in with ourselves, and with one another, to support one another and keep ourselves in shape and on track.

SECTION I BIBLIOGRAPHY

Campbell, J. (1968). *The hero with a thousand faces.* Princeton, NJ: Princeton University Press. The classic work on the quest of the hero as a metaphor for personal growth and transformation. The quest of the hero has the same basic structure as the fairy tale presented in this book.

Chemtob, C. M., Roitblat, H. L., Hamada, R. S., Carlson, J., & Twentyman, C. (1988). A cognitive action theory of posttraumatic stress disorder. *Journal of Anxiety Disorders, 2,* 253-275. The classic paper on survival mode as a post-traumatic symptom.

Cohen, J. A., Berliner, L., & March, J. S. (2000). Treatment of children and adolescents. In E. B. Foa, T. M. Keane, & M. J. Friedman (Eds.), *Effective treatments for PTSD: Practice guidelines from the International Society for Traumatic Stress Studies* (pp. 106-138). New York: Guilford Press. An authoritative review of effective child trauma treatments and what components the effective treatments tend to have in common.

Figley, C. R. (1995). *Compassion fatigue.* New York: Brunner/Mazel. An early classic.

Fletcher, K. E. (1996). Childhood posttraumatic stress disorder. In E. Mash & R. Barkley (Eds.), *Child psychopathology* (pp. 242-276). New York: Guilford Press. This chapter provides a good overview of child and adolescent post-traumatic stress disorder and posttraumatic stress.

Giaconia, R. M., Reinherz, H. Z., Silverman, A. B., Pakiz, B., Frost, A. K., & Cohen, E. (1995). Traumas and posttraumatic stress disorder in a community population of older adolescents. *Journal of the American Academy of Child and Adolescent Psychiatry, 34,* 1369-1380. Documents the wide range of clinically significant non-PSTD outcomes that trauma exposure can entail.

Greenwald, R. (2002). The role of trauma in conduct disorder. *Journal of Aggression, Maltreatment, and Trauma, 6,* 5-23. This article synthesizes research and theory on how exposure to trauma and loss can contribute to the development and persistence of problem behaviors. It lays the foundation for the Meaning of Behavior analysis.

Herman, J. L. (1992). *Trauma and recovery.* New York: Basic Books. A classic example of a phase model of trauma treatment; also provides a nice history of the treatment of PTSD.

Kendall-Tackett, K.A., Williams, L. M., & Finkelhor, D. (1993). Impact of sexual abuse on children: A review and synthesis of recent empirical studies. *Psychological Bulletin, 113,* 164-180. A classic paper showing the wide range of possible outcomes of exposure to sexual abuse.

Pearlman, L. A. & Saakvitne, K. W. (1995). *Trauma and the therapist: Counter-transference and vicarious traumatization in psychotherapy with incest survivors.* New York: W. W. Norton & Co. Good integration and treatment of the issues.

Perry, B. D., Pollard, R. A., Blakley, T. L., Baker, W. L., & Vigilante, D. (1995). Childhood trauma, the neurobiology of adaptation and use-dependent development of the brain: How states become traits. *Infant Mental Health Journal, 16,* 271-291. This classic paper describes the impact of early trauma on the child's neurological and personality development.

Saakvitne, K. W., Gamble, S., Pearlman, L. A., & Lev, B. T. (2000). *Risking connection: A training curriculum for working with survivors of childhood abuse.* Baltimore: Sidran. This is the source of the RICH relationship model. The book focuses on working with adults, but the relationship principles are essentially the same.

Stamm, B.H. (Ed.) (1995). *Secondary traumatic stress: Self-care issues for clinicians, researchers, and educators.* Lutherville, MD: Sidran. Another classic.

Terr, L. (1991). Childhood traumas: An outline and overview. *American Journal of Psychiatry, 148,* 10-20. This classic paper provides a good overview of trauma and explains the important distinction between discrete (Type 1) trauma and chronic (Type 2) trauma, and the effect that these types of trauma exposure can have on the child's development.

Tokayer, N. (2001). A brief note on the research support for the Risking Connection approach. In K. W. Saakvitne (Ed.), *Relational teaching, experiential learning: The teaching manual for the Risking Connection curriculum* (pp. 175-177). Baltimore: Sidran. Reviews the empirical and theoretical support for the RICH model, focusing on psychoeducation, empowerment, and therapeutic alliance.

van der Kolk, B. A., Pelcovitz, D., Roth, S., Mandel, F. S., McFarlane, A., & Herman, J. L. (1996). Dissociation, somatization, and affect dysregulation: The complexity of adaptation to trauma. *American Journal of Psychiatry, 153,* Festschrift Supplement, 83-93. This classic paper does address the impact of childhood trauma, even though the focus is on those traumatized kids as adults. A good explanation of affect dysregulation and more generally how trauma exposure can lead to a wide range of symptoms and psychopathologies.

SECTION II: EVALUATION AND TREATMENT PLANNING

The evaluation phase begins with the first meeting (actually with the first contact) and ends when feedback on the evaluation has been provided, recommendations have been offered, and the child and family have decided, with the therapist's guidance, how to respond to these. Typically this involves a treatment contract, that is, an agreement for the child and family to engage in treatment to address the issues raised in the evaluation. The evaluation should normally be scheduled to be completed as soon as possible, even within a single day, because of the following:

- Families tend to bring children for treatment in times of crisis.
- Children and families in crisis are most willing to engage in treatment; when the situation has quieted down, they may be less interested (until the next crisis).
- Even though many beneficial things should be occurring during the evaluation, it is not *called* treatment. Families in crisis should not be made to feel that they are being kept waiting for the official treatment to start.

In short, a rapid evaluation process will help families to feel that their pressing concerns are being taken seriously and responded to quickly, and will increase the chances of families choosing to engage in the recommended treatment.

Trauma-informed treatment—or any treatment—really starts with the first contact. It should go without saying that the person making the phone call or other initial contact should be treated with courtesy and *respect,* given all necessary *information* in an understandable form, that some *connection* should be made even in a limited first contact, and that *hope* should be conveyed. The RICH approach will maximize the likelihood that the family will show up for the first meeting.

It should also go without saying that every effort should be made to honor the relationships that the child and family form with the helping professional(s). Treatment does not arbitrarily begin after the "evaluation" has been completed and "treatment" starts. Treatment starts at the first contact. This is when the child and family begin to form a relationship with whomever they are interacting with.

A thirteen-year-old girl who had been sexually assaulted went through the three-session assessment with the intake worker at the community mental health clinic. Her case was discussed at a staff meeting and then assigned to a therapist. The girl never showed for her therapy appointment. She told her mother, "I already talked to that one lady. I practically told her my life story. She's the one I'll talk to. I'm not going to start all over again with a stranger."

Also, as the evaluation phase of treatment progresses, the child and family are telling their story, the therapist is giving feedback—a lot is happening. We may be tempted to underestimate how much treatment is really taking place even before we agree on a treatment plan and "begin."

An eleven-year-old boy went through a two-hour evaluation following a school referral for disruptive behaviors and failing grades. The evaluator provided a trauma-informed case formulation and treatment recommendations to the boy and his parents. However, implementation of the recommendations (for treatment) was delayed by four weeks until after the plan was approved at his individual educational plan meeting. When he returned to the same clinician to commence treatment, he said, "I don't need to be here. I don't have a problem anymore." Indeed he was doing much better with his behaviors and his school performance. He explained, "Once you explained everything to me [at the end of the evaluation], I knew what to do about it."

That so much may be accomplished during the initial intake/assessment phase of treatment is not accidental. We have much to accomplish at every phase of treatment. Following are the primary goals of the evaluation phase:

- Establish a sense of safety and predictability in the therapy.
- Enhance/reestablish primary attachment relationships.
- Provide trauma-related psychoeducation.
- Develop a case formulation.
- Identify goals and enhance hope in achieving them.
- Develop a trauma treatment contract.

The stated purpose of the evaluation phase is to learn about the child in order to understand what is wrong and how to fix it. However, the therapist can accomplish the remaining goals along the way by behaving in a manner designed to instill a sense of safety and predictability, and by presenting information in a manner designed to increase understanding of the child, empathy toward the child, and hope for healing.

Remember, we can't just say "trust me" or "you can feel safe now." We must do the work to give kids and families experiences with us that will allow them to learn to trust us and to feel safe with us.

YOU CAN TRUST ME!

Chapter 5

The Initial Interview—From "Hello" Up to History

How does a trauma therapist say Hello?

Actually, much goes into how we introduce ourselves and kick off the treatment relationship. The first goal is to establish a sense of safety and predictability in the therapy. We can do this by telling our clients what's going on and what to expect. The trick here is to tell them the truth, and to offer a truth that is reasonably enticing.

Psychotherapy was initially considered only suitable for intelligent, articulate, psychologically oriented clients, but now we try to treat a much wider range of people. This brings special challenges. The psychotherapy literature tells us that clients from minority groups are more likely than others to drop out of therapy so quickly that treatment never gets a chance to work (Wierzbicki & Pekarik, 1993). The same is true for individuals who are not so intelligent or verbal. This does not imply that these groups are similar, but both groups tend not to understand the appeal of the traditional unstructured talk-therapy approach. Children in treatment have many similarities to these groups, in that kids may not understand the purpose of unstructured talk, and they may not be particularly psychologically minded or verbal. So it's important to understand that kids as a group may be difficult to engage.

The literature also tells us that certain therapist practices can mitigate this problem and help these people to stay in treatment (Sue, 1998; Nader, Dubrow, Stamm, & Hudnall, 1999). The therapist can "acculturate" the client by explaining what therapy is, what the procedures are, how it works (and why these procedures might help), and what is expected of the client. It is also helpful when the therapist's style is directive, goal-oriented, and activity-focused rather than unstructured.

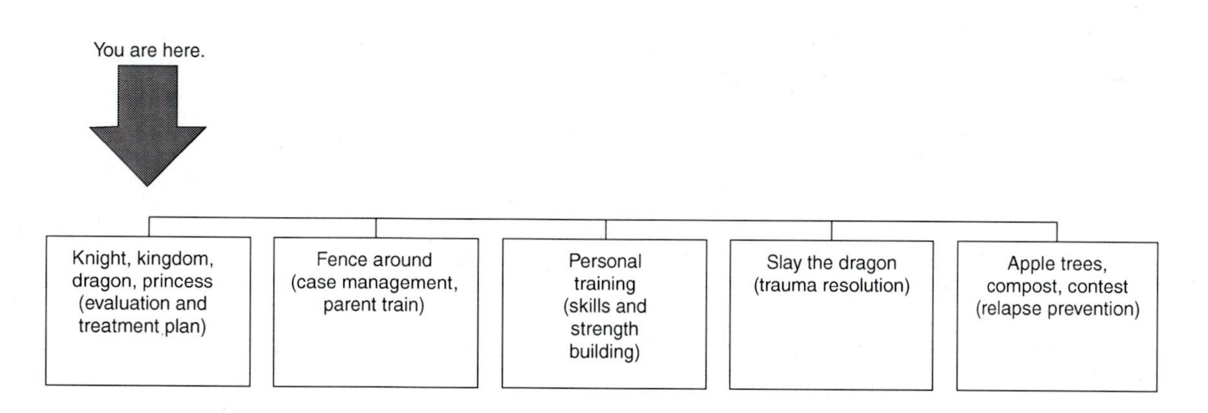

FIGURE 5.1. Steps in the fairy tale model.

ACCULTURATION

Clients who are not "therapy-wise" do not generally understand why an undirected "talking about whatever you want" is supposed to help them. As one incarcerated fifteen-year-old boy said, "They've been giving me counselors for years, but all that talking doesn't make a difference. I still do what I do." They want to know what to do to solve their problem, and they don't see how this kind of talk will get results. When the therapist explains the therapy procedures and why these procedures can be expected to help the client, clients are more likely to engage and to stick around. Therapists can also tell the clients what to do—how to behave in order to be successful in treatment. Then clients know, and have a better chance of doing it.

THERAPIST STYLE

The other issue here is what actually happens in therapy. Just "talking about your feelings" doesn't necessarily help (and might actually do harm if the feelings are overwhelming). The trauma-informed treatment approach consists of a series of tasks, and relies on a directive therapist to guide treatment accordingly, while also being sensitive and responsive to the client. When the client is helped to recognize the impact of his trauma (the dragon), to identify his goals (the princess), and to understand how the treatment plan might help him to overcome his problems and achieve his goals (personal training to slay the dragon and marry the princess), then he is more likely to engage and to stick around.

INTRODUCING TREATMENT

The therapist can start, then, by explaining what treatment is for and what is expected to happen in treatment. Here's an example of what a therapist might say at the beginning of the first session:

THERAPIST: Did your father tell you why you are here?

CLIENT: No.

THERAPIST: Usually kids come here because someone is worried about them, someone thinks that they could be feeling better, acting better, doing better in some way. My job is to learn a lot about you: what you care about, what you want for yourself, and what might be getting in your way. So I'll be asking you a lot of questions. Then I'll tell you what I learned. Then I'll give you some suggestions for how to get what you want, what to do about the things that are in your way. Did you know that this is what we'd be talking about?

CLIENT: Sort of. Not really.

Note that we are not talking about the child's problems at this point. We are acknowledging that problems exist and suggesting the possibility of solutions. However, the first focus is on acculturation, on what we're doing here, why, and how we are going to do it. This continues with an explanation of the rules. This word is chosen intentionally; children understand what rules are.

THE RULES

Here the therapist is primarily addressing the child, although the parent(s) may also be present.

THERAPIST: Before we get started with the questions, I want to tell you what the rules are for our meetings together. The first rule is about your privacy. That rule is that I don't tell other kids what you say. And I don't tell other grown-ups, either. What you say here is private. But there are exceptions. One exception is if you give me permission to tell someone about a certain thing. Also, if I'm afraid someone's in danger, the law says that I have to tell. So if you tell me that you have a gun and want to shoot someone, I have to tell your dad or the police or someone who can stop you and keep everyone safe. Also if you or some other kid is getting neglected—like they don't get fed meals at home—the law says I have to tell so that they can be taken care of and be safe. So here's a quiz. What would I do if you told me that you stole a pack of gum from the store, but don't tell anyone?

CHILD: You'd tell.

THERAPIST: Why?

CHILD: 'Cause I broke the law; it was wrong.

THERAPIST: Did you give me permission to tell?

CHILD: No.

THERAPIST: Is someone in danger, about to get hurt?

CHILD: Oh, you wouldn't tell, then.

THERAPIST: I might tell you that you did something stupid, but you're right, I would have to keep your privacy. [Therapist discloses any additional exceptions to confidentiality, e.g., disclosures to third-party payor, records kept for the agency, etc.]

THERAPIST: Okay, so that covers the rule about what I can say to other people. The next rule is about what you say. The rule is you are not allowed to say anything in here unless you decide you want to. So what if I ask you a question that you don't want to answer? How do you follow this rule? What can you do?

CHILD: Say I don't want to answer?

THERAPIST: That would be good. Can I count on you to do that?

CHILD: Okay.

THERAPIST: Let's practice. I'm going to ask a question that you don't want to answer, then you try that. What's four hundred fifty-four times sixty-eight?

CHILD: I don't want to answer.

THERAPIST: Good job! Should we practice again or are you good enough at that already?

CHILD: I'm good enough already.

The previous script is intended as an example of how to explain the rules. The point is that whatever your rules are, you should make sure to explain them. What information will you tell parents and what will remain between you and the child? If you are working in a juvenile justice setting, are you required to report instances of law-breaking? This is your chance to spell it all out.

Stating the rules makes them explicit. Therapy is a new setting for most children, and knowing the rules up front helps them to feel secure because then they know what to do and what will happen. The contents of the rules also convey safety and control for the child. This is reinforced by quizzing the child on the first rule and practicing with the second. The child can feel actively in charge of what she will say and what will be said about her. Finally, the quiz, and especially the practice, make the rules feel more true, more real. It's one thing to be told that a rule exists; it's another thing to experience it.

Note that the second rule is *not* phrased as "You don't have to answer a question if you don't want to." That's not a bad rule, but it carries the implication that the child can choose not to participate by refusing to answer a question. That sets up both the child and the therapist to feel as if they have failed. This rule, "You may not speak unless you decide you want to," carries the implication that the child is participating fully regardless of the choice. Later, when the child refuses to answer a question, the therapist can say, "I'm so glad you remembered my rule!" Thus both the child and the therapist remain successful.

Helping the child remain successful is a core element of trauma-informed treatment for a couple of reasons. First, in the fairy tale model, we are focused on personal training to help the child develop strength and skills. When failure becomes habitual, it's difficult to keep up the morale necessary to persevere. Also—and this is related—even a small failure may hit a sore spot and trigger a trauma-related overreaction. If kids are getting habitually triggered in therapy, they will learn that therapy is not a safe place and they need to protect themselves. Then they are more likely to be resistant and withdrawn, and less likely to get the job done. The more we can do to help kids feel successful when they are with us, the better chance we have of being successful with them.

After the rules we will ask questions. Consistent with the fairy tale model, it's very important to get the "once upon a time" information before we start focusing on the dragon and the problems it created. When we meet a child and focus immediately on his problems, he feels as if he is a problem and that is how we see him. On the other hand, if we focus on the positives—the history of successful relationships and achievements—the child feels as if we are getting to know *him,* not just what's wrong with him. Also, because the child is expected to be his own knight in shining armor, we need to be able to see this potential in the child and to know his strengths. We get this information by asking, by learning much about him, not just the problems.

STARTING WITH A PARENT PRESENT

Treatment is normally more effective when parents are involved; however, in certain settings parents may be unavailable. Even in such settings, it's worth making a creative effort to include parents whenever possible. Assuming we have one or more parents present when we start treatment, there are special procedures for the first meeting.

The therapist still explains the purpose and activities of treatment as well as the rules. The therapist then announces that after meeting all together for a while, time will be made for the parent alone, and for the child alone. The parent is then less likely to raise issues that should not be discussed in front of the child; if the parent does so anyway, this sets the stage for the therapist to tell the parent, "We can talk about that later."

We try to ask about "normal" things before asking about problems; this makes people feel more comfortable and respected. When the parent(s) and child are present together, a good starting point is to ask about the family. The therapist can ask a little about each family member, and create a genogram (diagram/map of the family).

Next, we make an exception to the typical first-session focus on the "once upon a time" material. We ask the parent about the presenting problem. First, most parents would feel that something was not quite right if, during the first meeting, they did not get to discuss the problem and why they are bringing their child for help. They might feel disrespected or that the therapist was not interested in the problem.

Also, one of the goals is to begin to enhance/reestablish primary attachment relationships. One way to do this is by asking parents what they most like about the child. However, if you ask this now, many parents will "spoil" their own answers by making such statements as, "Well, he gets along well with his siblings—when he's not fighting with them," or "She's good at doing her chores—if she's ever home." Many parents have such an urge to tell the therapist about the problem that it's best to invite this early and let them get it out of their system.

When a child is brought for treatment, she often feels like this is part of "being in trouble." By this time, the ongoing parent-child interaction may be fraught with anger, frustration, and rejection. Hearing the parent tell the therapist what's wrong is probably not big news to the child. On the other hand, the child may not have heard much lately about the ways she is positively viewed by the parent.

Once the parents have dumped their load of complaints, they are more able and willing to recall and discuss good things about their child. This reminder of positive attachment is a wonderful way to end the family portion of the initial evaluation session. If only briefly, it helps the family to feel close in a way they may not have for some time. This experience provides encouragement to all parties and makes them hopeful about the treatment.

Here is an example of how this part of the session might be conducted.

THERAPIST: Remember I said that parents bring their kids to me 'cause they're worried about them? Who's the most worried about you? And what is he or she worried about?

CHILD: I don't know. Ask her.

THERAPIST: I will. But I'm asking you first. If you're not sure, it's okay to guess. I want to see what you think she's worried about.

(Once the child has said as much as he will, ask the parent to confirm and elaborate if necessary regarding the primary concerns/complaints. If the parent starts to make a comment that is inappropriate or unnecessarily embarrassing to the child, remind the parent that he or she will have an opportunity to speak with you in private as well.)

THERAPIST: Now I'd like you to tell me the things you like most about [your child].

(Therapist writes these down in the list by the child's figure in the genogram. If parent qualifies these items with complaints, therapist ignores and redirects to focus on positives. Often the positives are remembered items that were more prominent before the presenting problem started/escalated.)

THERAPIST: I can see that there are a lot of things you really appreciate about your child. It must be frustrating to care so much for him and see him having such a hard time.

The therapist's summary statement (before transitioning to the parent-only meeting) conveys the impression/implication that the essence of the family is positive attachment and the essence of the child is the positive qualities. The presenting problem is seen as a disruption that is upsetting but can be dealt with. This type of subtle intervention is repeated frequently to enhance attachment and empathy and to convey that we are building on strengths to overcome problems.

MEETING ALONE WITH THE PARENT

The parent interview should cover the following:

- developmental history including temperament, attachment, medical, social, educational, legal (don't forget to ask about head injury and about prior treatment);
- detailed trauma/loss history;

- details of the presenting problem, including the situations in which the problem occurs, and the parent's typical response (or range of responses);
- the parents' discipline style including details of how and when it is implemented; and
- anything else the parent wishes to disclose without the child present (save this for last).

When asking about the child's trauma/loss history, it's best to give multiple specific examples of possible events, rather than asking the open-ended question. Recognition is easier than recall.

Also, this can be a sensitive topic. Parents often express guilt feelings when discussing their child's trauma/loss history. The therapist can point out that although it's natural for parents to feel that way, in fact most children do get exposed to significant trauma or loss. The important thing is to protect them as much as possible, and then to help them recover from the negative effects—which the parent is clearly making an effort to do.

This is a good opportunity for the therapist to start piecing together any possible connection between the child's trauma/loss experiences and onset or escalation of problems. Therefore it's important to question the parent with some specificity regarding observed changes following reported events. Then later when the therapist provides the case formulation, many of its components have been "field tested" with the parent ahead of time. Thus, rather than the therapist pulling a rabbit out of a hat, the case formulation arises naturally from the previous conversation, and the parent is more likely to accept the therapist's views.

There are several important reasons to learn a lot about the presenting problem, the context in which it occurs, and what happens when/after it occurs:

- This kind of attention shows respect to the parents, who have sought your help because of this problem.
- You want to be able to complete that Meaning of Behavior form, so you need to be able to identify the triggers that seem to set off the child.
- You want to learn the details of how the child is reinforced for the problem behavior. Remember, the problem behavior is the child's solution to the earlier problem of facing a trauma-related intolerable overreaction that was triggered by some minor stressor. How does the solution solve the problem? The better you understand how the problem behavior is working for the child, the better you'll be able to offer solutions.
- You want to learn about the parents' discipline approach because you want to know what solutions they've already tried. Also, many parents' discipline approaches actually contribute to the child's problem by reinforcing her problem behavior and/or by increasing her sense of insecurity. For example, many parents use an ineffective, inconsistent discipline style in which they first let things slide and then get so frustrated that they overpunish.

The parent training issues and methods can be gently introduced or anticipated here to help the parents become familiar with the concepts. It is important for the therapist to convey respect for the parents' intentions, e.g., not wanting to be hard on the child after all he's been through. Then later the parent training will be easier to sell because it will not be about contradicting the parent, but about helping him or her express his or her good intentions more effectively.

MEETING ALONE WITH THE CHILD

Kids can feel pretty nervous when a strange adult starts asking them personal questions. The more we can do to help kids feel safe and in control, the more comfortable and more likely to cooperate they will be. Also, the more we can help them to feel safe and in control, the more they will learn to trust us and to believe that we care for them and have their best interests as a priority.

A number of specific things can be done to foster the development of this therapeutic relationship and to help kids to feel safe with us.

Allow Certain Choices

Some children feel more comfortable when they are able to draw or play with a toy while talking. Although it is very important to get through the evaluation, we can allow kids to keep their hands occupied as long as they are also able to fully participate in the evaluation. Upon seeing the child begin to play with a toy, the therapist might say something like, "I don't know you very well. Will you be able to play with that toy and concentrate on our conversation at the same time?" This gives the child the option of playing with the toy, while also making clear that the conversation is a priority.

Help the Child Prepare

Before diving into the questions, remind the child about saying "I don't want to answer that." Think about driving a car, fast. This can be a little scary, but fun too. Now think about how fast you'd be willing to drive if you weren't sure if your brakes worked! Whenever we ask a child to "drive fast" or to take a new risk, it's nice to say, "Let's check and make sure your brakes still work." This reminder of how to "not answer" can help kids to feel in control, and then more willing to take the risk and answer questions.

Start Small

After the big buildup of "here come the questions," kids are relieved to be asked about their favorite color, favorite food, favorite activities, etc. The questions only gradually become more personal as kids become more comfortable. Children find these innocuous questions relevant—it's what they might want to know about one another—and like to be seen as a whole person and not just as a problem. Most kids will answer most or all of the questions, and will feel good at having expressed themselves—even if no apparent emotionally laden disclosure has occurred.

Warn Before Any Potentially Challenging Shift

The trauma therapist avoids surprising children with sudden shifts or potentially objectionable (personal and/or upsetting) questions. Thus the warning, "Here comes a different kind of question," or "Here comes a question that some kids don't like. Do you remember what to say if you don't want to answer?" The goal is not to surprise kids but to help them feel that we are looking out for them. In general, the more kids feel that they are in control and can say No, the more they are willing to go ahead.

Give a Menu

When the child has trouble answering an open-ended question or some other question, the therapist quickly (after about two seconds) intervenes with a "menu" of possible choices—types of appropriate answers. This helps the child be successful and can preclude the tendency for angry acting out (e.g., "Don't know, don't care") in the interview. The two-second rule is a good guide, but you can use your judgment or even ask about the silence. For example, "This seems to be a hard question to answer. Should I just give you more time or ask it in a different way?"

There are important differences between giving a menu and asking a leading question. Giving a menu is a way of showing what a right answer might look like, orienting the child to the possibilities, but clearly asking for the child's own answer. A leading question, on the other hand, pushes the child to give the particular answer that the therapist seems to be demanding. Here is an example, as a follow-up when the child did not adequately answer the question, "How do you know when you're angry? What are the signals?" A menu might be, "Well, some kids say they get swear words in their head, or fighting words, or their mind goes blank. . . . Some kids say that their face gets hot, or their heart starts pounding, or they fidget, or their hands turn into fists. . . . What happens with you? What are your signals?" A leading question might be, "Then you want to kill him, right?" A leading question can feel coercive to the child, and yields limited information of dubious value. Use the menu.

Provide Frequent Feedback

Therapy can feel safer for kids when the therapist offers frequent feedback. Many kids have been exposed to adults who, due to mental illness, substance abuse, or trauma-related reactivity, have been volatile. Kids in this type of environment learn to (try to) read minds, read signs, to figure out when the bad thing might happen, so that it can be avoided or at least prepared for. When a therapist plays the "blank slate" game, kids don't know what the therapist is thinking, and they are liable to fear the worst. Then they will feel unsafe, afraid to say certain things for fear that you'll get angry or not like them anymore.

On the other hand, if you provide frequent feedback, kids will feel that they know what's going on with you, and they won't have to worry about it. This doesn't mean that you make a habit of self-disclosure. Rather, it means that you let them know, selectively, what you think you are learning. For example, you might say, "So I'm getting the impression that you're smart enough to do well in school, if you decided to do the work. Do you think that's true?"

This gives you a chance to convey a positive impression, focusing on the child's strengths even while acknowledging the problems. Another advantage of providing frequent feedback along the way is that you get a chance to field-test the building blocks of your case formulation so that by the time you formally offer the case formulation, the child has already become familiar with many of its elements.

Offer Information

The therapist can share a couple of specific kinds of information during the initial interview. This strategy amounts to an informal psychoeducation regarding the impact of trauma. The goal here is to help kids understand themselves and their symptoms as within the range of normal responses to stressful past events. This also helps to build the case for the case formulation.

- *Why you are asking that question.* The therapist can simply explain this to provide information. For example, "The reason I was asking is that some kids, after they get a concussion like you did, they notice that some things are different, like they might get headaches, or have more trouble concentrating than they did before, or have a shorter temper. Did you notice anything like that for you, after the concussion?"
- *What other kids say.* At various points (e.g., when offering a menu or framing a question with multiple options) the therapist refers to what "other kids" say. Traumatized children often feel strange, alien, isolated, different. This type of questioning effects some of the universality normally available in group therapy: that the things that have made the child feel different are actually things in common with other children. Kids feel relieved to discover that they are "normal."

Honest Praise for Self-Advocacy

Kids may be hesitant to tell you that they have to go to the bathroom, that they don't want to talk about a certain thing that you've asked about, or that they are in a hurry to get out of the session because of some other high-priority commitment or activity. They may feel that advocating for their own needs would somehow be disrespectful to you or to the treatment. Although this consideration may be admirable in some way, the risk is that the child ends up taking care of the therapist instead of the other way around. If the child believes that her needs are not as important as yours, then in that way the therapy relationship may be replicating a prior victimization or exploitation and will not feel safe to the child.

This does not mean that there should be no rules in therapy; to the contrary, rules exist in large part to help the therapist maintain the focus on the child's needs. Traumatized kids respond well to structure and predictability; this helps them to feel safe. However, the therapist should be sensitive to the child's apparent discomfort and supportive of the child's needs, which hopefully the child will learn to assert with more comfort and confidence over time. For example, the therapist might say, "Of course you can go to the bathroom now. How could I expect you to sit there and concentrate when you have to go to the bathroom? I'm so glad you said something!"

What do kids learn when the therapist supports their needs being met? They learn that "This therapist cares about me and wants to make sure that I'm okay. This is not someone I need to defend myself against; this is someone who looks out for me, is on my side." Of course, the therapist will have to be alert for possible abuse of this flexibility, but in general it pays off nicely.

EXERCISE: PRACTICE THE INITIAL INTERVIEW

Using the following script, practice this portion of the initial interview with a colleague; then change roles and have the colleague practice with you. If you are on your own, just go ahead and try this with a new client, bearing in mind that you don't use this script until after you've done the acculturation, rules, and other activities that come first.

If You Are the Client

- Role-play a child of any age (old enough to talk in full sentences!). Tell the therapist your name and age.
- Do not look at the script. Don't do the therapist's job. Just respond as you would in the role you are playing. However, please don't give the therapist too much trouble, either! This is not the time to role-play your hardest case; give this therapist a break while he or she is trying to learn a new procedure.
- In an actual session, this portion of the interview comes after the rules. So when you are asked, "What do you do if there's a question you don't want to answer?" you can say, "No comment" as if you had just worked this out a few minutes before.

If You Are the Therapist

- Use the script verbatim, except that you may not need to ask all the questions (e.g., regarding drug use) to younger children who do not endorse the first questions along that line.
- If you don't get the answer you want/need, optional follow-up questions are provided in parentheses. For example, if you ask, "What's your favorite color?" and the child says "Blue," then you've got your answer and you can move on. If the child says, "I don't really

have one favorite," then you can use the parenthesized question and say, "Okay, what are your two or three favorites?"

- If the child declines to answer a question, thank her for remembering your rule, and move on to the next question.
- Do not ask extra questions to learn more about the child's responses. This might feel counterintuitive, but trust me for now and later you'll decide for yourself. The following are two exceptions:
  —It's okay to ask a clarifying question if you really don't know what the child means. For example, if she says she smokes "a lot" of cigarettes, you might ask, "Like how many cigarettes in a day?"
  —It's okay to ask brief follow-up questions on the positives that come up. For example, if he says he likes to draw, you might ask, "What kind of stuff do you draw?" This contributes to the focus on strengths.
- Write down what the "child" says. You would do this in a real session. This is your assessment data. It also shows respect: "What you say is important."
- Use the script *verbatim*. Say it word for word. Do not wing it. You have the rest of your career to do as you please. Right now, take this opportunity to learn as much as you can from this. This script is as carefully crafted as a sales pitch, and pulls for the responses you want. Please give it a try.

Exercise Follow-Up Questions

For the clients: What was that like? How did it go for you? Can you describe what worked with you and what didn't?

For the therapists: What was that like? How did it go for you? Can you describe what worked with you and what didn't?

Many therapists balk at using a script or indeed at doing anything with which they're not proficient or comfortable. It's important to recognize that when you are trying to learn a new skill, you are likely to feel de-skilled for an initial learning period. The phases of learning are observation, imitation, and then integration. If you skip the imitation stage, you will have less to integrate. If you are willing to experience the growing pains of actually learning the new method, you are more likely to improve your skills, as eventually you integrate the new skills with your current level of competence and comfort. It will happen!

For at least the first several kids, I encourage you to use the script in the session. If kids ask what you're doing with that book or piece of paper, you can just say, "I use this to make sure I don't forget to ask any of the questions." You are the professional here. Kids don't know how you're supposed to do your job, and they'll accept this answer. Some therapists continue to use the script as a regular practice.

Many therapists find it uncomfortable to just accept some short answer and move on; they say it feels mechanistic and uncaring. But what did your clients say? What is their experience? Many kids report, "I felt comfortable answering the questions because I knew you weren't going to pry." This is an important precedent to set, because in the next session we will be asking about trauma/loss history, and want the kids to feel safe to answer those much more difficult questions without fear of prying. We want to keep the treatment carefully contained so that kids feel safe and are not overwhelmed by being asked to handle more than they're ready for.

Many kids, even the ones who gave one-word answers down the line, also say, "I liked being able to express myself, tell you how I feel about things." When we ask these kinds of questions, kids feel that we want to know them. Even if they don't elaborate on their answers, they may feel that they are expressing themselves and being understood.

Child Interview Script

You remember I said I was going to ask a lot of questions to try to learn a lot about you? And do you remember not to say anything unless you decide you want to? And what do you do if there's a question you don't want to answer?

So here come the questions, ready?

What's your favorite color? (Possible follow-up: Okay, what are your two or three favorites?)

What's your favorite food?

What's your favorite music?

What's your favorite TV show?

What do you like in school? (Possible follow-up: Nothing? Not even recess?)

What don't you like in school? (What else?)

Some kids like to keep to themselves, some like to mostly be with one or two good friends, some like to hang with a crowd. Which way are you? (If "crowd," then: Would you say there are certain kids who are better friends to you? Or is everyone the same?)

You remember what to do if I ask you something that you don't want to talk about, right? I'm going to ask you some questions about your friends. Do your friends smoke cigarettes or not? Do they smoke weed? Drink? Other drugs? Would you say that your friends do pretty well in school, just get by, or are having trouble? Do your friends get in trouble with the law or not?

Now some of the same questions about you. You smoke cigarettes? Weed? Drink? Other drugs? How do you do in school? Do you get in trouble with the law?

What do you like to do with your friends? (Possible follow-up to "hang out": So if I was watching you guys hanging out and having a good time, what would I see you doing?) What else do you do with your friends?

What else do you like to do? What else?

What have people told you that you're good at?

I'm going to ask you a different kind of question now. If you could be any animal, who would you be? What would be good about being a [ ]?

If you could have three wishes, what would they be?

If you could wave a magic wand right now and all your problems would disappear, what would be different tomorrow? (Possible follow-up: If I'm watching on TV, what would I notice was different?) (Possible follow-up: Okay, so you'd be doing better in school. What would be different that would allow you to do better? Would the change be something inside you or outside you?)

Clearly this script is designed to start off slow, build rapport, and help kids to feel comfortable. However, we are also learning what we need to know. For example, it is critical to obtain as much information as possible about the child's strengths and achievements. Later, these will be used as a basis for hope.

The three wishes and especially the magic wand questions are good for identifying not only treatment goals, but also obstacles. It's also a good way to learn how the child perceives the problem. Does it come from inside or outside the self? For example, a boy who sees his tendency to fight as an internal problem might say, "I wouldn't get so mad anymore." A boy who sees the same problem as external might say, "People wouldn't act so stupid [make me so mad] anymore." When we know how this child sees his own situation, then we know how to talk about it in a way that is consistent with his viewpoint. Then our case formulation is more likely to be accepted.

OBTAINING MORE HISTORY WHILE FOCUSING ON STRENGTHS

The previous script, plus the acculturation preliminaries, can generally be covered in the first hour. The entire intake interview may require several sessions, depending on the length of the sessions. Following the portion of the interview detailed previously, the therapist can ask about the family and about the child's developmental history—although if a parent is available, then the family information is obtained first, and the developmental history directly from the parent, who will be a better informant. Then the therapist can ask about medical history (including head injury) and current status, educational history and current status, and legal history and current status.

You'll need a sufficiently detailed history so you will later be able to tie together any trauma/loss history with possible onset or escalation of problems. It is also important to continue to learn about strengths, abilities, positive relationships, and successes, since these will be the foundation for the child's work in treatment. For example, the therapist might ask about educational history as follows:

- When you were in the first grade, did you feel like you were about as smart as other kids, a little smarter, or a little slower? How were your grades in first grade?
- Did you get in trouble in school more than other kids, less than other kids, about average? Would you say you had more friends than other kids then, less friends, about average?

Once the baseline of school-related functioning is established, the therapist can go forward from there and develop a time line of changes that may have occurred.

THERAPIST: So how long did things stay this way in school until something changed?

CHILD: Until about fourth grade.

THERAPIST: Oh. What happened in fourth grade? What was different?

CHILD: I started getting into fights more, and my grades weren't so good anymore.

THERAPIST: Like how much more? How many fights in a week?

CHILD: Not every day, but at least once or twice a week.

THERAPIST: How come you were fighting so much more than before? What was different?

CHILD: I just was more mad.

THERAPIST: And were you still passing your classes? What were your grades like then?

CHILD: I was still passing but it was mostly Cs and Ds, and I failed one or two classes.

THERAPIST: And how long did things stay this way until they changed again?

CHILD: When I went to the middle school in sixth grade, I got with a new group of kids and started skipping classes a lot. . . .

The same type of interviewing can be practiced for the other topics (medical, legal). This results in a good time line of the child's history of functioning in multiple areas. We also know how well she was doing before the problems started. Later, we can point to those times as proof that she has the capacity to do well if it were not for the impact of the trauma/loss history.

Incidentally, by the time you finish this part of the interview, you have learned quite a bit about the presenting problems, but you haven't done it by asking "What's your problem?" or making the child feel as if she is a problem. Rather, you got to know the child and in the course of telling her story, information about her problems were revealed. This child is likely to feel that you see the good in her, that you see her as a normal kid—if with some problems—and that you care about her. That's a good start.

Chapter 6

Taking a Trauma History

By the second or third session, it's time to ask the big question: "What are the worst things that ever happened to you?" If we are going to conduct trauma-informed treatment, we need to get the trauma on the table so we can incorporate it into the case formulation and treatment plan. Therefore, the history must be done during the evaluation. Fortunately, it can be done in a careful, intentional way that helps the child to feel safe and able to make progress in treatment.

Even the order of the different topics in the intake interview supports the fairy tale model. First we ask about the good things, the strengths, the track record of achievements and positive relationships—the "Once upon a time" stuff from when circumstances were better. (Hopefully there was such a time! If not, we still do the best we can in terms of identifying strengths and resources.) Then we ask about history up to the present, in various areas of life, and start to learn about the impact that the dragon might have made in terms of problem development. Only then do we ask about the dragon.

When we do ask about the dragon, we do it in a specific, limited way. Remember, the personal trainer does not ask the knight to go from five pounds to a hundred all at once. The strategy is to provide progressively greater challenges, one step at a time, each one manageable with the therapist's help. You may have already taken the child through several challenges up to this point, for example:

- Trusting an adult enough to cooperate and answer questions.
- Telling the three wishes and the magic wand changes—these responses often reflect an awareness of the child's wounds and current problems. ("I wish my family had a nice house and never had to worry about rent." "I wish my brother never died.")
- Talking about the family (some problems may be found here).
- Talking about the problem history (as part of education and legal history).

That's a good start, but there's a long way to go before the child can be expected to slay the dragon, or to talk about the trauma and face the emotions. To invite this too soon is to risk failure. So when we get the trauma history, we are careful to ask for, and allow, only disclosure of the most basic facts, the bare minimum that will allow us to proceed with the case formulation.

Even though we are not asking for the whole story for each trauma event, the disclosure can be difficult for the child. It is probably the most challenging thing we have asked the child to do so far in treatment. So we continue to use the principles and practices of trauma treatment, to help the child to manage this experience, to feel successful, and to come out in reasonably good shape. Here are the steps we take:

1. *Warn.* Here comes a hill. Why don't you check your brakes again, just to make sure they work? In other words, we remind the child again about the rule: Do you remember what to do if there's something you don't want to answer?
2. *Make a "list."* We say, "I need to make a list of the worst things that ever happened to you." What does the word *list* imply? Brevity. This is going to be quick and easy, perhaps even im-

personal. We're not going to get into details. This establishes a limit, defines what will be happening. The child knows that he will not be expected, or allowed, to provide a lot of detail.

3. *What other kids say.* This is a crucial opportunity for psychoeducation. When it comes to the trauma history, which is often a secret, kids feel at their most strange, damaged, and vulnerable. Here, the therapist offers the menu of possible trauma/loss events without even waiting for the child to be silent for two seconds first. This accomplishes several purposes:
   - If you just ask the child to list the worst things that ever happened to her, you will get some answers. If you first give many examples of items that might be on her list, you will get more answers. This is the difference between multiple choice and fill in the blanks: recognition is easier than recall.
   - When you give these examples by saying, "Let me tell you the kind of things that other kids say," you are normalizing the part of the child's experience that may feel most abnormal. You have transformed this question from "How are you damaged and different?" to "In what ways are you like other kids?" This takes some of the pressure and stigma away.
   - Children often keep these experiences private and may be worried—for good reason—about how others might respond to a disclosure. When you describe what other kids have said, and you are calm and businesslike, you give the message that you can handle whatever this child will tell you. You've heard it before. You can talk about it; you will not freak out. This provides permission and safety.
4. *Get the list.* Once you have prepared the child, ask for the list of worst things. It is up to the child to determine what might belong on the list. The child may include items that surprise you, yet fail to include items that you are sure should be included. It's okay to suggest additional events that you may be aware of from the earlier interviewing (including the parent interview).
5. *Age for each item.* You also want to know at what age (or what grade) each event occurred. This can usually be done as the child is reporting each event, or it can be done just afterward. You need to know when events occurred to determine if the trauma/loss history can help account for problem onset or escalation.
6. *SUDS for each item.* SUDS stands for subjective units of distress scale and is technical jargon, not a term you should be using with kids. This is the 0 to 10 scale for how bad it feels when you concentrate on it right now. Some tricks are involved in getting the SUDS scores:
   - Some kids will claim that "It doesn't bother me anymore." Although they are not exactly lying, what they often really mean is something such as, "I don't let it bother me anymore. I try not to think about it." You don't need to argue about this. Just ask your question in a way that will get you the answer you want, e.g., "When you make yourself concentrate on it now, just for a second, how bad is it from zero to ten?"
   - Don't ask "How do you feel?" That's not exactly the question. We are trying to help the child to keep some distance, keep it a little less personal. So the question is "How bad is the feeling?" which is more objective, less intrusive. Or better yet, once they get used to the routine, "What's the number on this one?"
   - Asking for the SUDS is, in a way, doing exactly what we have been trying to avoid: having the child get into the feelings associated with the trauma memory. When therapists ask for the SUDS as they are asking about each event, they risk getting the child mired in the memory and unable to shake it. We do need to ask for the SUDS, so the best we can do is get it over with as quickly as possible. This is why we save it for last and do all of the events at once—well, one after another.
7. *What if the child refuses?* Sometimes the child will refuse to disclose one or more of her trauma memories. This is good. It means that she is following your rules. So what can you do about that? How can you get the information you want/need while still respecting her decision (and keeping your own promise about the rules)?

Here's an interesting point: when you are talking about not talking about the trauma, you are in fact talking about the trauma. So when the child says she doesn't want to talk about it, you have already accomplished one of your goals, which is to have her talk about it, at least a little, but not more than she can handle just now.

Another of your goals, though, is to get a time line of when the bad things happened, so that you can develop a case formulation. You can't just ask her, "How old were you?" because that would be talking about it, and she just told you that she doesn't want to talk about it. But you can ask her, "Is it okay to ask you how old you were?" Most children will readily disclose the age of the event they don't want to talk about. Later you can ask for the SUDS for that memory the same way you ask for the SUDS on the other memories on the list.

If the child will not even allow you to ask about the age of the event, don't worry; you can still do your job. Just write a question mark down on your list for the trauma and again for the age and SUDS. The fact that she is not telling you more is itself important information. She is letting you know that it would be too much for her to handle today. Does this mean that you have not established the trusting relationship that you were hoping for? Does it mean she's testing you? Does it mean that she's having a bad day but will have an easier time talking about the hard stuff next time? Does it mean that she is more fragile than other kids and will need that much more preparation before she is ready to slay the dragon? These are questions you will want to keep in mind.

8. *What if there's nothing on the list?* Sometimes a child who believes he is cooperating just doesn't have anything to put on the list. This can happen for several reasons. Sometimes even though you have provided the menu of common trauma/loss events, for some reason that doesn't jog the kid's mind regarding his own similar experiences, and he can't think of any. Some kids have a personal style that does not allow or acknowledge extremes, and so they are unable to respond to your question about "worst things" or things that "really hit you hard." Finally, some kids do not consider the upsetting events in their own history to be severe or bad enough to merit being put on this list.

Just because there might be some good reasons why your list is empty (or nearly empty), don't stop there. In general, for reasons that will become clear later, it's good to have at least two or three items on a younger child's list, and at least four or five items on a teenager's list. More is fine too; less will often be a problem.

So what to do? We definitely don't want to tell the kid, "No, I know you have more stuff to put on the list. Come on, give it up!" Fortunately, your clients don't know what your next question will be. So when you have a client who doesn't give enough events for the list, here are your next questions:

- How old were you for the worst thing that ever happened at school?
- How old were you for the worst thing that ever happened with other kids?
- How old were you for the worst time you ever lost someone you cared about?
- How old were you for the worst time you ever got disciplined or punished?
- How old were you for the worst time you ever saw parents or other grown-ups arguing or fighting?

These questions seem to help complete the list. Occasionally the child will still say, "Nothing like that ever happened," and we can accept that, as long as it's not the consistent answer for each question. Usually he will give the age that the event happened and explain a bit about it.

Notice that we do not ask, "Did this ever happen to you?" We already asked that, and came up empty. This time we ask, "How old were you when this happened?" Now we get an answer we can use.

9. *Finish the sandwich.* Remember, whenever we expose a child to challenging emotional content, we follow it up with some calming activity, then with something more thought-oriented to help with recomposure. Following the trauma history we have the child do a deep breathing exercise. This helps the child relax. Then we ask about the best things that ever happened.

This helps the child to refocus on something more positive, rather than staying stuck in the trauma. Although we avoid asking probing details about the trauma, it is okay to ask more about the good events; this helps to accomplish its purpose. Finally, we end the session with conversation about more casual issues, such as what the child will be doing later in the day or the week.

It is important to write down the details of the child's trauma history; you will need to refer to it on several occasions later in the treatment. Your notes on the trauma history might look like the "Worst Things" box that follows. Please review that box now. Perhaps you noticed the comment in parentheses after the "Breathing" notation. As a therapist, you may have a repertoire of interventions that can help kids calm down. Not every intervention works for every child. It's not the child's fault and it's not a problem. We just want to keep track of what works and what doesn't with a given child so that we can proceed accordingly. With the girl in the example, we are unlikely to attempt deep breathing again, and this note will remind us to try something else next time.

"Worst Things" Example

Worst things

Age	Event	SUDS
10	Uncle RJ died	6
5	Car accident	3
11	?	10+
13	Boyfriend broke up with me	7

Breathing (went through the motions but did not appear to relax)

Best things

Age	Event
All	My birthdays
14	Roller skating
13	Beach vacation

EXERCISE: TAKE A TRAUMA/LOSS HISTORY

Work with a colleague. When you have finished, change roles and do it again. If you're on your own it is worthwhile to complete the form for yourself, but you'll be missing much of the learning experience.

If You Are the Client

- This is not a role-play; be yourself. It is up to you to decide which events you wish to disclose. Disclose only to the extent that it feels comfortable and appropriate to do so.
- Do not use or look at the script; that's the therapist's job. Just be yourself.

If You Are the Therapist

- Use the Trauma/Loss History form provided, or duplicate the form on another piece of paper that you can write on. As you receive answers, write them into the form.
- Use the trauma history script. In the script, the words in brackets are instructions for you. The rest is to be spoken aloud. Do it verbatim—word for word.
- Remember to go in order. First, do the preparation, followed by the trauma/loss events and ages. When you have all of those, get the SUDS for each event. Then practice the deep breathing. Next, proceed to the best things. The script will guide you.
- Just because you will not be asking probing questions about the bad things that happened, this does not mean that you must shut off your humanity or your caring. You still can—and should—use your clinical skills to convey your compassion, your concern, and your comfort and ability to tolerate hearing what you are being told. How do you accomplish this? Different people have different styles, but the basic requirement is empathy, that combination of being both emotionally present and objective/composed. Good luck.

Form for Trauma/Loss History Exercise

Worst Things

Age	Event	SUDS (0-10)

(Breathe)

Best Things

Age	Event

Trauma/Loss History Script

Now I'm going to ask you about something that some kids don't like to talk about. You remember what to do if you don't want to say something?

Good. I want to make a *list* of the worst things that ever happened to you. Things that made you really sad or mad or scared, things that really kind of hit you hard. Maybe you already have something in mind, but let me tell you the kinds of *things that other kids say,* so you know what I'm asking about.

Some kids, it would be maybe a car accident, or another kind of accident, or seeing someone else get hurt really bad. Some kids, it's that someone in their family, or someone else they care about, got really sick or died. Or being taken away from their family. Or if someone hurt you, or made you do sex things, or threatened you, told you they would do something bad. Or seeing parents having really bad arguments or fights.

So what would be on your list? Okay, how old were you then? What else would be on your list? [Etc. until there are no more events to list.]

[Note: If the child denies *any* trauma/loss, then ask the following questions to fill out the list:

How old were you for the worst thing that ever happened in school?
How old were you for the worst thing that ever happened with other kids?
How old were you for the worst time you lost someone you cared about?
How old were you for worst time you ever got punished or disciplined?
How old were you for the worst time you saw parents or other grown-ups arguing or fighting?]

Now I'm going to ask you how bad the feeling is for these, on 0 to 10, where 10 is the worst feeling in the world, and 0 is no bad feeling at all. I'm not asking about how bad it was at the time, but when you make yourself think about it right now, how bad the feeling is right now. So for [that car accident], how bad is that feeling right now on 0 to 10? [Ask about SUDS—the 0 to 10 subjective units of distress scale—for each memory on the list.]

Did anyone ever show you how to do deep breathing, like to relax? I'm going to ask you to try my way of doing it for a couple of minutes, then you'll tell me whether we should ever do it again, or not. You will be taking a very deep, slow breath in, to my count of 3, then hold for 3, then breathe out slowly to a count of 3. Ready?

Breathe in 1, 2, 3; hold 1, 2, 3; out slow 1, 2, 3. Again, breathe in 1, 2, 3; hold 1, 2, 3; out slow 1, 2, 3.

This time, when you breathe out, look for any bad stuff—tension in your body, upsetting thoughts or pictures—and when you breathe out, imagine the air coming from that place, and the bad stuff going out with the exhale. Ready?

Breathe in 1, 2, 3; hold 1, 2, 3; breathe out the bad stuff, 1, 2, 3. Once more, breathe in 1, 2, 3; hold 1, 2, 3; breathe out the bad, 1, 2, 3.

How did that go? Would you say you feel better than before, worse, about the same?

Now I want to know about the best things that ever happened to you, or times that you felt really good. For some kids it would be a really good birthday, or they did something they're proud of, or they went someplace special, or were having a really good time doing something. What are the best times you can remember?

Exercise Follow-Up Questions

If You Were the Client

How did this go for you? Please describe your experience if you are willing. Since people have a range of experiences, we can begin to learn from one another about the variety of possible responses. What did your therapist do that made you feel more or less comfortable than you might have expected? Did talking about the bad memories upset you? Did the breathing or talking about the good memories have any effect?

If You Were the Therapist

How did this go for you? Please describe your experience if you are willing. Were you tempted to encourage your client to talk more? How did you handle that?

For the Group

As a therapist in that exercise, please raise your hand if you found something your client said personally challenging to listen to, or upsetting or hard to tolerate in some way. What did you tell yourself about that while it was happening? How did you handle it? Do you feel any remaining distress? How do you want to handle this distress now?

Many therapists who are new to trauma treatment struggle with the constraint of the list. When you ask kids about their trauma/loss history, some of them will try to tell you the whole story on the spot. It can be tempting to permit this. Many of us were trained to believe that when a client "opens up," that's a good session. He is choosing to open up; he obviously wants to talk about it, right? Wouldn't it be disrespectful to shut him up once he has started? What kind of message would he get from that?

Despite this temptation and these arguments, it is usually a bad idea to allow the child to disclose too much so early in treatment. The following several reasons suggest the therapist should exercise restraint on the child's behalf:

- Kids tend to be ambivalent about disclosing their trauma/loss history. They want to express it, yet they don't want to face it or expose themselves in that way. Just because the child is showing you one side or the other does not mean that she is not ambivalent. You must always take both sides into account. If you tell her, "This is important. We don't have time now, but I hope we can talk about it in more detail when it's the right time," you have addressed both sides of the ambivalence. If you just allow her to spill her guts, you have only addressed one side. The other side is likely to come out later. There is a risk that the child will feel overexposed and even tricked by the therapist into overdisclosure. Then the child is likely to feel unsafe and withdraw.
- If you allow the child to discuss the trauma in too much detail too soon, you are inviting fallout after the therapy session is over. You haven't yet had a chance to do the self-management training to help the child learn to cope better with upsetting feelings. So a higher risk exists that the child may become upset later on, and perhaps act out or underfunction. This is bad for the child and gives you, and treatment, a bad reputation.
- If you allow the child to talk too much about the trauma, you are less likely to have time to complete the follow-up activities in the session. The follow-up activities are critical to help the child manage and contain the emotion that may have been activated by recalling the trauma memories. This further increases the risk of after-session problems.

- If you allow the child to talk too much about the trauma, you are less likely to have time to complete the trauma/loss history in this session, and you'll have to do it again next time to get it done. The history is essential to making a case formulation. Once you have a case formulation and a treatment contract, things go much better, so you want to get to that point as soon as you can.
- You are the mental health professional with the specialized knowledge of how to conduct a trauma-informed treatment. You are the adult who is supposed to be providing a secure, supportive, and predictable environment, so the child can learn to feel safe. Chances are, the child is coming to you at least in part for impulse control problems. So whose judgment do you want to trust—yours, or the child's? If you allow the child's overdisclosure impulse to spoil your session and your treatment program, you have failed the child; you have not kept your own implied promise.

If this session has gone well, the child may have had a rather profound experience. He may have told you about something that he has never talked about before. Perhaps he was afraid of how someone would react; perhaps he was afraid that he himself couldn't handle it. Hopefully you reacted in a calm and supportive manner; and hopefully he was able to handle it well enough too, with your guidance. This is a great step! He has learned some important facts about himself, about you, and about what he might be capable of in treatment. He is stronger now than before, and he has more reason to hope.

It doesn't really take very long to ask the child about the trauma/loss history, but there's clearly a lot to it! The follow-up activities—deep breathing, list of good things, and the less intense final conversation—are all very important to help the child regain composure and come away with a good experience. These take time. So here's some advice: don't start on the trauma history with only ten or fifteen minutes left in your session! You might not make it through all the follow-up activities; it's too risky. If you have long sessions (close to an hour) then you can start partway through the session. If you have shorter sessions (closer to half an hour) it is best to start on the trauma history near the beginning of the session.

Chapter 7

Trauma-Informed Case Formulation

If all you get out of evaluation is a diagnosis, you don't have much to work with. If the intervention of choice was simply a pill or medical procedure, little understanding would be required, and a mere diagnosis might suffice. Keep in mind, though, that in child trauma treatment, both the child and the parents will be asked to perform a series of challenging tasks that require both energy and persistence. Also, many of your kids and families have probably already been through counseling, perhaps more than once, and the problems keep getting worse. So your explanation must be extremely good. It should demonstrate your knowledge and credibility while also providing a persuasive rationale for the treatment activities you'll recommend.

This is accomplished with a trauma-informed case formulation. The case formulation is the product, or outcome, of the evaluation. It's the therapist's explanation of what's going on with the child. The case formulation becomes the cornerstone of the entire course of treatment—it's the road map. In fact, when I provide consultation and the therapist isn't sure what to do, the problem is almost always the absence of case formulation to guide the treatment. With a good case formulation, you will have a deep, detailed understanding about who the child is, how the problem developed, which factors keep the problem going, and what to do about it.

Although the case formulation is formally offered following the interview portion of the Evaluation, in fact it begins much earlier. The therapist should be testing hypotheses all the way along, by providing mini-formulations with both the child and the parent, and requesting feedback. This helps the therapist correct misimpressions early on, and to pursue fruitful areas in more depth. It also allows the child and parents to gradually try on the therapist's perspective and give input into the formulation's development. In other words, the evaluation should be an interactive learning experience for the family. By the time the full case formulation is offered, the family should feel as if they are being told something they basically already know and understand—even if they did not know, and could not have articulated it that way, prior to the evaluation.

This type of interactive process of mini-formulations also gives the therapist an opportunity to zero in on specific details related to the formulation, and on the client's language. Later, when the full formulation is offered, the therapist can use the client's language and fill it in with the specific examples most relevant to the client. This enhances both the understandability and credibility of the formulation.

The case formulation is an opportunity to teach the child and family about the problem and how the child's trauma/loss history contributes to the problem. This accomplishes several purposes, as follows:

- It transforms the child from "bad" to sad, mad, or scared. It's tempting for a parent or other caregiver to be angry with a bad child, to reject him, give up on him. But what if the child isn't really bad, just wounded? How do you react to a wounded child? You want to help. Helping the parents see the child as wounded rather than bad opens the door for more empathy and for enhanced attachment.
- It externalizes the child's problem while internalizing the child's goodness. Like their parents do, many children also believe that they themselves have become bad, damaged,

tainted in some way. The case formulation helps them to see themselves as basically good, with some problems that have intruded but do not represent their core being. In other words, the dragon is the problem, not the kingdom itself.

- It normalizes (and depathologizes) both the problem and the solution. Kids suffering from posttraumatic symptoms and labeled as "problems" tend to feel that they are not normal, that they are stigmatized, broken, sick. The case formulation helps them to see themselves as having normal and reasonable reactions to unfortunate events. The case formulation also calls for simple and normative actions (such as becoming stronger and talking through the bad memory) to effect a cure.
- It emphasizes strengths and resources. The case formulation does not start with the dragon or the problems/symptoms. It starts with Once upon a time; with the kingdom's pre-dragon level of functioning, and with the knight in shining armor. It is the kingdom and the knight, together (or, the family/community and the child) who will work together to slay the dragon. The therapist must identify the child's strengths and resources because these will be the foundation of the child's success in treatment.
- It mobilizes people to productive treatment-related activities. When the child, parents, and others can understand where the problem comes from, when they can feel empathy, connection, and protectiveness toward the child (instead of anger and rejection), when they can feel capable and empowered to solve the problem, and when they have reason to hope for improvement . . . watch out!

The trauma-informed case formulation is essentially a story of the child's life, which shows how the child learned specific lessons (leading to the presenting symptoms) from specific experiences (the trauma). The story is presented in plain language in a way that makes good sense to

parents and children who may not be psychologically oriented. The structure is the same as the "meaning of behavior" form, but with "Once upon a time"—the child's strengths and resources—added at the beginning. Although the contents are individualized, all trauma-based case formulations should include the following elements:

1. Begin with available evidence of positive attachments, healthy development, successful functioning, good qualities, prosocial goals, supportive others, and other strengths and resources.
2. Call attention to specific traumatic experiences in the child's history.
3. Describe how other kids tend to react to such experiences:
   - *Negative beliefs:* They may learn that the world is unsafe—bad things might happen—and they better watch out. They may learn to believe that they are helpless, unworthy, or bad.
   - *Pile-up of feelings:* The bad feelings from the event (e.g., sadness, anger, worry) are so big that it's kind of too much. The feelings get stuck inside, and just pile up.
4. Describe how when something happens now that's a reminder (trigger) of the old event, it hits a sore spot, and the pile-up of bad feelings is so strong that kids get overwhelmed, bogged down, caught in their symptoms. Sometimes they end up doing things to get rid of the bad feelings, that later they wish they hadn't done.

Here is the same case example that was used to illustrate the Meaning of Behavior form. To make this a trauma-informed case formulation, the "Once upon a time" part (strengths, successes, resources) is added at the beginning. Remember that the child's identified problem behavior is actually a solution, from his perspective, to some other more pressing problem.

Casey is an eight-year-old boy who is referred for frequent fighting in school and in his neighborhood. He has a history of witnessing domestic violence—seeing his father push his mother and hit her—and had tried unsuccessfully to protect his mother from his father. Casey tells you that he does not pick fights but only defends himself when other kids gang up on him and call him names.

Here is an abbreviated example of how you might fill out the worksheet:

1. *Strengths/successes/resources:* Will stand up for himself and his family. Does not pick fights. Wants friends.
2. *Trauma/loss event:* Saw father push and hit mother.
3. *Lesson learned (negative belief):* I am powerless.
4. *Piled-up feelings:* Anger, fear, shame.
5. *Trigger situation: Theme:* feeling threatened or attacked; *example:* being teased by other kids.
6. *Problem behavior:* Fighting.

Here is the story (the explanation) you might provide. Notice that the order of events in the story is the same as the order of steps on the worksheet.

1. Casey really cares about his family. He is brave and willing to stand up for himself and his family even when others are bigger and stronger. He tries hard in school. He is a friendly boy and is nice to other kids. He told me that he really wants to get along with kids better and have more friends.
2. There were times that Casey saw his father hurting his mother. Casey tried to stop it from happening, but he couldn't. He was too small.

3. Kids learn from experience. Kids who have had this kind of experience often learn to believe that they are powerless, that they can't protect themselves or those they love, that they are not good enough.
4. Also, when something like this happens, kids often have very strong feelings, like being afraid that someone will get hurt, being mad, and being ashamed that they can't stop it from happening. These feelings can be so big that they just pile up inside and leave a big sore spot.
5. Now no one likes to be teased, it bothers everyone at least a little. But when Casey is teased, I can't help but wonder if it might be hitting that sore spot from the old thoughts and feelings that are piled up inside. Then his reaction is much stronger than other people think it should be. Then the bad feelings might be so strong that he can't stand it, and he has to get rid of it somehow.
6. So his solution is to attack the kids who are teasing him. When he hits them, this gets rid of the bad feelings. It gets out his anger. Also, he doesn't feel powerless anymore; he feels like he is able to protect himself.

Notice that the child's goals were included in the "Once upon a time" section. He wants more friends. Positive prosocial goals make kids feel normal. This boy is not "bad" or one who "just doesn't care." It's important to point this out. Also, this is his Princess; this is the thing that will motivate him to work hard with us. When we follow the case formulation with treatment recommendations, we will refer to his goals as the reason it is worth his while to follow our advice.

EXERCISE: DO IT YOURSELF

Try this exercise by yourself or, better yet, in a small group (three or four is ideal). Using the following vignette, do the following, in order:

1. Complete the Trauma-Informed Case Formulation worksheet (included in this chapter). Do this in order. Fill in everything you can for the first section, then the next, etc.
2. Tell the story (give the case formulation) out loud to others in your group. Follow along with the order used in the worksheet. Do your best but don't worry if it's not so smooth. It takes practice.
3. Have others give feedback: What one thing worked really well in that story and should be done the same way next time? What one thing could be done better, and how?
4. Have another person take a turn telling the story and receiving feedback. Repeat the process until everyone has had a turn.
5. Here are some tips to make the story work. It can be helpful to review these tips before each attempt at telling the story. You won't get these all at once; it takes practice.
   - Go in order. Follow the worksheet. It works.
   - Use simple language that the child, teacher, or high-school-educated parent can understand.
   - Use actual experiences rather than labels, for example, "he saw his father hit his mother" is preferable to "he witnessed domestic violence." This way you are conveying the facts, not making up labels. (On the other hand, sometimes it is more appropriate to be vague—"some bad things happened"—rather than disclose confidential information in a group that includes people who may not have a right to hear the details. You'll have to use your judgment in the situation.)

- Try to avoid accusing the child of having certain thoughts or feelings. It's better to talk about the thoughts or feelings of other kids in similar situations. If the shoe fits, wear it. This approach is experienced as less intrusive. Also, when you talk about other kids having similar experiences, the child in question feels more "normal," less like a freak, and may feel more comfortable listening to what you have to say.
- Explain that when the trigger event causes the same negative beliefs and feelings as those piled up from the trauma memory, it can hit the sore spot, leading to an extra-strong reaction. Try to use the phrase "hits the sore spot" because people understand that. Explain how the problem behavior gets rid of the bad feelings and has become a solution for the child.

Following are some additional examples of case formulations.

Example 1: John

Presenting Information

John is a ten-year-old boy in the fourth grade. He has dyslexia that was only diagnosed a few months ago and he is receiving special help with reading now. His grades and his disruptive behavior have been progressively worsening for several years. The request for evaluation followed a suspension for dumping his desk and walking out of a class during a quiz, as well as failing grades in several classes.

Formulation

Introduction: "Let me tell you what I've learned about John, and what I think can be done for him. Then we can talk about it and you can decide what you want to do."

Once upon a time: "One thing I've found out is that everyone I talk to really likes him! He watches out for his little sister, helps around the house sometimes, wants to do well at school, and has friends who like to play with him.

"But I know he has a lot of trouble with his reading, and that makes schoolwork hard to do. And the reason you're talking with me is because he also gets into a lot of trouble at school, not doing his work, making noise, and getting into fights. And you told me that sometimes at home he doesn't listen, either. So let me tell you why I think he is the way he is."

Then the dragon came: "Any kid who has this much trouble reading is bound to have a hard time in school—to have things go wrong, over and over again."

Negative beliefs: "Other kids in this situation have told me that when they see other kids doing stuff they can't do, they start to think that maybe they're stupid, even if that's not really true."

Piled-up bad feelings: "Other kids have told me that it can be pretty frustrating to hit that wall again and again. And when it's hard to read, it's hard to do almost any subject in school; even math has word problems this year."

The trigger: "So now, when he does try and something is hard, I wonder if it reminds him of all those other times, hits the sore spot where all the years of frustration are piled up. That much frustration can be hard to handle; it can feel like too much."

The problem behavior and how it's a solution for him: "So sometimes I think he decides right away he can't do it, and just gives up. And one thing I think is happening is that he's so sick of getting frustrated that sometimes he'd rather not even try, so he doesn't have to get frustrated again."

Exercise: Trauma-Informed Case Formulation

Marcus is a fourteen-year-old boy who was referred following his second suspension in a month for fighting, this time for beating someone rather severely. Testing from second grade showed an estimated IQ of 95 (the average range is 90–110) with better performance scores than verbal scores. At that time he was having some reading difficulties—dyslexia was suspected but never formally diagnosed—and responded well to a brief stint of tutoring. However, by fourth grade he was no longer earning academic grades higher than a C. He is generally quiet and attracts little attention in his classes, where he has been getting by with barely passing grades and minimal work. He typically gets suspended once or twice a year for fighting, and will not tell the vice principal (but will tell you) that he only fights when someone disrespects him or his family. He is quiet and respectful at home, with occasional temper outbursts. History of exposure to harsh physical discipline and witnessing domestic violence, which steadily escalated until Marcus was eleven when parents separated and divorced. He is no longer in contact with father and says that's the way he wants it.

1. Once upon a time (introduce positive impression of strengths, including relationships, competencies, successes, resources):

2. Then the bad thing(s) happened:

3. Leading to (for each possible trauma event, describe how other kids have reacted: negative beliefs, piled-up feelings):

4. Along with piled-up feelings:

5. Now, whenever the trigger (or "high risk") situation occurs (describe the trigger situations and how that leads to reactivity):

6. Then the bad thoughts and feelings are so strong that (describe the urgency of the reaction, and how the problem behavior provides relief for the child):

Exercise: Trauma-Informed Case Formulation

Michael is a ten-year-old boy who was diagnosed with ADHD at age nine after two years of school-related problems including impulsive/disruptive behavior, interpersonal conflicts, and poor work habits. Medication at age nine seemed to help at first, but after a couple of good weeks his school performance has been steadily deteriorating. At home he does his chores after repeated prompting, and gets along with his siblings, though with a fair bit of squabbling. His parents are currently separated; he lives with his mother, and sees his father several times per week. Trauma history includes a minor auto accident at age five, and the death of an uncle at age six.

1. Once upon a time (introduce positive impression of strengths, including relationships, competencies, successes, resources):

2. Then the bad thing(s) happened:

3. Leading to (for each possible trauma event, describe how other kids have reacted: negative beliefs, piled-up feelings):

4. Along with piled-up feelings:

5. Now, whenever the trigger (or "high risk") situation occurs (describe the trigger situations and how that leads to reactivity):

6. Then the bad thoughts and feelings are so strong that (describe the urgency of the reaction, and how the problem behavior provides relief for the child):

Example 2: Jody

Presenting Information

Jody is a seven-year-old girl in the second grade, previously high functioning, who began wetting her bed and having nightmares following the anniversary of the World Trade Center attack. She has also been picking on her younger sister more recently. Her house burned down three years ago (she was not home at the time). The event precipitating the referral was a crying jag at school when the teacher asked Jody why she hadn't completed a quiz.

Formulation

Introduction: "Let me tell you what I think I've learned about Jody, and you can tell me if this makes sense to you or not."

Once upon a time: "First of all, I've learned that Jody is basically a normal girl who likes to play, gets along with other children, does well in school, and listens to her parents.

"But you came for help because it seems that in some ways, she's not herself lately."

The dragons: "I think it's probably related to what happened when the World Trade Center was destroyed. Let me tell you the kinds of reactions that some other children are having; maybe Jody's going through something like this too.

"When something very scary happens, like a house burning down or a big building being destroyed, children can take this a lot of different ways."

Negative beliefs: "Kids with good parents grow up feeling safe and protected, and then something happens to show them that maybe things aren't so safe. Sometimes they become very worried that something else bad will happen. And also, this might not seem to make sense, but some kids will feel guilty when something bad happens, even though we know they could not have caused it. But kids get mad about something, and then something bad happens, and part of them might believe that their anger caused it."

Adding in a little psychoeducation regarding other posttraumatic symptoms: "When kids have been badly scared, sometimes they have bad dreams; sometimes they start wetting their bed again."

Piled-up feelings: "This type of event can also make a child feel helpless, sad, or angry. These feelings—the fear, worry, helplessness, sadness, anger, guilt—can just pile up, get stuck inside."

Trigger: "Then when something else happens to remind her of one of these feelings, even something small, the pile-up of feelings can kick in and she can have a strong reaction. So maybe something goes a little wrong at school, she feels a little mad or helpless, and instead of handling it like she used to, now it hits that sore spot, and it's so strong that it's too much to handle anymore."

The problem behavior and how it's a solution for her: "So then she just gives up and cries. This gets out some of the bad feelings for her, also when she gives up that takes the pressure off because she's not getting frustrated anymore, and people try to comfort her."

Example 3: Carla

A case formulation can take multiple traumas into account as well. Here is an example of the portion of the case formulation (the trauma, negative beliefs, and piled-up feelings) that pertains:

Carla is a ten-year-old girl in the fourth grade. She has a history of exposure to domestic violence at ages three to five, death of a cousin by auto accident at age six, and dyslexia that was only diagnosed two months ago. She was referred for failing grades and for refusing to do her schoolwork.

"When kids see one parent hurting the other one [like your child did], they often learn to believe that they are not safe, that bad things can happen, and that they are helpless, what they do doesn't matter. Also, sometimes the bad feelings that kids have are so strong that they just pile up, and stay stuck inside. Kids might feel mad about what happened, sad about it, and even ashamed that they couldn't stop it. I wouldn't be surprised if [your child] had some of this kind of reaction to what she saw a few years ago when things were bad at home.

"Then when her cousin died, that's another trauma piled on the first one. More helplessness, more belief that bad things are going to happen, more anger, sadness, shame. The pile just gets bigger.

"We also just found out a couple of months ago that Carla has dyslexia. Kids that have dyslexia and don't know it have lots of experiences at school, maybe many times every day, where they are trying as hard as the other kids, but they can't do it. Kids in this situation often learn to believe that there's something wrong with them, and that they're helpless, trying doesn't make any difference, bad things will happen no matter what you do.

"So Carla has been learning the same lessons over and over again. And the bad feelings have just been piling up. And now, when [a trigger] happens . . ."

When you were practicing your case formulations, you might have noticed a strong temptation to go right into what the child and family should do about all this. Good! That's what comes next, in the same session—but here, it's in the next chapter.

You might have also noticed that the focus, in these case formulations, was on the trauma-related issues. This is not to say that trauma is the only issue or the only reason that the problems develop or persist. There may be many other reasons; for example, the parents' habitual ways of responding might be repeatedly reinforcing the problem. However, the case formulation is not the time to be passing around blame. The purpose of the case formulation is to increase understanding of the trauma contribution to the problem. This helps people access their caring for the child, and to mobilize to improve the situation. Later on, we will use this understanding, caring, and determination to address the other issues as well.

Chapter 8

Making a Treatment Contract

Once the trauma-informed case formulation has been accepted, treatment recommendations can be made, and hopefully accepted by the child and family. Following the themes of the case formulation, recommendations will focus on helping the child feel more safe and secure, and become stronger and more effective, so that he will be able not only to manage the trauma-related symptoms, but to face the trauma memory directly and gain mastery and resolution. Specific treatment recommendations will most likely include

- Interventions specific to unique problems, symptoms, or situations;
- Parent (and other caregiver) activities to help the child feel more safe and secure;
- Child activities to help the child feel safer, stronger, and in control; and
- Child activities (later in the treatment) to help the child face and master the trauma memory.

Before trying to "close the deal" on the treatment contract, however, we must ensure that the child's (and family's) motivation is being effectively developed and tapped. Remember, without the princess to work toward, nothing else will happen.

MOTIVATION ENHANCEMENT

The case formulation is not only about the past and the present; it is also about the future. Motivation is an essential component, because without it, nothing else will happen. There are two main ways to enhance motivation during the case formulation:

1. Don't forget the princess! It is critically important to identify not only the parent's goals for the child, but the child's goals for herself. What kind of person do you hope your child becomes? What kind of life do you want to have when you are older? What kind of day do you want to have now, next week, next month?
2. It's not enough to yearn for the princess if it's only a fantasy. The child and the family must believe, at least tentatively, that success is possible. Remember hope? Many things should have already been happening that contribute to hope:

    - The development of the therapeutic relationship might already make the child feel more hopeful that safety is possible and that attachment is possible.
    - The therapist's obvious depth of knowledge about the presenting problem gives the therapist credibility, and makes the proposed solution seem plausible.
    - When the therapist talks about "what other kids say," and then indicates that other kids have been successful in treatment, the child might believe that he can do it too.
    - The family's increased sense of attachment as a result of the evaluation sessions shows them that their former closeness may not be altogether lost.
    - The child's ability to tolerate the disclosure of trauma/loss history provides the beginning of a track record for success with greater challenges.

- The therapist's recommendation of a series of practical steps toward problem resolution can bridge the gap between the problematic present and the desired future. Seeing how it's possible to achieve goals, step by step, makes the prospect of this achievement more plausible.

In other words, nearly everything you are doing contributes to a growing sense of hope. The child and family have been learning to feel better about themselves and one another through their work with you. They have also been learning to respect both your knowledge and your expertise. Hopefully, with the case formulation and treatment recommendations, you'll have them ready to work!

MOTIVATIONAL INTERVIEWING

Motivational Interviewing (MI) is a well-established counseling style/approach to conducting an evaluation and providing feedback that can be helpful for getting kids to identify their own goals and then to commit to a treatment plan in the service of those goals. Although MI has been used primarily with adults with substance abuse problems, in recent years it's been applied more widely, including use with people with post-traumatic stress disorder, and with teens. Several studies of MI with teens found that a single MI session led to the following outcomes (in the different studies):

- Ten percent had quit smoking cigarettes by six-month follow-up.
- Thirty-seven percent more in the MI group attended their treatment sessions (compared to the control group).

This approach recognizes that people with problematic behaviors are generally ambivalent about these behaviors. On one hand, the problem behaviors solve some other problem for them (e.g., help to get rid of a bad feeling); that's why they persist. On the other hand, these behaviors cause other problems!

When others complain about why these behaviors are a problem, it's natural for an ambivalent kid to respond by resisting, perhaps by saying, "I like it. I'll do it if I want to. It's none of your business!" On the other hand, when the other person supports his right to keep his behavior and acknowledges that some value must be found in persisting with that behavior, it's natural for an ambivalent kid to respond by filling in the other side of the ambivalence, perhaps by saying, "Yeah, but I'm sick of getting in trouble because of what I do. It's getting old."

When we tell kids what's right, then even if they accept this, they are accepting what we said. When we can guide kids to tell us what's right (for them), then they feel more ownership; it's what they said—it's theirs. In this empowerment model of treatment, we want kids to take the initiative as much as possible. We want them to feel that they are participating in treatment activities because of their own determination to achieve their own goals. We may be the guide or the coach, but we can't do the work; so it's got to be the kid's princess.

Here are the essential principles and procedures in the MI approach.

Free Will: What You Do Is Up to You

The therapist is explicit about the fact that the child is making her own choices. The therapist might say, "It's your life; what you choose to do is up to you." This respects the child's autonomy while stating the truth—the child does make choices, not only of behaviors but of their consequences. It's important for the therapist to be supportive of the child while also keeping some distance or neutrality, to avoid being sucked into a conflict about what the child should choose. For example, the therapist might say (or at least say internally), "I hope you make the choice that will help you get to your goal. But whatever choice you make, you know what happens at six-thirty tonight? I have dinner." In other words, root for your team, but don't bet your savings on what the team does. Another way of thinking about this is that we are supportive of the client but we are not invested in the behavioral choices she makes at any given time. When kids can't use their choices as weapons in a fight with the therapist, they are left fighting with themselves, and sometimes this leads to good things.

Empathy: Embrace the Client's Worldview

Empathy has been identified as one of the key components of effective psychotherapy, and it's central to this approach, too. When we embrace the client's worldview, he feels supported and respected; he feels that we are with him. This doesn't mean that we necessarily believe everything he says, or that we *only* see it the way he does. But we do convey understanding and acceptance. This is often accomplished with an active/reflective listening approach. For example, the therapist might respond to the child's explanation of what happened by saying, "So you were just kidding around, but then he started really fighting with you?" The alternative, to say, "It sounds like you started it," is nothing new; this is what others have been telling this child already. It hasn't helped; that's why they sent him to you. When you show empathy and acceptance for your client's worldview, then at least you are in the same conversation, and he feels that someone cares and understands.

Be Nonconfrontational

Getting in the kid's face and telling her what's wrong with her might work in the movies, but nowhere else. All you really get with the confrontational style is another free hour in your week. The research indicates that the in-your-face approach only leads to worse treatment compliance and increased dropout (Sommers-Flanagan & Sommers-Flanagan, 1995). Kids don't like to be "yelled at," so they block you out and write you off. The motivational interviewing style is nonconfrontational. We leave it up to the client to confront herself.

Identify Goals and Enhance Investment in Goals

The therapist guides the client toward identifying goals, things he cares about, wants for himself. Even this can be challenging for a child with trauma-related avoidance of hope; the child may habitually deny having goals to preclude disappointment. The therapist also guides the client to increasing his investment and commitment to these goals. This is done by helping the child get in touch with how much he wants these goals, and also by helping the child to believe that it's not just some fantasy; we can figure out practical steps that can make the goals seem more realistic and attainable.

Highlight Conflict Between Goals and Behaviors

The climax, or punch line, of the motivational interviewing approach is to highlight the conflict between the client's goals and her current behaviors. This is done, of course, in an empathetic and nonconfrontational manner. The therapist might say, "I'm confused. You told me that you want those good things to happen for you, and I believe you. I think you really do want that. But you're also doing this stuff that you told me can get in your way, keep you from getting what you really want. So it's hard to tell what you really do care about." When this dilemma is highlighted and given back to the client, it can have a strong impact.

Offer Specific (Concrete Actions) Advice

Once the client has endorsed the positive goals and claimed them for her own, the therapist can offer advice, specific actions the client can take to help her to achieve her goals. Even now, it's important to maintain the stance of supportive neutrality, so that the client can retain ownership of her goals and her initiative. The therapist might say, "Well, if that's really what you want, let me tell you what other kids have done in your situation to get to the kinds of goals that you're talking about . . ." Then the treatment plan is offered in service of the child's goals.

Arrange for Some Quick Successes

It is important that the treatment plan include some early treatment activities that will lead to quick, if small, successes. What happens when the child quickly sees that he is actually accomplishing the first things on the list? He believes, more than before, that this can really happen, and that he is already on the road to success. He becomes more confident, more hopeful, and more committed to treatment.

FINDING THE PRINCESS

A number of strategies are available for guiding kids to identify and invest in their own goals. Your strategy will be determined in part by the child's age and developmental status. Kids at different ages have different concerns, different concepts of future, and different perspectives on how much of the future might be relevant.

Preschoolers are very present focused; they just want to feel safe and happy. Most kids this young will do what their parents tell them to do, as long as their parents are effective authorities and as long as the child does not feel afraid. The parents are so influential that most of the motivational focus is with the parent. Motivational approaches for parents are addressed in Chapter 10.

School-aged children want to have a good day, but also are able to look forward to the near future. Kids this age want to stop wetting their bed so they can sleep over at a friend's house; they want to get a better report card so their parents will take them to the video arcade; they want to earn money to buy a special toy; they want to get better at a sport so they can get picked earlier for a team, and so they can help their team win. This does not mean that they would choose to be in treatment, even if the treatment can help them to get what they want. We must still count on the adults to make sure that the child shows up.

Even so, it's the child who will either work with us, or throw obstacles in the way. It's important first to identify what the child cares about, wants for herself, and then to make those goals the explicit focus of the treatment. Note that one goal she may have is to not come to treatment anymore. This is a legitimate goal to work toward and, of course, working hard on the other treatment goals will get the whole thing over with more quickly. It's also important to help the child believe that her parents really want her to work toward her goals. In case the child believes that her symptoms help her parents in some way, this intervention helps her to feel that her parents will be okay and that she has their permission to get better. Also, when the child and parents work together, this supports and enhances the relationship that may have been disrupted. Here are the steps in a relatively straightforward intervention to accomplish this motivational piece:

1. Acknowledge that it may not be the child's choice to come to treatment. "Your parents told me that you're going to have to come here every week for a while. Does that sound good to you, or would you rather be doing other stuff?"
2. Identify goals by using a "greatest hits" menu of other kids' goals. Make sure to include the goals you suspect this client might have. "Here are some things that other kids have told me they wished for. You tell me if you wish for any of these things, too.
   - Some kids wish they didn't have bad dreams anymore.
   - Some kids wish they got better grades in school.
   - Some kids wish they had more friends.
   - Some kids wish they didn't get picked on so much.
   - Some kids wish their parents didn't yell at them so much.
   - Some kids wish they didn't wet their bed anymore.
   - Some kids wish they didn't get in so much trouble."
3. Align the child's goals with the parents' goals for the child. "So you wish that you had better grades, and that your mom didn't yell at you so much? You know, when I was talking with your mom before, that's what she said she wanted for you, too. Did you know that?"
4. Mutually commit to these goals. "So while you are stuck coming here, is it okay if that's what we work on? Doing things to help you get better grades, and to get your mom to yell at you less?"

By the time most kids are twelve or thirteen, they are also interested in the long-term future, in what kind of person they will become, and what kind of life they will have as an adult. However, teens are also still very interested in the immediate as well as the near future, and in fact may be choosing instant gratification at the expense of long-term goals. This is especially likely for traumatized kids, who may say, in effect, "Nothing good's going to happen for me anyway. Nothing's going to work out, so I might as well just do what I want right now." The problem is that the bigger (or longer term) the goal, the more likely that the trauma-related "pessimistic future" will keep the child from feeling hopeful about it, or even admitting to having the goal at all. Of course, the more actively the child avoids plans, hopes, and dreams, the more difficult it is to get the child to invest in the future, and the more such a future focus is needed.

FUTURE MOVIES SCRIPT

The following "future movies" intervention (Greenwald, 2004, pp. 8-11) is one example of a way to help teens to identify their goals and to elicit increased investment as well as commitment to working toward these goals. It has been successful in extensive clinical experience as well as preliminary studies. It follows the motivational interviewing principles, and it is structured and scripted as carefully as a sales pitch to address the anticipated objections and obtain the desired responses. For example, the movie metaphor is used to allow kids to maintain some initial distance while discussing their hopes and dreams; this lowers the perceived risk. Later, the practical steps from today to the desired goal turn the goal from a fantasy into a realistic possibility.

> I've asked about your past and about how things are now. Now I want to know about your future. Let's say that ten years from now—how old will you be?—I stop at the video store on my way home from work, and pick up a movie called *The [client's name] Story*. It's about this kid who grows up in a city, starts out okay. Seems like a good kid but then some things go wrong for him, and he gets more angry, more stressed, the bad feelings piling up inside. He gets so stressed he ends up doing some things he doesn't really feel good about. He gets himself into some trouble, and I'm saying to myself, "This is a bummer. I used to work with kids like this. Looks like another good one going down the drain." But then

things start to change. First one good thing, then another, then another . . . till finally, by the end of the movie—you know that last picture, when the music's playing and the credits are rolling?—I'm smiling, and saying, "Way to go! You made it!" So tell me: If this was your story and things go the way you wish they would, what would your life be like?

(*Note:* With a real client, the therapist uses that client's history as the filler for this story. So it will have a little more detail and will directly relate the client's trauma/loss history to the onset or escalation of his problem behaviors. Then it will relate the "stress pileup" to the client's current reactivity and acting-out behaviors. This follows the fairy tale model, and is one way to present the trauma-informed case formulation.)

Follow-up questions, if called for: "What would you be doing for a living? Where do you think you'll be living? In the neighborhood you're in now, or someplace else in the city, or where? Your own house or an apartment? By yourself, with a buddy, with a girlfriend? Maybe married by then? What's she like? Will you have your own car? What kind? What color?"

Sample Movie Script Dialogue

THERAPIST: Okay, so if this is your life, what would be in that last picture, to let me know how good you're doing?

CLIENT: I'm in front of my house with my wife and my kid.

THERAPIST: When you have this picture, what kind of feeling goes with it?

CLIENT: Good, happy.

THERAPIST: Where do you feel that? Where in your body?

CLIENT: All over.

THERAPIST: And *what could you say to encourage yourself toward this goal?* Something like, "I can do it," or "I'm gonna make it"?

CLIENT: "Go for it."

THERAPIST: Okay. Now I want you to concentrate on this picture. Maybe it'll work better if you close your eyes. Concentrate on the picture, the feeling, where you feel it, and what you're saying to yourself.

THERAPIST: The thing is, the movie didn't just jump from the middle to the end; there were all these things that happened along the way to get there. So tell me, if this was your story, what happens in this movie? What would we see you doing tomorrow, next week, next month, next year?

CLIENT: You mean if this was me?

THERAPIST: Yes, if this was your story, the way you're hoping it would happen.

CLIENT: Well, I wouldn't get in trouble anymore.

THERAPIST: Okay. What would you do?

CLIENT: First I'd do good in school and graduate and make my mom proud.

THERAPIST: So what do you have to do to do good in school?

CLIENT: Have to go every day, pay attention, do my homework.

THERAPIST: And when trouble comes?

CLIENT: Just walk away.

THERAPIST: And after you graduate, do you see yourself getting a job, joining the service, going to college, what?

CLIENT: I'll probably work with my uncle, detailing cars, and go to college at night. Then learn about computers. There's good money in computers.

THERAPIST: So now I want you to imagine watching the whole movie in your mind, not from the beginning but from today all the way to that good end you were telling me about. All the things you were saying would happen to get there. You can do this with your eyes open, or closed. So start from today, and tell me when you're done.

How did it go? What happened in the movie?

I hope it goes the way you want it to, but what if it doesn't go the good way we've been talking about? What if you kept on doing the same old stuff, and things got worse and worse? What would that last picture be?

THERAPIST: Okay, so in the bad ending you see yourself behind bars?

CLIENT: Yeah. In a concrete room, like at the lockup.

THERAPIST: And what kind of feeling goes with this picture?

CLIENT: Bad. Sad.

THERAPIST: Where do you feel that?

CLIENT: In my mind.

THERAPIST: With this picture, *would it feel true to say to yourself, "It's not worth it" to go that way?*

CLIENT: It's not worth it. That's for sure.

THERAPIST: Okay, so just for a few seconds, I want you to concentrate on this bad ending, the bad feeling, where you feel it, "It's not worth it." Okay. Did that "It's not worth it" feel more true, less true, about the same? Okay, let's do this one more time. Concentrate on this bad ending, the bad feeling, where you feel it, "It's not worth it." Okay. Is it more true, less true, about the same?

Commitment to Goals

THERAPIST: So on zero to ten, zero is nothing, ten is all the way, how much of you really wants to go for that good ending you were telling me about?

CLIENT: Almost all of me, maybe eight or nine.

THERAPIST: Okay, and on zero to ten, how much of you still feels like doing the same old thing?

CLIENT: Maybe half. About five.

THERAPIST: So most of you really wants to go the good way?

CLIENT: Yeah.

THERAPIST: But sometimes that smaller part takes over and messes it up for all of you?

CLIENT: You could say that. I guess so.

Strengths and Obstacles

THERAPIST: If you were going to make a bet on a sports team, on who would win the game, how would you decide which team to bet on?

Right, you have the idea. Okay, so let's say I'm going to put a hundred dollars down on you making it to the good end. What would make me think this was a smart bet?

Well, I have some ideas about why this might be a smart bet. See if you think these ideas are right or wrong.

Well, you said you want to graduate high school and then get a basketball scholarship to college. Are you a good basketball player?

CLIENT: Yes. I was the best one in my high school before I got kicked off the team.

THERAPIST: Okay, I'll write down "good basketball player." See, that's something that will help you get to your goals. What else is there?

CLIENT: If I decide to do something, I don't give up.

THERAPIST: Okay, I'll write that down too. Also, you tell me that you have a close family?

CLIENT: Yeah, we'll do anything for each other.

THERAPIST: I'll write down, "close family," because it's easier to get to your goal when your family is behind you. What else?

Now, I bet there'll be someone else who's gonna say, "I'll bet you" and they'll think that they're gonna make some easy money. What would make them think that they have a smart bet?

What could stop you from getting to your goals? What could get in your way?

So it sounds like there are some good reasons to believe that you really could make it on the good track. And also some real challenges, some things that could get in your way.

On zero to ten, how confident are you right now that you'll be able to make it in the good direction?

And what would it take for you to feel a little more confident, for that six to be a seven? What would have to happen? (Follow up-questions/reflections as needed.)

In the previous intervention, following the Motivational Interviewing principles, after the goals were identified, the conflict is highlighted by focusing on the possible outcome of doing the same old (problem behavior) stuff. This conflict is further developed by focusing on strengths and obstacles. At each step, while the conflict is being highlighted, the client is guided to identify with the positive goals, while seeing the problem behaviors as a problem for himself (and not just for others). And at each step, the client is gaining a better understanding of what to do to get to his goals, and why he might really be able to be successful. By the end of this session, many kids will feel so capable and confident that they don't notice that they have shifted from talking about a movie to talking about their own plans.

There's another reason that it's important to include the component of identifying possible obstacles to achieving the goals. If obstacles are not part of the conversation, some kids will not perceive them. If kids don't perceive any obstacles to their goals, then they don't need your help! They're fine on their own, thanks anyway. When you can agree on significant obstacles or challenges, then you have something to offer, a strategy to help them to become stronger and to master the challenges. Don't think you can skip this part and get away with it—you'll pay later!

Many teens, at the end of the entire course of treatment, will say that the future movies session was their favorite part of the treatment. We are helping kids to identify their goals and to recognize their own strengths and resources. This feels good, and it often inspires kids and mobilizes them. This is the session they thank you for.

Clearly the motivational interviewing approach supports the fairy tale model. It focuses on empowering the client, helping her to identify "the princess" and then encouraging her to become more confident and to do what it takes to get ready to slay the dragon. Once the case formulation has been provided and the motivation has been identified and developed/enhanced as much as possible, it's time to offer the specific advice.

TREATMENT PLANNING AND CONTRACTING

The case formulation provides a detailed understanding. This leads directly to "What do we do about it?" The therapist can then recommend a treatment plan: build a fence around the child for safety and security, then help the child to become stronger, then to slay the dragon. The treatment plan also accomplishes several purposes:

- It extends the road map of the case formulation from the past and the problem into the future and the solution. The therapist may have been the first one to ever really explain the problem. This capitalizes on the therapist's credibility and improves the chances of acceptance of the proposed solution.
- It gives everyone a role. This is especially important for parents, who may feel guilty, inadequate, and disempowered. Parents can build the fence around the child by maintaining household routines, implementing a consistent discipline approach, and taking other measures to help the child feel more safe and secure. Teachers or others can do their part in some situations. The child can work on becoming stronger, in anticipation of facing and working through the trauma memories.
- People feel better when they can take an action that is expected to make a difference. In many types of psychotherapy, parents are just told to bring the kids, and the kids are just told to do or say whatever they feel like doing or saying. This can make people feel helpless. With a clear treatment plan, including specific actions at each step, people can feel that they are doing something that matters.
- It enhances faith in the treatment. When people can perform specific actions that are expected to directly help them in achieving specific goals, they understand why they are doing the actions. When people know why they're doing a treatment activity, they are more likely to believe in it, and to keep coming to therapy. Chances of engagement and success are increased, and risk of dropout is reduced.

With Older Kids/Teens

In the session after Future Movies (Greenwald, 2004), with older kids it can be helpful to create a graphic representation of the problem—including the trauma component—and the solution. This approach anticipates and addresses one of the major problems in treatment: that once kids get better at self-control and things calm down, they—and others—think that treatment was successful and it's done. The graphic, illustrating the trauma's ongoing impact on reactivity, can serve as a reminder that there's more work to be done (Nancy Smyth, personal communication, September 2002). The following transcript (Greenwald, 2004) shows how this might be set up. In that session, the therapist started out with a blank piece of paper, then drew the circles and filled them in during the conversation.

Note that, as in all of the scripts presented in this book, the words are chosen very carefully. This does not mean that you can't modify the words to fit your situation. However, the modifications should be done intentionally and not casually. For example, at one point in this dialogue, the therapist asks, "Can I touch your shoulder lightly?" It would be unwise to skip that or to say, "Now I'm going to touch your shoulder lightly." Asking permission is essential. On the other hand, you might choose to be even more careful with a given client, by asking, "Can I touch your shoulder lightly with this book?"

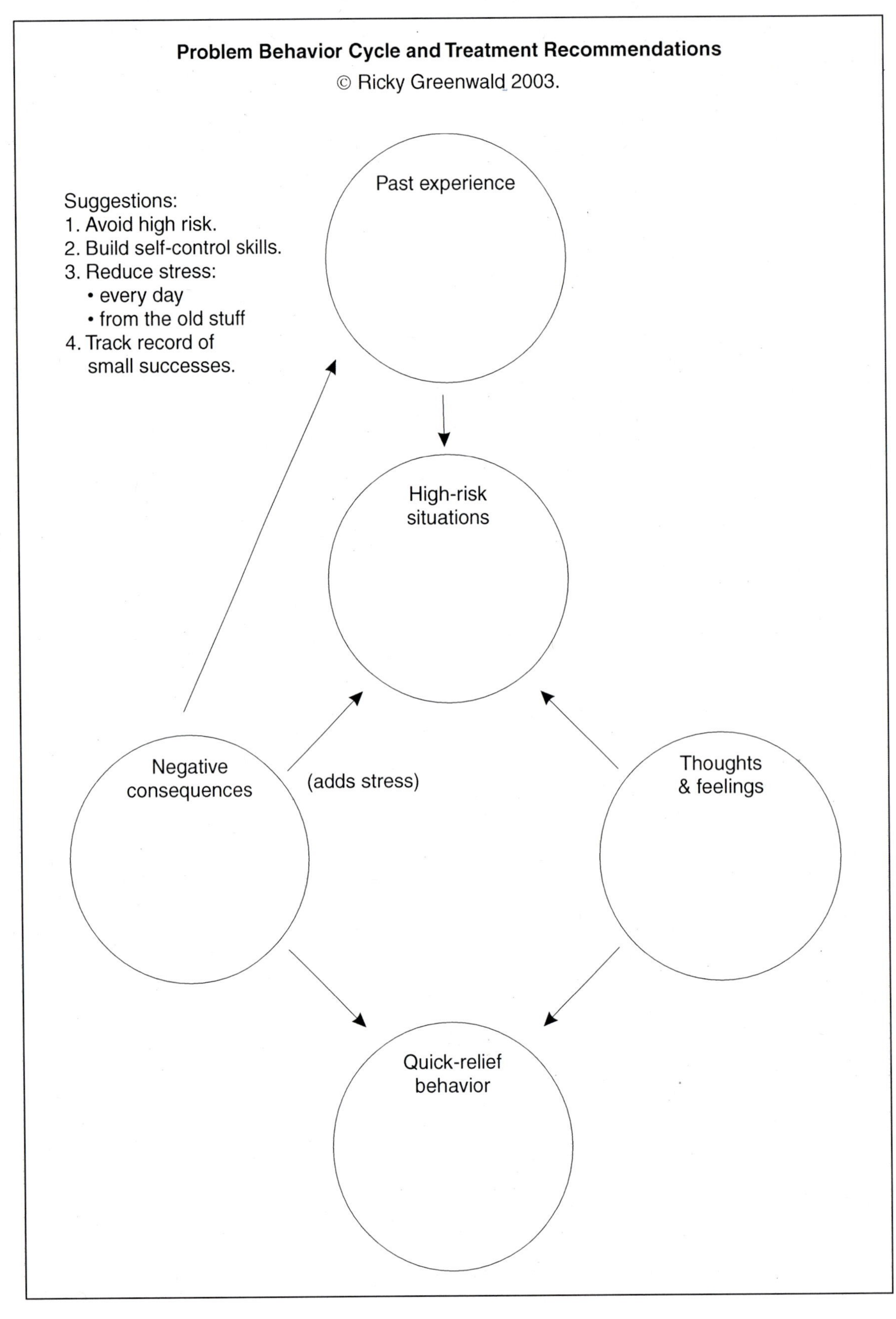
Problem Behavior Cycle and Treatment Recommendations
© Ricky Greenwald 2003.
Suggestions:
1. Avoid high risk.
2. Build self-control skills.
3. Reduce stress:
• every day
• from the old stuff
4. Track record of small successes.
Past experience
High-risk situations
Negative consequences
(adds stress)
Thoughts & feelings
Quick-relief behavior

Sample Dialogue

THERAPIST: Last time we met, we talked about your goals, the kind of life you want for yourself. We talked about your strengths, things that will help you get what you want, and also about some things that could get in your way. You said that the main thing that could get in your way is your temper. So are you losing your temper every minute of every day, or just at certain times?

CLIENT: Just once in a while, only if someone makes me mad.

THERAPIST: Like what would someone have to do to make you mad?

CLIENT: If they say something about my family, or if they stare at me or talk stupid.

THERAPIST: Oh, so there are only certain situations that could lead to you losing your temper. I'm going to write these down as your "High-Risk Situations." So when's the last time that one of these things happened?

CLIENT: Just yesterday.

THERAPIST: What happened yesterday?

CLIENT: On the bus, this guy bumped into me and then stared at me like it was my fault, like I was supposed to apologize to him.

THERAPIST: So when that happens, what are your thoughts and feelings?

CLIENT: I'm mad.

THERAPIST: What are you saying to yourself? What are the words in your head?

CLIENT: I want to hurt him.

THERAPIST: And what's happening in your body? What are the signals that you're mad?

CLIENT: My heart is beating and my hands are fists.

THERAPIST: So this is a pretty strong reaction. When you're like this, what do you feel like doing?

CLIENT: Feel like hitting the guy.

THERAPIST: Okay. But you told me that this kind of thing would get you bad consequences. Like what kind of bad thing might happen to you if you hit people?

CLIENT: Suspended from school, maybe get locked up again. The guy might try for revenge . . .

THERAPIST: So let me ask you another question. These high-risk situations you were telling me about—would you say that you mess up every time someone does one of those things?

CLIENT: No, usually I can control myself.

THERAPIST: Would you say that you have a better chance of controlling yourself when you are feeling good, relaxed? Or when you're already stressed?

CLIENT: If I'm already stressed, that's when the trouble happens.

THERAPIST: So when you get these bad consequences, like being suspended from school, or wondering if someone will try for revenge, does that make you more relaxed or more stressed?

CLIENT: Definitely more stressed.

THERAPIST: So the more you handle these high-risk situations by fighting, the more you end up getting stressed from the consequences?

CLIENT: Yeah, I guess so. Oh, I see. This is a cycle!

THERAPIST: Right, it can be. Now here's an interesting thing: You know how you told me the things that were your high-risk situations? Other kids, some of them don't mind that stuff, but other things bother them, things that are no big deal to you. I have an idea why these are the high-risk situations for you. Can I tell you?

CLIENT: Sure, go ahead.

THERAPIST: Okay. To explain this, can I touch your shoulder lightly?

CLIENT: Okay.

THERAPIST: Okay, pay attention, and tell me how much this hurts, on zero to ten. (Punches client's shoulder lightly.) How much?

CLIENT: Nothing. Zero.

THERAPIST: Now I'm going to ask you to imagine something that I would never do, and you would never let me do. Imagine that I have a baseball bat, and that I swing this bat as hard as I can, right to that spot on your shoulder. Not just once, but over and over again for ten minutes. And then tomorrow, the same thing, over and over again. Every day like that for two weeks. And then, you're walking down the hall, and someone bumps you in the shoulder—can I touch you there again?

CLIENT: Okay.

THERAPIST: Okay, now tell me how much this would hurt if someone bumped you like this, after that two weeks with the baseball bat (punches lightly as before).

CLIENT: A ten!

THERAPIST: How come?

CLIENT: 'Cause it's already all banged up and sore.

THERAPIST: That's what I think might be happening with your high-risk situations. Remember when I asked you about the worst things that ever happened to you, and I asked you on zero to ten how much those things still hurt inside? Some of the things on your list had pretty high numbers. I'm wondering if those things make a sore spot inside you, so when something else comes along that maybe feels like that in some way, it hits the sore spot and you react extra strong.

CLIENT: I think so; I think that's what's happening.

THERAPIST: So this makes sense to you?

CLIENT: Yeah.

THERAPIST: Okay, then we have a pretty good idea of what could get in your way, keep you from getting to your goals. So let me give you some suggestions for how to handle this stuff, so you can be in charge of yourself and get your life to go the way you want it to.

CLIENT: Okay.

THERAPIST: First of all, let's say you have a friend. He's twenty-one. He's an alcoholic but he's trying to stay sober. He's doing good so far. He needs a job, and he says to you, "That bar down the street needs a bartender. Think I should try for that?" What will you tell him?

CLIENT: No, don't do it.

THERAPIST: Why not?

CLIENT: 'Cause there's gonna be beer all around. Sooner or later he's gonna drink some.

THERAPIST: Good answer. So you already understand the first thing I'm going to suggest for you: Avoid high risk. If you know where the trouble is, sometimes you can just decide to stay away from it. Thing is, your friend took your advice; he got a job at the clothing store. But then he went to a birthday party and guess what?

CLIENT: They're drinking.

THERAPIST: Right. So even when you do everything right, sometimes you just can't avoid the high-risk situation. So here comes my next suggestion, and it's something you're already doing—my suggestion is to get even better at this: self-control skills.

CLIENT: Yup.

THERAPIST: Now you told me that if you're stressed, it's harder to use your self-control skills. So my next recommendation is to reduce stress. Now this one has two parts. One part is to get better at living a less stressful life, and at bringing your stress down once you are stressed. The other part is to bring stress down from the old stuff, those old memories that make that sore spot inside. There are special ways of talking about those old memories. It doesn't make them disappear, but it can help to make the sore spot smaller. This isn't something we would do right away, but maybe down the line.

My final suggestion probably won't be a surprise either: Success. The more you succeed at doing the things you said you cared about, the more strong you'll feel, the more confident you'll feel, and the harder you'll be willing to work on it.

So what do you think of these suggestions? Do they make sense to you?

CLIENT: Yeah, they make sense; some of it I've been trying to do already.

THERAPIST: So is this something you think you might want to work on together, when we meet?

CLIENT: I guess so.

With Younger Kids and Their Parents

At this stage parents almost always accept the formulation and embrace the plan. The really critical element at this point is to insist on the importance of the parents' role, so they don't think that they can just leave all the work to the therapist.

THERAPIST: There are several things that we usually do for kids in your son's situation. The first thing is to keep up the special help in reading that he's getting at school. Then there are things that you can do at home, that can help him to feel more secure and less worried. That will help him to calm down. Also, I can work with him to help him get over the old bad feelings that he still carries around. Down the line, we might want to do a behavior chart to help him get better habits, but we might not need it.

PARENT: That sounds good. I really think he needs that individual counseling, have someone to talk to.

THERAPIST: Yes, I think it should help. But the biggest job will be yours. If you can make him feel more secure at home, then my job will go much better. I can get a lot more done. You're much more important than I am. I'm just some guy he talks to once in a while. You're his mom.

PARENT: So what should I be doing?

THERAPIST: There are a few things, we talked a little about them before. When you told me that your husband is kind of hard on the kids, and you give in to them a lot? That kind of makes a kid feel insecure, 'cause the rules are always changing. Also you said that sometimes you get really mad and end up yelling at him, or making some big punishment you know you won't keep later. So you kind of lose control, doing things you don't really want to do. When you lose control, that can also make him feel insecure. He really needs you to be in charge, so you can protect him and keep him safe and under control.

PARENT: It's not easy. These kids, they do make me mad sometimes.

THERAPIST: I know it's not easy. I can give you some things to try. Then you try them, see how it works for you and where there's problems. I'll help you figure it out. It's a lot of work for you, but most parents find that once they get into it, their kids really do calm down and things are better.

Some parents may already feel like failures because they couldn't handle the child's problem on their own. When the therapist sets the parents up as active partners in the child's treatment, the parents are likely to become more confident and effective. The therapist should also be vigilant in pointing out the parents' contributions at every opportunity. Even when the child responds dramatically to an individual session, the therapist can accurately say that the parental support made it possible. The therapist's goal is not to get the glory but to help the family.

THERAPIST: So if your child skins his knee, gets a cut, what do you do?

PARENT: Wash it up; put on a Band-Aid.

THERAPIST: Okay. What if he breaks his leg? Do you put on a splint, or what?

PARENT: No, take him to the emergency room, to the hospital.

THERAPIST: Of course you do. The everyday things you can handle yourself, but sometimes a problem gets too big and you go to a professional for help. This is the same thing. This is what good parents do when it gets too big to handle on their own.

The last part of the agenda for the treatment contracting session is to have the parents give the child explicit permission to engage in treatment, and to make progress. Parental support can be conveyed simply by the parents, with the child present, reviewing the child's goals, for example, doing better in school and getting in less trouble, and encouraging the child to cooperate with the therapist. Feared negative outcomes associated with progress should be addressed as needed.

THERAPIST: Your dad was telling me that he wants you to learn to control yourself better, so you can do better in school and not get in so much trouble. You were saying you wanted that too, when we talked last week, remember? So you and I are going to work together to help you get better at controlling yourself. Do you think that when you're older, more strong, you can control yourself better?

CHILD: Yeah, when I'm bigger.

THERAPIST: So what we'll be working on is helping you get bigger and stronger so that you can handle things better, things that are hard now like when someone makes you mad. Okay?

CHILD: Okay.

THERAPIST: So here's what we'll be doing. Your dad told me that he might be getting more strict at home, to help you learn to do what you're supposed to do. And you and I will meet once a week. I can kind of coach you in some tricks to help you control yourself better. Also, remember what we talked about, how those bad feelings could be stuck inside from old things that happened, like from the hurricane and from seeing your parents fight?

CHILD: Yeah.

THERAPIST: Another thing we can do is talk about those old things, and try to make the bad feelings be smaller so they don't mess you up so much.

You might have noticed that no mention has been made in the treatment contracting of the final phases of treatment, relapse prevention, and harm reduction. This is intentional. At this stage, kids and parents are trying to figure out how to get rid of the current problem, so that's what we talk about. Once we've gotten through trauma resolution, though, and helped kids to get their lives back on track, then we can talk about the future in more detail. At that stage, kids and families are generally quite willing to talk about what they can do—anticipating future challenges and making strategies to handle these—to stay on track. Right now, though, it's just not the issue at hand.

OBSTACLES TO FOLLOWING THROUGH WITH THE CONTRACT

Finally, it is worthwhile to anticipate treatment obstacles and prepare coping methods in collaboration with the family. There are several common obstacles to treatment (Greenwald, 1999). Kids who believe that their symptoms are helping their parents may feel that family loyalty is more important than symptom relinquishment. Sometimes the logistics of getting the child to treatment regularly may prove challenging to a family. Paradoxically, sometimes the fact that the child has become so much better takes the pressure off in terms of follow-through. Each of these obstacles are addressed in the following text.

Obstacle: "Treatment Might Be Risky"

Some children believe that their symptoms serve an essential function in the family. For example, the child may believe that the focus on the problem protects the family by keeping them from focusing on something else that is more upsetting. Kids often fear that if they give up the problem they will be giving up the attention and closeness that they are used to having with their parents. If the child believes any of these kinds of things, then she may not be willing to really engage in treatment despite apparently agreeing to it.

To address this, the therapist can express concern regarding possible risks of successful treatment. The child may then acknowledge concern that "getting better" might lead to unwanted consequences. Once the child admits to this—sometimes only following specific questioning—it can be seriously discussed. Typical outcomes include contradiction by amazed parents, who assert that relationships will actually improve; discussion of specific ways of tracking possible changes in relationships; and a family commitment to exploring this issue in therapy following individual treatment.

Script

THERAPIST: Before we get too far, I just want to check and make sure that going ahead will be okay. (To child) If you get better, what would be the worst thing about that?

CHILD: Nothing. I don't know.

THERAPIST: Let me tell you what other kids worry about, and you tell me if any of these is true for you. Some kids worry that if they don't have the problem anymore for their parents to worry about, their parents might have more problems with each other. Some kids worry that if their parents don't have to worry about the problem anymore, the kid might not get as much attention, and they might not be as close to each other anymore.

CHILD: That one.

THERAPIST (to parent): Is that a worry for you too?

PARENT: Of course not. If we didn't have to deal with all this, we could spend time doing nice things instead.

THERAPIST: Like what kinds of things?

PARENT: Oh, watching movies, going to the park, playing games . . .

THERAPIST: You mean that if he didn't have this problem, he'd get just as much time with you, but doing more fun things?

PARENT: That's right.

THERAPIST: (to child) Would that be okay with you?

CHILD: That would be better.

THERAPIST: Well, it sounds good to me too, but I'm still just a little worried. Can we make a deal? After the problem is gone, can we get back together and make sure that things are going well in the family? That you're really doing those fun things? Then if something went wrong, we can fix it.

CHILD: Okay.

PARENT: Okay.

THERAPIST: (to child) So what would be the best thing about getting better?

Comments

- It is important for the therapist to deliver this intervention with a straight face, and to include a brief menu of possible risks that are most likely to be plausible to the child.
- This intervention helps the child to feel permission, support, and safety in attempting to relinquish symptoms. It also may serve to "hype" the treatment, with the therapist's paradoxical worry about success leading to increased motivation. The awareness of family dynamics generated by this discussion may also help the family to reorganize in support of the child's changes.
- This is also a good time to point out that the parents and child each independently identified treatment goals that they share.

Sometimes even this intervention will not be sufficient, for example, when the parent has given ambivalent messages regarding support of the treatment, or when the child's symptoms reflect concern about the parent's safety or well-being. For example, in the case of so-called school phobia, quite often the child is actually staying home to protect a parent from a perceived risk of loneliness, suicide attempt, sudden health emergency, or violence. Then the therapist can ask the parents to demonstrate their support of the treatment with concrete behaviors that can realistically allay the child's fears. For example:

Script

THERAPIST: Your daughter really needs to know that you will be okay even if she leaves you to go to school. Supposing that you get depressed while she's at school, who can you call?

PARENT: I can call my sister.

THERAPIST: Is she available during the day?

PARENT: Oh yes. We talk to each other all the time.

THERAPIST: Because your daughter will try to watch out for you until she really believes that the grown-ups are taking care of it. So if she comes home from school and she finds you drinking, or lying in bed crying, what will she think?

PARENT: That I'm a mess.

THERAPIST: Yes, she'll be thinking that you really do need her to stay home and take care of you. Supposing she comes home from school and finds the house looking good—maybe you've gotten a snack ready for her—what will she think then?

PARENT: That I can take care of myself.

THERAPIST: Yes. And that she can go to school knowing that you'll be okay.

Comments

- This type of intervention can assist parents in accomplishing a variety of self-care and safety behaviors, including calling on an adult for assistance, locking the door of the apartment to keep out intruders, etc. The therapist helps to identify a behavior that the parent can actually accomplish, and then defines this behavior as having a specific meaning, as demonstrating that the parent is okay, and that the parent supports the child's treatment.
- This intervention can also be more directly related to the treatment itself. For example, the therapist can define the parent's bringing the child to treatment sessions on time as proof of parental support for treatment.
- This is consistent with the therapist's overall approach with the parent: to create shared understandings of the impact of the parent's behavior, and putting the parent in the position of healing his child by doing things the parent is capable of doing. The capability is developed by helping the parent understand the value of the behavior, and by problem solving to help the parent overcome obstacles to implementing it.

Obstacle: "Something Came Up at the Last Minute"

Especially with multiproblem families, things tend to come up that prevent the families from coming on time—or at all—to their scheduled appointments. The trauma therapist views this disorganization and lack of predictability as a target of treatment, since consistency and routine tends to be part of the treatment plan.

The therapist can manage this treatment obstacle by explaining that consistency in attendance is important to treatment effectiveness, and asking about what kinds of things might prevent the family from achieving regular attendance. Obstacles may include child care issues, forgetting, transportation difficulties, etc. These should be problem solved in sufficient detail that the parent has a specific and realistic plan to surmount each identified obstacle.

Obstacle: "I Don't Have a Problem Anymore"

Paradoxically, the success of the Evaluation and Preparation phases of treatment may tempt the family to end treatment prematurely. Many families do not appreciate the extent to which healing from trauma is possible. When the family understands the child's problem better, and the child has made good progress with symptom management, the crisis has passed and the child has regained at least some of his former level of functioning. At this point kids often claim to be "better," and it can be difficult for the parents to know how to disagree with that claim. Avoidance may also be an issue; not only do children often prefer to avoid talking about the bad thing that happened, but their parents often wish to spare them that experience. Kids often say, "I'm doing fine now, so I don't need to talk about that [trauma memory]."

This obstacle can be addressed by predicting it and discussing it. It's important to explain that the trauma memory, if left untouched, can remain as an ongoing source of stress and vulnerability. Even if the child seems to be doing better in the moment, if he does not work through the trauma memory, the sore spot remains, and he will be more vulnerable to future stressors. Because of this obstacle, it is particularly important to have presented a persuasive case formulation that makes clear the central role of trauma in the child's presenting problem.

It is also important to establish that the parental role includes making decisions about the child's treatment. For some reason, otherwise responsible parents may tend to consider mental health treatment something that the child should do only if he wants to. Here it can be helpful to equate mental health treatment to medical treatment—the parent would not neglect the child's medical care just because the child complained about it. Of course, the child will not have to talk about anything he doesn't want to, but he should be made to attend treatment if such treatment is warranted.

SECTION II BIBLIOGRAPHY

Colby, S. M., Monti, P., Barnett, N. P., Rohsenow, D. J., Weissman, K., Spirito, A., Woolard, R. H., & Lewander, W. J. (1998). Brief motivational interviewing in a hospital setting for adolescent smoking: A preliminary study. *Journal of Consulting and Clinical Psychology, 66,* 574-578.

Greenwald, R. (2000). A trauma-focused individual therapy approach for adolescents with conduct disorder. *International Journal of Offender Therapy and Comparative Criminology, 44,* 146-163. The future movies intervention is introduced here.

Greenwald, R. (2002). Motivation—Adaptive Skills—Trauma Resolution (MASTR) therapy for adolescents with conduct problems: An open trial. *Journal of Aggression, Maltreatment, and Trauma, 6,* 237-261.

James, B. (1989). *Treating traumatized children: New insights and creative interventions.* Lexington, MA: Lexington Books. Nice example of therapeutic style in beginning treatment.

Lawendowski, L. A. (1998). Motivational interviewing with adolescents presenting for outpatient substance abuse treatment. *Dissertation Abstracts International, 59-03B,* 1357.

Miller, W. R. & Rollnick, S. (2002). *Motivational interviewing: Preparing people for change* (2nd ed.). New York: Guilford Press. The classic text on motivational interviewing.

Monti, P. M., Colby, S. M., Barnett, N. P., Spirito, A., Rohsenow, D. J., Myers, M., Woolard, R., & Lewander, W. (1999). Brief intervention for harm reduction with alcohol-positive older adolescents in a hospital emergency department. *Journal of Consulting and Clinical Psychology, 67,* 989-994.

Newman, E. (2002). Assessment of PTSD and trauma exposure in adolescents. *Journal of Aggression, Maltreatment & Trauma, 6,* 59-77. Overview of more formal trauma assessment strategies.

SECTION III: SAFETY AND STRENGTH BUILDING

Once we have developed a case formulation and have the child's and the family's agreement to work on the recommended treatment activities, we can move forward with the recommendations. In this section we focus on safety, skill development, and strength development (increasing affect tolerance), in preparation for facing and working through the trauma.

In the fairy tale model, the tasks at hand are to build a fence around the child so that she can feel safe and secure enough to concentrate on the other tasks, then to help her become stronger and more skilled in preparation for slaying the dragon.This entails the following:

- Case management for safety and problem resolution
- Parent (and other adult) training for safety and security
- Self-control skills training for safety and competence
- Progressive mastery of affective challenges—"getting stronger"

There are several reasons to go through these steps rather than going directly to the trauma resolution work. When we get to the Trauma Resolution phase of treatment we want the child to be able to say about the trauma, "That was bad, but it's over, and things are okay now." This is not achievable unless the trauma actually is over and things actually are okay now. Therefore, in preparation for trauma resolution, everything possible should be done to ensure that the child is—and feels—as safe and supported as possible.

Threats to safety and threats to sense of safety often, but not always, coincide. For example, ongoing exposure to a perpetrator of continuing physical abuse will make the child be unsafe and feel unsafe, whereas ongoing exposure to threats of a jailed perpetrator may not affect the child's actual safety but will probably make her feel unsafe. More rarely, a child may be unsafe without feeling unsafe, for example, if the parent is secretly abusing drugs while responsible for the child's care, or leaving the child with potentially irresponsible caregivers.

Perhaps the most common ongoing safety-related problems entail repeated exposure to triggers. For example:

A girl, whose father no longer hit her, would shrink away and instinctively put an arm in front of her face whenever the father yelled. Presumably she interpreted the yelling as a danger signal, a warning that the slap would soon follow, as it used to. When the therapist explained to the father that his daughter felt unsafe when he yelled, the father made more of an effort to avoid yelling, so that the girl would feel safer.

A girl who suffered with a reading disability for some years before it was diagnosed was repeatedly triggered every time she found her schoolwork too difficult. Whenever an assignment seemed challenging she would say to herself, "This is too hard; I'm sick of being given things I can't do. I'm not going to try anymore." As part of treatment, arrangements were made for the teacher's aide to respond extra quickly to this child's requests for help in school, to help her to begin to feel that she could manage frustration and succeed with school-related challenges. This intervention was provided in addition to the special instruction that had been instituted to help her with reading.

Another goal in this phase of treatment is to help parents and other caregivers "rehabilitate" themselves by reestablishing their roles as protectors and helpers in the child's life. When a child is hurt, the child's parent almost always feels like a failure. Whether the child's hurt came from actual irresponsibility on the parent's part, or whether it was just the bad luck that comes with living, parents typically feel that they are to blame, that they should have protected better. Then bad things can happen, for example:

- The parent may be traumatized by what happened to the child, and by the parent's own perceived contribution to that. This could lead to a range of posttraumatic symptoms and might add weight to any of the other problems on this list.
- The parent, overburdened with guilt, may try to "make up for" the child's hardships by allowing him to slide, overindulging, and not being strict or consistent anymore with rules or expectations.
- The parent, feeling inadequate or even depressed, may become more withdrawn and less active in parenting activities such as discipline, supervision of homework and chores, and doing enjoyable things with the child.
- When the child acts out—perhaps due to the sore spot trauma-related overreaction—the parent may then have a sore spot trauma-related overreaction to the child's behavior, which is a reminder of the parent's guilt and failure. Then the parent might react with loss of control and act out against the child, instead of responding appropriately.

When the child heals, the parent finds some relief. When we can give parents an active and constructive role in the child's healing, the parent heals, too. When the previous parenting capacities are restored or even enhanced, the child benefits. The parent becomes more effective in protecting, guiding, and nurturing the child, and the primary attachment relationship is reestablished on firmer ground.

Finally, it takes a great deal of strength, skill, and determination to slay the dragon. If we ask the child to attempt to face the trauma before she is ready, she is likely to feel overwhelmed and even retraumatized. Then she learns that facing the trauma—and trusting the therapist—is a bad idea. On the other hand, when we help her to gradually build up her strength and skill in facing emotional challenges, then she learns that she can in fact become progressively stronger and better able to handle things. While building capacity she is also building her track record of successes. This gives her more hope for success in the future, and increases her investment in her goals, and her determination to continue her efforts.

Chapter 9

Case Management

One of the first things we want to do is build a fence around the child, to help him to feel more safe and secure. Although many issues will be addressed with parent training and self-control skills training, certain issues can be addressed very early on, with case management. The case management may be done directly by the therapist, or by anyone in the family's system that can get the job done. These case management interventions can often have a significant impact on the child's ability to recover from past trauma, and should be effected as soon as possible.

What kinds of issues need managing?

1. Continued exposure to an abuser
2. Acute/pressing needs (e.g., medical, housing)
3. Parent at risk of being hurt (e.g., involvement with an abusive partner; suicide threats)
4. Continued exposure to an *unwarranted* trigger
   - Learning disability without special help
   - Bullying
   - Inadequate supervision
   - Erratic or absent discipline

The purpose of case management is to actually solve problems that are currently forcing the child to remain focused on survival and other pressing concerns, instead of being able to focus on activities that will lead toward healing. Case management involves intervening in such a way that the child's life situation has been altered. For example:

A mother brought in her teenaged girl who was showing apparent posttraumatic stress symptoms after having been bitten by a rat while asleep one night in their apartment. The girl was anxious, jumpy, and afraid to fall asleep. Rats had long been a problem in their apartment building and they had been unsuccessful in their efforts to get their landlord to solve the problem. The clinician who evaluated this girl said, "Of course you're afraid to go to sleep; you must be worried that another rat will get you. What you need is

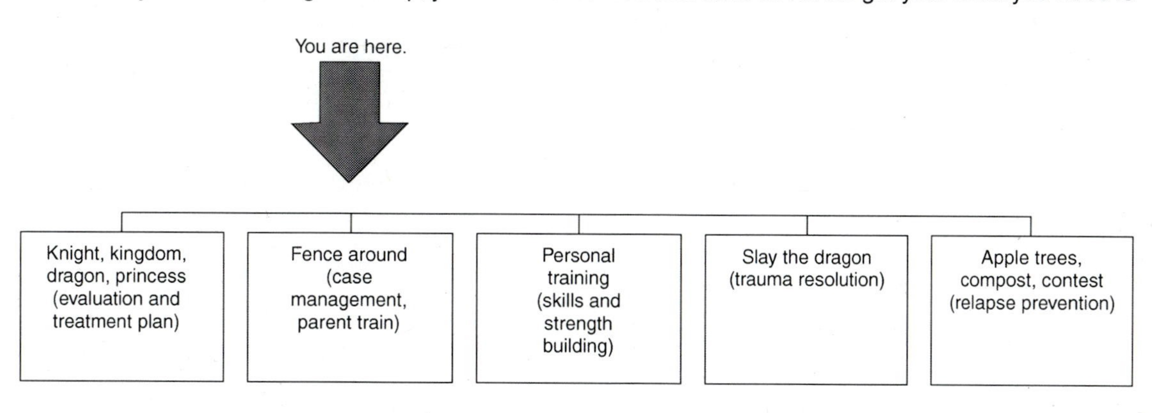

FIGURE 9.1. Steps in the fairy tale model.

a safer place to live. Let's work on that first, then we'll see how you're doing." The mother was then connected with a housing advocate who helped her to find a new apartment. When she brought her daughter back afterward, the posttraumatic stress symptoms were still present but much less pronounced.

A sixth-grade boy was referred for school-related problems: he gave up on assignments very quickly, was disruptive in class, and was rude to peers and teacher. His history included witnessing domestic violence (until his parents divorced) as well as the death of an aunt with whom he had been very close. A comprehensive evaluation found that the boy liked his teacher and really wanted to do well in school. However, he had ADHD, which made it difficult for him to stay focused and on task with his schoolwork. Schoolwork-related frustration hit his sore spot and became a trigger for his trauma/loss-related helplessness and hurt. Then he used his problem behaviors to make himself feel less helpless and less hurt. Once he was given medication, he was better able to focus on his schoolwork. He was still a hurt, angry boy with bad study habits. But he was being triggered much less often, and for the first time was able to say, proudly, "I can do it. I can be good in school."

Although the goal of case management is straightforward (solve the problem), getting it done is not always so simple. Ideally the change is accomplished by convincing those involved to support the change. In the previous example, the mother of the rat-bitten girl was immediately enthusiastic about finding a safer place to live, and followed through with everything she was asked to do. However, the parents of the boy with ADHD were reluctant to try medication for him, and this took some persuading. This persuading can be tricky, and might not happen all at once.

If the first persuasion attempt is not successful, then you may have to just go ahead without as sturdy a fence around the child as you might wish for. However, you may be able to negotiate for another chance later on. For example:

In a very similar case, the parents of the boy with ADHD refused to try medication for him at all. Even after hearing the recommendations and the reasons for same, they said, "We just don't want to give our boy medication. We don't like the side effects we heard about. We want to try to solve the problem some other way." Then the therapist said, "I understand; a lot of parents feel that way. They want to try everything they can before just giving their kid a pill. I gave you my recommendations, but you're the parents and it's your decision. So we can still go ahead with the other things. It will mean that we'll all have to put in extra effort because the medicine won't be there to help. And you never know, sometimes when kids feel better, some of the other problems fade away. Let's give it our best shot."

In this case, treatment proceeded on several fronts. The mother worked on a more consistent discipline approach at home and the father committed to more regular scheduled contact with the boy. The teacher used an incentive system for good behavior and academic achievement. In individual therapy, the boy worked to develop self-control skills, problem-solving skills re classroom challenges, and eventually worked through the trauma and loss memories.

After about four months, the therapist approached the parents again, and said, "You know, we've tried everything, and it's worked. He's happier, he tries hard, and the bad memories don't hurt him anymore. He's not an angry person anymore; he feels good inside. He's doing a little better at school, but he still has a lot of trouble with his schoolwork. After all of the things we did, the ADHD is still giving him the same trouble. Would you consider trying the medicine now?"

This time, the parents agreed, and medication was tried. The boy immediately did much better in school, to the point where he was no longer a behavior problem and was routinely completing his assignments. Of course, this dramatic improvement would almost certainly not have happened had the medicine been tried sooner; the improvement was partly because the other issues were no longer in the way. The point here is that case management can happen at any point, although it is generally preferable to take care of it right away.

The key to getting cooperation for the case management task is the trauma-informed case formulation. With rare exception, parents, teachers, and others who work with kids truly care about them and want to do what is right. However, what they are actually doing might not be the best thing for the child. The case formulation can help them to understand the child and what he really needs, and then the recommendations will give parents and caregivers a role in helping the child. For example:

The mother of an eleven-year-old boy did not want to discipline the boy because she wanted to make up for all that he had been through with an abusive father. The mother said, "I don't like to be hard on him." With the case formulation, the therapist was able to help the mother understand that her son acted out when he felt unsafe and that he escalated the problem behavior until she was finally forced to discipline him. When she understood that her discipline provided reassurance—and that when she disciplined for smaller offenses, she was less harsh—she willingly became more strict with her son.

The assistant principal (school disciplinarian) did not want to discipline a fourteen-year-old girl for bullying her peers, because he thought it would be more helpful to talk with her, as he had done several other times in the past year for similar offenses. The case formulation helped him to understand that the girl used bullying as a solution to feeling uncomfortable in challenging social situations, and that she repeated the bullying behavior because it worked for her; it provided relief, with minimal negative consequences. With this understanding, the assistant principal made a new response: he punished her (to make the bullying behavior less rewarding) and also contacted the parents and recommended treatment to help the girl to find a more acceptable way of managing the challenging situations.

EXERCISE: CONVINCE THE ASSISTANT PRINCIPAL (AP) OR THE PARENT

If you're on your own, just complete the worksheets as instructed. If you're with others, then in small groups (four is best), for each of the following vignettes, complete the worksheet to provide a case formulation and treatment recommendations using the fairy tale model. Then role-play the conversation you would have with the identified parties. Use what you've put on the worksheet to convince them to do what is best for the child. Repeat each role play until everyone in your group has been in each role.

You will notice that much of this is the same as you've done before; it's building on the case formulation. Here, though, you'll be taking it the next step, using the formulation as leverage to get some action. Here are some tips:

- Remember to use plain language, avoid jargon, and tell a story.
- Emphasize that kids learn from experience, and that they will learn from new experiences as well. What do you (the AP or parent) want the child to learn?
- Avoid criticizing the caregiver, even by implication, for not being perfect already. If you put down or disrespect the caregiver, he or she will block you out. Better to acknowledge that he or she does care and to recognize the efforts already made on the child's behalf. Acknowledge the good intentions that even the caregiver's wrong position represents. When you offer to help the caregiver do what he or she is already doing for the child, but more effectively, your suggestions are more likely to be accepted.
- This is a complex intervention. You have a better chance of being understood if you keep it simple. One way to keep it simple is to go in order—do your talking by following the form from beginning to end.

Damian

Damian is a thirteen-year-old boy who has a history of exposure to witnessing domestic violence as well as direct physical abuse, until his parents divorced when he was seven. His mother reports that he is respectful to her and helps out with the younger children when he is at home. He is a friendly, outgoing boy who seems to be popular with both boys and girls. However, his gregariousness has been escalating into

Exercise: Case Formulation for Case Management

1. Once upon a time (introduce positive impression of strengths, including relationships, competencies, successes, resources):

2. Then the bad thing(s) happened:

3. Leading to (for each possible trauma event, describe how other kids have reacted: negative beliefs, piled-up feelings):

4. Now, whenever the trigger (or "high risk") situation occurs (describe the trigger situations—theme and examples—and how that leads to reactivity):

5. Then the bad thoughts and feelings are so strong that (describe the urgency of the reaction, and how the problem behavior provides relief for the child):

6. This is what helps kids in this situation (outline the phases of treatment and what is accomplished in each phase):

7. Here is what you can do (explain what impact the current situation is having on the child, and what impact your recommended action would have, in relation to the fairy tale model):

verbal aggression: teasing peers, rudeness with teachers. The current referral follows an incident in which he physically intimidated a small female teacher by "getting in her face" without actually touching her or verbally threatening harm. You learn from Damian that (1) he did not intend to hurt her and (2) that she asked for it by criticizing him for not knowing an answer and making him feel stupid in front of the class. The AP (school disciplinarian) likes this boy—Damian "is a good kid, has a heart"—and wants to give him a break this one time. You're now having a meeting with the AP, mother, and Damian.

For this exercise, keep it simple and just focus on trigger situations related to the recent teacher situation. When you have finished with that, repeat with the second vignette, working with the parent to establish some strategy to reduce the impact of the biological mother's unreliability.

Angela

Angela is a nine-year-old girl who is in treatment for emotional and behavioral problems. She is bossy with peers and does not easily tolerate waiting for her turn or losing a game; you have seen her cheat, and even dump the game board. You know that she was sexually abused on several occasions by her stepfather during ages five and six until Child Protection intervened. Then mother refused to kick out her husband, so Angela went to live with her maternal aunt, who helped to raise her and who is currently in the process of adopting her. Visits with her biological mother are scheduled for two hours every Thursday after school. When the visits are accomplished as planned, Angela's behavior is rather stormy at home for the rest of the day: crying, yelling, stomping, disobeying. When her biological mother fails to show for the visit—this happens about half the time—Angela's behavior at home is even more stormy and lasts through the following day as well. Two months into treatment, you have formed a good relationship with Angela and are planning to work toward trauma resolution activities with her. You also have a good relationship with her aunt, who is an excellent parent. You're now having a meeting with the aunt.

For this exercise, keep it simple and just focus on trigger situations related to the biological mom visiting situation.

Follow-Up Group Discussion

For those on the receiving end (as the AP or parent), what kinds of statements made you feel confused, put down, or put off? What kinds of statements helped you to get the picture? What kinds of statements led you to feel empowered or enthusiastic about what the therapist wanted you to do? For those acting as the therapist, what specific behaviors contributed to you having done a good job? What did it take, what did you have to say to yourself, to get yourself to do those things?

Sample Responses

Here are examples of how the previous forms might have been completed. If you did not come up with exactly the same results, that doesn't mean that you were wrong. But you can use these examples as a guide to see what was intended.

Damian

1. *Strengths/resources:* Good heart, has friends, helps his mother, respectful at home, does well in school, has mother who makes many efforts on his behalf (including getting time off from her job to attend this meeting), school disciplinarian who wants what's best for Damian.

2. *Trauma/loss history:* Saw father hit mother many times; heard loud fights; was beaten by father several times; abandoned by father following parents' separation.
3. *Negative beliefs:* I'm unsafe; I can't protect myself; I'm inadequate; there's something wrong with me; *piled-up feelings:* shame, fear, anger, sadness.
4. *Trigger situations: Theme:* feeling put down in some way; *example:* teacher correcting in front of others.
5. *Problem behaviors and why it's a solution:* Threatening or intimidating another person can make him feel powerful and that he can protect himself.
6. *Overview of treatment recommendations/plan:* External controls that can make him feel extra safe and secure so he can relax a little and be able to focus on recovering from what has hurt him. Motivation for change, figure out what he wants and why current behaviors won't help. Then he'll be more willing and able to work on these issues in his meetings with me.
7. *How you can help right now:* Has to learn that "crime doesn't pay" so that it will be worth his while to choose another type of solution behavior. The more he gets away with this kind of thing, the more he learns that it works for him. Punishment can teach him that choosing aggression has a high cost. Punishment will also give a message to him, as well as others (students and teachers), that threatening behavior is not tolerated here; that makes everyone feel safer. Also can reduce frequency of triggering; perhaps speak to teacher about correcting him in private?

Angela

1. *Strengths/resources:* Wants friends, wants to please adults, capable of recruiting adults to care about her, capable of forming attachments/relationships, tries hard in school, does well in school, many interests, is not secretive, shows how she's feeling, is outgoing, can be a leader, has an aunt who is like a mother to her, who is dedicated to her care and who is generally effective as well, has a therapist who cares about her.
2. *Trauma/loss history:* Sexual abuse by stepfather, rejection/abandonment by biological mother.
3. *Negative beliefs:* I'm helpless; I'm worthless; I don't deserve to be loved; there's something wrong with me; I can't tolerate bad feelings; *piled-up feelings:* grief, anger, shame, despair, confusion.
4. *Trigger situations: Theme:* being abandoned or rejected; *examples:* When biological mother does visit but then says good-bye, and also when biological mother fails to show for the visit.
5. *Problem behaviors and why it's a solution:* Relief from intolerable feelings by expressing them in temper tantrums. The punishments give her containment and reassurance.
6. *Overview of treatment recommendations/plan:* I want to work with her on self-control skills and then on recovering from the trauma memories, not only the abuse but being rejected/abandoned by her biological mother. But first she needs to feel safe and secure, as if things are more or less okay right now, so that she doesn't have to be constantly focused on trying to make sure that more bad things aren't going to keep happening.
7. *How you can help right now:* She won't be able to concentrate on any of her treatment tasks while she's being freshly abandoned and rejected by her biological mother every week! She'll stay distracted by her repeated upsets and her fear of more to come. Can we try to figure out how to keep her from getting hurt the same way every week like this?

Standing Your Ground

Sometimes a case management intervention can be challenging or controversial. Remember that your first obligation is to do your best for the child, according to your skills, understanding, and professional standards. You want to be able to stand by your actions—to avoid legal liability for substandard practice, and to live with yourself.

A clinician evaluated a five-year-old girl who had been molested by a man, and who was somewhat nervous around men. The clinician prepared a written evaluation that included a recommendation for a female therapist. However, before the evaluation was turned in, he happened to speak with a male therapist in the same clinic, who had somehow already had a couple of sessions with the little girl, which he said were going well. To avoid "rocking the boat," against his better judgment the evaluator turned in a report with no reference to the gender of the therapist. A week later, the girl suddenly refused to work with the male therapist anymore.

A clinician was hired by the public school to evaluate a ten-year-old boy with mild mental retardation and emotional disturbance. The boy was being repeatedly frustrated because he was in classes with content too abstract for him to relate to; then he would start acting out and getting into trouble. The clinician recommended that the boy be provided an educational curriculum suited to his abilities and needs. The principal said, "You can't recommend that. We don't offer that kind of program here anymore," but the recommendation stood, and became part of the child's educational record. Within a few weeks, a new classroom was created for this purpose—and several other children with similar needs joined the class as well.

A child protection worker in a small town investigated an abuse allegation and found that the child had indeed been physically abused by the father, who was the custodial parent and a local police officer. The usual action in this situation would be to require the father to participate in an anger management program for parents. As a "professional courtesy" the worker did not require this but only recommended it. The father never attended, and the abuse continued.

When the Case Doesn't Get Managed

In many situations, you will be able to elicit cooperation and accomplish the case management tasks that you believe will help the child. Sometimes this will fail, and then you'll have to consider your options.

Accept Defeat Gracefully

One option is to just keep on working, and accept that not everything you want for the child will happen as you wish it would. This option is preferred when you really have no choice anyway. Even so, it can still be worthwhile to make the recommendation and the attempt; this plants the seed. Sometimes you'll have another chance later on.

A fourth-grade boy was referred for problem behaviors and loss of interest in former activities. Interactions in his family had also deteriorated. Recommendations included specified family activities, a classroom-based incentive program, and psychotherapy. The parents refused psychotherapy because of a prior experience in which they felt that a therapist had been intrusive. The evaluator was clearly not welcome to even discuss their position, but instead asked whether it would be okay for some of the same goals to be addressed by the school counselor. This was acceptable to the family, who also allowed the evaluator to provide consultation to the counselor and to the teacher.

A concerned teacher noticed that a certain child often came to school with dirty clothes and sometimes fell asleep in class. She contacted the school counselor, who contacted the parents, who refused to talk about it. The counselor made a report of suspected neglect to the local child protection agency, which refused to investigate. The counselor and the teacher decided to make an extra effort to make the parents feel welcome in the school, to be supportive of the child, and to be alert for other opportunities either to make some headway with the family, or to file another report for child neglect.

Advocate for the Child

Sometimes even if you are not immediately successful in effecting a change, you can do more. Perhaps your advocacy will lead to a resolution. Even if it doesn't, there is still value in the child and family knowing that you made the effort on their behalf. You may be the only person giving them the message that the child deserves to be safe and to be treated with respect.

A twelve-year-old boy was afraid at school because he was being repeatedly bullied by an older boy, who had severely beaten him on one occasion. The school did not discipline the offender and did nothing to protect the younger boy. Repeated requests for action made by the parents and by the boy's therapist got no results. The therapist then wrote a letter to the school principal detailing the events that had taken place, including the interactions between the boys, as well as the parent and therapist requests for the school to do something about it. In this letter, the therapist stated that the school has an obligation to protect its students, and that this is particularly true when a specific known danger exists. A copy of this letter was sent to the parents, the police, and the child protection agency. Perhaps due to the increased awareness of the school's legal liability that this "paper trail" engendered, the older boy's schedule was modified so that the boys would not meet each other at school anymore.

A nine-year-old girl was referred for treatment for posttraumatic stress symptoms after having seen her mother severely stabbed by mother's ex-boyfriend. The symptoms of anxiety and intrusive imagery were most severe in the evenings, when mother was not home because she was out with her current boyfriend, who was controlling and emotionally abusive. The therapist did not know the mother well enough to tell her who her boyfriend should be. However, the therapist was able to help the mother understand that her daughter was afraid for her mother's safety, especially when mother was with someone like the one who had hurt her. Mother agreed to call her daughter before bedtime to reassure her that everything was all right. Within a couple of weeks, mother spontaneously began to limit her late nights to two per week, on a schedule. Two months later, mother left the boyfriend.

Following is the intervention that led to the initial change in the behavior of the mother whose daughter worried when mother was out at night. Notice how the therapist focuses on the case formulation and the child's safety concerns. Notice also how respectful the therapist is of the mother's accomplishments and of the way she does care for her child. With this foundation, when the therapist makes a new suggestion, the mother does not take this as a slight; rather, she is able to hear it as helping her do what she is already doing, but better.

THERAPIST: Since you were attacked last year, your daughter has been really worried that something else bad might happen. We've been talking about how important it is for her to start feeling like things are safe now, so she can start to get over what happened before. What kinds of things have you been doing to make sure that things are safe now?

PARENT: He's in jail now, the guy who attacked me. I don't have to worry about that anymore.

THERAPIST: That's good to know. But we can see that your child is still worried, and I'm sure that you do other things to make sure that everyone's safe. What kinds of things do you do?

PARENT: Well, I always make sure the door's locked when we go out and when we're home. And I don't let her answer the door or the phone. She knows she has to let me do that. And I don't let her roam the streets like some parents do. She comes right home from school.

THERAPIST: That's good. You do a lot of the things already that I would have suggested. And what about you? What do you do to let her know that you're safe, that she doesn't have to worry about whether you're okay or not? I know that she says that the nights you don't come home, she's still pretty worried.

PARENT: Well, the problem is that my boyfriend doesn't have a telephone. But she's okay at home with her (older teenaged) sister there. I know she's safe.

THERAPIST: Yes, but she says that she doesn't know that you're safe. She doesn't really know when she gets home from school if you're going to be home that night or gone away, and when you don't call at night, I bet her imagination gets going.

PARENT: Maybe I could call her from a phone booth before she goes to bed, just to tell her good night so she knows I'm okay.

THERAPIST: I think that's a really good idea. And another thing: is there any way that you can tell her ahead of time if you're going to be out that night? Kids usually feel a lot better when they know what to expect.

The more the therapist works with the family on issues that are clearly related to being safe and to feeling safe, the more the trauma-based case formulation is reinforced. This lays a good foundation for the later focus on more abstract safety issues such as the parent setting consistent limits or avoiding yelling.

Force the Change

In extreme situations, change is necessary whether the parents (or other caregivers) like it or not. Many of these situations are covered by mandated reporting laws to protect the child's safety. Even in such extreme situations, there are opportunities to show respect and to empower the parents to come through for their kids.

A second-grade boy had so many school absences that soon a mandated report would have to be filed for educational neglect. The school principal said to the parent, "If your son misses two more days of school this term, the law requires me to report you for neglect. I don't want to have to do that, and I hope it's not necessary. I know you care about your son, so I'm sure that there's a good reason he's missed so many days. What is the reason? Is there anything we can do to help him get to school?"

A seventh-grade girl disclosed to her therapist that her stepfather had been "messing" with her. The therapist asked if it would be okay to invite the girl's mother into the session; the girl said yes. Several issues were addressed, including immediate actions to protect the girl, as well as the therapist's obligation to make a report to the child protection office. They decided to make the report together, which they proceeded to do, taking turns on the phone to talk with the worker. They were able to tell the worker about the actions they were already planning to take to protect the girl.

CASE MANAGEMENT PITFALLS AND REMEDIES

It can be heartbreaking to witness major disruption in the child's life (e.g., removal from the home), especially when it seems that the situation is being mismanaged by the authorities. Many children do in fact describe the intervention as being more traumatic than the original situation—even in retrospect, years later. Although sometimes disruption is unavoidable, it is often made worse than it needs to be.

When we are involved in making changes to a child's life situation, there are many things that we can do—and can encourage the allied professionals to do—to minimize the disruptive impact. Underlying these suggestions is the RICH relationship—that kids (and parents and colleagues) deserve to be treated with respect, to be given information, to maintain their connections as much as possible, and to have reason to hope for a better future. When kids and others are treated this way, there is less chance that we are adding new trauma to the old, and more chance that we are actually helping.

Here are some true stories of situations that kids have experienced at the hands of those who were supposed to be helping them. Unfortunately, those who work with abused children will be all too familiar with stories like these; this reflects common practice. Following the vignettes are specific suggestions for the various professionals involved.

Law Enforcement/Detective/Police Officer

A thirteen-year-old girl had truthfully disclosed to her basketball coach that her mother had allowed mother's friend to rape the girl. Later that night a police officer went to the girl's home, unannounced, and barraged the girl with antagonistic questions, in front of her mother. The girl was stunned, and felt that she was being "treated like a criminal," especially when the police officer threatened to arrest her if she lied. The girl said very little and disavowed the rape.

Suggestions

- Vary interview technique according to the individual you're talking to—not everyone is a criminal.
- Nonoffending parents already feel bad; they want to help. Be respectful.
- Make the victim feel safe to tell you what happened by interviewing her privately, or with a nonoffending parent.
- Victims are more likely to tell the truth if they're not afraid of you. An aggressive tone is aggressive! If they feel as if you're victimizing them, too, their primary goal will be to protect themselves from you.
- Use simpler language for younger children.
- Understand that kids may not feel comfortable with you right away, or tell the whole story the first time. Have patience.

Child Protection/Child Welfare Worker

Three weeks after an allegation of sexual abuse had been made, a twelve-year-old girl was awakened after midnight and taken by the child protection worker to the hospital emergency room for a medical exam.

A group of three siblings were removed from their home following substantiation that they were being abused by their mother's live-in boyfriend. Mother kicked out the boyfriend immediately and obtained a restraining order. The caseworker was on vacation and the supervisor did not return the mother's calls. When the caseworker returned two weeks later, she was backed up with work. She was slow in returning phone calls, slow in getting to the home to make a visit, and slow in getting the paperwork done. Although it took the mother only two days to make the home safe for her children, it took the children eight weeks to return home.

A ten-year-old boy in foster care was met at school by his caseworker, who took him to a new foster placement. He did not know to expect this, and did not know why it was happening. (It was because the current foster parent had lost patience with him.) His few belongings were in a plastic trash bag in the worker's car. His pet turtle, the only possession he cared about, was also in the worker's car, but it had been there all day and had died in the heat.

Suggestions

- Getting things taken care of in a timely manner can minimize the extension of the trauma. For example, an out-of-home placement can take days or weeks instead of months.
- Communication and coordination among the various players can avoid replication of exams, interviews, and services.
- Avoid the dramatic/urgent approach except when it is truly called for.
- Let kids know what to expect as much as possible.

- Help kids to keep their possessions and their existing relationships as much as possible.
- Keep the same worker on the case whenever possible. Kids and families learn to count on you. You are not interchangeable. You know them, and they know you.

Prosecutor/District Attorney

A nine-year-old girl was molested by a neighbor. The girl was interviewed about the molestation in great detail by the police detective, then by the hospital social worker (where she had her physical exam), and then by her new therapist. But after all that, it seemed for months that no one was going to do anything about it. Finally the prosecutor showed up, and asked her the same questions all over again.

Suggestions

- Talk to the victims and witnesses as soon as possible. Then they'll have a better memory for details, and will feel that you (and "the system") care and take this seriously. Also, expediting this process can minimize the duration of the trauma—many kids dread this meeting.
- Joint process with allied professionals can preclude the need for repeated interviews.

MD/Pediatrician/Emergency Room

A six-year-old boy was referred to child protective services when his teacher noticed bruising on his legs. The emergency room doctor, not an abuse specialist, diagnosed physical abuse without obtaining a second opinion. The child was placed in foster care for six months before the bruising, which continued to occur, was correctly diagnosed as a blood disorder.

A pediatrician noticed a number of old bruises on a five-year-old girl during her regular physical exam. The doctor did not want to "open a can of worms" and so said nothing. A month later, the girl was in the emergency room with several broken ribs.

Suggestions

- Don't fake it. If you're out of your area of expertise, refer the case, at least for a consultation or second opinion.
- Don't hide it. If you don't want to deal with child protection services, don't just drop the ball. Actively pass it to someone who will deal with it.

Mental Health/Counselor/Therapist

A thirteen-year-old boy told his therapist that his father (the custodial parent) had emotionally and physically abused him on a number of occasions. The therapist, assuming that child protective services would just make matters worse, took care of it by talking to the father herself. The abuse continued for another year until the boy began doing so much worse in school that he drew more attention to himself.

A four-year-old girl had been molested and was now in therapy. Her mother asked the therapist what was happening in therapy, and if she (the mother) could do anything to help her daughter. The therapist explained that it was important for the little girl to have privacy, so the therapist couldn't discuss it. No advice was given to the mother, except to keep bringing her child. This continued for more than a year with no great improvement in the girl's posttraumatic stress symptoms. Even then, it was the mother who finally stopped this and got a new therapist for her daughter.

A nine-year-old boy was referred to a therapist working in a specialty program for sexually abused kids. The boy had been sexually abused on two occasions by a neighbor; however, he was more concerned with the death of a grandparent two years earlier, and with his peer interactions. The therapist put the boy through the standard six-month group and individual treatment program, entirely focused on the sex abuse.

A ten-year-old girl disclosed that she had been molested by her older brother. The therapist thanked her for the disclosure, and later reported it to the authorities. Later that day, strange adults came to the girl's house, frightened her and her parents with questions and threats, and took the girl away! The girl had no idea that anything such as this might happen, and the "safety" intervention ultimately proved to be more traumatic than the molestation had been.

Suggestions

- Ask more questions before drawing conclusions. Really listen. Use a systems model of the child in the family/social context. Individual treatment can be important but is rarely sufficient to help this child become safer.
- Take responsibility and initiative to help allied professionals see the child the way you do. When others understand the case formulation, they are more likely to give support in a way that is good for the child.
- Facilitate communication among various players to avoid replication and ensure that critical needs are being addressed.
- Monitor yourself, practice self-care, and seek consultation to keep yourself on track.
- Use effective methods for trauma treatment.
- Share information with clients so they know what's going on and have a chance to prepare.

Many of these suggestions may require innovative approaches to providing services to children. It may take some effort to change the way your system works, or works with others. Remember, though, that the primary goal is not to make things convenient for ourselves, but to help the kids. Here are some examples of ways that agencies and organizations have made changes so that case management and related interventions are more helpful for kids:

- A child welfare agency used to have one worker to investigate child abuse cases, another worker to manage the child's case once the investigation was completed and the abuse charges proved valid, another worker to conduct home studies for potential foster and adoptive families, another worker to manage the cases of kids in foster placements, and yet another worker for kids in adoptive placements. After learning of the literature that showed that families are more likely to seek help sooner—before a problem gets out of hand—when they have a long-term relationship with their worker, the agency reorganized. Now, once the investigation is founded, a worker is assigned to a child (or sibling group) all the way through, no matter what happens to the child. This has required some additional training; however, it has reduced employee turnover, and also reduced the frequency of failed foster and adoptive placements.
- A hospital that received many referrals for suspected child abuse started a "one-stop" multidisciplinary child advocacy center where most of the required activities could take place. The staff includes a pediatrician, nurse, social worker, and psychologist, all with specialized training. This clinic works with designated allied professionals from child protection and law enforcement. When forensic interviews are conducted by the staff member, the child protection worker and the police detective can observe behind the one-way mirror. Subsequent treatment for medical as well as mental health needs is provided by the staff. This program requires regular meetings and good communication, as well as occasional multidisciplinary training events, to help the various professionals coordinate their efforts. However, the families feel taken care of, and the professionals believe that they are providing better service, reducing redundancy, improving treatment compliance, and improving chances for successful prosecution.
- A regular feature at the staff meetings of a community mental health center involved relating the latest horror stories regarding how their kids and families were being mismanaged by child welfare workers, probation officers, teachers, and others. They decided to stop complaining and try to solve the problem. After that, early in the treatment of a new child/

family, a meeting would be called of all involved (including the child, parents, and allied professionals). The case formulation would be presented as a basis for the treatment plan. Then each person at the meeting could define his or her role as part of this team effort. This approach did not always work because it was difficult to get everyone to show up or cooperate, but it did at least improve the situation.

Chapter 10

Parent Training

This chapter focuses on working with parents. However, many of the same principles and methods apply to foster parents, teachers, residential workers, and others who spend their day in the child's life space.

There is some overlap between parent training and case management, in terms of building a fence around the child. However, parents (and other caregivers) are also unique due to their responsibility for the child, their importance to the child, and their daily interaction with the child. Parents have a critical role in helping the child to be safe and to feel safe, and in encouraging and supporting the child on the path to healing. The many things that we wish parents would do include the following:

- Keep the child safe.
- Help to make sure the child can be reasonably successful at school and elsewhere.
- Bring the child to appointments regularly and on time, until we say that treatment is completed.
- Do not give up on the child.
- Enjoy the child more; reinforce positive behaviors.
- Stop hitting the child or blowing up at him.
- Use calm, reasonable, firm, and consistent discipline.

Although parents will generally recognize the importance of our wish list for their behavior, they are not always willing or able to come through for their children. This does not mean that they don't care about their kids. It means that something is in their way. Here is a list of the "Yes, but . . ." greatest hits:

1. I tried it (e.g., time out for discipline, instead of spanking) but it didn't work.
2. I don't want to bring it (the trauma memory) up; it will only upset her.
3. I don't want to be hard on him (enforce the rules); he's been through enough already.
4. She makes me so mad I can't help it (yelling, hitting).
5. He just doesn't care anymore, it's no use trying to help him.
6. I'm just so tired I don't have the energy.

Parent training is fine for teaching good parenting skills and practices, but it doesn't take care of the "yes-but" problem. If there's a yes-but, then the parents won't be using the skills they learned. We address this issue by using the fairy tale model as the foundation for the parent training approach.

Parent training for supportive behaviors, including calm and consistent discipline practices, is part of many child therapy approaches, and is a key component of trauma-informed treatment. One key distinction in trauma-informed treatment is the emphasis on the child's sense of safety, following from the trauma-based case formulation and recommendations. The other key distinction is the emphasis on respect and empowerment of the parent. Building on the parent's track record of caring about, and for, the child, the parent training is offered as a way to help the parents do even more of what they are already doing, or trying to do.

This is an important point because parents can be pretty touchy about being told that they need "training" to do what they have already been doing. Parents can also be touchy about receiving advice from someone who is different from the parent in terms of parental status, educational level, socioeconomic status, ethnicity, and/or gender. Parents who have experienced disrespect or even coercion from "the system" can be touchier still.

In short, the risk that your parenting advice will be rejected is high. You can make rejection almost certain by emphasizing that you know best and that the parent is the real problem. We convey this message when it is what we actually believe. This message is actually conveyed quite often by well-meaning professionals, even when effort is made to hide the true message within the jargon.

Although it is important to recognize problems, with the fairy tale model we work with the parent's strengths, so that's where we need to focus. The case formulation can help us do this. When we see the child as wounded, we can help the parent see the child that way too. The parents are *not* told—even by implication—"Your bad parenting practices have caused this problem." Rather, they are told, sometimes explicitly, "If it weren't for your child's particular problem, your discipline style would be of little interest to me. However, because of the trauma/loss experiences, your child is wounded, and there are special things that you can do, at least for a while, to help her to get better." Thus, instead of being blamed for the child's problems (parents tend to blame themselves already), parents are given an opportunity to be agents of their child's healing.

DID I HEAR YOU SAY "YES, BUT"?

At this point, many in a training audience roll their eyes, and say, "Yes, that's all very nice, but you don't know the parents I work with!" When we see a parent behaving inappropriately, in a way that only reinforces the child's problems, it is easy to feel justified in believing the worst about the parent. It is yet easier to believe bad things when the parent has other problems as well. But ask yourself: how would *you* respond to a misbehaving child if you truly believed that she was bad, did it on purpose, and just didn't care anyway?

On the other hand, think about some of the parents whom you see as problematic, uncooperative, incompetent. Imagine that the daughter of one of these parents breaks her arm. The parent takes her to the emergency room, where a cast is put on. Three weeks later the cast comes off and the physical therapist tells the parent, "Do this exercise with your daughter at home. Here, I'll show you how. Do it every day, ten times in the morning, and then ten times at night. Bring her back in a week and I'll see how she's doing." Most or all of your "problem parents" will follow through with this, right? Maybe not perfectly, but pretty well.

When parents feel blamed, disrespected, or otherwise attacked by the therapist, they are likely to protect themselves and reject the therapist. When parents see their child as bad, behaving badly on purpose, and not valuing the parent-child relationship, they are likely to protect themselves and reject the child. On the other hand, when parents feel respected and supported, they are able to be more open to your advice. And when parents can see their child as hurt, not "bad," they are more likely to come through with what the child needs to recover. Of course, no matter what we do right, not every parent will come through. But we can't know ahead of time which parents will surprise us and come through for their kids, when we give them a way to understand and a way to do something about it.

WORKING THE CASE FORMULATION

The key to eliciting parent cooperation is the case formulation and the fairy tale model. This helps parents see their child as still good, but wounded. It helps them to understand why the treatment recommendations make sense and will lead to healing. And it helps them to understand how important their own role is. With the case formulation, you can:

1. Advise parents to do things differently, not because they were doing it "wrong" before, but because their child has a special need.
2. Help parents to embrace a rationale that overcomes their "blocking beliefs." For example:
   - When the parent says, "I don't want to be hard on him (enforce the rules); he's been through enough already," the therapist can say, "Enforcing the rules makes him feel more secure. Then he knows what to expect, knows he can count on you."
   - When the parent says, "I don't want to bring it (the trauma memory) up; it will only upset her," the therapist can say, "If she sees that you can handle talking about it, then she can talk about it with you and get your help. Right now, because she doesn't want to upset you, she just keeps it inside, has to face it all alone."
3. Help parents become active agents in the child's healing and recovery.
4. Help parents identify personal obstacles to helping their kids, and what to do about them.

Sometimes parents really do need their own treatment. But if we just say this up front, we have overstepped our mandate (which is typically child-focused) and the suggestion may be perceived as offensive. On the other hand, if we work with the parent to gain an understanding of what to do and why, and then the parent still says, "I try to do it right, like we talked about, but I just get too angry and lose control," then we have an opening. Then we can say, "Is it okay to talk about what keeps you from coming through for your child the way you want to?" Then, without even knowing the details of the parent's history, we can offer a trauma-informed case formulation to explain the parent's own sore-spot reactivity regarding the child's behavior, and present options for taking care of it. At this point, many parents will engage in self-control skills training, and some will be willing to work toward trauma resolution as well.

PRACTICING RESPECT AND EMPOWERMENT

The fairy tale model's trauma-informed case formulation includes an emphasis on the "kingdom's" strengths and resources. This supports the empowerment approach. To make this fly, we must be able to identify and acknowledge the parents' strengths. Remember, the parents are the ones building the fence. The therapist should do as much as possible to convey support and respect for the parent, and to enlist the parent's active cooperation.

As the therapist learns about current discipline practices, even inappropriate and/or ineffective ones, the therapist can convey an understanding of the parent's positive underlying intent. For example, if the parent spanks the child for lying, the therapist might say, "It sounds like you really want your child to learn to tell the truth." Then when the therapist offers suggestions for modifying the parent's approach, the parent does not experience it as a put-down, but rather as a tip to help the parent do what he or she is already trying to do, but better.

PARENT TRAINING INTERVENTIONS

The following handout is an example of a way to build on the case formulation—work the fairy tale model—in a parent training approach. Typically this handout is not just passed to a parent, but is accompanied by a full session discussing each portion, step by step.

The core principles of the positive parenting form (and the parent training approach) are as follows:

- Problem behavior is a way children ask for reassurance. Reassurance calms kids down.
- You are the parent. You are the child's rock of security.
- If you are in charge, you are strong and can protect.
- Keep your promises.
- Only make promises that you can keep.
- When you stop a problem quickly, it's smaller and easier to handle.
- Minimize negatives; reinforce positives.

The following repertoire of interventions (Greenwald, 1999) can help parents understand the issues involved, overcome the obstacles, and acquire the specific behaviors necessary for effective discipline. The therapist needs to judge which interventions to use and which to skip, according to the demands of each case. (These interventions from Greenwald, 1999, *Eye Movement Desensitization and Reprocessing* are reprinted by permission of Jason Aronson, an Imprint of Rowman & Littlefield Publishers, Inc.)

Positive Parenting

Children who misbehave often feel scared, nervous, and insecure. They need gentle, but firm, consistent discipline. Then they will know that they can count on their parents. This will make them feel more secure, and they will calm down. Here are some ways to provide this sense of security to your children:

1. Keep Your Promises

Avoid making promises you can't keep. Then your kids will learn that they can count on you. This goes whether your promise is for a treat or for a punishment.

Don't promise good things unless you are sure that you can come through. And stick with small punishments so that you can follow through on those, too.

Train your children to learn that Yes means Yes and No means No.

2. Stop a Problem Quickly

Don't get into arguments with your child. You are not equals; you are in charge. You also want to avoid losing your temper. When you lose your temper, your child has pushed your buttons, and you have lost control. But your child needs you to be in control, to be in charge. Also, when you lose your temper, you may be tempted to yell, hit, or make promises that you can't keep (like a punishment that is too big). All these things will just make your child more scared and insecure.

You can avoid losing your temper by stopping a problem quickly, before it gets out of hand. Just tell your child one time what you want. Next, give one warning. Next, give a short time-out. After the time-out is done, the child still has to do what you say. That's it. No messing around.

When you stop a problem quickly like this, you don't have a chance to get frustrated and angry. Then you can handle it in a way you can feel good about.

3. Enjoy Your Child

Some children do bad things because they like to get attention from you. Why not give attention for good behavior instead?

As you become quicker and more effective with your discipline, your child will probably calm down and give you less trouble. Then you will have more time and energy to enjoy your child. Find things to do together that make your child feel special. It could be big things like going to the park or the beach for the day. It could be something small like fixing something together or cooking a meal together.

Remember, discipline and fun all come from the same place: your love and concern for your child.

Problem Behavior Is a Request for Reassurance

This is really just a reminder of the case formulation, as it applies to the child's problem behaviors.

THERAPIST: Sounds like your daughter can get pretty hard to handle sometimes.

MOTHER: Oh ya, she gets me going. It's like she's just asking to get smacked, until finally sometimes I do it, just to shut her up.

THERAPIST: Remember how we were talking about when she had to see you and her father fighting those times, and then he left? When kids go through that kind of thing, they get really scared inside. Like the world's not safe anymore, anything can happen. And then, even much later, they're still worried that something else bad might happen anytime.

MOTHER: Yes, she is worried like that, I know.

THERAPIST: So when she gets nervous, wonders if things are still safe, she asks you, by acting bad. Then if you can show you're in charge—in control—she feels safe again.

A Safe Child Has a Strong Parent

With parents of younger children, this intervention can help illustrate how, when the parent is in charge, the child can feel safe. This is most appropriate when the child has taken on a parental role, perhaps as the confidante, caretaker, or boss (if the parent is not in charge, the child is the boss). The therapist highlights this role confusion to the point of absurdity, which may jar family members into a new perspective on their interactions. First the confusion itself is presented, and then elements of resolution are addressed sequentially. Once parents demonstrate that they are bigger, older, and stronger, they are qualified to be in charge. Once they can prove that they are really in charge, they can use this parental role to help their child feel more safe and secure.

THERAPIST: You might think I'm stupid, but I'm getting confused here. Which one of you is the real mother?

CHILD: She is!

THERAPIST: I'm not so sure. When Mom tells you her troubles, then you're the Mom. (Then to the mother:) Do you have any adult friends you can tell your troubles to, so that Sara doesn't have to be your mother?

MOTHER: Yes, I talk to my neighbor sometimes, and to my sister . . .

THERAPIST: That's good. You want to keep grown-up talk with the grown-ups, so that your daughter can be a kid. But I'm still confused about who the mom is. Remember a little while ago, when you (to mother) told her to put the markers away, and she kept on using them? She was the boss then. I always know who the real mom is by seeing who's in charge. So I'm still confused. (To the child:) Are you in charge sometimes, when maybe your mom is supposed to be?

CHILD: Sometimes I don't listen good.

THERAPIST: Oh, so you might be confused sometimes too. No wonder I'm confused now.

MOTHER: Well I tell her, but she doesn't always listen.

THERAPIST: Right, that's why we're all so confused. But it's really important to know who the mom is, to know who's in charge. Let's see, a mom should be bigger, older, stronger . . . (to child:) Mom, stand up.

CHILD: I'm Sara!

THERAPIST: Oh, I'm sorry! Got confused. Okay, Mom—no, I mean Sara—stand up. And (to mother) Mom, you stand up too. Okay, good. Now which one of you is bigger?

CHILD: She is!

THERAPIST: Hmm. Let's see, you go up to here (puts hand by the top of child's head), and you go up to here, yup, she is bigger. Now, who's older?

CHILD: She is!

THERAPIST: Are you sure? How old are you?

CHILD: I'm six.

THERAPIST: And how old are you?

MOTHER: Twenty-seven.

THERAPIST: Bigger, and older. Well, maybe you are the real mom. But let's see who's stronger. (To child:) Go over and lift her up off the ground.

CHILD: I can't.

THERAPIST: Well, you never know. If you were the mom you could. Go give it a try.

CHILD: (tries) I can't.

THERAPIST: Okay, good try. Now (to mother) you lift her off the ground. (Mother does so.) Oh, bigger, older, and stronger too! Well, she might really be the real mom. But let's find out who the boss is! (To child:) What I want you to do is tell her to jump up and down. See if you can make her do it. (To mother, whispers:) Don't do it.

CHILD: Jump up and down.

MOTHER: No (smiles and does not move).

THERAPIST: (to mother:) Good job. Now, how does she get her way sometimes? I know! (To child:) Tell her again, maybe she'll change her mind. (To mother, whispers:) Don't do it.

CHILD: Jump up and down.

MOTHER: No (smiles and does not move).

THERAPIST: You're both doing a good job. (To child:) Keep telling her again and again. I bet you can get her to change her mind. (To mother, whispers:) Don't do it.

This role-play provides an excellent opportunity to emphasize the appropriate parental authority role. Children do tend to enjoy this activity even if they are unable to articulate that they feel more secure when their parents take charge. The parent can become somewhat inoculated to the child's coercive strategies, simply by going through each one systematically, with the child's playful participation.

THERAPIST: Hmm, I guess that's not working. What can we do? I know! Make that face that you make, you know (makes face). No, you do it better. Go ahead, make that face and tell her again.

CHILD: (makes face) Mom, jump up and down.

THERAPIST: Boy, she's tough, isn't she? Can you think of anything that might get her to do what you say?

CHILD: Maybe if I cry?

THERAPIST: Good idea, try that (by now, mother understands her role and does not need continuous prompting to stand her ground).

CHILD: I can't.

THERAPIST: That's okay. Just do your best, make believe.

CHILD: (moans) Mom, jump up and down.

THERAPIST: That was pretty good, but she's still not doing it. How about yelling? Will that work?

CHILD: I don't think so.

THERAPIST: Well, let's try one last thing. This time, yell at her to do it, and stomp your feet too. (Child stomps and yells.) Well, I guess this is the real mom after all. She's older, bigger, stronger, and it turns out that she's in charge, too. You can't boss her around. That's good news.

Once the parent is established as the more powerful person in the parent-child relationship, this should be tied immediately to the protective function. This can be accomplished through discussion or role-play, and can be modified to reflect any identified fears the child may have. The therapist can say something like, "Well, your mom seems pretty tough to me. Do you think she's tough enough to handle monsters?" Then the therapist may direct a role-play in which the parent is able to successfully protect the child from the feared object.

THERAPIST (raising arms and baring teeth): Here comes the monster! I like to eat little children. I think I see one! (walks slowly toward the child). (Whispers: "You think your mom can save you?")

MOTHER: Go away or I'll shoot!

THERAPIST: Ha ha! Here I come!

MOTHER: Bang! Bang!

THERAPIST (falls down): I'm dead.

If the therapist is uncomfortable in playing the monster role, a puppet or other prop can be used. Props can also be used for weapons or other means of protection. This role-play may be repeated a number of times, with variations, e.g., "Oh no, now two monsters are coming!"

Although the child is the most direct beneficiary of this game, the parent is also learning how important the strong parental role appears to be to the child. This can help to overcome parental ambivalence about taking charge.

Keep Your Promises

One of the most important concepts for parents to understand is that routines and rules are like the parent's promises to the child. This helps the parents realize how much their own behavior has been compromising the child's sense of security. It can be introduced gently, however, by conveying the assumption that the parent has positive intent but just didn't know better.

THERAPIST: Let me ask you something. If you tell your kid, "If you clean up your room in ten minutes, I'll give you some ice cream," and then in nine minutes, she shows you her room, and it's nice and clean, are you going to say, "That's nice, but I was just kidding about that ice cream"?

PARENT: Oh, I would never do that. Of course I would give her the ice cream like I said.

THERAPIST: I thought so. If you make a promise, you wouldn't let her down. But what about this: What if she doesn't do what you say, some little thing, and finally you get so mad that you say, "Okay, you can't go to the park tomorrow." And then tomorrow comes and you're not mad anymore, and you realize that the punishment was too big, and it's a nice day . . .

PARENT: Oh, I let her go. Usually I do give in later on.

THERAPIST: So you do break your promise in that situation?

PARENT: I guess so. I never thought of it that way.

THERAPIST: When you don't do what you say, you let her down. A lot of parents don't realize that. But when you say what's going to happen, she's counting on you to make it happen. She needs you to be a rock that she can always count on. You know how it is when you can't count on someone. It feels pretty shaky. Also, you have rules for good reasons, right?

PARENT: I like to think so.

THERAPIST: So let's say that she's not allowed to play in the street, and—

PARENT: That's a good example. A lot of fast cars go by our house.

THERAPIST: So let's say you tell her, "Don't play in the street or you'll have to come inside." And then she plays in the street, and she says, "Please, give me another chance?" and you let her stay out. What will she be thinking about that?

PARENT: Be happy she can keep on playing, think she got away with it.

THERAPIST: Part of her might be happy, but part of her is going to wonder, going to feel all shaky and nervous inside . . .

PARENT: Oh, like maybe I don't care about her.

THERAPIST: That's exactly right. Like maybe you don't care if she's safe or not. If you have a rule, to keep her safe, to help her learn to be a good person, whatever, you show you care by keeping your rules. And by doing what you say, so she knows she can always count on you. That will help her feel safer and she can start to calm down.

What Are Rules For?

This intervention helps parents to focus on their good intentions and how these can be compromised when they get too angry and lose control. This sets the parent up for the following intervention, which offers a specific method for disciplining without anger.

THERAPIST: This might seem like a stupid question but I'm going to ask anyway. Why do you have rules for your child? Is it to protect him, keep him safe, and to help him to learn to be a good person? Or is it so that when he breaks the rule, you can punish him and get revenge?

PARENT: My rules are to keep him safe, and to teach him right from wrong.

THERAPIST: So your rules come from love, from being a good parent.

PARENT: Of course.

THERAPIST: That's what I thought. Would you say that it's easier to be the kind of parent you like to be—coming from love like that—when you're calm? Or when you're angry?

PARENT: When I'm calm.

THERAPIST: So if you get mad enough, sometimes the revenge thing takes over?

PARENT: Well, sometimes, if I get mad enough, yeah, I might yell or come up with some punishment that's really too much.

Stop a Problem Quickly

This strategy serves multiple functions. It provides parents with practical steps with which to implement effective discipline. It helps parents keep their promises by using such small punishments that follow-through is less problematic. It helps parents to avoid losing their tempers by intervening before a problem situation gets out of hand. When parents can learn to intervene very quickly, with very small consequences, the child is reassured without having to escalate, and the discipline problem becomes much smaller.

THERAPIST: One of the biggest problems parents have in keeping their promises is that they get so angry that they make punishments that seem too big later when they're not mad anymore.

PARENT: Yes, I do that.

THERAPIST: One way to fix this is to decide ahead of time what punishments you will use, so you don't have to think up something when you're mad.

PARENT: That makes sense.

THERAPIST: Do you ever use time-out?

PARENT: Yes, sometimes I send her to her room, if I get mad and don't want her around. She can come back later, maybe in half an hour, if she wants to be good.

THERAPIST: I want to teach you a kind of time-out that you can use. You just pick a spot wherever you are, like in a chair or against the wall in the room you're in. And when she's in a time-out she can't talk, or play with anything, or kick the wall, or really do much of anything. And the time-out should last a minute.

PARENT: A minute? That doesn't seem like much.

THERAPIST: Maybe it should just be half a minute. I'm looking for a consequence that's so small that it won't break your heart to follow through on it. Can you stand it to keep her in a time-out for a minute?

PARENT: (laughs) That won't be a problem.

THERAPIST: Good. Because now I'm going to tell you to do this every chance you get, and to look for chances. You know how we were talking about one of the problems being that she can get you mad?

PARENT: That's for sure.

THERAPIST: Do you get mad right away, or only after a long time?

PARENT: No, it's just when I tell her and she keeps on doing it, won't stop, won't listen. Finally I get frustrated with her.

THERAPIST: That's what I thought. So here's what I want you to do: Tell her the first time. Then if she doesn't do it, tell her one more time, and count to three, not one, two, two and a half, two and three-quarters, just a straight, one, two, three. Then pow! it's time-out, one minute. Then she still has to do what you say. No arguing, that's just the way it is.

PARENT: That's it? That seems simple enough.

THERAPIST: The trick to this is that you don't have a chance to get angry, because you're not letting it drag on and on. And you can keep your punishment small because she hasn't done much. And the time-out isn't really even a punishment. It's just like, well, you don't follow the rules, so you're on the bench a little while; then you can come out and try again.

PARENT: I think I can do that.

THERAPIST: This week I want you to practice every chance you get. If you're not sure, go for it. And if you ever catch yourself starting to get frustrated or angry, you've probably let it go too far already, but you can still give a time-out right away. The funny thing about this is, the more strict you try to be, the less you end up giving those really big punishments.

If the child is hanging around, or can be brought into the session, I like to role-play the time-out procedure several times, first with me playing the parent, then with the parent playing herself. Sometimes the child likes to have a crack at the parent role as well. This exercise has several benefits. First, the parent gets to observe and then practice under observation. The child has a positive, even playful, first experience of this intervention, perhaps making it feel nonpunitive. Also, by role-playing obedient and disobedient behavior, the child may develop a stronger sense of control over her symptomatic behavior. Finally, the therapist can put a therapeutic "spin" on the whole enterprise.

THERAPIST: Your mom and I were talking, and she decided that she's going to be in charge more, so that you can feel safer at home. So now we want to practice something, will you help us?

CHILD: Okay.

THERAPIST: Okay, I'm going to tell you to put away the toys, but you keep playing with them. Ready? Put those toys away. (To the child: "Don't do it.")

CHILD: (keeps playing)

THERAPIST: I told you to put those toys away (To the child: "Still don't do it"). One, two, three. Now you have to do a time-out. Stand up over there in that corner. Yeah, right over there. No, you can't play with that during a time-out. Here, I'll hold it for you. Okay, good, just stand there. I'll time you for a minute and tell you when you're done. That's good, you're done now. Good job! This time it's your mom's turn. Do you think she can do that like I did? Will you help her practice it?

Slot Machine

The importance of keeping one's word consistently can be illustrated with the slot machine metaphor. This intervention also helps to prepare parents for the challenge of standing their ground, and highlights the value of sticking with it.

THERAPIST: So you understand now that whatever you say is like a promise to your kid. In the same way, it's really important to stick with what you say. You know how at the checkout counter at the store, there's always some kid who says, "Please, Mommy, please please please?"

PARENT: Right, and she finally says, "Okay, here. Just shut up already!"

THERAPIST: Oh, you've seen that too? The funny thing is, that parent is actually training her kid to be a pest, to act that way.

PARENT: What do you mean?

THERAPIST: Well, I'm gonna tell you how Las Vegas works, why they make so much money. It's the same principle; it's something you can use at home. Let's say I'm putting quarters in a machine, and every time I put a quarter in, I get four quarters back. What am I gonna do?

PARENT: Keep putting quarters in.

THERAPIST: That's right. And then what happens if one day I put in a quarter, and nothing comes back?

PARENT: You quit.

THERAPIST: Soon I quit. First, though, maybe I put in a bunch more quarters, say, "What's wrong with this machine?" maybe bang it a couple of times. But you're right, eventually I say, "I guess this machine just doesn't work anymore" and I quit, go try some other game. But what about this: what if I'm putting quarters in a machine, and mostly nothing happens, but every once in a while I get a jackpot?

PARENT: That's like the slot machines.

THERAPIST: That's right. The real ones, they work this way for a reason. Because what's going to happen if I put in a quarter and nothing comes back?

PARENT: You keep on trying.

THERAPIST: That's right. Maybe put in ten more quarters, maybe a hundred, and each time, I'm saying to myself, "Keep trying, the next one could be the jackpot."

PARENT: And then you're a millionaire and you quit your job.

THERAPIST: And that's just the same thing that the kid at the checkout counter is doing, when she says, "Please, Mommy?" and she says, "No," and it's "Please?" "No." "Please?" "No." "Please?" "No," ten times. She's saying to herself, "Keep trying; the next one could be the jackpot."

PARENT: So when she bugs me and I give in . . .

THERAPIST: That's right. Jackpot.

PARENT: I see what you're saying.

THERAPIST: So the trick is to just remember, yes means yes and no means no. Once you say it, just stick with it. Otherwise, you're training her to keep on bugging you, go for that jackpot.

PARENT: I've got it.

THERAPIST: I want to warn you, though, that this might get harder at first. Remember what happens when the machine doesn't work anymore?

PARENT: She might try harder.

THERAPIST: Right, she might put in all those extra quarters, hit the machine . . . which means that she might really try to push you, see if she really can count on you now, or if you're just kidding. And what happens if you just get tired, finally give in?

PARENT: Jackpot.

THERAPIST: Right. So if you're going to make this work, you really have to stick with it. Once she learns, though, that you mean what you say, well, why bother putting in all those quarters? Have to find a different game.

The Damn-Shit-Fuck Progression

If the principle of early intervention needs to be further emphasized, this should do the trick. The dramatic language can help parents to remember the point. Also, it ties the child's misbehavior to his insecurity, hopefully eliciting the parent's desire to reassure, rather than the parent's aversion to punish. Of course, this particular expression should be used only when it would not be too uncomfortable or otherwise inappropriate.

THERAPIST: When your kid does something wrong, I think he's asking for help. He's asking you to set him straight so that he feels safe. When he feels out of control, he needs you to help him, until he can control himself again. But if he messes up and you just let it go, he gets more and more nervous. Then what do you think happens?

PARENT: Well, he just keeps going.

THERAPIST: That's right. There's something I call the Damn-Shit-Fuck Progression which I think happens with your child. When he says Damn and nothing happens, he gets more nervous, and asks for help even louder. Then he tries Shit to see if you'll help him. If you don't come through then, he'll go to the next step.

PARENT: I've seen that before. He just gets out of hand.

THERAPIST: When he's nervous, he really needs you to take charge, to show him that you're in control. When you give the time-out, he's reassured, and he can calm down. Otherwise, he'll just go to the next level, until you finally come through.

Physical Restraint

Occasionally, a parent will say, "But she won't stay in the time-out." Then the therapist says, "Make her stay. You're in charge." Then the "how" must be addressed in some detail. In most cases, the parent can simply insist, or even stand in front of the child to block escape. Sometimes it is necessary to teach physical restraint techniques, which requires being able to count on the parent to implement this complex intervention effectively and safely. The parent must be able to proceed in a caring, authoritative and nonreactive manner, so the child feels safe rather than attacked. Physical restraint should only be taught by a therapist with formal training in a trauma-informed physical restraint method, which, though occasionally essential to child trauma treatment, is beyond the scope of this book.

Alternate Time-Out System

The standard approach to time-out, as previously described, may be too difficult for some reactive parents to manage effectively. Sometimes kids in time-out argue, make faces, tap their feet, or do other objectionable or distracting things. If the parent can't help arguing or yelling at the child, the problem behavior is being reinforced even within the time-out, which is counter to the time- out's purpose. The following alternative time-out system offers parents increased physical control of the child, while keeping the parents away so they are less tempted to reinforce the negative behaviors (Dutton, 2004).

The parents must designate a time-out room, such as the child's bedroom, in which there is nothing, including the walls and the furniture, which the parents are not willing to risk. The room should probably not contain a TV or electronic game system, but other toys are okay. If the child does not go immediately when given the time-out, she is physically transported by the parent. If she does not stay in the room voluntarily, the closed door forces her to do so. The child completes this time-out by being quiet for the specified period, perhaps five minutes, or one minute for each year of her age.

During a time-out, the parent goes about her business, regardless of what happens in the room. The child may be screaming and destroying everything within reach, for minutes or even hours; the parent ignores her. Only after the child has been quiet for the designated period does the parent make contact. Then, the parent is to only praise the child for behaving well for the past few minutes and thus completing the designated time-out. Note that the child is not required to sit silent and motionless, but merely to occupy herself quietly in her room.

This system relies on the principle that the child will do whatever is reinforced by the parent's attention. When the child misbehaves, the parent immediately sends her to the time-out room so that no reinforcement is available. When the child behaves properly by successfully completing the time-out, the parent does reinforce that positive behavior. Negative behavior diminishes when the child learns that it will not be reinforced. If the parent can stick it out, this system can be effective even with very challenging children.

Beyond Time-Out: Natural Consequences

Beyond time-out for annoying or disobedient behavior, the therapist can help the parents to apply the principles of trauma treatment to the variety of discipline challenges that may arise. The goal is to support the child's sense of safety and security while providing appropriate limits as well as learning opportunities. These principles include the following:

- Keep your promises. Be willing to follow through on the consequences you select.
- Avoid retaliation or revenge. By definition, these represent parental loss of control.
- Avoid depriving the child of meals, sleep, school, or (if possible) other worthwhile activities.
- Use consequences that are fair, make sense, and offer opportunities for a positive outcome.

These principles can guide parents in evaluating disciplinary options. For example, physical discipline (e.g., spanking) is generally problematic because it represents retaliation—loss of control—by the parents, and because it gives the child something else to be afraid about. The restitution approach has the advantage of being rehabilitative rather than punitive: it is clearly fair, and the child may actually make up for his misdeed, thereby repairing damaged relationships as well as self-esteem.

The concept of "natural consequences" helps many parents grasp the constructive intent of this approach to discipline. The parent's role is not exactly to punish, but to ensure that the child has an opportunity to learn from his mistakes by taking responsibility for them. Examples of natural consequences include the following:

- Make a mess, clean it up.
- Break something, fix it or replace it. Replacement can be done with cash or labor (e.g., extra chores).
- Break my trust, you lose it until you earn it back. For example: You didn't come back home by dark tonight, so you can't go out after dinner tomorrow. And I lost half an hour worrying while you were late, so you owe me a half hour of chores.
- Work before play, especially if the work isn't getting done. Poor grades? No TV until your homework's done.

Although such consequences are often necessary, a positive emphasis is a preferable means of eliciting wanted behavior. If parents seem to be getting bogged down around a particular problem behavior, the therapist can suggest a focused incentive program to encourage the child to do better. Sometimes the carrot-and-stick approach works: having both positive and negative consequences for the same events. For example, if the child doesn't get ready for school on time, he may have to go to bed fifteen minutes early that night. On the other hand, if he is ready every morning, he may get a treat Friday after school.

One of the important components in either a formal behavioral program or a more general approach to discipline is the parent's attitude of supportive neutrality. When the child is facing known consequences for a behavioral choice, the parent can help him see that he has chosen the consequence with his own actions. This takes the parent off the hook and helps her feel less mean. When the parent can see the child as struggling with the consequences of his own choices, the parent is in a position to be less personally reactive, and more able to focus on the child's needs.

THERAPIST: So when he tells you that you're mean because he has to go to bed early, how do you react to that?

PARENT: I get mad. I feel like I am mean, and I'm sick of his grumbling.

THERAPIST: Try saying this: "You told me you wanted to go to bed early; you told me this morning with your actions. It's not my choice; it's yours." Say that.

PARENT: You chose that yourself. You were late this morning and that was the deal.

THERAPIST: How does it feel when you say that?

PARENT: Like it's not my problem.

THERAPIST: That's right. You're being a good parent. You're keeping your promises, and you're letting him learn from his mistakes so he can do better.

PARENT: But I know him. He'll just grumble some more.

THERAPIST: That's not your problem either! In fact, it's his job to grumble. He's trying to find out if he can really count on you or not. He'll push your buttons. What are they? The "guilt" button, the "mean" button. What else?

PARENT: Oh, he knows them all.

THERAPIST: So your first job is to come through, keep your promise. Then you can help him learn by telling him that it's his choice. He can be happier if he makes better choices. And if he still is grumbling, if you want you can help him with his feelings. Try saying this: "You don't sound very happy about going to bed early."

PARENT: You don't sound happy about going to bed early.

THERAPIST: That's it. You can help him learn to handle things he doesn't like. But it's not your problem.

You're in Charge

Parents must understand that out-of-control children need someone else to be in control, and to help contain them, until they can control themselves again. This concept can be conveyed in many ways, and is a recurring theme in the parenting sessions. First, the parents must grasp that the child's sense of security rests on the adult being in charge. Then parents must learn to identify specific situations in which they may be relinquishing their authority, and learn how to recover it.

THERAPIST: We talked before about how your child feels scared inside, how every time some little thing makes her nervous, all those old scared feelings kick in.

PARENT: Right. You said, from the hurricane. I didn't realize that before. And the fighting, I know they didn't like that, but I didn't know it was still bothering her.

THERAPIST: Sometimes it's hard to know what kids are thinking. What happens with kids is that those old feelings can get stuck inside, and now any little thing can hit that sore spot and make her start feeling scared again. But you know how you can tell when she's scared?

PARENT: No, she never talks about that stuff.

THERAPIST: Kids don't know much about how to talk about stuff. She shows you she's scared, she shows you by doing something she's not supposed to do. Then when you put her in her place, she feels safe because you're in charge. She can count on you.

PARENT: Right, we talked about that, the time-outs.

THERAPIST: But there's more to it. If you argue with her, or if you yell, you've lost control, and that can spoil the help you're giving her.

PARENT: Just from yelling at her?

THERAPIST: Sure. When you're in charge, acting like the parent, what you say goes—no fuss about it. But if she can get you going, get you to argue with her, negotiate points, then you're just like another kid—just like her, instead of in charge. Or if she can push your buttons, get you mad, well, you've given her control again. She's gotten you to yell and fight with her, just like you were another kid. When you're the parent, you don't have to do that. When she's out of control, she needs you to be the parent, to be in control.

Parents may have difficulty maintaining their own self-control and avoiding the arguing, yelling, or hitting which may have been habitual. The following strategies can contribute to success in this effort:

- Viewing the child's misbehavior as reflecting fear can help the parent feel sympathy for the child instead of feeling personally affronted.
- Using the quick, small punishments can preclude opportunities for parental frustration.
- The "not my problem" approach can further depersonalize parent-child conflict.

When this child-focused approach is insufficient for parental self-control, individual work with the parent may be required. Self-control and anger management techniques can be helpful. Another approach is to view the child's misbehavior as triggering a traumatic memory for the parent; in other words, the child's behavior may be hitting the parent's trauma-related sore spot. The therapist can then do a case formulation with the parent, with a limited focus on how this might be happening, and then work with the parent on resolving his or her own trauma.

The Stepfamily Trap

In many families, one parent—typically the father—plays the role of the overly harsh disciplinarian, while the other parent—typically the mother—plays the overindulgent role. This is most common when the mother has custody of her children and the father is actually a stepfather who has married into the family; however, many intact families, and same-sex-parent families, have a similar dynamic. The problem is, the more the father disciplines harshly, the more indulgent and protective the mother becomes; and the more the mother neglects to discipline, the more the father feels obliged to step in. This creates a positive feedback cycle of increasing polarization, resulting in considerable family tension. When the father is punitive and the mother indulgent, the child cannot really count on either parent for appropriate guidance and support.

The therapist can explain these dynamics to the parents, and tell them how to resolve it: by having the mother (or the one who has been "soft") take the lead as the disciplinarian. Her relationship with her children will not be damaged by exerting her authority—it will actually be strengthened. When she becomes the primary disciplinarian, this gives her husband the opportunity to back off, and to develop a more positive relationship with the children.

Preventing the Parent Split

Some kids will try to play one parent against another in a different way: by going to the parent who is more likely to give them their way. This could be a different parent depending on the occasion. For example, one parent may be more permissive regarding privileges, whereas the other may be more generous with money. The problem is that when a child is allowed to split his parents, rules are not rules and parents are not in charge. Although the child may persist in attempting to split because of the immediate reinforcements, the more significant outcome is that the child will feel insecure and unprotected. Another outcome is that the parents are likely to resent each other, and may even feel that they must "outbid" the other parent for the child's affection.

The therapist can explain these dynamics and work with the parents to develop a system of teamwork. This system is specific to each family, but typically involves the following:

1. Parents agree on certain rules up front, and agree to stick to them even if only one parent is present.
2. Parents agree to check with each other when the child makes certain types of requests, to make sure that the other parent hasn't already given an answer!
3. Parents make a rule that if the child has already received an answer from one parent, that's the answer. If the child then tries to get a more favorable answer from the other parent, the child faces a predetermined consequence.

When parents use the same rules, they are not in the position of competing for the child's affection, and they are not in the position of undermining each other's authority. Also, the child can have parents who are in charge and who keep their promises.

Focus on the Positive

Parents can be encouraged to give frequent praise for their children's positive behavior, rather than only giving attention in response to misbehavior. In some situations the parent can learn to ignore negative behaviors and focus on positive behaviors of other children, perhaps thereby encouraging the problem child to join in. The therapist can also suggest that the parent regularly devotes some time to doing an enjoyable activity with the child. In conjunction with the effective discipline approach, this can help shift the family's energy to more positive interactions. Also, as noted previously, specific behaviors can be developed and encouraged through the use of incentives.

THE THERAPIST AS THE PARENTS' PERSONAL TRAINER

In the initial session focused on the parenting approach, the therapist is likely to focus on the Positive Parenting handout and perhaps a few of the other interventions described previously, according to what seems most on target. Don't try to get everything done at once. It's better to focus on a small number of tasks that can realistically be accomplished, and then later build on success. Parents should have sufficient opportunity to discuss and rehearse this discipline approach in session until they feel prepared to implement it at home. A caution against overly high expectations can help parents feel successful with even small progress.

THERAPIST: In this meeting, I just gave you the ten-week course! So I don't expect you to get it all at once. Habits take time to change. Also, kids are good at finding the loopholes! What I would like you to do is try this out, do your best, and then come back and tell me which parts worked, and which parts didn't work for you. Then we can try to solve the problems and you can do even better after that. We're not expecting any dramatic changes right now. We're just getting started.

Chapter 11

Self-Control Skills Training

Kids can do several things for themselves that will help them to feel more safe and secure and strong. These fall under several categories:

- Avoiding high-risk situations
- Self-management regarding anxiety symptoms
- Self-control regarding behavioral choices

AVOIDING HIGH RISK

There are two types of high-risk situations. One type is when kids are at high risk of being triggered to acting-out behavior. The other type is more literally a high risk in that kids are in some special kind of danger. When kids avoid the latter type of high-risk situations, they can feel safer because they are safer. In each case, helping kids to get better at avoiding high risk is an excellent step. And in each case, this is done by specifically identifying the high-risk situations, and then planning, and practicing, how these situations can be anticipated and avoided. Sometimes this can involve family members and making practical changes in lifestyle. For example:

- A certain babysitter does not provide adequate supervision; the parent agrees to use a different one.
- The child is afraid on the night the parent stays out late going to classes; the parent agrees to phone the child just before bedtime.
- The mother's ex-boyfriend, who assaulted her, has not been found/arrested; the mother gets the lock on her door changed, and tells several neighbors to be on the lookout for the man and to call the police if they see him.
- The father, who has had health problems, agrees to have an adult family member check up on him during the day while the child is in school.
- The child's "high-risk" time for getting into trouble and/or danger is during school, when he cuts classes and goes places with his friends. The child, parents, and teachers set up a system in which the teacher signs a card every time the child goes to class, and the child shows the signed card to the parent every day after school. This monitoring helps to keep the child in class.

Often the child's exposure to high risk situations is under her own control. Then the therapist can work with her directly, by helping her to identify the situation and come up with effective

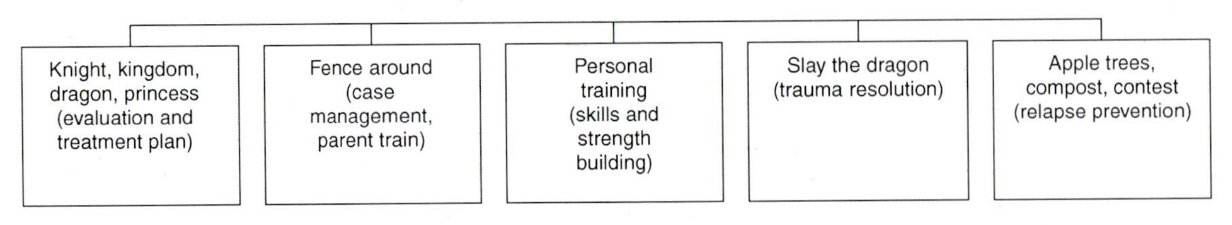

FIGURE 11.1. Steps in the fairy tale model.

ways of avoiding it. The next step is to have the child practice the coping strategy, first in imagination and then in real life. Here's an example of how this might go.

THERAPIST: We've been talking about why you're here, so that we can help you to be safer and to feel safer. So tell me, where is it that you feel the most unsafe?

CHILD: I don't know.

THERAPIST: Do you feel the most unsafe at school, at home, on the street, somewhere else?

CHILD: At school.

THERAPIST: In class, at recess, at lunch, when do you feel most unsafe?

CHILD: On the way to school and then in the hallways and at recess, that's when those boys bother me the most. I eat lunch in the art room; they don't bother me there.

THERAPIST: Good. Are there times at recess or in the hallways or on your way to school that you feel more safe than other times?

CHILD: Only if I'm with my friends.

THERAPIST: Are you usually with your friends, or usually by yourself?

CHILD: I'm usually by myself, but not always.

THERAPIST: If you decided that you wanted to feel more safe at school, do you think it might be a good idea to go with your friends more instead of by yourself?

CHILD: I think so.

THERAPIST: Do you think you might really do this, or will something be in your way?

CHILD: I like to go with my friends but sometimes I forget, or sometimes they get started, like they've already left the classroom, before I'm ready.

THERAPIST: So what could you do if you decided that you wanted to go with them?

CHILD: Get ready faster?

THERAPIST: So you mean, get ready faster when it's time to leave class?

CHILD: Yes.

THERAPIST: So what do you have to do to get ready to go?

CHILD: I have to get stuff ready for the homework, take the papers and book that I need, put my pencils and notebook in my pack . . .

THERAPIST: And you usually wait until the bell rings to do that?

CHILD: I guess I can start getting ready earlier, so when the bell rings I can just go.

Comments

Several interventions were demonstrated that are consistent with the overall trauma-informed approach:

- When the child did not immediately say where she felt most unsafe, the therapist did not merely repeat the question—that could make the child feel stupid and unsuccessful in the therapy. The "menu" restated the question to include helpful examples.
- There may be other problem-solving options as well, for example, turning to adults for assistance in controlling a bully (or prior assailant). This particular script assumes that such options have already been pursued in prior sessions as part of initial case management.
- The therapist has not told the child what to do. Rather, the therapist reminded the child of the child's (and parents') own goals, and then asked a series of questions to help the child find her own solution.
- If the child does not come up with a solution, the therapist can offer a menu, e.g., "Let me tell you the kinds of things that work for other kids in this situation, and see if you think that any of these might work for you."

Script Continued

THERAPIST: So if you did this, you could walk with your friends, and you might feel safer in the hallway going to your next class?

CHILD: Definitely.

THERAPIST: I'm going to ask you to imagine doing this; let's just see how it goes. What class would you be leaving?

CHILD: Math.

THERAPIST: And what time does math get out? When does the bell ring?

CHILD: At ten past ten.

THERAPIST: What time would you need to start getting ready, to get out right when the bell rings?

CHILD: Maybe five minutes ahead of time.

THERAPIST: Okay, so I'm going to ask you to imagine watching a little movie, in your mind. In this movie, you're in math class, and you're checking the clock now and then, and at five past ten you start getting ready to go. Then when the bell rings, you're ready to go. You go with your friends, walking to your next class, feeling safe. So you can do this with your eyes open or closed, whatever will help you concentrate. Start at the beginning, you're in class looking at the clock, keep going until the end where you're walking down the hall with your friends. Tell me when you're done. Ready?

CHILD: Done.

THERAPIST: What happened? How did it go?

CHILD: I just saw what time it was, put my things in my pack, and I was out the door with everyone else.

THERAPIST: Then what? How was the hallway?

CHILD: Oh, I just walked with my friends, and no one bothered me.

THERAPIST: Way to go.

Comments

1. Many children already have a general idea about what they should be doing differently. However, they're not doing it. Practice makes a difference—it improves competence and confidence, and these in turn improve motivation and likelihood of actually doing it.
2. To practice it, there needs to be an "it"—not just some general idea. Considerable specificity and concrete detail is necessary for the child to imaginally rehearse (visualize) the coping behavior. As a rule, if the therapist can't easily visualize the "movie" that the child is watching, more detail is needed.
3. If the child is having difficulty producing the needed detail, the therapist can ask, "If I'm watching you on TV, what do I see you doing?" This orients the child to the request for description of concrete, observable (and repeatable) behaviors.
4. There are several steps to follow in directing an imaginal rehearsal:
   - Interview for the details of the problem/situation, solution/coping behavior, and reinforcer/outcome.
   - Describe the contents of the movie in detail, and in sequence.
   - Summarize the movie to orient the child to the beginning, the steps along the way, and the ending.
   - Instruct to start at the beginning, go through to the end, and tell the therapist when it's over.
5. It's important to practice not only the behavior itself, but the preceding situation as well as the outcome. The details of the preceding situation (e.g., math class, five past ten) become reminders to initiate the behavior. The outcome is the reinforcer; rehearsing a behavior that is reinforced makes real-life repetition more likely.

SELF-MANAGEMENT OF ANXIETY SYMPTOMS

Even when kids are good at avoiding the high-risk situations, there are still other situations that are not actually high risk, but that trigger a trauma-related reaction such as anxiety or fear. Kids can learn to control their own emotional and physiological responses to these situations, so that they are not so vulnerable to the triggers, and not as likely to need to avoid a range of actually safe situations.

Again, this self-management training is accomplished by specifically identifying the triggers and by helping the child to identify, and practice, effective coping skills. Here's an example (continuing from the previous vignette) of how this might be done.

THERAPIST: Where else do you feel unsafe?

CHILD: Sometimes, like, riding a bus with my mother, I see teenaged boys and I get nervous, like maybe they'll do something to me.

THERAPIST: Could they really do anything to you there on the bus?

CHILD: No.

THERAPIST: But it still feels unsafe to you. You get that feeling?

CHILD: Yeah, I know nothing's gonna happen but I can't help it; I still get scared.

THERAPIST: Okay. How can you tell when you're feeling scared? What words are in your head? What's going on in your body?

CHILD: I don't know.

THERAPIST: Like, are you saying to yourself, "Here comes trouble," or "I'm scared," or "Watch out," or "I'm doomed," or what?

CHILD: I just say "Oh no, oh no" over and over in my head.

THERAPIST: And let me tell you some things that other kids notice in their bodies; you can tell me if anything like this happens to you. Some kids say that their heart starts beating faster or pounding, or they get sweaty, or they get all tense, or their stomach feels funny . . .

CHILD: My heart beats faster, and I get a kind of sick feeling in my stomach, and all over my body I kind of feel weaker, and kind of tense and still, like I'm afraid to move.

THERAPIST: Let me tell you something about how your body and your mind work together. When you're in danger, your mind tells your body, and then your body does all these things to take care of the danger. Like maybe once when you were in danger, you learned to keep still to keep from making things worse, and now that's how your body reacts, to try to keep you safe. The thing is, when your body does all that stuff—heart beating fast and all—your brain notices. Then your mind says, "Wow, look what my body's doing! I must be in big trouble!" So your mind gets your body going, and then your body gets your mind going even more. Do you follow that?

CHILD: Yes.

THERAPIST: The thing is, this can happen even on the bus, when you know in your head that you really are safe, that nothing bad will happen there. But once your body gets going, it makes you believe that you're in danger and you feel worse than you have to. See how that works?

CHILD: You mean when my heart's beating that makes me think I'm scared?

THERAPIST: Yes, that's it. Even when you know better. But you know what? You can make yourself feel safe then, if you decide to. You can control your body, get your body to give your mind a different message.

CHILD: How?

THERAPIST: Do you remember that deep breathing thing we did last week?

CHILD: Yes.

THERAPIST: Well, when you do that, you calm your body down. And when your body calms down, your mind starts to think that things are really okay. And you know what happens then?

CHILD: What?

THERAPIST: When your mind thinks things are okay, your body calms down even more. Here, I'll show you. Let's find an example. When was the last time that you were on the bus and felt scared?

CHILD: Just yesterday.

THERAPIST: Okay, I want you to remember being on the bus yesterday. Look for the time on the bus when you were the most scared; get a picture of that in your mind. Notice what you're seeing, what words are in your head, what you're feeling, what's going on in your body. Got it?

CHILD: (Nods.)

THERAPIST: Concentrate on this. Now I'm going to ask you how bad the feeling is, on zero to ten. Ten is the worst the feeling could be; zero is no bad feeling at all. How bad is the feeling right now?

CHILD: Five or six.

THERAPIST: Okay. Now I'm going to ask you to do that deep breathing, like last week. Ready? Deep breath in, one, two, three. Hold it, one, two, three. Out slow, one, two, three. Deep breath in, one, two, three. Hold it, one, two, three. Out slow, one, two, three. Deep breath in, one, two, three. Hold it, one, two, three. Out slow, one, two, three. Good. Now, on zero to ten, where are you now?

CHILD: About a three.

THERAPIST: All right! We're going to do a little more of the breathing. This time, when you breathe out, look for any bad pictures in your mind, or bad thoughts or feelings, or any place where your body doesn't feel good, and when you breathe out, you can breathe out from there and let it go with your breath . . .

Comments

- After the therapist acknowledges and seriously addresses the child's realistic fears, the child is more likely to be open to acknowledging that some of her fears are not realistic. If the therapist skips the first step, the child will likely feel discounted and perceive the therapist as not credible.
- Awareness of the signals of (in this case) fear are essential. There would be no point in learning coping behaviors without knowing when to use them. As in the previous imaginal rehearsal, the components of the fear response are used as a signal to initiate the coping behaviors. In fact, following the above, the therapist might well direct an imaginal rehearsal in which the child practices using the deep breathing in the feared situation.
- The therapist can also use self-talk, visualization, progressive relaxation, or other methods to help the child with self-calming. Such skills should be practiced repeatedly so that the child becomes competent and accustomed to practicing self-calming in specified situations.

For those kids for whom the fear and anxiety symptoms are particularly distressing, the therapist can guide the child to repeatedly concentrate on a distressing situation/image until the SUDS gets to a designated "maximum tolerance" level, and then use distraction, self-talk, and relaxation methods to bring the SUDS down. When this is done over and over within a session, the child learns to feel that she can handle any anxiety that comes her way.

THERAPIST: We're going to practice you handling getting anxious at those times when you really are safe. On zero to ten, what's the most you are willing to be upset right now?

CHILD: I could handle a six; I don't want to go higher than that.

THERAPIST: Okay. So in a little while I'm going to ask you to think of something upsetting, like being on the bus yesterday, and then calm yourself down. What ideas do you have about how you can calm yourself down?

CHILD: Well, I can breathe like that again.

THERAPIST: That's a good idea; it worked for you before. Any other ideas?

CHILD: Well, I know that I'm not really in danger on the bus.

THERAPIST: Right. So one thing you can do is just tell yourself something like that. What would you say to yourself?

CHILD: I feel scared but I'm really safe.

THERAPIST: That might help; I think that's a good idea. Something else that works for some kids is to think of something else instead, something that makes them feel good. Like the Safe Place we practiced with before, or playing with your dog, something like that.

CHILD: I can think of my dog.

THERAPIST: So you have a lot of strategies now, ways to calm yourself down. So here's what we're going to do. I'm going to ask you to think about when you were on the bus yesterday. When the picture is in your mind, tell me.

CHILD: Got it.

THERAPIST: Where is it now on zero to ten?

CHILD: Maybe a four or five.

THERAPIST: Okay, I want you to keep concentrating on it until it's a six, then stop. Think about the picture, the bad thoughts and feelings, make it more intense until it's a six, tell me when you're there.

CHILD: It's a six now.

THERAPIST: Okay, now use your strategies to calm yourself down. Tell me when it's a two.

This is repeated several times—up and down, up and down—until the child is clearly good at bringing down the distress level. It can also be practiced using different images and scenarios. After this session, many kids have a new sense of confidence that they can handle whatever anxiety comes their way.

SELF-CONTROL OF BEHAVIORAL CHOICES

Self-control skills training is frequently offered as a stand-alone intervention. The relatively limited impact of anger management training programs for antisocial youth (Kazdin, 1997) may be explained by the failure to incorporate this as a component of trauma-informed treatment, and implemented in the proper order of interventions (Greenwald, 2002a). The odds are better when kids first identify and invest in their own goals, making the skills work meaningful to them, and when this intervention is eventually followed by trauma resolution work to reduce the trauma burden and related sore-spot reactivity.

Even so, self-control skills training can itself reduce posttraumatic stress symptoms. For example, in a randomized study of war veterans with PTSD and severe anger management problems, those receiving standard PTSD treatment plus anger management training reported reduced intrusive imagery, whereas the standard care control group did not (Chemtob, Novaco, Hamada, & Gross, 1997). Prior to treatment, when these men were perceiving threats and acting out (in defensive aggression), their fears would tend to be confirmed, because their own behavior engendered hostility in others. This repeated experience would tend to reinforce their perception of the world as a dangerous place where such defensive aggression is required. Once they began to control their responses, they probably experienced much more favorable responses from others. Thus, they had repeated opportunities to learn that the world was not so dangerous after all, anymore. Perhaps, once they felt they were out of the "war zone," their trauma memories did not seem quite so salient, leading to a reduction of intrusive images.

These findings can also be applied to kids. One of the ways that kids learn to feel safer is by having their environment actually become more favorable—more predictable and supportive, less hostile. Kids learn to feel stronger by getting better at successfully coping with challenging situations that used to overwhelm them because of the trauma-related reactivity. When kids with impulsive/acting-out problems improve their self-control, they will probably also feel safer and stronger.

The following method of teaching self-control skills training to kids integrates the effective components of several approaches. It builds on the preceding steps in the treatment approach that has been presented already. When self-control skills training is presented as part of an agreed-upon treatment plan in the service of the child's identified goals, he is likely to be invested in trying hard to master the skills. Also, it integrates the child's long-term goals with current issues and pressing concerns. This is accomplished by:

- doing a check-in at the beginning of the session, and asking for something good and something bad that happened since the prior meeting;

- choosing one of those things—good or bad—as an example of the child's everyday challenges regarding self-control (the event can be used whether the child was successful or not);
- reminding the child that this challenge is a good example of the kind of thing that could get in his way; that mastering this challenge will help him to achieve the goals he has identified. You are then working on present and future concerns at the same time.

To help a child change a long habit of impulsive acting out, it's important to understand not only the trauma-related reactivity driving the impulse, but the reinforcement that the child receives following the acting-out behavior.

Imagine that your dog has gotten into the garbage and made a mess. Three days later you scold the dog. What does the dog learn from this? First, getting into the garbage is great fun! Second, the dog's owner is mostly okay, but every once in a while gets upset out of the blue. Oh well.

Kids with problem behaviors have this experience over and over again. The relief is experienced right away, and the negative consequences happen so much later that they don't seem relevant. What happens some other time doesn't matter because it does not feel connected to the problem situation or to the behavior. Learning occurs best when the consequence—whether reinforcement or punishment—is close to the behavior.

With kids, the problem behavior is being repeated because it works in some way: it provides relief from the intolerable thoughts and feelings. Negative consequences somewhere down the line do not feel very relevant to the child in the moment. To make matters worse, the child often experiences the so-called appropriate behavior as a punishment, because the frustration is immediate, and the reward is too far in the future to be reinforcing. Thus, the problem behavior is

reinforced by the immediate relief it provides, and the appropriate behavior is punished by the lack of relief. The long-term consequences are too distant to be influential.

In order to help kids to change their habits, we must find a way to flip the reinforcement schedule. We must find a way to make the problem behavior less appealing, and the wanted behavior more appealing. This can be done by rehearsing the challenging situations, along with the different behavioral choices, and pairing these choices with their long-term consequences. Our first goal is to "spit in the soup"—to make the problem behavior less appealing, because now it is more closely associated with an unwanted consequence. Our second goal is to "sweeten the pot"—to make the desired behavior more appealing, because now it is more closely associated with the wanted consequence.

With younger kids this rehearsal can be done with role-plays. With older kids (teens and preteens) it can be done with imaginal rehearsal. Either way, it is essential to have the child practice the behaviors, and to immediately follow this with the experience of the long-term consequences, so that the association of choices and consequences can be reinforced.

CHOICES HAVE CONSEQUENCES

"Choices Have Consequences" is an imaginal rehearsal intervention used with older kids (and sometimes their parents), to help them to get better at handling challenging situations the way they would like to. It occurs at the point in treatment where self-control skills training is called for. In the fairy tale model, that's after the case formulation, treatment contract, and case management has been taken care of. The child, and the caregivers, have already done their best to make things safe, supportive, and secure, and to reduce high-risk situations. Now it's time to manage those situations that cannot easily be avoided. As with any intervention, it should be directly tied to the child's stated goals.

The child's high-risk situations, or challenging situations, have already been identified on the "circles and arrows" page that includes the treatment plan. This gives the general idea, but to practice self-control skills, a specific situation/example has to be used. This can often be obtained just by asking the routine question at the beginning of the session: "Tell me something good and something bad that happened since we last met." Often, the child will report some event in which either she failed to exert self-control, or succeeded. Either way, that event can be used as the example. The therapist might say, "We've been talking about the things you wanted for yourself, how you want your life to go. You told me that if you keep on getting into fights, that could keep you from getting to your goals. Is this a good example of the kind of thing that can happen, that could get you into a fight?"

If such an example is not provided, the therapist can ask for one. "We've been talking about the things you wanted for yourself, how you want your life to go. You told me that if you keep on getting into fights, that could keep you from getting to your goals. When's the last time that something like that happened, when you did get into a fight?" If the child says, "Not for a long time," the therapist can say, "When's the last time that something happened that got you mad, where you could have gotten into a fight if you didn't control yourself?"

The goal here is to get a typical, everyday example of the challenging situation. We don't want to get some major trauma event here, nor do we want to get a minor event that might be too closely related to a major trauma. Using the personal trainer strategy, we want to add only a few pounds at a time. We don't want these examples to be overwhelming; we want the child to have a good chance of handling it, to be successful. Therefore, it's generally more effective to use examples related to peer provocation or to authority figures such as teachers; avoid examples tied to family, especially to parents.

Once the example situation has been identified, the therapist follows the structure of the circles and arrows diagram. The child is asked to imaginally view a "movie" including the following:

1. The provocation or challenging situation—a specific, concrete image of what is happening in a specific moment in time—the moment just before the choice is made.
2. The thoughts, feelings, and physical sensations that follow this. These are the signals that a choice is about to be made.
3. The "bad" (acting-out) behavioral choice.
4. The "bad ending" or negative consequence, paired with the words, "It's not worth it."

Then the child is asked to identify a coping strategy that would get him to the good ending instead of the bad one. "What could you do, in this situation, that would take you toward the good ending?" Many kids do know what to do here. However, if not, the therapist can always offer a "menu" of "what other kids have done" in this situation. Then the child is asked to imaginally view a movie similar to the first one, except that the good behavioral choice is made, leading to the good ending.

Finally, the child is told to start the movie the same way, but the ending will be determined by the behavioral choice: "Good choice goes to the good ending; bad choice goes to the bad ending." This "surprise ending" is repeated until the child chooses the good ending twice in a row.

Here is an example of how this intervention might be set up:

Choices Have Consequences Sample Script

THERAPIST: You told me last time that getting into fights was in your way, keeps you from getting what you want in your life. And you said that you get into fights when someone makes trouble for you, like when someone stares at you or says something disrespectful. Give me an example of when that's happened lately, even something little.

YOUTH: Well just this morning this kid got into my face. I was ready to whack him good.

THERAPIST: How come you didn't?

YOUTH: There was a teacher there, and I didn't really want to get in any more trouble.

THERAPIST: So what did you do? How did you control yourself?

YOUTH: I just tried to ignore him and concentrate on something else.

THERAPIST: So it sounds like you're doing things to get to that good ending we were talking about.

YOUTH: I guess so.

THERAPIST: Okay, good. I said I would give you some stuff you could practice to get stronger toward your goals. Today we're going to start on something to help you get even better at how you handled that thing this morning. I'm going to ask you to watch a little movie in your mind. It starts out with—what was this kid's name?

YOUTH: Jeff.

THERAPIST: When he was getting in your face, what was he doing? What did he say?

YOUTH: He was bragging, and then telling me I didn't know what I was talking about. But he was the one with no clue; he was just talking stupid.

THERAPIST: Okay. At the beginning of this movie, Jeff is in your face like he was this morning. The next thing in the movie is the signals inside, the thoughts and feelings. What was going on inside you?

YOUTH: Mad.

THERAPIST: How can you tell you're mad? What are the signals? What words are in your head? What's going on in your body?

YOUTH: My arms are tight, my hands are making fists, and no words really; my mind's kind of blank. And really mad. It builds up until I can't stand it sometimes.

THERAPIST: Okay. In this movie, it starts out with Jeff in your face. Then you notice yourself getting more and more mad. Then in this movie, you do the thing you might feel like doing—you whack him good. Then the ending of this movie is that bad ending you told me last time, with you behind bars saying, "It's not worth it." So start at the beginning, and when you get to that ending, tell me when you're done.

This is a real "workhorse" of self-control skills training and can be used with any number of challenging situations. A few of the following tips will help it to go smoothly and work well:

- It is essential to use a specific situation. If the therapist can't visualize it as if seeing it on TV, it's probably not specific enough yet. You need to know who's saying what, etc.
- This intervention is designed to change only the client's behavior. Only use this when the client's own coping behavior is identified as a problem to be improved.
- Before "running the movie," make sure that the statement "It's not worth it" feels true to the child, for the bad ending that's been selected. If not, extend the bad consequences farther into the future until "It's not worth it" does feel true. For example, the child may not feel bad about losing a privilege following some misbehavior; but he may indeed feel bad about where this habit might lead: to prison.
- The therapist should present a neutral response to the child's selected outcome. Many kids will experiment with the bad choice before ending up with the good one. The therapist shouldn't become excited either way. That way, the child is deciding for himself, and not to please the therapist.
- This is a rather quick intervention, with a very concrete focus. This is not the time or place to ask probing questions about feelings or to work for insight into the source of the problems. We already did that in the case formulation. Now we are focusing on practical coping skills. So don't go therapizing; just help your kid to get the job done.

The following two exercises will help you learn, step by step, how to set up and conduct the Choices Have Consequences intervention. The setup is the more complicated part. Once you become proficient, it only takes a few minutes, but getting used to it does take some practice.

EXERCISE: MAP OUT A PROBLEM

Pair up with a colleague (or try this with a friend or client). This is not a role-play. You will each be yourselves, and you will each get a turn as therapist and client. If you are working alone, complete the form for yourself. (Cynthia Cushman contributed to the development of representing problems with this type of graphic representation.)

If You Are the Therapist

This can be a challenging exercise because it requires skill and practice to get it right. You may have to say more than you see in the script to elicit all the details you need. Also, this exercise will probably be harder than actually doing the intervention with kids—it just tends to happen that way!

Here are some tips that will clarify what you're trying to get in each of the circles. Before you decide that you've finished the job, I suggest that you check back here and review these tips again. People often find that they need to do a few more things to make it right, and it's important to make it right.

- The *high-risk situation* is often, but not always, the same as the trigger situation that we have used in previous exercises. The high-risk situation is the moment in time just before the decision is made to either do the quick-relief behavior or the behavior that will lead to the good ending. For example, if the problem behavior is yelling at mother on the telephone, the high-risk situation is the specific thing that mother says, e.g., "You really should have come by last Sunday," just before your client is tempted to yell. If the desired behavior is going outside to take a walk, the high-risk situation is the moment that the client would be going outside, or might otherwise decide to sit down and read the paper. Get specific here, e.g., "In the kitchen, it's seven a.m., just finished my cup of coffee and put the empty cup in the sink."
- The *thoughts and feelings* and physical sensations are the *signals* that a choice is about to be made. These might be the same as some of the negative beliefs and piled-up feelings from the earlier exercises, but they might be different, too. The focus here is on the client's subjective experience in the moment. Your goal is to identify the thoughts, feelings, and sensations that push the client toward the quick-relief behavior.
- The *quick-relief behavior* is the behavior that your client is tempted to do instead of what he wishes he would do. This should be a specific action in the moment that the choice is made, not the whole series of steps that leads to the bad end.
- The *effective behavior* is the behavior that the client wants to do in that challenging situation to advance toward his goals. Again, it's not a whole series of behaviors, just one thing in that moment. The quick-relief behavior and the effective behavior should be mutually incompatible choices—the client must do one or the other. For example, do you yell, "Mom, would you please get off my case already?" or do you say, "Mom, I've got to go now. Talk to you soon"? Do you walk out the door to start on your walk, or do you pick up the newspaper? In these examples, one choice goes to the quick-relief circle, the other choice goes to the effective behavior circle.
- The *negative consequence* (the "bad ending" of the movie to come) should represent the worst-case scenario, the definitely unwanted extreme. Make sure that once your client describes the general situation, you ask the next question in the script and get a visual image that represents this. If you can't easily visualize it like you're watching it in a movie, it's probably not specific enough yet. The image should represent a moment in time when your client can see herself in an unwanted situation.

  Also, you want to make sure that "it's not worth it" feels true for the client. If that statement does not feel true, then have the client project the problem farther into the future, to a more extreme bad ending. Until "it's not worth it" feels true for the client, he has no reason to change his behavior.
- The *positive consequence* (the "good ending" of the movie to come) should represent the best-case scenario, the definitely wanted extreme. Make sure that once your client describes the general situation, you ask the next question in the script and get a visual image that represents this. If you can't easily visualize it like you're watching it in a movie, it's probably not specific enough yet. You can ask questions such as, "Where are you? What are you doing? What are you wearing? Who else is there?" and "What time is it?" You won't need to ask all questions to all clients; the point is to get an image that's specific.
- The *thoughts and feelings* circle is filled in with internal signals, the red flags that a choice is about to be made. Each of the other circles are filled in with a specific image. An image is specific when the therapist can easily visualize it as if watching it on TV. An image is specific when it includes a (day and) time, a place, and an action.

If You Are the Client

Think of a problem that you would like to work on right now. It must be a behavior that is, in theory, within your power to change. Here are some examples of behaviors that people often choose to work on for this exercise:

- Controlling an angry reaction
- Being more assertive in a certain type of situation
- Getting more exercise; controlling overeating
- Procrastinating less
- Getting certain chores done more efficiently
- Doing the things that are a higher priority in your life

EXERCISE: CHOICES HAVE CONSEQUENCES (GREENWALD, 2004)

This is a continuation of the setup that you did with Map Out a Problem. In an actual session the setup would only take a few minutes, and you'd just go right into this. If you are working with a partner, continue with that partner. If you are on your own, be your own therapist and take yourself through the client's experience.

If You Are the Therapist

You should be working from the already-completed Map Out a Problem form. Use the following script. Say the words in italics out loud; the rest are instructions for you.

If You Are the Client

Think of a problem behavior of your own that you would like to get better at doing in a more positive/constructive way. This can be an "acting-out" behavior such as losing temper, overeating, etc., or it can be a less visible problem behavior such as failing to be assertive, procrastinating, etc. Don't read the script—that's the therapist's job. Just be yourself and cooperate as best you can.

Script

Run the movie (in imagination, eyes open or closed); say, *"Now I want you to watch this in your mind like it's a movie. Start with [the provocation/situation], then notice [the thoughts and feelings], then [the bad behavior], then the bad ending with 'it's not worth it.' Start at the beginning, tell me when it's done. Ready?"* Then ask what happened; make sure it was run properly and ended with "it's not worth it."

Set up the good movie same way, using the challenging situation, the thoughts and feelings as signals, then with the good choice and good ending. *"This time the movie starts the same way, with [the situation] and [the thoughts and feelings]. This time, do what it takes to get to the good end. Start at the beginning; tell me when it's done. Ready?"*

Map Out a Problem—For Behaviors to Be Improved

1. So are you always doing this, or just in certain situations? Like what's a recent example, the last time that happened? Doesn't have to be anything big. (Or: When's the next time this could happen?)

2. When you're in this situation, what are the thoughts, the words in your head? Your emotional reaction? The signals in your body?

3. If you let this take you over, what do you do next? (This is, or leads to, the problem behavior.)

4. If the problem habit continues, gets even worse, how bad could things get? What picture could represent that? Does "it's not worth it" feel true? To go that way, I mean.

5. What if you got a handle on this, got it under control, what would you be doing instead (of the problem behavior)?

6. So if this effective behavior got to be a habit, what good things would that lead to? What picture could represent that?

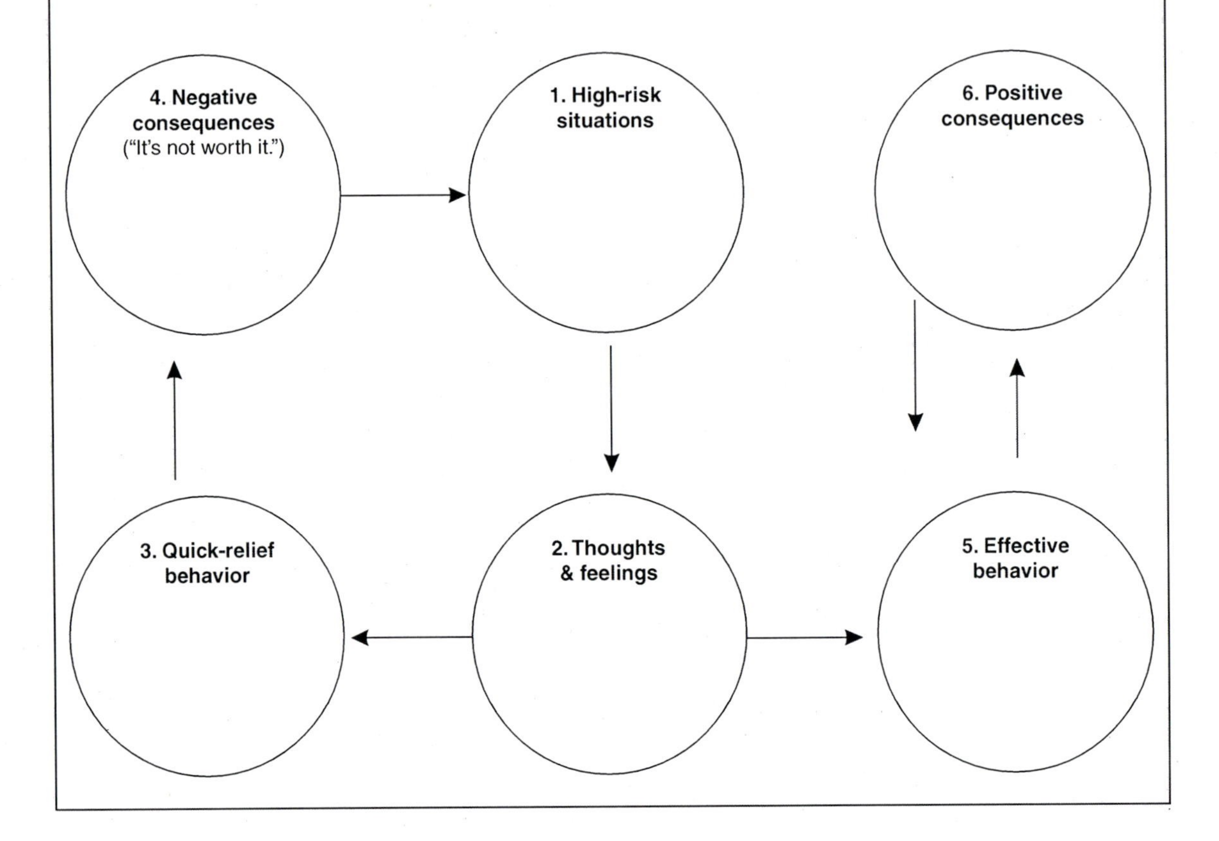

Run the movie; ask what happened; make sure it was run properly.

Set up the surprise ending the same way: bad choice, bad ending; good choice, good ending. *"This time, the movie starts the same way, with [the situation] and [the thoughts and feelings]. This time, I don't know what's going to happen; it depends on you. The rules are, 'Bad choice goes to bad ending and It's not worth it. Good choice goes to good ending.' Ready?"*

Run the movie; ask what happened; make sure it was run properly.

Repeat the surprise ending movie routine (the previous script) until the client chooses the positive end two times in a row. Every time, remind: *"Bad choice, bad ending; good choice, good ending."*

Repeat the entire routine with other challenging situations.

Follow-Up Questions

How did this go for the clients? What was your experience like? How did it go for the therapists? Raise your hand if, as the client, you are now less likely than before to handle this situation the way you want to? No more likely and no less likely? More likely than before?

Many people (not all) feel encouraged by this exercise, and believe that they are now more likely to handle the target situation the way they want to. This may be true, but ask your client (or yourself): How long did it take you to develop the habit you're trying to change now? How long do you think it might take to get the new habit? What does it take to get a new habit? Practice!

If you find that change is coming very slowly, that can still be counted as progress. Habits take time to change. But the more you practice, the more you'll get it.

Chapter 12

Getting Stronger

Getting stronger is an ongoing theme in this treatment approach, so this chapter could easily have come earlier. Getting-stronger interventions appear all along the way. For example, during the treatment planning conversation, the therapist might ask a younger child, "Do you think that when you get bigger and stronger, you'll be able to handle this stuff better?" When the child agrees (the common response), the therapist can say, "So one of our goals is to help you to get bigger and stronger." There are several advantages to focusing on getting stronger:

- It is consistent with the fairy tale model. It emphasizes empowerment and helps to justify a variety of treatment activities.
- It offers a normative and positive "spin" to the treatment: we are just trying to help you to get through this developmental challenge.
- It takes advantage of kids' natural desire to become bigger and stronger, and to show this to parents and others ("Look, Ma, no hands!").

A STRENGTH-BUILDING APPROACH

Getting stronger involves the ability to tolerate upsetting things (the technical term is "affect tolerance"). When kids can't stand the bad feeling even for a moment, they are likely to do just about anything to avoid it or get rid of it. This leads to pervasive avoidance, impulsive acting out, and other problems. When kids are better able to tolerate feeling bad for a little while, then they have a better chance of handling the situation the way they would like to.

Of course, success feeds on itself: as kids become more able to handle challenges the way they would like to, the stronger they feel. This paves the way for the next challenge. This is the "personal trainer" strategy in the fairy tale model. We give kids progressively greater challenges while also helping them learn to manage each challenge as it comes. Eventually, the child will be ready to slay the dragon.

Several principles guide the strength-building approach:

1. Focus on the natural desire to become bigger and stronger.
2. Offer challenges: can you do this?
3. Build on strengths and successes.
4. Take one step at a time.
5. Downplay expectations to preclude sense of failure:
   - Poor/limited performance was expected.
   - Good performance surpasses expectation.

With Older Kids

So for example, immediately following Choices Have Consequences (the self-control training activity described in the previous chapter) the therapist might downplay expectations as follows.

THERAPIST: It seems like you have this down, you know what to do now in that situation?

CLIENT: Yup, I've got it.

THERAPIST: So how long did it take you to get that bad habit that you're trying to change now?

CLIENT: I don't know, years I guess.

THERAPIST: So how long do you think it'll take to change to the new habit you've been practicing?

CLIENT: I don't know.

THERAPIST: You think it'll happen overnight? Or you think it might take a lot of practice over time?

CLIENT: Practice.

THERAPIST: I think so too. So don't worry if you're not perfect all of a sudden. But the more you remember to practice this, the sooner you'll get the new habit down.

Following this conversation, it is very hard for the client to fail. If he comes back the next week with no progress, the therapist can say that this was expected. Usually at least some progress is noticeable, though. For example, if the problem behavior is still happening sometimes but not as often, the therapist can again say that this was expected and that the progress is encouraging. If, as sometimes happens, the problem behavior has not recurred despite repeated opportunity, the therapist can say, "Well, it wasn't supposed to happen that fast. I'm glad to hear that you did so well this week, but I'm not sure it's a habit yet. If things don't go perfect next week, that just means that it takes a long time to make a new habit." This way the client gets credit for outperforming expectations, and if he backslides, it's still not a failure, only par for the course.

With Younger Kids

The specifics of the strength-building approach are different with younger kids. With younger kids, the therapist can encourage the confusion of physical and inner strength, which children seem to readily accept. Then the child's sense of physical strength can give her the confidence to face difficult emotional material. This is done as follows:

1. Discuss what she or he does to get stronger, e.g., walking, sports, eating well, sleeping, etc.
2. Imaginally rehearse "I'm getting stronger" while doing these activities; end with strength image.
3. Have the child perform exercises, e.g., push-ups. Keep a count. It'll be higher next time!
4. After the exercise, say, "I wonder if you're strong enough to . . ."
    - Act like a good sport if I beat you at this game.
    - Talk about the bad thing for three minutes.

Here is an example of how the therapist might work this theme with a child.

THERAPIST: We were talking about you getting stronger. How strong are you? Make a muscle, let me see.

CHILD: (makes a muscle)

THERAPIST: Oh, you're already pretty strong. How many push-ups can you do?

CHILD: Maybe five.

THERAPIST: Let's see. Go ahead.

CHILD: (does eight push-ups while therapist counts out loud)

THERAPIST: Eight, that's pretty good! What kinds of things do you do to make yourself strong?

CHILD: I don't lift weights or anything.

THERAPIST: Do you only eat potato chips all day, or do you eat good meals?

CHILD: I get potato chips sometimes, but I have to eat the regular meal first.

THERAPIST: Well, eating nutritious food helps you grow and get stronger. Do you stay up all night long, or do you go to bed and get some sleep?

CHILD: I go to bed at nine o'clock; that's my bedtime.

THERAPIST: Good; sleeping helps you grow and get stronger too. Does someone pick you up and carry you around everywhere you go, or do you walk around with your own feet?

CHILD: I walk! I walk to school and to the store.

THERAPIST: Well, exercise makes you get stronger. Do you ride a bike, or get any other exercise?

CHILD: I ride bikes with my friend, I play tag at recess, and play some basketball in the park.

THERAPIST: Good, so you do a lot of things to make yourself strong. No wonder you can already do so many push-ups. The more exercise you get, the stronger you get. When you think of yourself getting stronger, what is the picture you have?

CHILD: Me lifting up a house.

THERAPIST: I'm going to ask you to do two things at once; see if you can do it. Think of yourself lifting up a house. You have the picture now? Good. Think of that picture, and take a really slow, deep breath. Was that easy, or hard?

CHILD: Easy.

THERAPIST: Well, let me try to make it even harder. Think of that picture again, of lifting up a house, and say to yourself, "I'm getting stronger," and take another slow, deep breath. How did that go? Were you able to concentrate on all that?

CHILD: Yes.

THERAPIST: Wow, you did that too! No matter how hard I make it, you can do it. What were those things you do to make yourself stronger?

CHILD: Eating, riding my bike, playing basketball.

THERAPIST: Okay, think of those things now, and say to yourself, "I'm getting stronger." Deep breath. Okay. Now say that again, out loud: "I'm getting stronger."

CHILD: I'm getting stronger.

It is important to mix imagery and statements about getting stronger with actual proof of this. The direct experience of getting stronger makes the statement credible. Thus the push-ups. Jumping jacks also work, or sit-ups, or how fast the child can make it from here to that tree. The point is for the child to feel, and show off, how strong she is. Then we can build on this strength to help the child to face the next challenge. For example:

THERAPIST: It sounds like those kids are still picking on you. But I'm glad to hear how well you did in school this week. You remember what you and your dad said, that you come here because you want to do things to get better at getting along with other kids.

CHILD: Can we play now? (holds up a board game)

THERAPIST: Yes, I'll play this game with you. But first, I want to check on something. Last week you did eight push-ups. Can I see how many you can do today?

CHILD: (does ten)

THERAPIST: Ten! Well, it looks like you're getting stronger.

CHILD: I am getting stronger. I ate my vegetables every day at dinner; my dad says they give me vitamins. And I race my dad to the car and I can beat him sometimes.

THERAPIST: Last week when we played this game, do you remember what happened when I got ahead?

CHILD: Huh?

THERAPIST: Last week, when I got ahead you didn't like it, and you started taking extra turns to make sure that you would win.

CHILD: Oh, yeah.

THERAPIST: But remember what you told me? How other kids wouldn't want to play with a bad sport?

CHILD: Kids like to play with someone who follows the rules, who takes their turn.

THERAPIST: I think that's true. And I see that you're getting stronger. So here's my question for you: Are you strong enough now that if I get ahead in this game, you can handle it and be a good sport?

CHILD: I think so.

Later in treatment, the challenge is to get the child to be willing to face the trauma memories. This tends to be a greater challenge with older kids, who may be less "compliant," and with kids

who have poor affect tolerance. Persuading kids to take the next step can be especially challenging when, paradoxically, the other phases of treatment have been successful. In that case, the child may doing pretty well by now. So why bring that bad stuff up?

If you have been using the circles and arrows diagram and the treatment plan with the different steps, then "reducing stress from old memories" will sooner or later be the next task on the list. Even some kids who have been going along with the program until now are reluctant to face the trauma memories. So it's worthwhile to make an extra pitch at this point, going back to the diagram and reminding the child of how this work can help her get to her goals. Again, working the strength-building theme can be useful. Here's a typical conversation to get a kid to agree to try the trauma resolution work, including a sports metaphor that can be helpful.

THERAPIST: Okay, so the next thing on the list is to go after those old memories, to bring down the stress from those, so that you don't react so strong to the high-risk situations anymore.

CLIENT: I don't think I really need to do that. I'm doing pretty good now. And I don't want to talk about that stuff anyway.

THERAPIST: So let me ask you something. Say you're on the basketball team and your coach wants everyone to come to the practices. Are you going to say, "I don't need to come to the practices. Maybe if we start losing games I'll come." Or are you going to go to the practices?

CLIENT: Go to the practices.

THERAPIST: How come?

CLIENT: Gotta do what he says to stay on the team. Also, practice makes perfect, the more we practice, the more we're gonna win.

THERAPIST: I thought you'd say that, because you've been showing me with all the practice you've been doing here, and with how much better you're handling things. So now, say you're winning all your games, and then your coach says, "I want you to start coming early to practice, to do all these extra exercises." And you say, "What for? We're already winning all our games?" And the coach says, "Yeah, but so are the other teams that we're gonna face in the play-offs!" So do you do the extra exercises, or do you say no?

CLIENT: I guess I'll do them. I want to win the play-offs too.

THERAPIST: Well, this is why I'm suggesting that you work with me on the old memories. Because you've told me that you want to be successful tomorrow too, and not just today; because you have a lot of plans for yourself. Let me tell you what I've seen happen to other kids. I've seen a lot of kids who got better at self-control, things were going pretty well, and they said they didn't want to work on the old memories. So they did fine for a while, maybe a month or two, maybe a year or two. They were handling all the regular high-risk situations fine. But then some big problem comes along, maybe they lose a girlfriend they really care about, or someone in their family dies, some big stress. And that's too much for them, and they go downhill again. So that's why I'm suggesting that you take care of this stuff now, while you're doing well, while you're strong already. So you can get even stronger and be able to handle the really hard stuff whenever it comes.

CLIENT: Okay, I guess I'll give it a try.

THERAPIST: When you've done this, I think you'll be glad. Other kids that have done this, they've told me afterwards that things don't get to them as much as they used to, like they don't get so mad anymore. But it's the same rules as always. So if we're talking about something and you don't want to anymore, you can always say that it's time to stop.

RISKS OF STRENGTH BUILDING

With the personal trainer strategy, we are always pushing kids to do their best, to take the next step, the next challenge. Hopefully we are also providing adequate support so that when kids agree to take these steps, they will be successful. However, despite our best efforts, there is plenty of room for things to go wrong. Sometimes kids will refuse to take the next step; sometimes they will take that step, but it will be too much for them to handle. So we want to be prepared for the problems so that we can handle them successfully when they come.

One common challenge occurs when the child says that she is discouraged, tired, or "doesn't care" about this work. It's the therapist's job, on one hand, to encourage the child—without being pushy—and on the other, to allow her to make her own decisions. This is best done by focusing the child on her own goals, her own reasons for doing the work, so that the issue does not become a confrontation between the child and the therapist. Then the therapist can maintain the position of ally, regardless of the child's choice in a given session. Here are the steps in this approach:

1. After the beginning-of-the-session check-in, the therapist can remind the child of her stated goals. Then the task is being introduced in service of the child's goals. "We were talking before about the things you wanted for yourself, and what you could do to help you achieve your goals. Last time we talked about avoiding high risk, so today we were going to work on self-control skills."
2. Then if the child declines to participate in the planned task, the therapist can accept this and move on, keeping the focus on the child. "Usually you work hard with me, so I'm wondering what's different today. Maybe you're tired? Or there's something else on your mind that makes it hard to concentrate?"

The other common challenge occurs when the child overexposes to upsetting material. We are most focused on this risk when we get to the trauma resolution work, but it can happen at any point along the way. Here are points of particular risk for this:

- Answering the question about three wishes or the magic wand
- Answering the question about who is in the family
- Answering the question about something good and something bad that happened since the prior meeting
- Answering the question about trauma/loss history
- Talking about (and visualizing) good ending to the "future movie" (this challenges the avoidance strategy of not getting one's hopes up)
- Talking about (and visualizing) the bad endings to the "future movie"
- Talking about (and visualizing) the bad ending to the "choices have consequences" movie
- Talking about any current concern (e.g., peer conflict, love problems, the health of a family member)
- Talking about an upsetting memory

How can you tell if the child has gone too far for comfort? There are a number of signals, and it's important to be alert to these. If you fail to catch this, it will probably keep going, maybe get worse, until you do finally figure out what's going on. Here are some of the ways that kids can let you know that they're in over their heads:

- Saying, "I don't want to talk about this anymore"
- Crying
- Changing the subject

- Overtalking about a tangential detail, or about something else altogether
- Fidgeting, moving around, finding things in your office to mess with
- Humor or other "incongruent" emotion that does not fit the content of what's being talked about
- Getting angry
- Silence
- Looking down or away
- Suddenly being done with the session, even though it wasn't time to be done

ADDRESSING THE PROBLEM

So you're noticing that something might be wrong. What to do about it?

The first thing is to make sure you are correct about what you think is happening. This is done simply enough by asking. However, you want to avoid asking in a way that is intrusive or that further opens the wound. The wrong way to ask: "I notice that you're having some trouble talking about this. What's the worst thing about it?" Here's a better approach that will get you your answer while feeling respectful and supportive to the child: "I notice that you're looking down at the ground and not saying anything. Are you just trying to think of what to say next? Or is it getting to be hard to talk about?"

Sometimes you can problem solve and help the child to keep on going. This does not necessarily mean just giving a pep talk (although sometimes it may). It means really figuring out what's going on and trying to solve the problem. Only then might you make a decision, together, that it's okay to push on. Some problem-solving strategies:

1. If the child says that it is hard: "You told me that you really cared about your goals. Now that I see you doing the work, sticking with it when it gets hard, I am taking you more seriously."
2. If the child says that it's too boring:
   - Consider that the child might be feeling overwhelmed, and trying to manage this by feeling less, or trying to avoid continuing. The child may also be angry about being in this position. The child may also simply be bored.
   - For self-control skills training: "Good, this is what we want. We want you to practice so much that it's like instinct. Because in the moment, you might not have a lot of time to think. The more you practice, the better chance you have of being ready."
   - For talking about the trauma/loss memory: "Good, this is what we want. The more boring it is, the less it can hurt you. Let's do it [tell the story] again!"
3. If, despite the therapist's attempts, the child still says that he's had enough: The therapist accepts this and moves on to the next part of the session, containment procedures.

CONTAINMENT PROCEDURES

A number of interventions can be used to help the child "put the bad stuff away" and regain composure:

- Say that the hard part is over now.
- Have the child visualize putting the bad memory in a secure container (script for this in Chapter 14).
- Teach deep breathing (script for this in Chapter 1).
- Teach "safe place" (script follows).

- Put toys/materials away.
- Talk about plans for improved behavior (including utilization of coping skills).
- Talk about plans for later in the day or for the weekend.

When we ask about trauma/loss history, we do some of this in a planned, systematic way: we follow with deep breathing, then talking about the best things that ever happened. In practice, we should be doing these things in a systematic way at the end of every session. Even sessions that don't seem "heavy" or intense may still be different from the rest of the child's day. You may be the only person with whom he feels so safe and comfortable, the only person to whom he shows a certain side of himself. So every session should have some kind of ending routine that helps the child put the session away, regain composure, and reorient to what's next for him.

After a particularly challenging or emotional session, some of the extra containment/relaxation interventions should be used, as a lead-up to the usual ending routine. One such intervention is the Safe Place guided visualization.

EXERCISE: SAFE PLACE

In pairs, take turns leading one another through the Safe Place visualization. When one person has done it, switch roles and do it again.

If You Are the Therapist

Use the following script. Say aloud the parts in italics. The rest is to guide you. Only use the prompts if you need them. If you are already getting a good answer, accept it and move on. This is a conversation, so once you've said something, wait for a response before you move on.

If You Are the Client

Be yourself and cooperate.

Safe Place Script

Think of a place where you feel good, safe, relaxed, where nothing bad can happen. (Prompt: Could be a place you know, a place from a long time ago, a place you make up; maybe from when you were a kid, being with a certain person, or in a certain room or house.)

Got it? What is it?

So get a picture in your mind, who's there, what it looks like, how you feel to be there . . .

What kind of feeling goes with that? Where (in your body) do you feel it?

Would it feel true to say, "I'm safe," or "I'm okay," or what would be the right words (to go with this picture)?

Now I want you to concentrate on the picture, what you're saying to yourself, the feelings. . . . Concentrate, and take a couple of slow, deep breaths.

Discussion

Clients share your experiences. Therapists share your experiences.

Problem Solving the Safe Place Intervention

The Safe Place is a popular visualization for calming and self-soothing. It can be used in session to help calm down, and it can be practiced elsewhere as well. Most kids (and adults) can learn it easily, and they like it. Sometimes kids will teach other kids how to do it too. However, the Safe Place has a couple of tricky aspects, things that can go wrong and need to be caught and corrected.

Occasionally, the child can't come up with a safe place. An alternative is to think of an activity that feels good, comfortable. Clients have chosen a range of activities, from roller skating to making a cup of coffee in the morning. The goal is to find a visualization that feels good, comfortable, relaxing, safe.

A more common problem is that the safe place isn't so safe after all. Supposing that one of the child's problems is that he gets bullied, and the safe place he picks is playing football in the park. When he starts concentrating on the safe place image, what do you think is going to happen? Sooner or later, the bully will show up. Then the safe place is spoiled. A similar situation can occur with abused kids who choose their home or bedroom as the safe place.

The safe place is no use if it's not really safe and spoil proof. This is why the therapist must ask what the safe place is. Then use your own judgment—asking more questions if necessary—to determine whether this safe place is really good enough. If not, then it's okay to say, "I don't think this one will work for what we're doing. Can you think of another one?"

A final point: when we are helping people to calm down, put the hard stuff aside, and regain composure, how do we know when it's finished? We know by asking, and by observing. Don't ask the client to concentrate on the upsetting situation again; that will just bring it back. You can ask, "Where are you now on zero to ten?" If you observe continued signs of distress, that's an answer, too. The goal is not merely to go through the motions, but to make sure that your clients leave the session in good shape. This will help them feel that they are on a good track in their work with you, and they will be ready to try again next time.

SECTION III BIBLIOGRAPHY

Child Welfare League of America. (2004, February). *Creating parenting rich communities.* Available online at <http://www.cwla.org/programs/r2p/biblioparenting.pdf>. Annotated bibliography including general parenting research and parent training research and information.

Kazdin, A. E. (1987). Treatment of antisocial behavior in children: Current status and future directions. *Psychological Bulletin, 102,* 187-203. Review of the literature on training in self-management skills for kids with problem behaviors.

SECTION IV: TRAUMA RESOLUTION

The goals and tasks of the trauma resolution phase of treatment include the following:

- Select an order for memories to be addressed.
- Identify upsetting elements of the trauma memory.
- Face and master the upsetting elements of the memory.
- Repeat with other trauma/loss memories.
- Identify trauma-related triggers—reminders that trigger a trauma-related reaction.
- Face and master the triggers.

One way of describing the goal of trauma resolution is that after successful resolution, the child will say, "That was bad, but it's over, and things are okay now." Therefore, it's very important that things *are* okay now, or as close to that as possible, before attempting trauma resolution. Another way of stating this is that the child must have reason to believe that he is no longer in the "war zone" if he is to relinquish survival-mode as a primary orientation. Therefore trauma resolution should not be attempted until the following has occurred:

- The most significant case management tasks have been implemented.
- The parents are doing their part to help the child to feel more safe, secure, and supported.
- The child has developed adequate self-management skills to be prepared to handle the potentially highly challenging trauma material.

There may or may not be a clear line between the previous phase of treatment and this one. Many of the same methods may be used. For example, following the check-in at the beginning of the session, the therapist may ask for a demonstration of strength ("I want to see how strong you are. How many jumping jacks do you think you can do today?") and then say, "Do you think you're strong enough now to talk about the car accident for two minutes?" Or the exposure methods (that will be described in the following text) may first be applied, as a sort of trial run, with the recent upsetting event (e.g., getting in trouble that day in school) that the child may have reported. Thus, the child will feel that her continuing progress in becoming stronger and more competent allows her to master progressively greater challenges.

When you hear people talk about "trauma treatment" or "trauma work," they are usually referring to the trauma resolution portion of the trauma-informed treatment approach. Of course, you wouldn't want to try trauma resolution until you've done all the other stuff to get ready for it. There are a number of trauma resolution methods available, which will be reviewed in the following text. Then one method—exposure—will be presented in much more detail in the following chapters.

Chapter 13

Trauma Resolution Methods

Quite a bit of controlled research has been conducted on the various methods of helping kids to work their trauma memories through to resolution. The clear result is that not all methods are equal. Some tend to be slow and haphazard whereas others work relatively quickly and thoroughly. The big dividing line is between the so-called "traditional" child therapy methods such as play, art, and talk, and the so-called "structured, focused" trauma resolution methods such as prolonged exposure (PE) (Foa & Rothbaum, 1997), cognitive processing therapy (CPT) (Resick & Schnicke, 1993), and eye movement desensitization and reprocessing (EMDR) (Shapiro, 2001). The structured, focused treatments win hands down (Chemtob & Taylor, 2002). They are faster—often by months or even years—and more effective.

The mental health field has an odd and untenable tradition of being practitioner centered rather than client centered. It is not unusual to hear a therapist say, "I'm a play therapist" or "I'm a family therapist," or "I use a psychodynamic approach." However, in my opinion this is inappropriate when it is a rigid position, and it represents a serious problem with the field. Would you want to go to a physician who only prescribes certain treatments and not others, regardless of what might be proven effective, or what might be best for you? Therapists should be saying—as some do—"I work with children with problem behaviors," or "I work with kids with anxiety problems." Therapists should not merely use their own favorite methods and hope that their clients will happen to be a good match for the methods; therapists should use whatever works best to help our clients. This does not mean that we cannot have a primary orientation or way of understanding our work. However, it does mean that we should not eschew tools that may be helpful to our clients, unless we have something truly equivalent to offer.

You need a good sword to slay a dragon. Given our current knowledge, it is no longer ethical to attempt trauma resolution with an unstructured approach. That's like trying to slay the dragon with a stick. It's just not fair to the client, because it doesn't get the job done. This does not mean that we cannot use play, art, and talk modalities with children. However, for trauma resolution, these methods should be used in a carefully structured and focused way (as discussed in the following text).

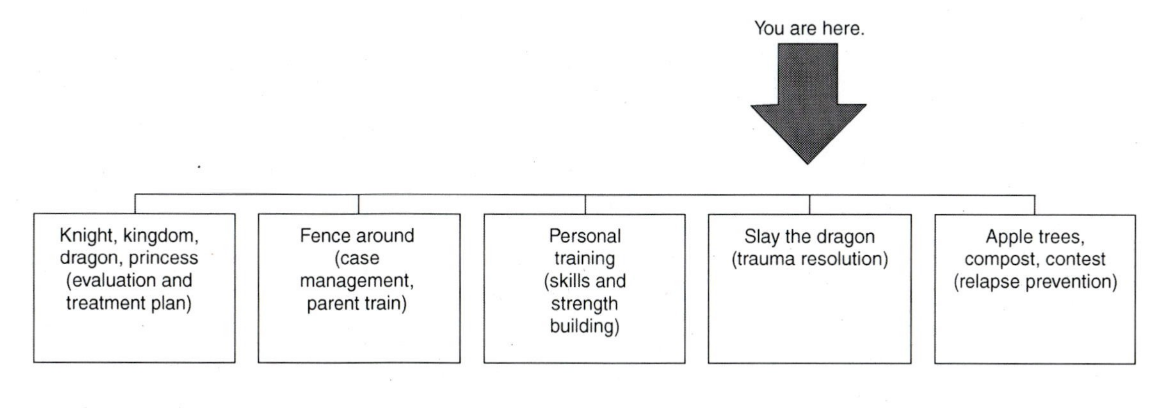

FIGURE 13.1. Steps in the fairy tale model.

Choosing which structured, focused trauma resolution method to use is another question. Several methods have proved effective, and as yet there is no method of choice, no clear front-runner. The two major trauma resolution methods, and a couple of others, are described and reviewed following. This chapter has more of a scholarly focus than the others, because selection of a trauma resolution method should be based on actual evidence of effectiveness, efficiency, and acceptability to clients.

First, the structured focused methods all benefit from the preparatory work that has been detailed previously in this book. Some of the trauma resolution methods explicitly include some of the preparatory steps, but that is not the focus of this chapter. No matter which trauma resolution method you use, you should still do all the other steps presented in this book, including the preparation as well as the follow-up. The focus here is on what distinguishes the methods from one another during the trauma resolution phase of treatment.

EXPOSURE

Exposure is a long-established method that has many years of study supporting its efficacy. Although there are a number of variants of exposure, the core of this method involves having the client tell the trauma story in detail, over and over again. "Start at the beginning, talk in the present tense as if it's happening right now, and along with each thing that happens, say what you're thinking and what you're feeling. Then when you get to the end, we'll do it again. And again. And again." Many of the exposure variants involve homework as well, for example, listening each day to the cassette tape recording of the story told in the exposure session, or writing down the whole story again each day.

One of the theories about why exposure works focuses on the "information processing" aspect (Foa, Steketee, & Olasov, 1989). This model articulates the processes underlying what I have referred to eariler as "digesting" the trauma memory.

Another theory about why exposure works involves habituation, or desensitization. The idea is that somehow by facing the trauma memory over and over again, it gradually loses its sting. This theory underlies a key component of the exposure approach, which is to guide the client to face the memory for a prolonged period. By facing the memory, avoidance is prevented, so that a new lesson can be learned. Remember that as long as the memory is being avoided, the avoidance is being reinforced and the memory keeps its threatening aura. However, when the memory can be faced while in a safe environment, the client has a chance to learn that the memory is no longer dangerous. Habituation/desensitization and avoidance prevention are the main principles guiding the structure of the exposure treatment approach.

The idea of "getting back on the horse that threw you" shows that we have a commonsense understanding of the problems associated with avoidance. We know that if you are thrown by a horse and then don't get back on soon, you are likely to continue to be afraid of riding. On the other hand, if you get back on the horse again and have more good experiences riding, the bad experience will be put in perspective and won't have the power to limit your activities.

Exposure works when it lasts long enough. If the client only faces the memory for a minute, gets anxious and upset, and then stops, the avoidance is reinforced by the relief of not thinking about the memory anymore. He got off the horse before the horse even took a step. The problem is that people want to avoid these trauma memories for a good reason: because facing the memory is so uncomfortable and hard to tolerate. It's important to find a way to help the client tolerate the memory long enough to get past the avoidance, to the new lesson.

Some exposure principles and strategies are nicely exemplified in "in vivo exposure," in which the client faces the feared thing "in life" rather than in imagination only. The following is an example case study.

Jamie

Jamie is a nine-year-old boy who has been bitten by a dog. Every time he even thinks about dogs, he becomes anxious. He now refuses to go near any dog, even his cousin's dog with whom he used to always like to play.

The therapist asks Jamie to list all the dog-related things that can make him anxious or fearful—everything from being near a big, scary dog, to seeing a picture of a dog. Then Jamie is asked to rate on zero to ten how much it bothers him to imagine each of the items. Then the list is ordered from least distressing to most. His list looks like this:

Seeing a picture of a puppy (1)
Seeing a picture of a scary dog (3)
Seeing the cute dog behind the window at the pet store (4)
My cousin's dog on a leash (4)
Playing with my cousin's dog (6)
A scary dog on a leash (8)
A scary dog not on a leash (10)

The therapist has Jamie practice various coping skills such as have been described in previous chapters. Jamie learns to distinguish between his body's "danger signals" (e.g., rapid heartbeat) and actual danger. He learns to calm himself with deep breathing, thinking about something that makes him feel safe (being tucked in at night by his mother), and telling himself, "I'm safe."

Next, they work with the first item on the list. The therapist shows Jamie a picture of a puppy. The goal is for Jamie to use his coping skills as needed, in order to keep on looking at the picture until it doesn't bother him anymore. This takes about ten minutes. He is able to look at it, touch it, etc., while reporting that it's a zero and doesn't upset him at all.

The next challenge is to do the same thing with the picture of the scary dog. This time Jamie's imagination starts to run, his heart starts to pound, and he says, "Can't we do this some other day?" The therapist reminds him that quitting now will only reinforce the avoidance and give the fear more power. The therapist also prompts him to be resourceful, by saying, "What can you tell yourself?" Jamie says, "It's only a picture; it can't hurt me." Jamie does stick with it, and after about fifteen minutes of staring at the picture and making himself feel calm, he is just as comfortable with this picture as with the other one.

This is how the in vivo exposure works. At each step, Jamie faces the thing that he is afraid of. He does not stop too soon, because that would only reinforce the avoidance (by giving him relief). Instead, he uses his coping skills to stick with it. Finally, in each case, he learns that the feared thing is not actually dangerous, and he doesn't have to be afraid anymore. Of course, this only applies to things that are actually safe. The therapist does not send him to face a scary dog that is unleashed!

In vivo exposure works. However, the therapist must be aware of several potential pitfalls, as follows:

- It's important to prepare the client properly in terms of motivation, coping skills, and understanding the rationale and method of the treatment itself. Otherwise, the risk is greater that the client will quit part way through an in vivo exposure session. This just reinforces the avoidance and doesn't help the client.
- It's important to start small and progress gradually. If you start with too great a challenge (an item with a high distress rating) or make too great a leap in distress level from one item to the next, it might be too overwhelming; the coping skills may not be adequate. Then the

client is more likely to quit before having achieved the elimination of the distress, and this, again, reinforces the avoidance.
- It's very important that the client not be bitten by the dog! Then the client would learn that he was right to be afraid. This reinforces the avoidance too!

Imaginal exposure is similar to in vivo exposure in many ways. Imaginal exposure is done in the therapist's office, using imagination and memory, rather than facing the actual "thing" such as a picture of a dog, or the dog itself. However, many of the principles are the same. The client is encouraged to use coping skills in tolerating the feared memory. The client is encouraged to not give in to the urge for avoidance, but to stick with the memory until it doesn't bother him anymore. The therapist's job is to prepare, guide, support, and monitor the client so that he can use his coping skills effectively and handle the memory, so that he does not become overwhelmed, or "bitten by the dog." This imaginal exposure method will be described in detail in the following chapters. It is primarily appropriate for adolescents (and adults).

For younger children, the structured, focused trauma resolution methods must often be modified in ways that incorporate other child therapy techniques. For example, play therapy can be used in a structured, focused way to assist in trauma resolution (Gil, 1991; James, 1989). When imaginal exposure is used with younger children, it may entail creating a "book" with the child, using pictures and words to tell (and retell, work through) the story of the trauma memory (Deblinger & Heflin, 1996). The research on this modified exposure for kids shows that it works pretty well, especially when the other treatment components (parent training, self-management skills, etc.) are included (Cohen, Berliner, & March, 2000). These modifications will also be described in the following chapters.

EMDR

The other leading trauma resolution method is eye movement desensitization and reprocessing (EMDR). EMDR will be discussed in some detail here, because it will not be taught in this book, and because knowledge of this method is important. EMDR began in 1987, when a psychology graduate student named Francine Shapiro noticed that her own upsetting thoughts faded when her eyes spontaneously moved rapidly from side to side. Over the next several years, she and her colleagues developed and refined this discovery into a systematic therapeutic approach.

EMDR is a complex method that combines elements of behavioral and client-centered approaches. To oversimplify, the client is asked to concentrate intensely on the most distressing segment of a traumatic memory while moving the eyes rapidly from side to side (by following the therapist's fingers moving across the visual field). Following the initial focus on the memory segment, after each *set* of eye movements (of about thirty seconds), the client is asked to report anything that "came up," whether an image, thought, emotion, or physical sensation (all are common). The focus of the next set is determined by the client's changing status. For example, if the client reports, "Now I'm feeling more anger," the therapist may suggest concentrating on the anger in the next set. The procedure is repeated until the client reports no further distress and can fully embrace a positive perspective. Shapiro (1995, 2001) has presented this method in detail. Similar to other methods, EMDR can be modified in various ways to work with children at different developmental levels (Greenwald, 1999).

Shapiro has proposed an information processing model as the theoretical basis for EMDR. Others (Hyer & Brandsma, 1997; Sweet, 1995) have pointed out that the components of EMDR are very similar to the components of other structured focused trauma treatments, suggesting that the effective methods may share common factors underlying their effect. The debate about whether the eye movements actually contribute to treatment effect is far from settled; but available data suggest that they do (e.g., van den Hout, Muris, Salemink, & Kindt, 2001). Other than the eye movements, EMDR is very different from exposure because the client is not required to stay with the upsetting part of the memory for an extended period. In fact, free association is encouraged, and (within limits set by the therapist) clients will go wherever their mind takes them. If exposure works by preventing avoidance, then EMDR works in some different way (see Rogers & Silver, 2002; Smyth & Poole, 2002). If exposure works because of information processing, then it's possible that exposure and EMDR share the mechanism of effect, even if this mechanism is activated differently in the different treatments.

A review of randomized treatment studies, published as part of the International Society for Traumatic Stress Studies' Treatment Guidelines, found EMDR to be an empirically supported efficacious trauma treatment (Chemtob, Tolin, van der Kolk, & Pitman, 2000), with the reservation that EMDR had not yet been directly compared to other validated focused PTSD treatments such as prolonged exposure. Since the publication of that review, several studies meeting most of Foa & Meadows' (1997) "gold standard" criteria have directly compared EMDR to validated cognitive-behavioral therapy (CBT) treatments (including an exposure component) for PTSD. Findings across studies indicate that both treatments were, in general, comparably efficacious (Ironson, Freund, Strauss, & Williams, 2002; Lee, Gavriel, Drummond, Richards, & Greenwald, 2002; Power et al., 2002; Taylor et al., 2003). One study (Taylor et al., 2003) found a greater effect for prolonged exposure; the others slightly favored EMDR. Two of the studies (Ironson et al., 2002; Power et al., 2002) suggested that the therapeutic effect may have occurred more quickly for EMDR than for CBT. One study (Ironson et al., 2002) found that the level of distress both during and between sessions was lower for EMDR; this study also found a lower dropout rate in the EMDR group.

A recent meta-analysis that used a "change per therapy hour" statistic found that, in controlled comparison studies, EMDR was consistently more efficient than CBT (Rogers & Silver, 2003). These findings suggest that EMDR may be at least equal to other CBT approaches in efficacy and acceptability while being more efficient, in that with EMDR, much less homework is required, and the treatment effect may be achieved in fewer sessions.

Less research on EMDR has occurred for children and adolescents as compared to adults, but several controlled studies of varying quality testing EMDR for kids have been reported. Puffer, Greenwald, and Elrod (1998) reported on a wait-list design study of twenty children and adolescents who were assigned according to convenience of scheduling to EMDR treatment or delayed treatment groups. Treatment was a single session; the focus was a single trauma or loss. The first author conducted all treatment and assessment, using several measures, at pre, post, and 1-2 m follow-up. No change occurred during the 1 m no-treatment delay, and significant improvement was recorded between the first and last scores on all measures. On the best measure of trauma symptoms (Impact of Events Scale), of the seventeen participants starting in the clinical range, eleven moved to normal levels, and three others dropped twelve or more points, while the other three stayed the same. Problematic design features include lack of randomization, lack of independent assessment (although no subjective scoring was involved), and use of a therapist with only partial EMDR training. Also, three participants had ongoing sources of distress, making recovery unlikely. Still, the results were quite positive, although somewhat more variable than in other studies.

Several studies have compared EMDR to "standard care" or to a nonspecific treatment. For example, Soberman, Greenwald, and Rule (2002) compared standard care plus three sessions of EMDR to standard care for twenty-nine boys ages ten to sixteen with serious conduct problems who were either in residential or day treatment care. They found that EMDR led to significant reductions in both reactivity to the targeted memories and severity of the primary identified problem behaviors. Limitations include use of a single therapist and lack of independent assessment.

Scheck, Schaeffer, and Gillette (1998) compared two sessions of EMDR with two sessions of active listening (AL), treating sixty females between the ages of sixteen and twenty-four, who were actively pursuing high-risk behaviors (substance abuse, unsafe sex, criminal acts, suicide attempts, etc.) and who had histories of trauma. This study included random assignment, twenty-four well-trained therapists, independent blind assessment, and multiple standardized measures. Although both groups improved posttreatment, EMDR outperformed AL on all five measures, with significant differences on four of the five. The EMDR group's posttreatment gains were also clinically significant, with mean scores falling within one standard deviation of the nonclinical norms on all measures, whereas for the AL group, only one of the measures was in the normal range. Two measures readministered at ninety-day follow-up showed maintenance of gains for the EMDR group. This study found no differences in the responses of the young adults compared to the older adolescents (J. Schaeffer, personal communication, November 1996), in that EMDR was equally effective. This study was limited by failure to assess behavioral outcomes.

Rubin and colleagues (2001) reported only nonsignificant trends favoring EMDR with a challenging child guidance center population (N = 39, ages six to fifteen). Participants in each treatment group had the same therapists, and randomization determined which children would have EMDR included in their otherwise similar eclectic treatment. Reasonable efforts were made to ensure treatment fidelity for EMDR. Unfortunately, the researchers relied on a single outcome measure (the Child Behavior Checklist) that does not assess posttraumatic stress, and that is known to be relatively insensitive to change.

There are only three EMDR/child studies in which EMDR has been compared to a credible alternative trauma treatment. Chemtob, Nakashima, Hamada, and Carlson (2002) reported very positive results in using EMDR with thirty-two children and adolescents traumatized by Hurricane Iniki in Kauai. Only those who did not respond to a generally effective previous cognitive-behavioral small-group treatment program were offered EMDR. The design featured a delayed-treatment control group, independent assessment with several standardized measures, and five therapists with varying levels of EMDR training and experience. The treatment protocol was clearly specified, and a number of efforts were made to ensure treatment fidelity. The participants averaged a 58 percent reduction on the primary trauma measure following three sessions, with results holding several months later. The primary limitation was the lack of an alternative-treatment control group at the time that EMDR was being delivered. Thus, although EMDR did work for these nonresponders to the prior treatment, we still don't know how the participants might have responded to additional sessions of the other treatment.

Jaberghaderi, Greenwald, Rubin, Zand, and Dolatabadi (2004) compared EMDR to CBT for fourteen sixth-grade girls in Iran who had been sexually abused and who suffered from clinically significant posttraumatic stress symptoms. Participants were randomly assigned and received up to twelve sessions of either CBT or EMDR treatment. Assessment of posttraumatic stress symptoms and problem behaviors was completed at pretreatment and two weeks posttreatment. Both treatments showed large effect sizes on the posttraumatic symptom outcomes, and a medium effect size on the behavior outcome, all statistically significant. A nonsignificant trend on self-reported posttraumatic stress symptoms favored EMDR over CBT. Treatment efficiency was calculated by dividing change scores by number of sessions; EMDR was significantly more efficient, with large effect sizes on each outcome. Limitations include small N, single therapist for each treatment condition, no independent verification of treatment fidelity, and no long-term follow-up.

Finally, de Roos, Greenwald, de Jongh, and Noorthoorn (2005) compared EMDR to CBT in a community mental health center for thirty-eight children and adolescents who had been exposed to the Enschede (Netherlands) fireworks disaster. The study included eight therapists each using both methods, training and supervision by an expert in both methods; manualized treatments; session checklists reviewed for treatment fidelity; blind independent assessment with multiple standardized measures; and random assignment to treatment condition. Both treatment conditions also included parent sessions. Both treatments showed large effects, with clinically significant reductions on all outcomes, including PTSD diagnosis, posttraumatic stress and related symptoms, and problem behaviors. EMDR was significantly more efficient, with greater change per session on most measures, and termination criteria achieved in an average 3.17 sessions compared to an average of four sessions for CBT.

In sum, the child/adolescent literature on EMDR is basically consistent with the adult literature. It's clear that EMDR works well, probably about as well as the other proven-effective trauma resolution methods. It's possible that EMDR works better than other trauma resolution methods, and it's likely that EMDR works more quickly. However, the literature is only suggestive on these latter points, and more research needs to be done.

Meanwhile, no evidence supports any reason to avoid using EMDR for the trauma resolution portion of treatment. Negative "side effects" (e.g., clients becoming more upset) have been reported, but mainly by those attempting to use EMDR in ways that were clearly inappropriate (see Greenwald, 1996). Clinicians formally trained in EMDR generally agree that EMDR is less risky than alternative trauma resolution methods (Lipke, 1994), perhaps because clients can more easily tolerate EMDR as compared to exposure, and/or because with EMDR, so much resolution occurs within the session.

Perhaps the main drawback—and the reason it is not taught in this book—is that EMDR is a relatively complex treatment approach that requires considerable training and supervised practice to master (Greenwald, 1996). Evidence suggests that even those with the basic training in

EMDR don't always perform it properly (e.g., Jensen, 1994) and that when EMDR is done properly, it yields better results (Maxfield & Hyer, 2002).

Many clinicians have chosen to obtain EMDR training because of the word-of-mouth reports as well as personal experience. Many therapists and clients will describe their experiences with EMDR as being qualitatively different and more effective than other therapy experiences they have had. Although the research literature has not yet established EMDR as the trauma/loss treatment of choice, it has at least established EMDR as a responsible choice.

OTHER VALIDATED TRAUMA RESOLUTION METHODS

Cognitive processing therapy (CPT) is another validated trauma treatment method with many similarities both to the preparatory methods described previously in this book, and to imaginal exposure. Most of the research supporting CPT with adults has been conducted with rape victims; however, it has been applied more widely. To date only one controlled study supports CPT's use with adolescents with PTSD (Ahrens & Rexford, 2002).

Of note is the unique trauma resolution procedure used within CPT. Rather than having the client tell the trauma story to the therapist, she is asked to write it down for homework. Then in therapy, she may talk about her experience of writing it down, and the therapist can provide support and guidance. Then she writes the trauma story again for homework. In the Ahrens and Rexford study, this procedure was tolerated by juvenile delinquents who may be expected to have very limited willingness to tolerate the upsetting feelings associated with their trauma memories. Perhaps the writing provides a sense of distance and control that the standard imaginal exposure does not.

Traumatic Incident Reduction (TIR) (Gerbode, 1989) is not yet considered a primary treatment option because so few controlled studies have been reported, and none (that I know of) with kids. Of note is the unique trauma resolution method used within TIR. Rather than telling the trauma story out loud to the therapist, the client is asked to visualize it, step by step, as if he were watching it in a movie. Then the therapist asks what stood out for the client most during that viewing; the client responds, and the therapist practices "active listening." Then the entire process is repeated multiple times until the memory is no longer distressing.

Many other trauma resolution methods are available; however, these either have not been applied to children, or no controlled research supports their efficacy, and therefore they are not included in this review. This does not mean that they don't work—only that at this time I do not have a basis to recommend them.

DISCUSSION

Although all of the reviewed methods involve some element of exposure to the memory, some methods are more similar than others. The standard imaginal exposure and the modified-for-kids exposure are very similar in structure, although the technique is modified to be developmentally appropriate. The exposure component of cognitive processing therapy is also fairly similar, in that it is also highly structured around telling, and repeating, the trauma story, although in CPT this is done by writing it rather than speaking it.

The structure of EMDR is substantially different. The client is asked to start with the worst moment in the trauma, and then follow where this leads—a kind of free association procedure. Sometimes the whole story gets reviewed; sometimes it doesn't. The client does not necessarily go over and over the same material, but rather focuses on some parts and not others, and for relatively brief periods. According to the primary theories and practices underlying imaginal exposure, this should not work. Since EMDR does work, a different theory is needed to explain it. This theory would be closer to the information processing or digestion model, which is of course a metaphor for brain processes that are not yet well understood. Even so, the result is that the memory is no longer distressing, and the client is able to tell the story in a coherent way.

TIR seems to fall somewhere between imaginal exposure and EMDR. The client is asked to go through the entire story from beginning to end by visualizing it rather than saying it or writing it down. Then she is asked to report on what stood out for her, and to discuss that as she sees fit. Thus it has a variant of the storytelling component common to imaginal exposure, as well as a variant of the free-association component common to EMDR.

All of these methods have certain factors in common:

1. Each requires careful preparation so that the client will be willing to do the procedure, and be able to tolerate it.
2. Each involves directly facing the trauma memory in a systematic way.
3. Each continues until the distress is reduced or eliminated.
4. Each results in the client being able to tell the story (often, previously fragmented) in a coherent and comfortable way.

Chapter 14

Preparation for Exposure

TARGET SELECTION AND MEMORY BREAKDOWN

The focus in this book will be on using exposure as a trauma resolution method, whether standard exposure for teens, or modified exposure for younger kids. However, in general, the same strategies and principles will apply when other trauma exposure methods (e.g., EMDR, CPT) are used instead of exposure.

Selection of Memories for Exposure

Several strategies may be used to decide which trauma memory (assuming, as in most cases, that there are more than one) to address first. Most exposure traditions focus only on the primary identified trauma, that is, the one that apparently precipitated the referral. Another approach, more common with clinicians who use EMDR, is to go in chronological order, starting with the earliest memory and moving forward. A third strategy, which can also be combined with either of the first two, is to go in order from lower to higher SUDS ratings, that is, from least to most anticipated difficulty.

Go for "the Big One"

This strategy is often used in the exposure tradition. This may be the best choice for children who were previously high functioning and who had not been exposed to major trauma or loss prior to the primary identified trauma event. One advantage to this strategy is that—if it works—by focusing on only one trauma memory, the trauma resolution phase of treatment can be completed relatively quickly. Another advantage to working with the "precipitating event" memory is that this strategy is relatively easy for kids to understand. If their case formulation story indicates their problems from this event, then it makes sense to them to go after the memory of this event.

However, problems can occur with this approach. For many kids, starting with "the big one" may prove overwhelming—too much too soon—and backfire by giving the child an upsetting experience that does not even lead to feeling better. Also, sometimes when the child starts with a later trauma memory, the trauma resolution work does not go very smoothly because of the influence of untreated earlier memories.

This is a tricky concept but important to understand. When a child has earlier unprocessed trauma memories, the unprocessed material is kept "behind the wall" and sometimes comes out when triggered by a thematically related stressor. This is the "sore spot" reaction. When a new trauma event occurs, part of the child's response to the new event will be an overreaction, because of the material behind the wall kicking in. The child doesn't know that she is overreacting; her subjective experience is that the current event warrants her reaction. Later, it works the same way. When we ask for the SUDS on that trauma event, some of the reported distress will really be from the sore spot reaction from earlier memories, even though it feels to the child as if it's all related to the identified event.

This is important because when you are trying to help a child process a trauma memory, you want to have a good chance of being successful. When some of the distress attached to the memory is actually from earlier memories that you're not talking about, it's more difficult to get resolution on the memory you are talking about. You can find yourself going through the identified memory over and over, not getting anywhere with it, and not knowing why. On the other hand, if the earlier memory is resolved first, the work with the identified memory is likely to go more smoothly.

Dave was a thirty-four-year-old man who came to treatment complaining of stress on the job for the past three years. However, nothing at his work site had changed; everything had been the same for eight years. What did happen three years ago was that his aunt had died. Dave said, "She was like a mother to me, since my own mother died when I was six." He gave the rating for the memory of his aunt's death as a "ten plus" and the memory of his mother's death as a "four."

Although he didn't quite understand why the therapist wanted him to work through the earlier memory (mother's death) first—"that one doesn't bother me"—he agreed to do so on the therapist's suggestion. Working through this memory took three full sessions using EMDR and included considerable intensity of emotion at several points, far more than the four of the initial distress rating. Dave said, "I had no idea that I was still carrying so much pain from that."

Then he faced the more recent memory (aunt's death), which had initially been identified as the primary source of distress. It was still a sad memory, but it only took one session to resolve. There was just not that much left of it once the earlier memory's sore-spot reaction had been removed.

Go in Order

This strategy is often used in the EMDR tradition. When more than one significant trauma/loss memory is on the list, often the preferred option is to address each memory in chronological order, starting from age zero and moving forward. By addressing trauma memories in chronological order, each trauma only carries its own distress burden—no sore-spot reaction piled on—and can be more readily resolved. Then when addressing later trauma, the prior traumas have already been resolved, so less distress remains.

Personal Trainer Modifications

Finally, with either strategy, you must also consider whether your client is ready to handle the memory you want to target first. It is often preferable to start with a less distressing trauma memory as a way to help the child become more competent in the method and gain a track record of success, prior to addressing the more challenging one you might have in mind. For example, what if you want to go in chronological order, but the earliest memory on the trauma history list is rated as a ten? Perhaps you'll decide to start with a later memory on the list that has a lower rating, as a stepping-stone to facing the more difficult one. Remember, as a "personal trainer" you want to give your clients challenges that they can handle. You don't want to offer too great a challenge and invite failure. Better to go a step at a time.

Selecting the order of trauma memories for exposure is guided by clinical judgment. Go for the big one and the hope of quick relief? Use a systematic approach and go chronological? Start small and build up, slower but safer? Fortunately, order selection is not a single make-or-break decision. The therapist is constantly presenting just-manageable challenges to the child and supporting the child's capacity to manage them. If the challenges seem too easy, the therapist can introduce greater challenges; conversely, if the challenges seem too difficult, the therapist can help the child to contain the memory, relax, and back off. Then the therapist will know to go slower for a while so the child can be successful and make progress.

Breaking Down the Memory

The goal of exposure is to help the client gradually face and process—or "digest"—the various components of the trauma memory, with the result being desensitization to the memory, along with a more mature and adaptive perspective on the event and on his own part in it. In this process, the discrete fragments of the memory (and associated thoughts and feelings) tend to become better organized and ordered, to form a coherent narrative. The narrative includes the details of the memory but does not end there; it ends *now,* with the client accepting the pain and loss, learning and growing from it, and moving on to a new and more satisfactory state of being.

Exposure with adults typically involves having the client describe the memory in great detail, including actions, thoughts, and feelings, and in the present tense to further encourage emotional engagement. This is repeated multiple times in the presence of a supportive but directive therapist who keeps the client on task. However, even with adults this can be extremely challenging, and many therapists who practice exposure report a high dropout rate. With kids, it is even more important to conduct the exposure in a manner that is not overwhelming, so that it can be tolerated.

One way to do this is to "titrate" exposure to the memory by having the child face only a portion at a time, rather than the whole memory at once. Breaking down the memory is a procedure that entails making a list of components of the memory prior to doing the standard exposure routine. This intervention helps to titrate exposure in two ways. By asking first for a "list" of component events for the memory, rather than asking for the whole story with thoughts and feelings, the client may be able to discuss the memory with relatively less emotional content the first time around. The list approach can be a nicely contained step. Also, once the list is made, the trauma memory may be broken down into more manageable portions. Then the client might only work on a certain portion of the memory at one time, rather than the entire memory. These steps are not always required, but they're good options to have available.

Breaking down the memory is a fairly simple procedure. It is similar in many ways to the method for obtaining a full trauma history, except that now the list is focused on components of a single memory. Once the trauma memory has been selected for exposure, the therapist helps the child to identify discrete portions of the memory, put them in the order they occurred, and rank each portion with a SUDS score from zero to ten. The SUDS ratings are used in several ways:

- They help the child learn more about how she feels in relation to the memory.
- They help the therapist plan a strategy for approaching the exposure work (see Chapter 15).
- Finally, they serve as a baseline, so that later on, the therapist can say, for example, "you started out as an eight on this part and now you say it's only a three. Would you say you're making some progress?" Without this baseline measurement, it's easy for kids to forget where they were, and then it's harder for them to tell how much they've accomplished.

The therapist and child together also identify posttrauma information and events that relate in some way. For example, if the perpetrator of an assault is in jail, or if the child is no longer in physical pain, this is an important component of the narrative even if it did not occur at the exact time of the index event.

Get to the Good Ending

It is critical to success in this method to make sure that the child's story goes all the way to a good ending. This is true both for the memory breakdown and for the exposure itself. Even if there is no ending that is really happy, it's essential to find an ending point in which at least the bad part is really over.

Bryson was an eight-year-old boy who complained in session one day about having missed recess that morning because he pushed a boy who had insulted him. He gave this a SUDS rating of eight. The session was interrupted and then picked up again the next day. The counselor reminded him of what they'd been talking about the day before, and asked again for a SUDS rating. This time it was a zero. Why? Bryson explained, "Oh, we're friends again!"

Remember, one of our goals with exposure is for the child to be able to say, "That was bad, but at least it's over now, and things are okay." Really understanding—on a gut level—that the bad part is over helps people to let it go and move on. One reason traumatized people stay stuck is because some part of them doesn't realize that the bad part is over now. The memory isn't organized into a story; it's still in fragments. The fragments that include the worst parts of the memory don't know that it's over now.

So when we help someone to organize the story, we must make sure the story goes all the way to a good end, to when the bad part is really over. This can be tricky; it can be hard to find a good end to many stories. For our purposes, a "good ending" doesn't necessarily mean that what happened was good, or even that the ending was good. The goal is to get the client past the distressing fragments of the memory to a felt sense that it's really over. Here are some examples of good endings to bad memories, which the therapist helped the client to identify:

A fourteen-year-old girl had been teased mercilessly by her peers throughout elementary school. Although only two teasing-related memories were on her trauma history list, smaller but similar events were a daily occurrence for some years. So at the end of the event in her memory, she also knew that she faced the same kind of thing the next day. The therapist asked her, "Do you get teased now?" Fortunately, she was no longer getting teased, but got along well with her peers. The ending to her teasing memory story was in the present: the last event in this memory was seeing herself having lunch with her friends at school, the day before this therapy session.

A ten-year-old boy's older brother's fiancée had died two years ago in a car accident. The boy missed her then and now; she had been like part of the family and they had been close. The good ending was seeing himself return to school and other normal activities the week after the funeral.

A seven-year-old girl had been injured the year before in a fall from a friend's apartment window. She had broken bones and many cuts, and had to return to the hospital for treatment on multiple occasions over several months. The story of the trauma memory included those hospital visits. The good end was saying good-bye to the last doctor, and then seeing herself playing jump rope with her friends.

A five-year-old boy was severely beaten on several occasions by his grandmother when he stayed with her for the summer. He still has to see her at family events, but his parents have told him that grandmother is not allowed to babysit him anymore. The good ending was when his parents told him that, and then seeing him safe with them at their home.

A twelve-year-old girl had been near a building that got bombed. Although her daily life routine is unremarkable, she lives in an area where bombs or other attacks could happen again. Her good end was that no one she cared about had been hurt in the bombing; she visualized eating dinner with her family members all present that evening.

These examples illustrate several possible strategies for identifying the good ending. Ideally, the good ending can represent a true resolution of the event. Sometimes this resolution can be found soon after the event, and sometimes it needs to be found much later. Unfortunately, some events do not have true resolutions, for example when there is lasting damage (e.g., the loss of a family member; a permanent physical injury) or when the event seems especially likely to recur (e.g., in an area regularly targeted by criminals or terrorists). In such instances the best we can do for a good ending is identify a time when the bad event and its aftermath was as finished as possible, and things were as much back to normal as possible.

It's important that the good ending be represented in an image of an actual event, an actual moment in time, when a particular thing happened. Many people will describe a status as their good end; then it's up to the therapist to help the client convert the status into a representative image. For example, if the client describes her good ending as, "I wasn't afraid to ride on the bus anymore," then the therapist might ask, "What picture represents that for you; what do you remember doing that let you know that you weren't afraid anymore?" For another example, if the client describes his good ending as, "I didn't feel bad; I wasn't worried about it anymore," the therapist might ask, "So when you didn't feel bad, and weren't worried about it anymore, what were you doing?" The point is, this is a story. In a story, things happen. So for the good ending, it must be an actual event that happens. An event has a time, a place, and an action. If the therapist cannot visualize the good ending as clearly as if seeing it on TV, it's not specific enough yet.

Sample script

Here is an example of how a breaking down the memory session might go.

THERAPIST: Today we're going to talk a little about the memory, just enough to make a list of the different things that happened. Let's see, what are the different parts of the memory? What was the first thing, like if this whole thing was a movie, what would be the beginning?

CHILD: Getting into the car.

THERAPIST: Okay, getting into the car. Who was getting into the car?

CHILD: Me and my brother and my mother; we were going to the store.

THERAPIST: Okay, and what's the next thing?

CHILD: We're driving along and then we stop at the stop sign but the car behind us didn't stop; it crashed into us.

THERAPIST: Okay. Driving along. Stop at the stop sign. Car crashed into us. What happened after that?

CHILD: Then the ambulance came and took me to the hospital, and then they put on the cast and the bandages and then we went home.

THERAPIST: Okay. Ambulance came and took me to the hospital. Put on the cast and the bandages. Went home. Then what?

CHILD: Then I didn't go to school the next day but I went after that. And then the cast came off a few weeks later. That's all.

THERAPIST: Got it. And what about your mother and your brother? What happened to them?

CHILD: They came to the hospital with me and they got some bandages too but they weren't hurt bad.

THERAPIST. Okay, I'll put that down too. Now after the cast came off, is there any more to the story, to the movie about this car accident?

CHILD: I don't think so.

THERAPIST: What about how you kept having the bad dreams and being nervous about getting into a car, and then you came here and got stronger and able to handle it, and getting back to normal?

CHILD: Oh, yeah.

THERAPIST: So what happened that really let you know that you were back to normal again?

CHILD: I didn't need the light on when I went to bed. And I could get in a car to go someplace without feeling worried.

THERAPIST: Like when did you get in the car without feeling worried, where were you going?

CHILD: To the store with my mom.

THERAPIST: Okay, now I have a list of all the things you told me, that would be part of the story. Now I'm going to go through the list, one at a time, and ask you to give me a number to tell me how bad the feeling is now when you concentrate on it. On zero to ten, ten is the worst that the feeling can be, and zero is no bad feeling at all. So just for a minute, concentrate on getting into the car that day, and notice how you're reacting inside right now. How bad is that feeling right now, if ten is the worst and zero is nothing?

CHILD: Maybe a three.

THERAPIST: Okay, and how about when you stop at the stop sign?

CHILD: That's an eight.

THERAPIST: And when the car crashes into you?

CHILD: Ten. Ten plus!

THERAPIST: And when the ambulance comes?

EXERCISE: BREAKING DOWN THE MEMORY

If You Are on Your Own

Follow the therapist instructions with someone who will let you practice on him or her, or with a client who you are sure can handle this and for whom it is an appropriate intervention at this time.

If You Are the Client

- This is not a role-play, be yourself.
- Choose a memory (from your trauma history list or otherwise) that you rate six or lower on the zero to ten scale, and that you are willing to talk about today.
- Do not look at the script; that's the therapist's job.
- Remember what to do if you feel that you need a break or if there's something you don't want to talk about. Just because you agree at the beginning does not mean that you will feel the same way later on. Take care of yourself.

If You Are the Therapist

- Use the form in this chapter, including the script that's on it. Verbatim, of course!
- You'll be making a list of each event that happened in the memory. You don't need or want a lot of detail here, just the bare bones of the event. Write each event down on its own line, in the open space of the form. Write the next event on the next line. Use another page if you need more space.
- Remember, this is only a list. Don't pester your client with questions about thoughts or feelings. Don't pester your client with questions about minute details. Just get the thing that happened, write it down, and go on to the next thing that happened.
- Make sure you go all the way to a good end that is a specific event, just like the rest of the things on the list.
- When the list is done, follow the script to get the SUDS on each item. Write that down on the edge of the line for that item.
- In a session, you might decide to just continue with the standard exposure. In this exercise, finish with a calming activity. Try the "Container" intervention (the script is included in the following text). Then see if your client would like to do some deep breathing or a safe place visualization.

THE CONTAINER

The Container is yet another intervention that can be used to help calm the client. The best time to use a container is after you've been talking about a memory that may have been upsetting (even if the client does not show upset). The goal is to help the client feel as if the memory is put away again. In the script below, this is a conversation. You must wait for answers to your questions before you go on to the next one. You don't want to give your client too many ideas; it's better if she comes up with her own imagery. The questions are designed to help her to make it specific enough that it works:

What kind of container can you think of that could hold this memory until you need to get to it again?

What would it be made of? How big would it be? How would you close it (keep it secure)? *Where would you keep it?*

What I want you to do is imagine packing this memory away in [the container]. *When it's all put away, let me know.*

How did that go? Does it feel all put away?

Problem Solving

Once in a while, the container doesn't really work. You will know this because when you ask, "Does it feel all put away?" your client will say, "No." Then you must help your client improve the container so it will work. You can do this by asking questions, for example, "What kept it from being all put away?" Then your client will probably tell you that the container was too small, too weak, or not adequately secured. Then you can ask for solutions, for example, "What would it take to make the container work better?" Again, your job is to guide the client to come up with her own imagry. Once the client has improved the container to solve the problem, you try the visualization again.

Once the memory is put away in the container, check with your client. How's he doing now? If he's not all the way relaxed, follow this with deep breathing or safe place. Then, finish up with

Breaking Down the Memory

Today we're going to talk a little about the memory, just enough to make a *list* of the different things that happened. Let's see, what are the different parts of the memory? What was the first thing, like if this whole thing was a movie, what would be the beginning? Then what?

When would you say it felt like this was really over? What event or picture represents that?

Make a list of the different parts of the memory, in chronological order. Go all the way to the end, to where things are okay again.

Event segment	SUDS

Okay, now I have a list of all the things you told me, that would be part of the story. Now I'm going to go through the list, one at a time, and ask you to give me a number to tell me how bad the feeling is now when you concentrate on it. On zero to ten, ten is the worst that the feeling can be, and zero is no bad feeling at all. So just for a minute, concentrate on [the first part of the story], and notice how you're reacting inside right now. How bad is that feeling right now, if ten is the worst and zero is nothing?

(Put the current SUDS next to each item on the list, above. Then either go directly into exposure [on the whole memory or a selected section], or do some containment/closure activities.)

any debriefing or even small talk, whatever is needed to help your client regain composure and be ready for whatever's next in his day.

Discussion Questions

Clients should describe their experiences. Therapists should describe their experiences. How many therapists had their own emotional reaction to the client's story? What did you do with it; how did you handle it? Is there more you need to do? Clients, how many had a higher SUDS in the memory than what you had expected? What can we learn from this to help us understand our clients? Clients, raise your hand if you feel worse off than before? Same as before? Better off than before?

Chapter 15

Conducting an Exposure Session

Once you have selected a memory to target for exposure, and broken down the memory (see previous chapter), you'll need to decide on an exposure strategy. Should you work with the story a chunk at a time, or all at once?

A CHUNK AT A TIME

You choose this strategy when you have to, when in your opinion the child will not be able to handle the whole story all at once. The younger the child, and/or the more emotionally fragile, the more often this strategy is used. For example, you might judge that the child is not ready to face the most upsetting portions of the memory right away, but can get started on some other portions and so build strength. Or you might judge that the child does not have the attention span or ability to tolerate staying with the entire story long enough to get much accomplished. You want to help the child be successful, so you aim for a smaller bite.

If you are going to do exposure a chunk at a time, you can't skip the step of breaking down the memory. You need to know what the components of the memory are so that you can make an informed decision about where to start and how to proceed. The two main ways to implement this strategy are by going in order of what seems manageable, or by going in the sequential order of the event.

In Order of What Seems Manageable

This is a good strategy when you feel that the child is ready to handle the memory, but isn't quite ready to face the worst part yet. So in the first exposure session, you have him focus not on the whole memory, but on a chunk that you agree to start on. Typically, this chunk will include more than one line on the memory breakdown form; it'll be a portion of the memory that includes several of those lines in sequence. Once you work through that chunk (using the exposure procedure described in detail in this chapter), you go on to another chunk. You might continue this strategy for some time, or at some point you might switch to working with the entire memory all at once.

So where do you start? One approach is to select the chunk that seems easiest to handle. You can determine this by looking at your memory breakdown form, which will list the SUDS ratings next to each event. This is the personal trainer style again, going one step at a time, starting small and working your way up. Another approach is to start with the last part of the memory, perhaps from some time after the worst part is over, all the way through to the good ending. This may be tolerated relatively well because the child keeps on encountering a reminder that it really is over now. It is important to work this ending chunk at some point before you have the child face the worst part of the memory. Later, when the child is facing that worst part, it will be easier for her to tolerate because she will be more able to remember, and truly believe, that it's over now.

In the Sequential Order of the Event

This is a particularly good strategy for younger children (pre-teen to much younger) who may be better suited developmentally to working with an art, play, or drama focus rather than straight talking. Although many strategies exist for working with younger children using these symbolic modalities (e.g., see Gil, 1991; James, 1989), the focus here will be on the sequential approach (Deblinger & Heflin, 1996) that has been subjected to extensive research (Cohen, Deblinger, & Mannarino, 2004).

MAKING A BOOK TO TELL THE TRAUMA STORY

In this approach, the child and the therapist work together to make a book of the story of the trauma memory. In this book, perhaps each item on the Breaking Down the Memory form will have its own page. For each page, the child draws a picture to represent the portion of the memory being depicted. While he is drawing the picture, the therapist may be prompting the child by asking what the characters in the picture are doing, thinking, and feeling. Either the child or the therapist (using the child's words) might write a caption or a narrative to go along with each of the pages. This approach has the following advantages:

1. Prompting for actions, thoughts, and feelings helps the child to fully engage with that portion of the memory so it can be digested.
2. The fact that it's a picture allows the child to maintain a certain distance, which may make the memory easier to tolerate while it is being faced.
3. The act of drawing keeps the child active and engaged. This gives her something to do, which counters restlessness.
4. The drawing itself provides a way to manage and express any distress related to the memory.
5. The time it takes to draw the picture allows the child to stay with that portion of the memory long enough to overcome the avoidance and to acheive some digestion.
6. Only one portion of the memory is being focused on at a time. This may keep it from becoming overwhelming for the child.

Even in the sequential approach, it's okay to skip the most difficult pages if the child is not yet ready for those. However, eventually those should also be completed, and then put in their place in the sequence. Usually, once the child has progressed to the good ending, she will feel more able to go back to the hard parts and get through those as well. Sometimes additional strategies can also be helpful, for example, using additional strength-building interventions such as those described earlier in the book.

Many therapists also routinely use incentives to help children to get through exposure. This can be as simple as, "Once we get our work done, we'll have time to play," or it can involve an agreement for the child to earn a certain reward or prize for accomplishing a specified task in treatment. Although incentives can be useful, it is important not to use such large incentives that the child would ultimately feel coerced. It's also important to do all the preparatory steps to gain the child's understanding, motivation, and cooperation, and to help her to build her coping skills and affect tolerance. If incentives are attempted as a shortcut for skipping those steps, it won't work.

Once the pages of the book are completed, including the title page, the book can be bound, perhaps with tape or staples. The final task in this exposure procedure is for the child, in the therapist's presence, to show the book to her parents and tell them the story from start to end. Many children are proud of their work and look forward to this session.

We want the parents to be proud of their child as well, and to show their compassion and pride while the child is showing the book and telling the story. However, if parents are seeing this book and hearing the story from the child for the first time, they are likely to feel overcome with their own emotions. Then the focus would be on the parents and not on the child. Worse yet, the child might feel that the parents need her care. To help parents to come through for their children, the therapist meets with them alone and prepares them for the "show-and-tell" session by going over the story with the parents in detail. This gives the parents a chance to have their own reaction to the story in private. Then when their child shows the book and tells the story, the parents are more prepared to support the child the way they want to.

After the story has been presented, the therapist works with the child to prepare questions for the parent, and also works with the parent to prepare questions for the child. The ensuing structured conversation about the trauma helps to further reestablish the parent-child bond and communication. This facilitates the transition toward the end of therapy and helps the parent take over some of the therapist's role.

The rest of this chapter will focus on the "talk" format for exposure, assuming that the entire memory will be used. However, the same method can be applied to the talk format for working on a chunk at a time, and the principles apply to the sequential drawing method as well.

ON THE WAY TO EXPOSURE

Several last-minute things need to be done on your way into the exposure session. These will help your client understand why you are asking him to do this and how it relates to his goals, and will also help him feel that he has ready access to whatever makes him feel safe, secure, and in control.

Restate Rationale

You need to remind your client about why you are asking her to do this activity. Don't think that just because you talked about it last week, she still knows! Kids tend to shy away from talking about their trauma memories and can easily forget why it seemed like a good idea when you talked about it before. Kids may feel that bringing up the trauma memory will only make them upset and make things worse for them. Also, kids who are doing better in various ways, often because of your help and guidance, may feel they don't need to talk about the trauma because they're already doing well. Here's an example of what you might say to reorient your client to the reason for doing exposure today:

> You told me that you wanted to [restate child's treatment goals here, e.g., do better in school, have more friends, stop having bad dreams, have a good job someday]. We were talking before about how the bad memories on your list make stress pile up inside you, give you that sore spot, and get in the way of the things you want. So we've been doing these different things to help you get stronger and more in charge of what happens to you. We've talked about avoiding high risk and staying safer, you've done a lot of work to get stronger and better at handling things, and you've figured out ways to keep your stress down.
>
> The next thing we said we would do is to talk about the bad memories on the list, one by one. The reason I'm thinking that this is a good time is that you are getting stronger, I think you can handle this now. I'll be asking you to tell what happened in [the selected memory] over and over. It might be hard; it might hurt your feelings while you're doing it. Remem-

ber, though, that the more you do it, the stronger you get, and the smaller your sore spot gets, the less power the memory has to mess you up.

The rationale may be presented in different ways, according to developmental level and according to the way the therapist understands what exposure actually accomplishes. For example, you may wish to use the "digestion" metaphor, or you may wish to focus on how facing the memory over and over again interferes with avoidance and allows desensitization to occur. Whatever rationale you give for exposure, it is always important to tie it to the child's stated goals, and to present it as the next step in a series of treatment activities in which she has so far been successful.

Sometimes even after you give this rationale, kids will object to doing exposure because they are so much better now that they "don't have a problem anymore." Then you'll need to offer an additional rationale that will hopefully be persuasive. Normally this will focus on remaining symptoms and on future challenges. For example:

> Years ago, when I was working with someone who is doing as well as you're doing now, I would think that we were all done. So if this was a few years ago, I might shake your hand, say "good work," and send you on your way. But here's what happened. Those kids mostly did pretty well as long as things in their life stayed the same. But when some new challenge came along, some new stress, like maybe their girlfriend broke up with them, or someone in their family died, then things would go downhill and they'd end up with the same kinds of problems they had before. So maybe a couple of months later or a couple of years later, I'd see them again. The reason is that we hadn't helped them to digest the trauma memories, so they still had the same sore spots. When something big came along, it hit that sore spot and it was just too much. So I've learned the hard way. Now I always suggest that while you're doing well and feeling strong right now, you take care of the sore spots. Then when some new challenge comes along down the line, you'll have all your strength and you'll have a better chance of handling that, too.

Here's another way of conveying essentially the same message.

THERAPIST: Supposing you're on a basketball team, and your coach tells you, "You can't just come to the games. You have to come to the practices, too, and do push-ups, run laps, everything. You don't really like doing push-ups or running laps. What are you going to do?

CLIENT: Come to practice; do what the coach says.

THERAPIST: Why? You don't really like doing some of that stuff.

CLIENT: Have to, to stay on the team. Also, it makes me stronger so I can play better, help the team win.

THERAPIST: I thought you'd say that. Okay, so the season is going along, and your team is winning every game. Now your coach says, "I want you to start coming in for extra practices; we're going to be doing more different exercises and drills from now on." Why do you think your coach would say that? You're already winning every game.

CLIENT: I don't know.

THERAPIST: I think it's because the coach wants your team to win the play-offs, too. You know who you're going to face in the play-offs?

CLIENT: The other teams that have been winning all their games!

THERAPIST: Right. So are you going to tell your coach, "Forget it; we're already doing fine. I'm not going to those extra practices"?

CLIENT: No, I want to win the play-offs too.

THERAPIST: Well, that's where I think we are right now. You've done a lot of work with me, to be safer, get stronger, better at handling things, and it's really paid off. You're stronger now and you're doing pretty well, wouldn't you say?

CLIENT: Well, I'm not getting in trouble much anymore.

THERAPIST: So it's like the team that's winning the games, and now it's time to get ready for the play-offs. So if I just wanted you to win today's game, I'd say that you were all set, and I wouldn't ask you to do any more work. But I want you to win tomorrow's game, too. I want you to win the play-offs. Remember the things you told me you wanted for yourself? To get through school, learn a trade, get a good job, have your own family?

CLIENT: Yes.

THERAPIST: Well, sooner or later, some big challenge is going to come your way. Maybe break up with a girlfriend you care about, maybe lose a good job, maybe someone in your family dies. You know how life is; things happen.

CLIENT: It's always something.

THERAPIST: So now that you're doing well and feeling strong, it's a good time to get ready for the big challenges that'll come your way down the line. The stronger you get now, the smaller you can make those sore spots, the better chance you'll have of handling even the big things. Then you'll have a better chance of staying on your track to your goals.

If even this isn't enough, and your client still resists, perhaps you are asking for more than the client believes she can handle. Then it may be wise to back down just a bit, perhaps by suggesting that you start with an easier (lower SUDS) memory than you may have initially had in mind. You are still holding your ground in terms of recommending that your client complete the trauma resolution work, but you can offer a way for her to get into it more cautiously.

THERAPIST: Even though I can see that what I'm saying makes sense to you, a lot of kids are still not really sure that they want to talk about those memories that still hurt inside. Some kids think it might be too hard, more than they can handle. And some kids just don't believe that it would work for them, that they could really feel better about the memory than they do now. Do you have any of these questions about doing it?

CLIENT: I just don't see how talking about it is going to help. It'll just stir things up.

THERAPIST: Must be kind of confusing for you. Because you know me pretty well by now, you've had pretty good luck with my suggestions so far. But you're not sure about this one.

CLIENT: Yeah, nothing against you. I'm just not sure about this.

THERAPIST: Well, if it's not going to work for you, of course you shouldn't do it. But if it is going to work for you, you'd probably end up being really glad that you did do it. So I have an idea for you. My suggestion is that you kind of check it out, but not with one of the really bad memories. My suggestion is to pick out something that happened in the last few days that maybe bothers you some now, but that you know is really no big deal. Kind of like sticking your toe in the water to see how it is before you decide whether you're going to go swimming or not. How does that sound to you?

Reminder of Strength Resources

Before expecting the child to face the challenge entailed in talking about the trauma memory, it's good to remind her of the things that make her feel strong and secure. The client might get

this from being reminded of her goals and of all the success she has already achieved on the path to her goals; this was shown previously in presenting the rationale. Another strategy, particularly for younger children with whom the same approach has been used all along, is to refer directly to physical strength. The therapist might say, "Let's see how many push-ups you can do today," as preparation for saying, "Okay, I think you're strong enough to talk about this now."

Some therapists also like to use a variety of "helpers," which can symbolically represent strength, attachment, safety, or other resources to help the child face the trauma memory. Helpers are a standard element of trauma processing for kids within the EMDR tradition, and more detail on how to develop such helpers is available from other sources (Greenwald, 1999). These helpers can be toys, imagined weapons, celebrities or fantasy characters from the mass media, or people that the child knows personally, such as family members. By this time in the treatment, the therapist is likely to know the child fairly well, and may suggest, "Would you like to hold that [toy] sword while we talk?" or "Would it help to imagine that your father is here with you now?"

If you are using a helper, sometimes the child will incorporate the helper into a fantasy version of the story being told. That is, instead of telling the story as it actually happened, the child may tell it the way he wishes it would have happened had the helper been available. If this occurs, don't worry, just keep going. Sometimes kids need to tell it the "wishful" way one or more times; this helps them gain the strength to tell it the harder way. However, if the child only tells it the fantasy way over and over, the therapist can actively encourage the next step, for example, by saying, "This time, can you imagine that your father is here with you while you tell the story the way it actually happened?"

Practice with Stopping

By now it is your habit to remind your clients of how to follow your rule if there is something they don't want to talk about. Every time you are about to do something that might be touchy, you remind them again. It's like a friendly warning: there's a hill up ahead, remember how to use the brakes if you need to? When it's time to do exposure, we go a little farther, in effect saying, "Here comes a very steep hill. It's time to check out the emergency brakes, too!" One way to do this is by practicing a new way to stop.

THERAPIST: We're going to be talking about something that might be hard for you sometimes. So you might need to take a break. That doesn't mean that you can't handle it, just that you need to take a break. So if you want a break, what can you do?

CHILD: I can say I want a break?

THERAPIST: Right. Let's practice that right now, I'm going to be talking and you interrupt to tell me you want a break, okay? Bla bla bla bla . . .

CHILD: Stop! I want a break!

THERAPIST: Good, you can do it. I want to show you another way, too, that you can do it without even telling me. Remember the safe place image that you use here sometimes?

CHILD: Yes.

THERAPIST: Okay. What did you have for breakfast this morning?

CLIENT: Cereal.

THERAPIST: Here's what we're going to do. You start out by concentrating on what you had for breakfast. Then I'll call out "Switch" and you go as fast as you can to the safe place. When you get there, let me know. Okay, think about breakfast . . . Switch.

CLIENT: I'm there.

THERAPIST: Good. What did you have for dinner last night?

CLIENT: Chicken and potatoes.

THERAPIST. Okay, think about the chicken and potatoes . . . Switch.

CLIENT: I'm there.

THERAPIST: That was fast. Do you think you're pretty good at this, or do you want more practice?

CLIENT: I'm good at it.

THERAPIST: Okay, so if you decide you want a little break, you can go any time to your safe place. You don't have to ask first.

As with the initial "rule" about what to do if there's something you don't want to talk about, we give the clients practice with this new method of putting on the brakes. Telling them about it is nice, but not really enough. Clients develop belief in these brakes when they've had the experience of using them. The more kids feel that they are in control, the more willing they are to attempt a challenge such as exposure.

EXPOSURE PROCEDURE

Here are the instructions we give to an older child or adolescent who is about to do exposure:

1. Tell the story (or the selected part of the story) from beginning to end.
2. Tell it in the present tense, as if it's happening right now.

3. Say what's happening, also what you're thinking and feeling.
4. Now and then I'll ask a question to help me understand something, or to see how you're doing.
5. When you finish, I'll ask you to do it again, and then again. This is how you'll get stronger.

When the child is telling the story of the trauma memory, he will probably not be following your instructions exactly. That's okay. This is a process. It can take many retellings, over one or even several sessions, for the work to get done. Your goals, meanwhile, are (1) for the child to make at least a little progress each time, to digest at least one or two more bites, and (2) for the child not to get bitten by the dog, not to get overwhelmed. As long as you are achieving your goals, you can just let him tell it the way he is telling it.

Then when he's through, you give the instructions all over again, and he tells it again. This time, you'll probably notice that some parts of the story are different—a little more detail here, a little more emotion there. This is your signal that the work is getting done. If this is happening, trust the process. Don't pester him with questions; just let him talk. Trust the process; it works.

Your goal is to keep a balance, to help the child stay feeling strong enough to handle it, but also engaged enough with the memory that there is something to handle—too much and he gets overwhelmed, too little and nothing is being digested. In the middle ground, as long as something is moving, the therapist mostly witnesses and stays out of the way. The therapist should keep several strategies in mind during an exposure session, to keep the child on track.

Structure First

If you notice that the story is being told without much emotion or detail, that can be a good thing. In the previous session, we did this on purpose when we broke down the memory with the "list" approach. We accept a superficial narrative, especially early in the procedure. This allows the child to build the structure of the story before filling it in. Remember, until now the memory may have been a jumble of unorganized fragments. Giving the story order and structure helps the child to feel more secure and grounded. In particular, we want her to be secure in knowing, and feeling, that the good end is connected to the difficult middle, before she gets too involved in the emotions related to the difficult part.

Be Permissive

You might also notice that in telling the story, the child suddenly shifts from present tense to past tense. What does that mean? What just happened there? It probably means that she reached a more emotionally difficult part of the memory and felt the need for more distance. You might also notice that the child is telling lots of detail, thoughts, feelings, and then suddenly skims through one portion of the memory very quickly. This is probably another strategy for managing something difficult. Your job is to be glad that your client knows how to manage the intensity of the exposure to this memory. This saves you the trouble! So when you notice these things, especially early in the story, be permissive. Just accept what is said and let your client keep going. Later, when she is feeling stronger, she will probably dig in more.

Repeat

When the story has been told, give the first three instructions again, verbatim. As the child gets used to hearing these instructions, he may start to prompt himself, for example, "Oh, I went to the past tense. Okay, now I'm walking in . . ." This is fine, but don't think that's a reason for you to start doing it. Stay out of the way. The next time the story is finished, give the instructions again. By now you can probably use a shorthand version: "Okay, start again from beginning to end, present tense, and what you're thinking and feeling."

You might notice that your client thinks that this is enough already. He's already told it (once, twice, three times). Okay, some interesting things came out, but that's enough. Nothing else is going to happen. You might also notice that you're feeling the same way! That's okay. Have your client tell the story again anyway. And again. And again. And again. You will probably notice that each time, more progress is made.

Regardless of my assurances that you should keep going, chances are that when you're on the spot, you will still be skeptical and unsure about this. I don't know why this should be, but I am predicting it because it's so typical. The problem is, if you don't believe in your heart that there's value in persevering, it's going to be difficult for you to convince the client to keep going when he's telling you he's sure he should be stopping now. You need to experience this for yourself, as a client, with someone who will encourage you to keep going long enough to fully resolve the memory. Even then, it'll take practice and experience as a therapist for you to become accustomed to this. Ideally, while you're learning and practicing these methods, you are also being supervised by someone who is already good at trauma treatment.

Monitor

I've just been telling you over and over again to trust the process and stay out of the way. Now I'll tell you when to jump in. It comes down to monitoring your client. Remember in the instructions, you said, "Now and then I'll be asking you a question"? You were preparing for this eventuality.

Remember, you want her to be engaged but not overwhelmed. How can you tell if she is indeed in that middle ground where good things can happen? Or in the danger zone? Or in comfortable avoidance? You do this by observing and, if necessary, by asking.

- Too much? If you are concerned that too much exposure is happening, your job is to help the client to gain a little more distance and composure. You can check in, ask for SUDS, see if the client is okay or feeling overwhelmed. Note that some clients can tolerate a very high SUDS and still be okay. If needed, you might suggest deep breathing, taking a break, or skipping the hard part of the memory for now and going to an easier part.
- Too little? If you are concerned that too little exposure is happening, you can start gently prompting your client to report all details, to stay in the present tense, and to describe what she is thinking and feeling. Remember that the client may have many good reasons to avoid greater engagement, so you don't want to push too hard at the wrong time. Use your clinical judgment. If you are confident that your client really can handle this with some encouragement, then go ahead and push a little.

EXERCISE: PRACTICE WITH EXPOSURE

If You Are the Client

- This is not a role-play. Be yourself.
- Choose a memory (from your trauma history list or otherwise) that you rate six or lower on the zero to ten scale, and that you are willing to talk about today. If you participated in the Breaking Down the Memory exercise, you might want to continue with the same memory.
- Do not look at the script; that's the therapist's job.
- Remember what to do if you feel that you need a break or if there's something you don't want to talk about. Just because you agree at the beginning does not mean that you will feel the same way later on. Take care of yourself.

If You Are the Therapist

- When your client tells you what memory she'll be working on, help her to identify a good end that's a specific event.
- Use the following instructions, one through five, the first time. Verbatim, of course!
- Do your best to restrain yourself and allow your client to do her work. Don't pester her with questions about details, present tense, thoughts or feelings. Don't tell her your own insights or interpretations. Just be present and let her tell her story.
- Make sure the story goes all the way to the good end.
- Repeat the first three instructions, again verbatim. Have the client tell the story again.
- Do this as many times as you have time for and as your client will tolerate.
- When you have finished with the exposure portion of the exercise, use the "Container" to put the memory away. Then see if your client would like to do some deep breathing or a safe place visualization.

Exposure Instructions

1. Tell the story from beginning to end.
2. Tell it in the present tense, as if it's happening right now.
3. Say what's happening, also what you're thinking and feeling.

4. Now and then I'll ask a question to help me understand something, or to see how you're doing.
5. When you finish, I'll ask you to do it again, and then again. This is how you'll get stronger.

Discussion Questions

- In a group, clients, please share your comments and experiences.
- How many (clients) found that the SUDS turned out to be higher than you had initially rated it?
- How many (clients) feel that you are worse off than before? The same as before? Better off?
- Therapists, please share your comments and experiences.
- How many therapists had some difficulty restraining yourself from making comments or other interventions?
- How many clients felt that the therapist cared about you? What did you notice that made you think that?
- How many therapists had a personal emotional reaction while conducting this session? How did you handle this? How do you feel now? Do you need to do anything else to take care of yourself?

SELECTING THE TARGET MEMORY FOR EXPOSURE

Here's a reminder about the difference between workshop practice and clinical practice. In a workshop setting, we count on participants to decide for themselves what memory they want to work on today. In clinical practice, we do not ask our clients, "What memory do you want to work on today?" That would be an abdication of our professional responsibility. Imagine going to a physician and being asked, "What examination methods would you like me to use today?" or "What medication or treatment would you like me to prescribe today?"

As therapists, we are the ones with the professional training and knowledge. It's up to us to develop a case formulation and treatment plan. It's up to us to develop, in collaboration with the client, of course, a strategy for selecting the order of memories to target with exposure. Our clients don't know what we know about how treatment works or how to make these choices. That's our job.

I'm making this point for two reasons. First, when something is practiced in a workshop setting, it can feel natural to do it the same way in clinical practice. So it's important to alert you to any differences. Also, many therapists have been previously trained to believe that it's good clinical practice to let the client determine what is discussed, so the way you practiced this in a workshop setting might also be consistent with some of your clinical practice habits. Although trauma therapists do try to take the client's current concerns into account, and if possible integrate these into the treatment session, trauma therapists do much more than follow the clients. Trauma therapists guide clients through a carefully structured series of tasks, designed to help them gradually become safer and stronger, digest the trauma memories, and prepare for future challenges.

When Have You Done Enough Exposure?

Are we done yet? How do you know when you have finished with exposure for the memory you've been working with? Although this question has no definitive answer—practices differ among the various trauma resolution traditions—there are some useful guidelines.

No More Changes

You notice that the story is the same, again and again. (When the child first complains that it's getting boring, the therapist says, "Good, that's what we want. That means that it's losing its power. Now tell it again.") No new detail is forthcoming, the emotional issues have been worked out and no longer seem to have any charge, and the client has an easy time telling the story fully.

No Irrational Negative Self-Statements

In an unprocessed memory, often negative beliefs exist about the self, such as "It was my fault," "I'm bad," "I'm not safe," etc. These are the kinds of beliefs that hurt your client—they're part of his sore spot. When your client has really digested the memory, he will have a healthier way of seeing the memory and his part in it. Now he will make statements such as, "I did the best I could," "I'm safer now," and "I learned from this."

Low SUDS

You don't need to get to a SUDS of zero to be done (unless you're using EMDR). With exposure, even when you've done all the work, sometimes the SUDS level stays at a low or moderate level for days or even weeks afterward. As long as you've really worked the memory into the ground, and the other criteria are met, you're probably okay. However, if any portion of the memory is still highly distressing, it can probably use more work.

Symptom Reduction

If you are doing exposure on one memory of many on the trauma list, you are not likely to see much in the way of quick symptom reduction, because so many other memories remain that are also driving the symptoms. However, if you are doing exposure with the primary identified trauma, you should expect to see some symptom reduction within days or weeks. You are most likely to see reduction of symptoms that are most closely related to posttraumatic stress, such as nightmares, bed-wetting, and intrusive imagery. However, other symptoms may also diminish.

Ideally the SUDS should be no higher than about a three, and lower is even better. Ultimately the child should feel strong, in control, and bored with discussing the trauma.

The Session After Exposure

When you are working with a child in the trauma resolution phase of treatment, and you have been doing exposure, you should be doing specific things in the session after the exposure session.

Regular Check-In

It's important to do your regular beginning-of-the-session check-in, for several reasons. The check-in maintains the routine that is part of the structure and predictability of your treatment. It also serves a purpose, which is to find out what's happening. If there is some crisis or pressing concern, you will want to know that right away, so you can take it into account and perhaps address it. It can be very frustrating to go ahead with your own agenda only to find out that your client can't concentrate because of some other concern that you weren't aware of. Finally, the check-in might give you some clues about the child's response to the work done in the previous session.

Ask About the Memory

You want to know how the previous session's work might have affected your client during the week, and you want to know the current status of the memory. So you might say something like, "We talked about a hard thing last week. In the last few days, did you think about that more than usual, less than usual, or about the same? And on zero to ten, where is it now?" After an exposure session it is fairly common for the client to think more about the event than usual, at least for a while, and then to feel more relief and leave it alone. But don't be surprised if the memory is worse than when you left it, better, or the same. Anything can happen.

Finish Work on the Memory

If the memory is still unresolved, then you can do more work with it. Does a blocking belief need to be challenged and corrected? Does a hot spot exist that can be worked over? Or is it just a matter of having your client tell the story more times?

Do Exposure with the Next Memory

If the memory you've been working on has been fully digested, it's time to do exposure with any remaining memories that are still disturbing to the client. You'll want to use the same kind of judgment and strategies that you've been using already, to select the next memory to target with exposure, and to help your client get through it. Of course, now that your client has made it through exposure successfully with one memory, she is stronger and more experienced, so she will be able to handle a little more challenge in the next one.

The trauma resolution phase continues until all the significant trauma/loss memories have been resolved and are no longer a source of distress.

Chapter 16

Problem Solving in an Exposure Session

Doing exposure well takes practice, and even though it may seem pretty simple, there's a lot to it. It will be difficult to do exposure well, and to fully use the suggestions here, without supervised practice. Much of deciding if, when, and how to intervene during an exposure session is clinical judgment. The practice and supervision will help you learn where the judgments fall.

Many sessions will go smoothly, and then the basic procedures and principles described in the previous chapter will get you through nicely. Other sessions will not go so smoothly. This chapter will give you ideas on what to do in response to some of the most typical problems that come up during exposure. Actually, these typical problems are all variants of the same basic problem: that the memory is difficult to get through. However, the memory can be difficult for various reasons, each calling for a different problem-solving strategy.

When the exposure session is going smoothly, meaning that movement (change) occurs from one time to the next, then at the end of one telling of the story, the therapist can simply repeat the instructions and have the client tell the story again. On the other hand, if the therapist has concerns about how the session is going, the end of a telling of the story can be a good time to check in, ask questions, and try to figure out what's going on. This doesn't mean that it's okay to ask pointed or intrusive questions that will push the client to open up again to the difficult part of the memory! The goal of the questioning is to learn whether the client is still in the productive middle ground, or if not, what the nature of the problem might be. Understanding the problem allows the therapist to choose the best intervention to solve the problem.

PROBLEM: ONE PART OF THE STORY IS ESPECIALLY DIFFICULT

Sometimes most of the story is going smoothly, seems easy to tell, but one place in the memory is a real sticking point (or maybe a couple of places). You might have a feeling that much of the memory is too easy and nothing's happening there, while the part that's difficult is not really getting much airtime.

Signals That This Might Be Happening

- One or two places in the memory seem much more difficult than the rest.
- The difficult places do not move or change from one telling to the next.
- Therapist is wondering what to do about this (this really is one of the signals!).

Questions the Therapist Can Ask at the End of a Telling

- How did it go for you this time? What struck you the most?
- What's the worst part of the memory right now? Where is that on zero to ten?

Intervention Strategy

- Work the "hot spot." Go through the portion of the memory that includes the hot spot—perhaps from just before that part to just after it. Do this over and over again. It's okay to leave the rest of the memory alone for a little while.
- After you've made some headway on the hot spot, go back to working with the story of the whole memory again. Hopefully things will keep on moving now.
- The hot-spot strategy can be repeated if necessary, and/or tried with other spots in the memory.

PROBLEM: THE CLIENT SEEMS OVERWHELMED

If the client is feeling overwhelmed, he cannot digest anything. Also, there is a risk that he will experience the exposure session itself as a new trauma. In the early days of exposure, a large percentage of clients dropped out of treatment for this reason. Now that we are better at catching this problem and helping clients stay in that productive middle ground, we don't lose so many of them. It's a bit tricky to achieve this balance, though. On the one hand, we are asking our clients to talk about an upsetting thing that happened to them, in the present tense, along with details, thoughts, and feelings. Surely we are expecting some anguish and tears! Yet we don't want them to get bitten by the dog. We want them to face only what they can handle and digest. So it's important to remain sensitive to the client's status, and to try to keep them from trying to take too many bites at a time.

Signals That This Might Be Happening

- *Expression of distress.* The child may say that he is feeling bad or is having a difficult time.
- *Body language.* This can include crying, tearfulness, changes in breathing or posture, etc. It can also include restlessness or fidgeting.
- *Shift to past tense.* Going from present to past tense is a distancing strategy. It is used frequently in exposure sessions that are going well, so it's not automatically a problem. But it is an indication that the client is trying to back off. You can take this into consideration along with the rest of what's happening, and see if you think there's a problem.
- *Shift to superficial.* Again, at times a superficial account is appropriate within an exposure session that's going well. Early on, many kids will lay down the structure of the story with one or more rounds of a relatively superficial recounting. Much later, after the details have been told and worked through, the story might again become relatively superficial because the details are no longer interesting. However, when you see your client telling the story in some detail, and then getting to a difficult part and skimming over it in a superficial manner, the client is probably practicing an avoidance strategy. This is not automatically a problem if progress is being made, but should be taken into consideration.
- *Humor.* If your client makes a joke about something that's really painful, usually it's best if the therapist can respond both to the underlying pain and to the fact that the client is attempting to gain some distance from the pain. It's okay not to laugh.
- *Boredom.* When the memory is really worked into the ground, boredom is a goal, a sign of success—it means that the memory has lost its charge. However, sometimes a client will complain of boredom prematurely, before the work is even close to being completed. Although sometimes this can be a sign of actual boredom, often it is an indication of avoidance.
- *Overtalking.* Beware of clients who give way too much detail about things that don't matter, such as what she ate for breakfast the week before the event. You'll know this when you hear it. Another method of overtalking is when clients seem to spend all their time talking *about* the exposure session in one way or another, rather than doing it. Think, "Avoidance."
- *Wanting to be done* (for any of a variety of "reasons"). I'm all better now; this is boring; this is stupid; this isn't doing anything; can we play now?

Questions the Therapist Can Ask in the Moment of Concern

- Where are you now on zero to ten? Is this okay for you, or does it feel like too much?
- Are you telling me that it might be too hard to talk about this part right now? Should we go to another part that's not so hard?
- Do you feel like you want to just keep going? Or should we take a little break?

Intervention Strategies

- Allow some avoidance (e.g., a shift to past tense, a superficial telling of a certain part). Then just give the regular instructions the next time through, and let the client set her own degree of closeness or distance to the memory.
- Bring the SUDS down. This can be done with deep breathing, safe place visualization, or other strategies.
- Shift to another less challenging focus.
- Go to the good end; focus on things being okay now.

PROBLEM-BLOCKING BELIEFS

Sometimes the "sticking point" in a distressing memory is a child's negative belief, for example, that she was at fault in some way. Such beliefs are not always rational, and even the rational ones are generally not objectively true, even if they may work within a child's logic and limited fund of information. These are called "blocking beliefs" because they block further progress in digesting and resolving the memory.

Some beliefs are directly related to the exposure process itself. For example, a child may believe that she can't handle the emotion associated with the memory, and so remains at a superficial level in each telling. Another example would be a child who believes that if she talks about the memory, she will get so angry at her parent that their relationship will be destroyed. This type of blocking belief prevents the child from being willing to fully participate in the exposure.

Sometimes the problem beliefs work themselves out over repeated exposure. If this does not seem to be happening, the therapist can try cognitive restructuring interventions, including Socratic style questioning as well as psychoeducation. In other words, we give bits of information and ask questions to lead the child to a different and more useful way of looking at it. Here is an example of how a therapist might introduce information to shake loose a blocking belief, while allowing the child himself to generate as much of his own understanding as possible.

CHILD: I should have told her to watch out for that car; it's my fault.

THERAPIST: Did you know the car was coming?

CHILD: No, but I should have known. I should have been watching.

THERAPIST: Did your mother give you that job, to watch for cars behind her?

CHILD: No . . .

THERAPIST: Did you know that if you were always twisted around to look behind you, you could get more hurt than you did?

CHILD: No.

THERAPIST: Your mother told me about this accident, too. Did you know that even if you had seen that car and said, "Watch out!" your mother still couldn't have gotten out of the way?

CHILD: No, I didn't know that.

THERAPIST: The rule is, it's the driver's job to watch for other cars, and it's the kids job to sit with a seat belt on, and not to mess around, so that the driver can concentrate on driving. Did you have your seat belt on?

CHILD: Yes.

THERAPIST: And were you screaming and jumping around so your mother couldn't concentrate on driving?

CHILD: No, we were just talking.

THERAPIST: So you were doing your job. Were you driving that other car, the one that crashed into your car?

CHILD: No!

THERAPIST: So whose fault do you really think it was, your fault for doing your job just the way you were supposed to? Or the other driver who wasn't paying attention and crashed into you guys?

CHILD: The other driver.

THERAPIST: That's what I think, too. Now go back to when you're sitting at the stop sign, and tell the story again.

Signals That This Might Be Happening

- The client seems stuck, not making progress.
- The client states a blocking belief, either spontaneously or in response to questioning.

Questions the Therapist Can Ask at the End of a Telling

1. What was the hardest part this time? Where is that now on zero to ten?
2. What keeps that part from getting better?
3. What are you saying to yourself about that?

Although the general approach to blocking beliefs is the same regardless of the specific belief, specific interventions seem to work best in response to particular blocking beliefs. Some of the most common types of blocking beliefs, along with suggested interventions, are listed in the following:

Blocking belief: I'm still in danger.
Suggested intervention: Is that true? Please explain. Can he hurt you from jail? Etc. (Note that if the client really is still in danger, this should be addressed as much as possible prior to trying exposure.)
Blocking belief: It was my fault/I should have done X (when this is irrational/incorrect).
Suggested intervention: Provide information; ask clarifying questions.
Example: An eleven-year-old girl had come home from school at age five to see her grandfather on the floor, having a heart attack. In the exposure session, she is stuck on, "I should have called nine-one-one." Even though she has been told previously that it was already too late, that an ambulance could not have saved him, she is not thinking of that right now. She's stuck on blaming herself.

THERAPIST: Do you remember what the doctor told your mother about that?

CHILD: What?

THERAPIST: That he would have died anyway, even if someone did call nine-one-one.

CHILD: Oh, yeah.

THERAPIST: So how old were you when this happened?

CHILD: Five.

THERAPIST: Did you know nine-one-one when you were five? Had someone taught you that?

CHILD: No, I just learned it maybe last year.

THERAPIST: Yeah, I think most kids learn nine-one-one when they're maybe nine or ten years old. So you weren't old enough to know nine-one-one then?

CHILD: I guess not.

THERAPIST: And the doctor said it wouldn't have helped anyway?

CHILD: I guess not.

Blocking belief: It was my fault (when this is true).
Suggested intervention: What have you learned from this? What do you know now that you didn't know then? What would you do (in that situation) now? Is there anything you can do to make up for what happened?

This is a particularly tricky situation, because when the child actually did cause the bad event, it's not an irrational belief that can be refuted. Still, there's no point in living a miserable life just because you did something bad. The goal here is not to relieve the child of legitimate guilt, but to help her figure out how to learn to live with this and move on in a productive way. Kids can often recognize that they have learned and grown, that they are different now, and that they would do something different in that situation now. It can also be helpful for the child to find some way to help others, as a way to make amends for the earlier wrong.

Blocking belief: I'm a bad person because of this.
Suggested intervention: Who did the bad thing? Did you deserve this? What would you say if it happened to someone else?
Example: A ten-year-old girl had been molested by her uncle a few months earlier. At that time her uncle had blamed her for his behavior, saying that the dress she was wearing, and the way she looked, made him do it. In the exposure session, she is stuck on the idea that she is a bad person because if she caused it, she must have wanted it to happen.

THERAPIST: So when you put that nice dress on, what were you thinking about?

CHILD: Just that it was a nice dress. I like to wear it; it's pretty. My parents gave it to me for my birthday.

THERAPIST: You weren't saying to yourself, "I think I'll wear my nice dress today so that my uncle will mess with me"?

CHILD: No! I never thought of that.

THERAPIST: I didn't think so. So how old is your uncle?

CHILD: I don't know, maybe thirty?

THERAPIST: And how old are you?

CHILD: Ten.

THERAPIST: And who's bigger?

CHILD: He is.

THERAPIST: So who usually decides what happens, the bigger older person who's in charge, or the smaller younger kid?

CHILD: The big person. But he said that if I hadn't worn that dress—he said I made him do it.

THERAPIST: Do you think that when you grow up, you'll have a family of your own?

CHILD: I think so.

THERAPIST: What if you give your daughter a really nice dress for her birthday? And then some big grown-up man messes with your daughter—and he says it's her fault because she was wearing that nice dress. Whose fault would it really be?

CHILD: The man's.

THERAPIST: It wouldn't be your daughter's fault for wearing that nice dress you gave her?

CHILD: No, she can wear a nice dress; there's nothing wrong with that.

Blocking belief: If I feel better (about the person's death) that would mean that I didn't care. Alternately: If I am no longer in mourning, that would mean that I am no longer in a relationship with this person.
Suggested intervention: What would [the dead person] want for you to do?

This is a very common blocking belief in exposure sessions focused on bereavement. The essence of this blocking belief is that the child's primary goal is to maintain a relationship with the dead person. That's more important to the child than getting rid of sadness. The problem is, right now, the only way the child can see how to maintain the relationship is to keep the sadness.

In this situation, telling the child to go ahead with the exposure—in other words, let's get to work on getting rid of the sadness—risks giving the message that the therapist does not care about helping the child to maintain the relationship. But that's the child's primary concern. This creates an impasse, and nothing gets done.

It's better to work with the child on the child's goals. Although you can simply ask, "What would [the dead person] want for you to do?" it's even better to have the child ask the dead person directly. Then instead of giving her own opinion of what the dead person would say, she can get the actual statement. Since most people have some experience in talking with dead people, this is usually not too hard to accomplish. For example:

THERAPIST: So how would you talk with your grandmother? Some people would go to the graveyard; some people would go outside at night; some people would do it while they're sleeping, in their dreams; some people would write a letter and then burn the letter so the smoke goes up . . . What would work best for you?

CHILD: I would go outside at night and talk to her in the sky.

THERAPIST: Okay, now what I want you to do is imagine going outside at night and talking to her in the sky. You can do this with your eyes closed, if you want. Imagine telling her how much you still care about her, and how you are staying sad to show her that. Ask her if that's okay with her, if that's what she wants you to do. And notice how she answers . . .

This is not an exhaustive list of blocking beliefs or problem-solving strategies, but it gives you the general idea. Notice that although the therapist does introduce information in certain circumstances, in general the therapist avoids telling the child what to think or believe. Rather, the information and questions are designed to guide the child to reach his own conclusions. Then they are his and there is a better chance that he'll integrate these conclusions into his story.

After the blocking belief has been addressed and possibly resolved with this cognitive intervention, you can go back to working on the memory as before. Perhaps the first time, you might want to work just on the hot spot related to the blocking belief. Normally when the blocking belief has been addressed, you will see renewed progress when you return to the regular exposure procedure.

EXERCISE: PRACTICE WITH EXPOSURE

This is the same exercise as in Chapter 15. It's a good exercise to practice, and this time around you know more about how to do it than you did before.

If You Are the Client

- This is not a role-play; be yourself.
- Choose a memory (from your trauma history list or otherwise) that you rate six or lower on the zero to ten scale, and that you are willing to talk about today. If you participated in the Breaking Down the Memory exercise, you might want to continue with the same memory.
- Do not look at the script; that's the therapist's job.
- Remember what to do if you feel that you need a break or if there's something you don't want to talk about. Just because you agree at the beginning does not mean that you will feel the same way later on. Take care of yourself.

If You Are the Therapist

- When your client tells you what memory she'll be working on, help her identify a good end that's a specific event.
- Use the following instructions, one through five, the first time. Verbatim, of course!
- Do your best to restrain yourself and allow your client to do her work. Don't pester her with questions about details, present tense, thoughts or feelings. Don't tell her your own insights or interpretations. Just be present and let her tell her story.
- Make sure the story goes all the way to the good end.
- Repeat the first three instructions, again verbatim. Have the client tell the story again.
- Do this as many times as you have time for and as your client will tolerate.
- When you're done with the exposure portion of the exercise, use the "Container" to put the memory away. Then see if your client would like to do some deep breathing or a safe place visualization.

Exposure Instructions

1. Tell the story from beginning to end.
2. Tell it in the present tense, as if it's happening right now.
3. Say what's happening, also what you're thinking and feeling.
4. Now and then I'll ask a question to help me understand something, or to see how you're doing.
5. When you finish, I'll ask you to do it again, and then again. This is how you'll get stronger.

Discussion Questions

- In a group, clients, please share your comments and experiences.
- How many (clients) found that the SUDS turned out to be higher than you had initially rated it?
- How many (clients) feel that you are worse off than before? The same as before? Better off?
- Therapists, please share your comments and experiences.
- How many therapists had some difficulty restraining yourself from making comments or other interventions?
- How many clients felt that the therapist cared about you? What did you notice that made you think that?
- How many therapists had a personal emotional reaction while conducting this session? How did you handle this? How do you feel now? Do you need to do anything else to take care of yourself?

SECTION IV BIBLIOGRAPHY

Ahrens, J. & Rexford, L. (2002). Cognitive processing therapy for incarcerated adolescents with PTSD. *Journal of Aggression, Maltreatment & Trauma, 6,* 201-216. The first report of CPT being used successfully with adolescents.

Deblinger, E. & Heflin, A. H. (1996). *Treating sexually abused children and their nonoffending parents: A cognitive behavioral approach.* Thousand Oaks, CA: Sage Publications. This is the classic text/manual on doing modified exposure with kids, using the strategy of making a book to tell the story of the trauma memory. Much of the research showing that exposure works with trauma-exposed kids has used this manual as the basis for their treatment.

Gil, E. (1991). *The healing power of play: Working with abused children.* New York: Guilford Press. An alternative structured/focused approach to trauma resolution using play.

Greenwald, R. (1999). *Eye movement desensitization and reprocessing (EMDR) in child and adolescent psychotherapy.* Northvale, NJ: Jason Aronson. A thorough presentation of EMDR for kids, within a trauma-informed treatment approach. Plenty of vignettes and session transcripts to see how it really goes.

James, B. (1989). *Treating traumatized children: New insights and creative interventions.* Lexington, MA: Lexington Books. Another example of both traditional and innovative child therapy methods applied to trauma treatment.

SECTION V: MAKING THE MOST OF IT

When you've finished the trauma resolution phase of treatment, the child is much closer to regaining a developmentally appropriate level of functioning. Sometimes this just happens—once the trauma is cleaned up, symptoms seem to just melt away, and more normal functioning takes over. Sometimes, though, problems remain. These can be taken care of more easily now that the unprocessed trauma is no longer driving the symptoms. For example, this might be an excellent time to revisit skill development. Now that the trauma is out of the way, kids will have a much better chance of learning better study habits, self-management skills, and other things they may have been working on.

Some of the persisting symptoms might be clearly trauma related. For example, a child may avoid a certain type of activity or place that reminds her of the trauma, even after the trauma itself is no longer particularly distressing. Another example is related to the "hyperarousal" symptom—the child might still have an unreasonably strong reaction to something that is, in some way, a reminder of the trauma:

A fourteen-year-old girl who had been abducted by men driving a red car continued to become anxious whenever she saw a red car.

A twelve-year-old boy who had been overly reactive to his frustration in math class, perhaps initially because this reminded him of his trauma-related helplessness, continued to be overly reactive and to give up too easily.

Family relationships should also be reevaluated, since these may have been modified as a function of the parent training and/or the child treatment. For example, a child who has been overprotected may start to be given more responsibilities. Also, some children believe that their symptom serves an important function in the family; once the symptoms are reduced or eliminated, the therapist has an obligation to check and make sure that the family is okay, and has found another way to take care of what the symptom was being used for:

An eleven-year-old girl had "school phobia" because she was afraid to leave her mother alone during the day. Her mother had a medical condition and this fear was somewhat realistic. In a family meeting following the trauma resolution work, the therapist checked to make sure that there was still a trusted adult checking in with mother during the day.

A seven-year-old boy, at the beginning of treatment, had been reluctant to participate. Then in a family meeting, in response to the therapist's questions, he had expressed concern that if his mother didn't have to worry about him and yell at him any more, they wouldn't be as close. The family made an agreement that as his behavior improved and his mother didn't have to discipline him so much, they would find other things to do together, such as play games and watch movies. After the trauma resolution was completed, in a family meeting the therapist asked how often they were doing things together such as playing games and watching movies.

The issue of the child's vulnerability should also be addressed at this time. Before, the focus was on safety and stability in the present. Now the focus can be on the future. What can be done to limit vulnerability to further trauma exposure? If something bad happens anyway, what can be done to limit deterioration and facilitate recovery? Also, for kids who have been unwilling or unable to complete the trauma resolution work, how can remaining trauma-related vulnerabilities be managed in the future, especially in times of increased stress?

The following chapters focus on how to follow up on trauma resolution work, how to consolidate the gains made in the prior treatment phases, addressing the issues described previously. A range of interventions may be used, including family systems interventions, in vivo exposure, and relapse prevention. The concepts and procedures directly build on previous interventions.

Chapter 17

Reevaluation and Consolidation of Gains

After trauma resolution has been completed, some of the easiest remaining problems to take care of are those that are trauma-related. Often these problems or symptoms will melt away, but sometimes they have taken on a life of their own. Then they tend to be very responsive to cognitive and behavioral interventions, because the driving force behind the problems is no longer present.

There are a number of effective strategies for overcoming leftover trauma-related symptoms, including in vivo exposure as well as the use of incentives; these can also be combined. Use of incentives is discussed in more detail in the final section of the book.

IN VIVO EXPOSURE

The central principle of in vivo exposure is that the fear underlying the avoidant behavior is disproved, and "extinguished," by persistently engaging in the avoided behavior. It's only by facing the situation that you've been avoiding that you can find out that the feared thing isn't going to happen. Of course, for this to be successful, it's important for the child to be able to tolerate the thing she has been avoiding. The therapist helps her to prepare for this by breaking it down into manageable steps and then rehearsing coping skills to address any anxiety associated with doing it.

THERAPIST: I want to check with you again this week, how much has that thing been on your mind, the memory we've been talking about so much?

CHILD: I don't really think about it anymore.

THERAPIST: That must be nice. If you make yourself concentrate on it right now, how bad is the feeling right now, from zero to ten?

CHILD: It's the same as last time, maybe a one or two. It doesn't really bother me.

THERAPIST: And are you back to sleeping in your own bed again, or still sleeping in your Mom's bed?

CHILD: Oh, I still sleep in my Mom's bed; I'd be too scared to sleep in my own room anymore.

THERAPIST: You know, after all the brave things I've seen you do, I bet you could handle sleeping in your own room, too. Your mom told me that when you're good at sleeping by yourself again, she'll let you do a sleepover at your cousin's house. Is that something you want to be able to do?

CHILD: I've been asking her for months when can I sleep over at their house.

THERAPIST: Okay, so let's help you get ready for sleeping by yourself, so that you'll be more confident that you'll be able to handle it. We're going to think about each step of this, from thinking about going to bed, to going to your room, to your mother saying good night to you, to you getting into bed, staying there, falling asleep. . . . I want you to imagine a movie in your mind, with each of these steps. It starts when you are thinking about going to bed, and it ends when you wake up in the morning. Go ahead, start the movie, and then tell me when you're done.

CHILD: I didn't get all the way through, I started hearing noises and got nervous and went to my mother's bed.

THERAPIST: In this movie, about how long did you last in your own bed?

CHILD: Maybe ten or fifteen minutes.

THERAPIST: That's not bad for a start. Do you remember how before, we were talking about the difference between actually being unsafe, and actually being safe but feeling unsafe?

CHILD: Yeah.

THERAPIST: Do you think that in your bed at night you are really unsafe, or are you really safe but maybe feel unsafe?

CHILD: I'm safe but I don't feel safe.

THERAPIST: Do you remember what to do when you know you're safe, to help yourself calm down and feel safe?

CHILD: Like the breathing and stuff?

THERAPIST: Right, it's the same thing we were doing before. The deep breathing, saying to yourself, "I'm safe," thinking about your Safe Place, thinking about doing something fun. . . . Which of these do you think would work best for you while you're lying in bed?

CHILD: Maybe the safe place.

THERAPIST: Okay, let's try that. I want you to do that movie in your mind again. This time, when you're in your bed and the noises start, what can you say to yourself?

CHILD: That I know I'm really safe.

THERAPIST: Okay, so when the noises start, you say to yourself, "I know I'm really safe," and then concentrate on your Safe Place. In this movie, stay in your bed for half an hour, then if you want, you can go to your mother's bed. Okay? So start at the beginning, think about going to bed, and tell me when the movie's over.

CHILD: Done.

THERAPIST: How did it go this time, how long did you stay in your own bed?

CHILD: I stayed for a half an hour, and whenever I got nervous I did that stuff you said.

THERAPIST: And how bad would you say it got, on zero to ten, what was the worst it got?

CHILD: Maybe a four or five.

THERAPIST: How long do you think you could stay in your bed, for real, without it getting too hard?

CHILD: I think I could do it for half an hour, as long as I knew it was going to be over soon.

THERAPIST: I think that's a good way to start. Every night this week, I want you to stay in your own bed for half an hour before you go to your mother's bed. Is there a clock near your bed so you can check how much time you have?

CHILD: Yes, it has glow-in-the-dark hands so I can see what time it is at night.

THERAPIST: Okay, let's try the movie one more time. You'll go to your own bed, when you hear noises or get nervous you tell yourself it's really safe, think of your safe place. And after half an hour you can leave, go to your mother's bed. Ready?

CHILD: Done.

THERAPIST: How did it go that time?

CHILD: Easy.

THERAPIST: Okay, good. I'm going to talk to your mom about this too, so you both remember. So every night this week, you go to your own bed for half an hour, right?

CHILD: Right.

THERAPIST: And after all the ways that I've seen you be brave, seen you get stronger and stronger, my bet is that you're going to be able to do this. What do you think?

CHILD: I think I can, too.

As with imaginal exposure, the ideal for in vivo exposure is a moderate level of distress. Too low is too easy and little is accomplished; too high is too difficult, too great a risk of failure and feeling overwhelmed. Challenges close to a SUDS of five are preferred. If the SUDS attached to an avoided situation or behavior is much higher than five, the challenge can be broken down into more manageable components.

With an older child, it may be more important to present a rationale, e.g., "It's important for you to stay in bed for at least X minutes, to prove to yourself that it really is safe there. If you keep leaving the bed after only a minute or two, you'll never really be sure. But if you stay there a long time and nothing bad happens, you can learn to feel safer and safer."

As with many interventions, in vivo exposure can be supported by incentives, such as the anticipated overnight at the cousin's house used in the above example. It is important for the therapist to work closely with the parent to guide the parent in encouraging and reinforcing desired behaviors. Just as important, though, is to build on the child's own growing sense of strength and self-efficacy.

In the previous example, the child is likely to overstay in her own bed, even fall asleep there, on one or more occasions. This is not assigned, so that if it does not happen, the child does not feel that she has failed; but if it does happen, the child feels extra successful for having surpassed the assignment.

FAMILY STRENGTHENING INTERVENTIONS

Near the beginning of treatment, the therapist may have raised issues regarding how the presenting symptoms may have been affecting the family's sense of closeness, and/or the child's normal development. As treatment comes to a close, it is worth revisiting these issues. Now that the child is no longer so disruptive, is the family really less close? Or are they (as they had predicted) just as close, but focused on more enjoyable activities? Now that the child is no longer impaired by his fears, do his parents treat him like a normal child his age? Do they let him walk to the corner store? Do they expect him to do chores? Or are they still extraprotective, such as had been appropriate when he required special care?

There is no single way to approach these issues. In general, the therapist may directly inquire, with the child, the parents, and the family together, as seems most fitting. Most commonly, the parents can be guided to correct any remaining problems with a combination of awareness, psychoeducation, and sometimes specific suggestions or assignments.

THERAPIST: Do you remember when we first decided we were going to work together? Do you remember that I was worried about whether you and your parents would be less close if they didn't have to be busy yelling at you and punishing you all the time? But you all said that the family would still be close, but that you would have more fun together instead of just arguing. So I wrote down the kinds of things you thought you would be doing. Let's see, here it is. You said that you would watch movies together, play cards together, but also just enjoy each other more just doing regular things like going to the store or maybe helping to cook a meal or something. So let me ask you first: Do you think that you are more close with your parents than before, having more good times together? Or is it worse than before, or about the same?

CHILD: I think we're more close because I act better. I'm more good now, and they don't have to yell at me so much anymore.

THERAPIST: And if I was watching your family on TV, what would I see you doing together? What would I notice that would make me think that things were better?

CHILD: When Dad asks me to take out the garbage I don't argue with him. I just do it—well, most of the time, anyway—and you would see us watching a movie together.

THERAPIST: What about you? How do you see it? Better than before, worse, about the same?

PARENT: Things are a lot more peaceful at home. I think it's nicer for everyone.

THERAPIST: And would you say that when you don't have to yell at your child, you can ignore her now, or are there things you still do together?

PARENT: Oh, we do plenty of things together. We go to the store, errands, we do things at home, she helps me with chores, we watch TV or movies. It's just nicer now.

THERAPIST: You told me that that's how it would happen, I guess you were right. That's good, I didn't know if I should be worried about that or not.

As always, it's important to learn each person's perspective, and to obtain specific, concrete information. The therapist asks for specifics, gives examples, and persists. In this example, the problem had been resolved, and the therapist was just checking up to be thorough before terminating. On the other hand, if problems are uncovered, the therapist would explore the nature of the problem and work with the family to correct it.

THERAPIST: I've been pleased to see how well your son has done in talking about the bad memories. I know he feels a lot better now and he's not having the bad dreams anymore. You've also told me that he seems happier in general, and more interested in things again.

PARENT: Yes, you really helped my son; I'm so thankful.

THERAPIST: I'm glad he's doing so much better. You really came through for him, too: you brought him here, you gave him all that extra attention while he was so clingy and wanting to be near you all the time. You really helped him to feel secure so he could get back on his feet.

PARENT: Well, he's my baby.

THERAPIST: You know, that's what he told me too! But now that he's feeling better, he says he doesn't want to be treated like a baby anymore. Isn't that good news?

PARENT: I know. He doesn't want to have a bedtime anymore, wants to watch anything he wants on TV. . . .

THERAPIST: Fortunately, you have the good sense to know that you're in charge, and that he still needs that from a parent. But I think there are some things you can do, to kind of push him a little, help him feel more grown-up and responsible, like other kids his age.

PARENT: Like what?

THERAPIST: Well, you know how you were walking him to the bus stop? For a while, that was just the right thing to do, made him feel really safe. It was just what he needed. But now—

PARENT: Oh yeah, I can see how that would be embarrassing. And I can see the bus stop from my window anyway. I guess I don't have to be right there where the other kids can see me.

THERAPIST: I think that's a really good idea. You can still see that he's safe, he can still know that you're watching. But when you let him go by himself, you're giving him the message that he can handle it, that he's okay, that he can do things that other kids his age can do. If he thinks you believe in him, he'll believe in himself even more.

As with the earlier parent training, the preferred approach is to identify the parent's positive intent, give credit for ways that they are already successful in expressing that intent, and then find other things they can do to express the intent even more effectively.

This intervention often involves helping the parent make a shift from a previously appropriate parenting role to a current role that involves giving the child more responsibility. This shift may be difficult for a parent who is in a habit of providing an extra level of protection for a child that has been especially vulnerable. The therapist does not accomplish this by saying that the parent was wrong, but by saying that, to be a parent to a growing child, the parent must occasionally make shifts to respond to the growing child's changing parent-related needs. Parents know this; the therapist's job is to help the parent recognize this as one of those moments when a shift is needed.

In the previous example, only one parental behavior change was mentioned. In an actual session, the therapist might say, "I wonder what other ways you can show him that you believe he can handle things that other kids his age can do?" And if this does not yield a good response, the therapist can suggest examples of normative levels of responsibility for a child that age—for example, doing chores, or going places with friends—and ask where the child is relative to the norm.

Ideally, a small number (two or three) of parent behaviors are targeted for change in this intervention. A single change might not be sufficient to encourage generalization; too many changes might be hard to remember to do, leading to failure to implement the planned changes. A small number of changes, selected according to a guiding principle (e.g., showing that we believe in him), are likely to be implemented successfully, and can be built upon.

OTHER INTERVENTIONS

After trauma resolution, the therapist should take a good look at the child's overall situation, a sort of reevaluation. Check for case management and safety issues, skills and habits, and family dynamics. Anything that still needs work, this is the time to do it. At this point, the intervention strategy should be appropriate to the problem; it's not a trauma issue anymore. Fortunately, at this point, non-trauma-related intervention strategies have an excellent chance of working, since the trauma is not in the way anymore.

Chapter 18

Relapse Prevention and Harm Reduction

Let's go back to the fairy tale model. Once the dragon is slain and the guy has married the princess, well, that's nice, but we're not done yet. What can we do to keep more dragons from coming along? And if one should come, what can we do to be ready for it? Now that we've worked out the problems that were bothering the child and family in the moment, it's time to focus on the future.

Relapse prevention refers to a range of interventions designed to keep a vulnerable person on track despite the challenges and adversities that may arise. It can help to prevent recurrence of an unwanted event; prepare coping strategies for a stressful situation; and if/when the bad thing happens anyway, relapse prevention and harm reduction strategies can minimize damage and speed recovery. In child trauma treatment, the goals are (1) to prevent recurrence of trauma; (2) to prepare coping strategies for anticipated challenges; and (3) in the event of a new trauma, to develop response behaviors including rapid recognition of the traumatization, along with symptom management and help seeking. Some of the same concepts and methods that have been used throughout the treatment can be used here.

The approach to relapse prevention is very similar to the approach to self-management skills training that was used earlier in the treatment. In fact, the Choices Have Consequences intervention can be used here as well. The strategies in relapse prevention are to

1. Emphasize the child's goals, strengths, and positive intent. Blaming the child only knocks her down and makes her weaker and less capable of handling challenges.
2. Externalize the problem. If the problem is personality or temperament, the client is stuck with who she is, and thus powerless to cope. If the problem is situational, the client can do something to avoid or manage situations.
3. Identify future high risks and strategies to avoid these.
4. Identify specific signals as cues to specific actions.
5. Identify the signals as early in the risky situation as possible, so that the client gets better at managing the situation before it goes too far.
6. Label failures as "expected" and not as signifying total failure. If one slip means total failure, the child is more likely to give up. If a slip is expected, the child can still feel that she is on track, and can maintain her efforts.
7. Utilize all available resources to help the child implement her coping strategies. For example:
   - Pair behaviors with their consequences.
   - Invoke "the rules," "what Mommy says," or other external authorities that may strengthen the child's stance.
   - Involve parents and others in the planning of coping strategies; for example, mother agrees to take the child's statements seriously if she reports being assaulted again.
8. Rehearse/practice the coping strategies.

It can be very tempting to end treatment when the child seems to be "all better now." The therapist and the child are feeling satisfied and successful, and for good reason. Everyone did their job. The child is feeling better and acting better; nothing's wrong now. So why not quit? Because if you don't prepare for the future, you could be in for some nasty surprises.

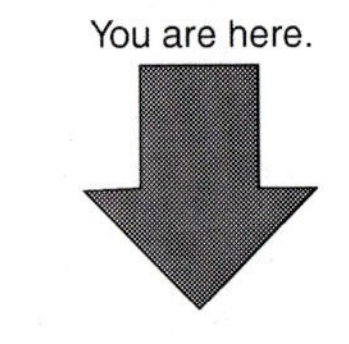

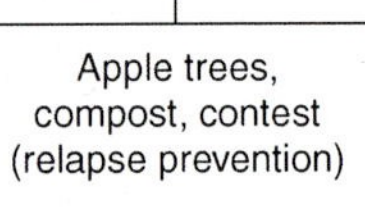

FIGURE 18.1. Steps in the fairy tale model.

WHAT CAN YOU DO TO KEEP BAD THINGS FROM HAPPENING?

The child as well as family members should be involved in making plans for avoiding potential problem situations. This will probably involve continuing to use safety-oriented practices that were hopefully initiated much earlier in the treatment. The latter part of the treatment is also an opportune time for the therapist to prepare the child and parents for upcoming developmental challenges—and related safety concerns—that can reasonably be anticipated.

Coping Skills in Challenging Situations

Of course, it is impossible to prevent every potentially risky situation, so it's also important to prepare the client for challenges that are likely to be faced. In the following case, the therapist hadn't yet made the effort to identify and address the client's vulnerabilities.

Martha was a nine-year-old girl who was in treatment for having been molested on multiple occasions by an uncle, some years before. She had been in treatment for six months and had completed the trauma resolution work. The current focus of treatment was on her remaining bad habits such as interpersonal problems related to her bossiness with peers.

One day at about noon, the therapist got a call from Martha's mother: "Do you know where she is?" The therapist said, "No, isn't she in school?" Martha's mother called back an hour later to report that Martha had been found, in the home of another girl in her class. When found, they were in the living room, eating popcorn and watching TV. The other girl's mother was there, too.

It seemed likely that Martha's earlier experiences of having been molested had predisposed her to doubt herself in the face of authority and to allow herself to be coerced. When the therapist heard this story, it became apparent that addressing Martha's vulnerability could not wait! Martha came to treatment later that day, and the therapist then initiated some relapse prevention strategies.

THERAPIST: Your mom told me that you weren't in school today. She got pretty worried about you.

CHILD: Yes, I was at my friend's house.

THERAPIST: I heard about that. How did that happen?

CHILD: Well, I was at the bus stop to go to school, and my friend was there, and her mother said we could come inside, so we did, and we watched TV and ate popcorn.

THERAPIST: I'm wondering what was happening inside you while your friend and her mother were inviting you to their house, but you knew you were supposed to be waiting for the school bus. What were you saying to yourself then? What kinds of feelings were you having?

CHILD: Well, I had kind of a funny feeling and I knew I wasn't supposed to go. But I sort of thought that because it was her mother, it must be okay. And I thought we were just going inside for a minute, like until the bus came, but then when I said, "Aren't we supposed to be going to school?" the mother said it was okay and I didn't really know what else to say.

THERAPIST: So it sounds like you knew it was wrong and you were kind of uncomfortable, but you weren't really sure what to do.

CHILD: Yeah.

THERAPIST: And then your mom got so worried she called the police, and now you got into big trouble with your mom.

CHILD: Yeah.

THERAPIST: So would you say that this whole thing was your idea? Or would you say that you were really just trying to go to school but that someone tricked you?

CHILD: Well, kind of, I guess they did trick me. I thought it was just going to be for a minute.

THERAPIST: Did you know that that's how a lot of bad things happen? There's a lot of tricky people out there trying to get other people into trouble.

CHILD: No, I didn't know that.

THERAPIST: Do you want to get tricked anymore? Or do you think you've had enough of that?

CHILD: I don't want to get tricked anymore.

THERAPIST: Should I tell you the secret so you know how to keep people from tricking you?

CHILD: Okay.

THERAPIST: Well, when someone tries to get you to do something, you can ask yourself, Is this something I'm allowed to do or not? and you can notice if you have an uncomfortable feeling or a funny feeling. And if it seems like maybe there's something wrong with it, like maybe someone's trying to trick you, you know what you can do?

CHILD: What?

THERAPIST: You can say no, and you can get away. Do you think you can say no?

CHILD: Yes.

THERAPIST: Let me hear you. Say it strong.

CHILD: No!

THERAPIST: That's not bad. Now let me see if I can trick you. I know! I'm going to be a guy who's walking along while you're playing in your front yard. Ready?

CHILD: Okay.

THERAPIST: Hello little girl. Can you tell me which way is the McDonald's from here?

CHILD: It's over that way.

THERAPIST: Can you show me? If you come with me, I'll buy you some ice cream.

CHILD: Um . . . no!

THERAPIST: You did it! I tried to trick you but it didn't work. Let me see, maybe I can trick you this time. Okay, we're on the school playground, kind of away from other people, and I'm another girl who you want to be friends with but don't know very well. Hey, come here. I have a cigarette. Want to smoke it with me?

CHILD: My mommy says I'm not allowed to smoke.

THERAPIST: I'll be your best friend.

CHILD: No, thank you!

THERAPIST: You did it again! You're pretty good at this!

HARM REDUCTION

What if something bad does happen in the future? What can you do to keep yourself on track?

Another part of relapse prevention is called harm reduction. The focus of harm reduction is to help your client anticipate and identify signals that the bad thing has happened, that things are going wrong for him, and to catch himself. In the following case example, this preparation was not done.

Kevin

Kevin was a thirteen-year-old boy who was brought in for treatment because of depression, social withdrawal, and loss of interest in former activities. With a trauma-informed evaluation and case formulation, the problem seemed to have come from a single trauma memory of having been molested by a stranger a few years before. Following the trauma resolution phase of treatment, the boy showed a rapid and remarkable transformation: his posture improved, he got a haircut, he smiled, he became more talkative with his family, and he became reinvolved in baseball, which had previously been a passion of his. Treatment was ended with congratulations all around.

Three months later, Kevin was brought back into treatment, having just been arrested for breaking a large number of windows at his school by throwing rocks at them one evening. Kevin was a "good kid" and not the type to do anything destructive, but he had in fact done this. Here's the story.

Since treatment, Kevin had been doing quite well for two months. Then one day the neighborhood bully, who was about Kevin's age, took Kevin's younger brother's skateboard. Kevin found the bully, fought him, and was able to take the skateboard back. In this neighborhood, that was not such an unusual encounter, and Kevin thought little more about it. Until the next day, when Kevin was hanging out on the corner with a few of his friends. The bully's father walked up and, without words or warning, punched Kevin, pushed him down, kicked him a couple of times, and walked away.

Then Kevin went into a tailspin. He hid out in his room most of the time, telling himself bad things about himself and the world. He stopped going to baseball practice. He was unable to concentrate well in school, and did little of his assigned homework. Every day he became more confused and more depressed. Finally one evening, not knowing what to do with his tortured emotions, he found himself in the schoolyard. Feeling moments of relief by throwing rocks at windows, he kept on doing it until the whole wall of windows was broken.

Harm reduction can be taught in about the same way as other relapse prevention strategies. It's just that the focus is on a different point in the anticipated challenging situation. The goal here is to anticipate and identify signals that something has gone wrong, so that it can be addressed before more damage is done. Had this procedure been done with Kevin, there is a good chance that he would have asked his mother to bring him back to the therapist long before he was at the point of throwing rocks at windows. Here is an example—with a different child—of a harm reduction intervention.

THERAPIST: You know how, after that kid at school showed you the knife and made you do all that stuff, you kept it a secret for a long time?

CHILD: Yeah, he said he'd kill me if I told.

THERAPIST: Right. And so you kept it a secret a long time. Remember how bad that felt? And how you were doing worse in school, and getting in trouble and stuff?

CHILD: Yeah.

THERAPIST: How long was it before you told? Maybe a year?

CHILD: About that; I guess so.

THERAPIST: And once you told, your mom brought you here, and we talked about it a lot, and you got so strong that it doesn't mess you up anymore.

CHILD: Plus, that kid didn't kill me, cause they kicked him out of school and he's not allowed to go near me or I can call the police.

THERAPIST: So if you have a friend someday that this kind of thing happens to, what would you tell your friend to do?

CHILD: Tell her mother or her father or her aunt or something.

THERAPIST: I think that's a good idea. Cause then she can get the kid in trouble, and she can start to feel better, like you did.

CHILD: Yeah.

THERAPIST: What if something else really bad happens to you someday? I hope it doesn't, but what if it does? What could you do?

CHILD: Tell.

THERAPIST: Who would you tell?

CHILD: My mother.

THERAPIST: What if your mother's on vacation and she's gone away for a few days?

CHILD: I can tell my auntie.

THERAPIST: Would you have to wait a while or can you tell her right away?

CHILD: Right away as soon as I get home from school.

THERAPIST: I think that's a good idea. But let me ask you a question. What if you're not sure if you should tell or not, and you decide to keep it a secret? But then you notice that you're starting to feel bad. Then what can you do?

CHILD: I can tell. If I feel bad, I should do something, right?

THERAPIST: I think you're right. Feeling bad is a good signal that you should tell. How can you tell that you feel bad? What are the signs?

CHILD: I stay in my room a lot and cry.

THERAPIST: And then you can tell your mom or your auntie?

CHILD: Yeah.

THERAPIST: You remember when we talked about this with your mom? She really wants you to tell her if anything else bad ever happens. Remember she said that?

As with the self-management training interventions, it's always important to transform concepts into concrete behaviors and events. In the previous example, "feeling bad" was transformed into a concrete indicator of distress, "stay in my room and cry." Then two years later, when she is staying in her room a lot and crying, there is a better chance that she will recognize this, catch herself, and do something about it. This chance is further improved when the distress signals, and the corrective behaviors, are practiced in role-plays or imagination.

ENDING TREATMENT WHEN TRAUMA RESOLUTION HAS NOT BEEN COMPLETED

Relapse prevention and harm reduction strategies should be used at the end of every treatment, regardless of how much has been accomplished already. Treatment may end for a variety of reasons, perhaps because the child is moving, or the insurance policy will not pay for more sessions and the family cannot afford to pay out of pocket. Sometimes treatment ends because the child absolutely refuses to engage in trauma resolution activities, despite the therapist's best efforts—so there's nothing left to work on. No matter why treatment is ending, the therapist should prepare the child as well as possible for the challenges to come.

Julio was a fifteen-year-old boy who came to the United States as a refugee from the Guatemalan civil war at age eleven. He had average to high-average intelligence and an accent so good that he sounded native to the United States. He was in treatment while in a three-month program at a residential facility operated by the juvenile corrections system in his state. Within the facility, Julio's behavior was excellent. He did well in school, got along with others, did not lose his temper, and did not break rules. The concern was very specific: When he was released, would he go back to stealing cars, or not?

Julio was cooperative in therapy, in part because he was so interested in figuring out what he could do to make sure that he was never incarcerated again. He was able to identify long-term goals that he cared about and was willing to work for. He declined to identify the events on his trauma history list, but considering where he had come from, it is likely that his trauma history included witnessing of assault, torture, and murder, as well as the loss of significant family members, possibly including parents and siblings. However, as noted in the chapter on trauma history, the specific details are not absolutely necessary in order to provide a trauma-informed case formulation. The real treatment impasse arose a little later, when the "personal training" phase of treatment was over, and the therapist suggested that it was time to start slaying the dragons.

JULIO: No, I don't need to talk about all that stuff [the trauma].

THERAPIST: What do you mean? You told me about the goals you have for yourself, things you really care about. I thought that you would want to give yourself the best chance of getting there.

JULIO: I do care, I'm going to make sure I get there. But now that you explained to me about the traumas behind the wall, and the sore spots, I know what to do.

THERAPIST: What?

JULIO: I'll just make the wall stronger so those things don't mess me up anymore.

THERAPIST: How will you do that?

JULIO: I know how.

THERAPIST: So it sounds like you really don't want to talk about the bad things that happened. You really want to kind of keep them behind the wall and keep them from bothering you.

JULIO: That's right.

THERAPIST: And you also really want to get to your goals, to live the kind of life you were telling me about.

JULIO: That's right.

THERAPIST: And you're feeling pretty confident that you can do both: make the wall stronger, keep those memories out of the way, and get to your goals.

JULIO: Yup.

THERAPIST: Well, my job is to make suggestions and your job is to make decisions. It's your life. So I'm going to explain a little more about my suggestion, and then it's up to you to make your decision. I've seen other kids try your strategy, and sometimes it works. The problem is, sometimes it only works for a while. Then some new stress comes along and adds to the pile-up. Then even the stronger wall just isn't enough, and the trauma messes them up again, and they end up doing things that get them in trouble all over again. I'd hate for that to happen to you. That's why I'm suggesting that you do the work now, to take care of the trauma memories so they can't hurt you anymore.

JULIO: I get what you're saying, but I'm going to do it my way.

THERAPIST: Okay. I hope that sooner or later you do take care of that stuff behind the wall; when you do it, I think you'll be glad you did. But no one can tell you when it's your time. It could be next year or twenty years from now. You'll have to decide that for yourself.

JULIO: Maybe never.

THERAPIST: Maybe never. Now you're making a decision that I'm kind of worried about, I'm afraid that your way, things might go bad. But I hope you prove me wrong. Supposing that it turns out you're right, say, one year from now, what will you be doing? What will be happening in your life?

JULIO: I'll be going to school every day, keeping my grades up. I'll have a job after school. I can walk by nice cars without needing to drive them away. . . .

THERAPIST: In other words, you'll be doing the things you said you would be doing, to get toward your goals.

JULIO: Yup.

THERAPIST: And I hope it doesn't happen this way, but what if it turns out that I was right to be worried? What if your wall isn't strong enough, and you're getting off track? What would be going on a year from today?

JULIO: I'd be stealing cars again, cutting school sometimes. My aunt would be on my case all the time. . . .

THERAPIST: And if you noticed these things happening, what could you do to get yourself on track again?

JULIO: Talk to a counselor. Do what you said.

THERAPIST: How do you find a counselor?

JULIO: Ask my aunt, or ask the guidance counselor at school.

Another therapist might have kept Julio in treatment for longer and tried to work on building affect tolerance to the point where Julio might have been more willing to consider trying the trauma resolution work. That might have been a better strategy. Also, unfortunately, we can't be sure that the counselor whom Julio might find a year from now will know how to help him with trauma resolution. The point of this example was not to second guess the therapist, but to show how a therapist might help a client to prepare for future challenges even when treatment was not completed according to the therapist's agenda.

In many ways, this final part of treatment replicates what was done earlier, but this time with a focus on the future rather than the present. The earlier focus was on being safe today; now we are focusing on being safe tomorrow, next month, and next year. The earlier focus was on avoiding high-risk situations this week; now the focus is on avoiding high-risk situations farther in the future. The earlier focus was on managing everyday problem situations in a way that led to a good ending; now the focus is on anticipating more significant and challenging problem situations in the future, and managing those.

ENDING TREATMENT

When is it finally time to end treatment? It may be so if the following occur:

- Presenting problems are resolved.
- The child reports little or no distress when recalling the trauma memories.
- The child reports little or no difficulty in managing trauma-related triggers.
- The family has made a positive adjustment to the child's improved functioning.
- The child is oriented toward a positive future and is behaving in ways that will make such a future likely to occur.
- The child and family can anticipate future challenges and stressors, and are prepared to respond to these effectively.

Chapter 19

Challenging Cases: Applying the Fairy Tale Model

Early in the book, the fairy tale was presented, with elements of the fairy tale then related to corresponding steps in a comprehensive trauma-informed treatment approach. Since then, you've been learning how to do various interventions in each of these steps in the treatment approach. Now that you've been through each of the steps, it's time to pull it all together again, to work with the model as a whole.

Here is a retelling of the fairy tale. Please don't skip this even though you remember it from before. People consistently tell me that they were glad for getting the story the second time. Read it carefully. As you read it this time, notice what's the same as before and what's different or new.

THE FAIRY TALE REVISITED

Once upon a time there was a small kingdom, about the size of a small town. Things were pretty regular there. People did their jobs; kids went to school. Some people went to church or temple and some didn't. Some people would go to a friend's house on the weekend, get together for a barbecue, play games, or have a party. Most people got along, but not everyone. And that's how things were: pretty regular.

Until one day . . .

The dragon came. One day the dragon ate a cow right out of a farmer's pasture. Another day the dragon ate a dog right out of someone's front yard. People got pretty scared! The parents told their kids that they weren't allowed to go outside anymore. The thing is, kids aren't very good at not going outside. So the parents stayed home to guard their kids, to keep them safe from the dragon.

Soon no one was going to school anymore, and not so many people were going to work, either. Everyone was so afraid of the dragon that they mostly just stayed inside their houses. And people started wondering, "How come our kingdom has a dragon, anyway? The other kingdoms don't have one." No one knew why, but they wanted to know, so they started making guesses. One group of people blamed another group of people; that group of people blamed some others . . . and pretty soon, everyone was blaming someone and they were all mad at each other.

It didn't take long until this kingdom got a bad reputation. People from the other kingdoms, well, they didn't know about the dragon, but they sure knew what was going on. They would say, "That kingdom's messed up. The people don't go to work, the kids don't go to school, nobody gets along, they're all mad at one another. All they do is stay inside all the time. They're messed up."

And that's how things were. Until one day . . .

A knight in shining armor came along. Well, he wasn't really a knight, and he didn't have any armor. He was just some guy who happened to be passing through. But the people in the town saw something in him.

"You!" they said. "You can slay the dragon; you're just the one to do it!"

The guy said, "No, sorry, I'm not a dragon slayer. You have the wrong guy. I've been walking a long way. I'm looking for this certain princess I'm in love with. But I don't know what kingdom she lives in." He pulled a picture out and showed it around. "Have you seen this princess? Do you know where I can find her?"

The people said, "Yes, she's our princess. She lives here. And what a coincidence: she really wants to get married—to whoever slays the dragon!"

When the guy heard this, he said, "Well, in that case, I'm your man. Take me to your dragon!"

So they took him to the dark place where the dragon was sleeping. The guy saw the dragon and said, "Whoa, this is a bad idea! I can't handle this dragon! No way! It's huge; it looks really strong. It's covered with scales—it breathes fire. Let's just forget the whole thing!"

The people said, "No, you can do it. We know you can! You can work out, do exercises, build yourself up. We'll help. We'll get you a personal trainer. And remember the princess!"

The guy said, "Oh yeah, the princess!" He was in love with this princess and he really wanted to marry her. "Okay, I don't know about this, but I'll give it a try and see how it goes."

So they gave him a personal trainer and took him to the schoolyard to start on his exercises. But he couldn't stay focused! Every time he got started on some exercise, he would suddenly stop and look all around. He was afraid the dragon would get him while he was out there, exposed. So he wasn't making any progress. This clearly was not working.

So they took him to a clearing at the edge of the forest where there were high trees on one side. Then they worked to build a high fence around the rest of the clearing. Everybody pitched in: cutting lumber, putting it up, securing it, cooking for the workers. . . . Even the little kids helped by bringing water to people, carrying messages, doing whatever they could. It wasn't long until they had a high fence around the rest of the clearing. Then the guy could concentrate on his exercises.

Things went better after that. Every day he worked hard with his personal trainer: he did push-ups, sit-ups, lifted weights, ran laps, did all kinds of exercises. Every day the trainer added a pound or two to the various weights. Every day the guy became a little stronger, a little faster, a little more agile. Eventually they got an athletic teenager to dress up in a dragon costume, and they did role-plays so the guy could practice his dragon-fighting moves.

Finally, the day came: he was ready. He went to the dark place where the dragon was, faced the dragon, fought it, and slew it.

He did marry the princess, but things didn't just go back to the same old way that the kingdom used to be.

For one thing, they now had a hero in their midst. People from the other kingdoms were saying, "That kingdom has a dragon slayer. I wish ours had one." And everyone in the kingdom felt proud, walked a little taller; they knew they'd all helped out and been a part of it.

But they were still asking each other, "How come our kingdom had a dragon, anyway? I wonder if we'll get another one?" They still didn't know. They were worried about this, and they really wanted to know. So they hired a consultant.

The consultant took a good look around. Then she called everyone together for a big meeting to tell them her findings. "You have two problems here. First of all, you throw all your garbage in the dump. It's this huge pile of garbage that stinks for miles around. That smell attracts dragons." So they decided that everyone would put their garbage in a compost pile in their own yard. No big smell to attract dragons, and compost is good for the gardens anyway.

The consultant also told them, "Here's your other problem. On the edge of the kingdom where the farms are, there are all these low fields. It's flat, flat, flat for miles! Dragons are lazy, and this place, it's just too easy for a dragon to cruise right in." So they decided to plant clusters of apple trees here and there in the fields. They liked apples anyway, and this way it wouldn't be such smooth sailing for any dragon that was wandering by.

Well, it didn't take long before they had so many apples that they didn't know what to do with them. So every year in the fall, they had a big apple festival, and people would come from all the kingdoms for miles around. There were all kinds of contests for the tastiest apples, the biggest apples, the best apple pies. They also had plenty of food, games, and music—everything a festival should have.

The highlight of the festival, on the Saturday night—the event that everyone would go to—was the dragon-slaying contest. Of course, they didn't have a real dragon, so whoever had won the year before got to play the dragon. All year long, teenagers from all the kingdoms were practicing, training, hoping that they'd be the one to win the big contest at the next year's festival. Not only was this great fun, but if another dragon ever did show up, they would be ready!

Then, they did live happily ever after—more or less. The end.

So what did you notice in the fairy tale this time that was different from the first time?

Give yourself credit for that. The story is exactly the same as before. What's different is you. You know more now, so you are able to notice more elements of the story. You are able to see how these relate to the trauma treatment approach.

For much of this book, you have been working with one step at a time. The new task, for this chapter, is to work with the model as a whole. On the following page is a summary of the fairy tale model and the corresponding component in the trauma-informed treatment approach. In case you're wondering, this also is exactly the same as when it appeared earlier in the book.

Applying the Model

You probably figured out some time ago that this treatment approach is not just for kids with PTSD, or just for kids with presenting problems clearly related to trauma. Most therapists who learn and practice this system end up saying, "This is just good therapy. I've been using this with all my clients." They are still doing many of the things they used to do, with kids, families, and any others involved, but now they are doing it in a way, and in an order, that takes trauma into account.

Even so, any theory or model has an area of "best fit" and other areas where the fit may not be so good. One of the goals of this chapter is to help you to test the fairy tale model with your own challenging cases, to see if, and how well, it might fit your cases and provide you with useful guidance.

Another goal of this chapter is to give you more practice in using the model and internalizing it. When you learn a new way of thinking about how to do your work, at first your focus is on what's new. In the long run, though, you don't want to be focused on the fairy tale model; you want to be focused on the kids you're working with. So it's important to practice the model until you get used to it. Eventually, instead of focusing *on* the fairy tale model, you're focusing *with* it—it'll become your perspective, the way you see a case. This takes practice.

When you are working with the fairy tale model, of course it's great if you've started your case that way, and done all the steps in order. But you may have many ongoing cases that you've started some other way, or picked up from someone else. You may also have cases that you are trying to do according to the fairy tale model, but they are especially confusing or challenging in some way. And even within the fairy tale model, kids don't sit still for us to go along according to our own agenda. Sometimes events happen in their lives that throw off the course of treatment, and when we next see them, they're not in the same place we left them.

Because we can't force kids to be where we think they should be, the best we can do is figure out where they actually are. When you know where the child is in the treatment model, you will have a much better idea of what's needed, and what you should be doing. Here is a more detailed summary of the goals and tasks for each phase of treatment.

The Fairy Tale Model of Trauma Treatment

Stage of treatment	Corresponding element of the fairy tale
Evaluation including Strengths/resources Trauma/loss history	I see your strengths; you're the one who can slay the dragon. We need to know about the dragon to make sense of the problems.
Motivational interviewing, goal setting	Without the princess, nothing will happen.
Trauma-informed case formulation and psychoeducation	Identify the strengths/resources as reason to hope for a chance of success. Take the dragon into account; then the problems make sense.
Trauma-relevant treatment contracting	Recommend fence-around, personal training to get stronger, and slay the dragon.
Case management for safety and other needs; parent training for safety and security	Build the fence around so you're not worried about being attacked at any moment. Then you can concentrate on your tasks.
Self-management skills training for physical and psychological safety as well as improved affect regulation	The personal training approach to build skill and strength.
Trauma resolution	Slay the dragon.
Relapse prevention and harm reduction	Compost instead of using the dump, to stop attracting dragons; stands of apple trees so it's harder for dragons to come along. Teens training for the dragon-slaying contest, so if another one does come along, we'll be ready.

Phases of Trauma Treatment

1. Evaluation and treatment planning

Goals: Understanding, hope, commitment to action

Establish safety in the therapy context: say rules, give certain choices and controls, start slow, limit disclosure.

Obtain trauma history in a careful, contained way.

Provide psychoeducation about trauma and its impact.

Provide a trauma-informed case formulation.

Identify goals and use these to enhance motivation and commitment to treatment.

Agree on a treatment contract.

2. Safety and strength building

Goals: Safety, skills, success, courage

Case management for safety, stability, and minimization of unnecessary stressors/triggers.

Parent training for child's sense of safety and security.

Self-management training for control of anxiety symptoms.

Self-control training for coping with triggers/stressors, and for improving behaviors and outcomes.

Progressive challenges to increase sense of competence, strength, affect tolerance.

3. Trauma resolution

Goals: Work through trauma

Develop a plan for which trauma memory to address first.

Additional safety and controls.

Develop an exposure strategy: standard talk-story, writing it down, drawing/making a book, using directed play therapy, etc.

Exposure, EMDR, or other trauma resolution procedure.

Containment, relaxation, recomposure.

Reevaluation and further exposure on that memory.

Exposure (or EMDR, etc.) with other memories if necessary.

4. Consolidation and relapse prevention

Goals: Resolve symptoms, prepare for challenges

Skills training, desensitization, in vivo exposure, and/or incentive plan to overcome remaining symptoms.

Identify and resolve remaining problems.

Identify anticipated challenges and develop/rehearse coping strategies.

EXERCISE: APPLY THE MODEL

For each of the vignettes below, speculate about where the child is, which phase of trauma treatment. Then make a suggestion as to what the therapist might do to help the child progress. It's okay to refer to the Phases of Trauma Treatment page for ideas. Remember that until the tasks of one phase have been completed, the child is unlikely to be successful in a later phase of treatment. Also, sometimes a child may leap forward or backslide for one reason or another. Although there is rarely a single "right answer" in this field, some suggested responses are included following the vignettes. So if you want to formulate your own answers first, don't look ahead.

1. A ten-year-old girl has had two trauma resolution sessions and has done well in each. When she comes for the next session, although she does not report anything special in the beginning-of-the-session check-in, she seems angry and abrupt. When the therapist reminds her of how well she has been doing in treatment, and suggests picking up where they left off, the girl refuses. The therapist reminds her of her goals and how this work is helping her to achieve them. The girl responds, "I don't want to do it. I just don't care about that anymore." What is the phase of treatment? Based on that, what should the therapist do?
2. A nine-year-old boy is in treatment for disruptive behavior in school, and for peer problems such as teasing and fighting. The first two sessions were focused on rapport building and seemed to go well. In the third session, the therapist is trying to teach him some self-control skills, but the boy is barely cooperative and will only agree to participate half-heartedly for a few minutes at a time, in exchange for time playing games. The therapist complains to the boy, "This is supposed to be for you. Why does it feel like I care about it more than you do?" What is the phase of treatment (or what's missing)? Based on that, what should the therapist do?
3. A seventeen-year-old boy with a history of conduct problems is in treatment because it is required by the alternatives-to-incarceration program to which he has been adjudicated. He has been cooperative in the first several sessions, and appears to be sincerely invested in achieving positive long-term goals. But when the therapist offers him the treatment plan, he rejects it, saying, "I don't need to do that stuff. I don't need counseling." The therapist reminds him of his goals, and the boy says, "Yeah, but I'm going to do all that. I don't have any problems." What is the phase of treatment (or what's missing)? Based on that, what should the therapist do?
4. A distraught grandmother calls the clinic to arrange treatment for her thirteen-year-old grandson, for whom she is the custodial parent. She describes a number of possible posttraumatic symptoms, including low energy, nervousness, heightened startle response, and being afraid to go to sleep. The precipitating event was that the boy had been bitten by a rat while asleep. The grandmother professes her own guilt: usually she stays up and scares the rats away by swatting at them with newspapers, but on the night in question, she fell asleep by accident, leaving her grandson vulnerable. She has been complaining about the rat problem for some years, but neither her landlord nor the city has done anything for her. Now her grandson has posttraumatic stress. What is the phase of treatment (or what's missing)? Based on that, what should the therapist do?
5. A fifteen-year-old girl is brought to the in-school therapist because when she took off her sweatshirt earlier in the day, a peer noticed fresh cut marks on the girl's arm and reported it to a counselor. By now the school principal has notified the parents, and the therapist is expected to do whatever is necessary to make sure that the girl is safe and taken care of. What is the phase of treatment (or what's missing)? Based on that, what should the therapist do?

6. A fourteen-year-old girl has been doing well in treatment, and in the last session worked her most significant trauma through to resolution. That trauma was also the first one, chronologically, on her list, which includes four other traumas rated at a SUDS of eight or higher. In the next session, the girl reports that the treated memory doesn't bother her anymore. The therapist suggests proceeding with the next trauma on the list, but the girl says that that memory doesn't bother her anymore either, that it's a zero. The therapist checks to make sure that she's really concentrating on it (some kids claim zero when they really mean that they are making sure not to think about it) and she still reports no distress. They go through the same routine with all the other untreated trauma memories on the list, with the same results. What is the phase of treatment (or what's missing)? Based on that, what should the therapist do?

Suggested Answers

Case 1

Phase of treatment: The girl is clearly not in the trauma resolution phase today. Since it appears from the vignette that the case formulation, motivational component, and treatment contracting were done already, the issue probably lies elsewhere. She says she doesn't care about her goals, but the therapist knows she does. So what's going on? Chances are that something has happened to make the girl feel unsafe or insecure in some way, and the phase of treatment would be Safety and Strength Building.

Intervention: The therapist must find out what's on the girl's mind and help her address it somehow.

The story: In this case, the girl's mother had become upset with her for a minor offense a couple of days prior to the session, and threatened to send her into foster care if she misbehaved again. The therapist was able to talk with the mother and the mother agreed to explain to her daughter that she had spoken in a moment of anger but did not mean it. Once the "fence around" the girl had been repaired and she felt secure again, she was able to continue with the trauma resolution work in the following session.

Case 2

Phase of treatment: In the fairy tale model, they are still in the first phase of treatment. The therapist is wishing that the child is ready for Strength Building, but the foundation is not there. Whenever the therapist is trying harder than the child, wants it more than the child does, it is probable that the princess hasn't been identified. Right now the child's only goals are to have a good time, to play games. That's not adequate. If he doesn't have treatment-related goals, some personally meaningful reason to work with the therapist, not much will happen in treatment.

Intervention: If the beginning of the Evaluation has already been completed, then the therapist can work with the child on identifying what he would like to improve in his life and making a treatment contract to include treatment activities that will help the boy to achieve his goals. However, in this case, it appears that the therapist has not been following the model at all. He'd best start from scratch and do it right, otherwise he will continue to encounter problems.

Case 3

Phase of treatment: One small but important thing seems to be missing here. The boy does not seem to perceive that any challenges or obstacles stand between him and his goals. If the boy believes that he is on track to his goals and nothing is in his way, why would he need the therapist?

Intervention: The therapist should find ways of highlighting potential obstacles. Two ways of doing this are described in Chapter 8. First there is the listing of strengths and obstacles, including the gambling metaphor and the question, "Why would that other person bet that you're not going to make it?" Later comes the Problem Behavior Cycle, which has the advantages of being visual and of incorporating the trauma history as the source of the vulnerability. Once there is agreement about possible obstacles, the boy might decide that it's worth working with the therapist to become more capable of mastering the challenges he faces.

Case 4

Phase of treatment: This was a trick question. In this case, we're in a pre-evaluation phase, because something urgent must be taken care of before evaluation is even appropriate. If we do an evaluation now, all we will learn is that the boy is afraid to go to sleep, and that he has symptoms appropriate to someone who is living with fear and without sleep. The principle is "safety first," and urgent safety and survival needs come before anything else.

Intervention: Safety first. In this case, the therapist connected the grandmother with a housing advocate, and stayed in touch with her over the following weeks while she went through various steps to obtain a safer place to live. Once that was accomplished, the therapist invited the grandmother to bring her boy in for an evaluation. At that time, living in a new rat-free apartment, the symptoms were mostly gone. This is a common issue in critical incident and disaster response. Naive mental health professionals may ask people how they are feeling or if they want to talk about it, when what's really needed is something more practical. When people are in crisis they need to know what's going on, where their loved ones are, what they will eat, where they will sleep, how they will get home. Safety and survival come first. Often the best "mental health" intervention is giving someone a blanket, a sandwich, or crucial information.

Case 5

Phase of treatment: In this type of situation, most therapists are trained to conduct a safety assessment for risk of suicide. This might include questions about suicidal ideas, intent, plan, and means to achieve it. If this was your response, don't feel too badly, you're not the only one. But I would argue that these are overly intrusive questions, coming from a stranger. And bullets are not whizzing by. The knife is not in her hand right now. Yes, we are concerned, but this concern allows us to take all the time we need to do the job right. I would say that because this is the first meeting, we are at the beginning of the evaluation phase. So there is a presenting problem, everyone has one. This particular presenting problem does have sufficient urgency to require that much of the evaluation is done in the first meeting.

Intervention: Introduction to treatment, rules, favorite color, etc. In this particular case, the therapist spent an hour and a half with the girl, and they got all the way through the initial interview, family, developmental, medical, school, trauma/loss, and best things history. By this time, the girl felt so comfortable with the therapist that she was glad to explain about the problem with her boyfriend over the weekend and how that made her so upset that she cut her arm. When she contracted for safety, the therapist trusted her because they had a relationship; the girl was not just making a frivolous promise to get some strange adult off her back. The girl did keep her promises, and also continued with treatment to a good conclusion.

Case 6

Phase of treatment: Yes, this does happen sometimes, and it's real. It appears that the trauma resolution phase is complete before the therapist expected it to be. So how can this be? What happened? Three main possibilities exist, which are not mutually exclusive. First, the high SUDS ratings for the later traumas on the list could have been mainly "sore spot" reactions, overreactions that had more to do with the earlier memory than with the identified later event. When the earlier event was digested and no longer a source of distress, the discrete reactions of the later events (the reaction not related to the "sore spot") just didn't amount to much, weren't significant on their own. Also, when the client works through one trauma memory, the new lessons can somehow generalize to other trauma memories as well. You can't count on this happening, but sometimes you find that it did. Even when this does occur, you often still must treat the other trauma memories, but maybe it'll go easier because of the work that's been done on the first one. Finally, the client's life situation may have changed in a way that makes the later trauma memory less relevant. For example, a teenaged boy had "getting locked up" at age fourteen as a SUDS of ten. However, by the time he got around to being ready to work on that memory, it was only a two. The therapist told him that it had been a ten before and asked why it was so much lower. The boy said, "Well, look how well I'm doing now. I know I'm not gonna get locked up again!"

Intervention: It looks as if it's time to move on to the posttrauma resolution reassessment, to see what symptoms and problems have disappeared on their own, and what might need to be actively addressed. However, if I'm the therapist for this girl, I'll probably keep checking the SUDS levels for those untreated trauma memories, at least for a couple of weeks, just to be sure.

THE IMPORTANCE OF USING THE MODEL

Hopefully what you are getting from these examples is the idea that kids will show us where they are by what they say and what they do. They are not always where we think they are or where we wish they would be. But at least they give us clues that we can track down to learn what's going on, and from there we can use the model to figure out what needs to be done. Sometimes a pressing concern or change in life situation causes progress or setback. Sometimes the therapist has skipped one or more steps and ends up paying for this later when the child is unable or unwilling to do what the therapist wants.

I have been providing supervision and consultation to therapists for many years, and I've learned that certain therapy impasses occur with some frequency. One of the reasons I wrote this book is that I got tired of trying to teach the whole system over and over again to therapists within the one-hour conversations we were having. Although the system is not so hard to learn, it can't be done on the fly. Here are some of the more typical problems that therapists report, along with my fairy tale model response.

THERAPIST: So that's what's going on. I'm just not sure what to do, where to go from here.
CONSULTANT: What's the case formulation? What's the treatment plan?

THERAPIST: I'm trying to get him to work with me, but it feels like I'm pulling teeth.
CONSULTANT: What are his goals that he believes treatment will help him to achieve?

THERAPIST: This feels like a good case for [EMDR, exposure], but I don't know if she's ready yet.
CONSULTANT: Have you done skill building to develop coping skills and affect management? Have you tried the trauma resolution method with a recent minor event? Do you have a trauma/loss history? What about starting with an earlier (or a lower SUDS) trauma from the list?

THERAPIST: I just don't see how I'm going to get anywhere with this kid, the way the home environment is.
CONSULTANT: You're probably right. So the first thing to do is work with the parents to make things more predictable and supportive.

In these cases and many others, because therapists skipped steps, they got in trouble or got lost. You can't make a treatment plan without a case formulation. You can't get the child to work on the treatment plan unless she has her own goals that she believes the treatment is supporting. You can't expect a child to focus on goal-oriented treatment activities while she is feeling threatened or unsafe in her daily life. You can't do trauma resolution without having done the strength building.

The fairy tale model is a comprehensive system; it covers the bases. When you do the steps in order and you don't skip any, the child tends to be ready and able to do the next one. Of course, some kids can go through the steps faster than others. And because life happens, kids don't always stay in order. Still, proceeding in order and doing all the steps gives you a good chance of getting the job done. When the situation isn't what you thought it was, you can use the model to figure it out and get your bearings.

EXERCISE: CASE CONSULTATION USING THE FAIRY TALE MODEL

Think of a challenging case, something current, that's on your mind for whatever reason. It doesn't have to be a "trauma case." If you are doing this by yourself, use a copy of the following form and fill in each of the sections. If you are with a group, have one person present the case and then the group members can serve as consultants to complete the form together.

It is essential in this exercise that you proceed in order, and restrain yourself from jumping in with questions or suggestions that are out of order. One goal of this exercise is to test the model on your case: if you stick to the fairy tale model, can you provide a good consultation? Will all of your questions be asked? Will all of your suggestions for interventions have a place in the model?

Another goal of the exercise is to practice using the model in a systematic way that will help you integrate it into your way of thinking about your work. If you just jump in with questions and suggestions as you think of them, you are not doing anything you don't already know how to do, so it's less likely for learning to happen. By going in order, you are, in fact, using the model. It takes discipline to wait for the right moment for your questions and suggestions. It can be helpful to make a note when you think of something, so that you have it for the right moment.

Discussion Questions

For the Presenter

How did this go for you? Did you feel respected and supported? Did this consultation have any impact on your understanding of the case? Did this consultation give you any ideas for what to do? Did the fairy tale model seem to fit this case?

For the Consultant(s)

How did this go for you? Did you get a chance to ask all your questions? Did you get a chance to make all your suggestions? Was there a place for them?

SECTION V BIBLIOGRAPHY

Marlatt, G. A. & Gordon, J. R. (1985). *Relapse prevention: Strategies in the treatment of addictive behaviors.* New York: Guilford Press. The classic text.

Case Consultation Form

Summary

1. Presenter summarizes (in about two minutes):
   - Client's age, gender, family status/situation, school/work/living status/situation
   - Presenting problem/symptoms including some details
   - History of treatment: How many sessions so far? What was done in each session?

2. Consultant asks clarifying questions, in order, to the extent needed to complete the case formulation:
   Once upon a time—Strengths/resources:

   Then the dragon—Trauma/loss history:

   Leading to
   Negative beliefs:

   Piled-up feelings:

   Now when the trigger happens (theme and example):

   it hits the sore spot. This brings back the negative beliefs and piled-up feelings, which are intolerable. Then the person tries to get rid of that by using this solution behavior:

3. Consultant asks, in order, about what has already been done at each phase of treatment. Here is where suggestions can be included, also in order.

Trauma-Informed Treatment—Sequence of Interventions

Fairy Tale Model Stage of Treatment

Evaluation

- Acculturation: purpose of treatment, treatment activities.
- Rules/expectations/agreements.
- Rapport/trust-building.

Once upon a time . . .

- Strengths/resources, internal and external (the knight and the kingdom).
- History of functioning and problem development.

The dragon

- Trauma/loss history (then deep breathing, then best things).

The princess

- Motivational interviewing/goal setting.
  —Long-term goals (for teens especially); shorter-term goals too.
  —Practical steps to get from here to there.
  —What the bad ending would look like.
  —Strengths/resources in support of goals.
  —Obstacles to achieving the good ending.
- Trauma-informed case formulation and psychoeducation.

Remember: Case Formulation + Princess = Treatment Contract

- Trauma-relevant treatment contracting:
  —Fence around, personal training, and slay the dragon; or
  —Enhance safety and security, avoid high-risk/trigger situations, stabilize, self-management skills, trauma resolution.

Safety, stabilization

Fence around

- Case management regarding safe housing, reliable medical care, appropriate educational placement, etc.
- Parent training for increased household routine, consistent/supportive discipline, etc.
- Avoiding/preventing dangerous situations.
- Controlling/limiting bullying and other abuse.
- Avoiding "high-risk" situations including trigger/sore-spot situations when possible.

Skill-building, strength-building

Personal training

- Safe Place, deep breathing, etc. for self-soothing/calming.
- Self-management training for anxiety.
- In vivo exposure to overcome fears.
- Choices Have Consequences (set this up with Map Out a Problem) for control of behaviors.
- Incentive system for habit improvement.

(continued)

(continued)

Trauma resolution

Slay the dragon

- Introduce Exposure (or EMDR, CPT, or other trauma resolution activity).
- Decide the order for targeting memories (start small!).
- Break down the memory (if you need to, as a step).
- Do the exposure (or other method).

End of session:
- Container with any incompletely processed memory.
- Debrief, calming activities, assist in regaining composure.

Next session:
- Continue with same memory;
- or if it's done, go to the next one; or if all done, move on.

Consolidation of gains

Marry the princess

- Revisit case management and self-management practices now that the sore spot is smaller. Get daily functioning as good as it can be.

Relapse prevention and harm reduction.

Compost; Plant apple trees; Dragon-slayers in training

- Revisit case management and self-management practices, now focused on anticipated future challenges. In particular:
  —Avoid/prevent high-risk situations.
  —Prepare to cope with challenging situations.
  —If things should go badly, how to recognize the signs and catch yourself before it gets too bad.

SECTION VI: 24/7—HELPING THE CHILD IN DAILY LIFE

To get the most out of this section of the book, it's essential that you have read the first section already; that's Chapters 1 through 4. This section is especially for those who spend "daily living" time with kids. You might be a parent (perhaps foster and adoptive) or a worker in residential treatment, day treatment, school, camp, shelter, corrections facility, or another kind of program. You have a critical role to play in the child's treatment.

What kids experience and learn in their daily life is very important. Not all the healing takes place in the therapy hour. In fact, the healing that will occur in the therapy hour depends to a large extent on what happens in the rest of the child's life. Kids whose life experiences allow them to feel ever more safe, secure, strong, and successful will have the best chance of being able to do the work in therapy, recover from their wounds, and move forward with their lives.

You have special opportunities to influence kids because of your personal relationship and because of the time you spend with them. You also have special challenges for the same reason; personal relationships and time together can lead to emotional investment—and sometimes emotional reactivity—on the part of the adult. This section of the book will provide guidance on how to help kids to feel safer and more secure, and to become more strong and successful. The same methods you will be using to help your kids can also help you to keep yourself from overreacting, so that you can focus on the job you are trying to do.

Ideally, you are working closely with the child's therapist, who is also (ideally) using the fairy tale model of trauma-informed treatment, or something similar. The therapy will go better when you are actively supporting the child's participation and when you are telling the therapist about what's going on in the child's life. The therapy will also go better when you are helping the child feel more safe and secure and to become more successful in daily life. You should also be talking with the therapist about the efforts you are making with the child. The therapist can give you suggestions and help you to problem solve when things are not working out as planned.

In the fairy tale model, there are many points in treatment when the adults in the child's life play an especially important role:

I. Evaluation and Treatment Planning
  A. Goals: Understanding, hope, commitment to action
    1. Bringing kids to treatment.
    2. Providing information to the therapist.
    3. Participating in the child's reestablishment of attachment to parents and parent figures.
    4. Demonstrating support for the child's participation in treatment.
    5. Committing to adult participation in the treatment.

II. Safety and Strength-Building
    A. Goals: Safety, skills, success, courage
        1. Helping to create a supportive environment so the child can feel more safe and secure.
        2. Helping the child to develop effective coping skills and other good habits and behaviors.
III. Trauma Resolution
    A. Goals: Work through trauma
        1. Keeping up the supportive environment so the child can concentrate on the work in therapy.
IV. Consolidation and Relapse Prevention
    A. Goals: Resolve symptoms, prepare for challenges
        1. Work with the child and the therapist to help the child solve any remaining problems and further improve good habits and skills.
        2. Work with the child and the therapist to anticipate future challenges and to plan and prepare accordingly.

In sum, the adults in the child's life are active in every stage of the child's treatment and recovery from trauma and loss. The adults can directly support the treatment, for example, by bringing the child to the therapist. However, the primary role of the adults is to create a safe, supportive environment for the child, and to help the child learn and practice self-management skills. This will be the focus of the chapters in this section.

Chapter 20

Creating a Safe Environment

One of the early, and ongoing, steps in treatment is to create a safe environment for the child. This is important because we want kids to be able to feel that although bad things have happened in the past, things are okay now. We want kids to be able to feel that although adults allowed bad things to happen in the past, it might make sense to start trusting adults again. Finally, we want kids to be able to feel that because things are getting better now, there's reason to hope for further improvement, and to work for it.

THINGS ARE OKAY NOW

If we expect the child to "get over" the bad events that happened, she must have some reason to believe that the bad events really are over, and in the past. Is it true to say, "At least things are okay now"? Only then can she start to separate the present from the past and feel that she can move on. Are things really okay now? Or are the old problems being "reenacted," replayed over and over again, in some other way? Until kids can really believe that things are different (and better) now, they will not let down their guard enough to do their work in therapy. As long as kids perceive that they are still in the war zone, in constant danger, they'll stay defensive, focused on survival.

A ten-year-old girl had been raped by her babysitter (who was now in jail). Her older brother constantly bullied her and took her toys, and her parents allowed this without comment. She was learning the lesson of the rape over and over again every day: that she was helpless against stronger people who would do whatever they wanted to her.

A five-year-old boy whose father had abandoned the family believed that it was because his father didn't like him, that there was something wrong with him. On the playground, the other children teased him mercilessly; they told him that they didn't want to play with him because he was clumsy and stupid. He was learning the lesson of the abandonment over and over again every day; that something was wrong with him.

A twelve-year-old boy had been molested by a neighbor when he was nine. He had attention deficit/hyperactivity disorder that was not being treated, and he kept on getting frustrated in school when seeing that other kids were getting their work done but he was not, even though he was trying. He was learning over and over again that he was helpless and that there was something wrong with him.

A fifteen-year-old girl grew up being neglected and poorly supervised, which led to a number of unfortunate events. Now, in the residential facility, she's figured out which staff members will let her get away with not doing her chores properly, and even with sneaking off to meet with other residents who smoke together. She is learning, over and over again, that she is not important and that adults don't care enough to take good care of her or protect her.

ADULTS ARE OKAY NOW

One of the unfortunate lessons that kids learn from having experienced trauma or loss is that the adults did not protect them or keep the bad event from happening. Adults become "spoiled" as a source of protection and guidance. Many kids will then lose faith in adults, and rely only upon themselves—and sometimes their peers. Although this may be understandable, it's not good! In fact, kids still need the love, protection, and guidance that adults can provide.

When we can take control and help kids to feel safe again, something good happens. When we can help kids to feel safe, we are rehabilitating ourselves in kids' eyes. Then kids can start to trust adults again, start to look to adults for love, protection, and guidance. Kids become willing to attach again. When kids are open to the good adults have to offer, they have a better chance of getting back on a healthy track in their development.

THINGS CAN GET BETTER

Kids learn from experience. When the bad events happened, they learned from experience to expect more bad things to happen. After that, many kids train themselves not to expect good, because when you don't get your hopes up, you don't get disappointed. The problem is, when you don't get your hopes up, and you're not expecting anything good to happen, it's hard to get yourself to work hard in school or therapy. Why should you? Maybe it's boring or hard, and nothing good's going to come of it, anyway.

When kids start to feel safe and secure, something good happens. That's just it: something good has happened. Now they have a new kind of experience to learn from. When kids start to see that things have gotten better—that things can get better—it's harder to stay pessimistic. Hope starts to grow.

When kids feel hope, they are more willing to work on getting better at handling challenges, and on getting stronger. The more progress kids make, the more successes they experience, the more confident and hopeful they become.

The "personal trainer" approach helps kids become stronger, more capable, and more confident, one step at a time. Meanwhile, the child is working on similar goals during his meetings with the therapist. When he becomes strong enough and brave enough, he will be ready to slay the dragon, to face and work through the trauma memories. Then he will be able to do even better with daily life challenges. This is our goal.

So how do we help kids feel safer? What does it mean to create a safe environment?

When kids feel safe and secure, and do not need to focus on survival or self-protection, they are more able to focus on healing and on healthy development. We want kids to know, to believe, that their basic needs are being met. We must give kids experiences that will help them learn this.

Here, the concepts of physical safety and emotional safety will be presented separately for convenience. However, they actually overlap, because when kids are safe, they also have more of a chance to feel safe. In general, the principle is that we want to go beyond merely meeting kids' needs, to also teaching them—through experience—that they can count on this.

PHYSICAL SAFETY

- *Protection from attack.* For kids to be safe, they must be protected from being attacked. This means that they are not being sexually abused by family members or anyone else.

They are not being bullied and beaten by peers. They are not being assaulted or beaten by parents or other caregivers.

- *Protection from other dangers.* For kids to be safe, they cannot be exposed to dangerous risks or experiences. This means that they are not exposed to dangerous weapons that could be used by them or against them. They are not being transported by drunk drivers; they are not being supervised by someone who is too depressed, irresponsible, drunk, or high to take care of them. They are not allowed to ride in a car without wearing a seat belt. When they are sick, they receive medical care.
- *Other basic needs.* For kids to be safe, they must live in a safe place. It should be dry enough and warm (or cool) enough that they can be healthy. They should be able to sleep without worrying that rats will bite them or that neighbors will sneak in and do harm. They should have enough to eat, of food that is nutritious.

EMOTIONAL SAFETY

- *Protection from attack.* For kids to *feel* safe, protection from attack must be much more extensive. Kids can feel safe when they are not being verbally attacked by being yelled at, insulted, disrespected, or put down in some way. Kids can feel safe when they are not being threatened with violence or disrespect. This means that no one else is being hurt or threatened either. Remember, when an adult punches a wall or kicks an animal, a child sees this (correctly) as a threat.
- *Predictable routines.* Kids who have been exposed to trauma have learned that bad things can happen, so they are prone to assume the worst. When they don't know what's going to happen, they worry! Adults can help with this by structuring the day, and various activities, into predictable routines. For example, if food is served at set mealtimes, kids can learn to count on that. Many activities can be routinized, including waking up, getting dressed, getting ready for meals, eating meals, going to school, coming home from school, doing homework, getting ready for bed, and going to sleep. The more kids know what to expect, and what is expected of them, the more safe and secure they can feel.
- *Consistency by adults.* If kids are to regain trust in adults, they need to be able to count on us to do what we say we will do. That means that we enforce our rules, every time, the same way. That means that we keep our routines up. That means that we keep our other "promises" too, so that kids know that we mean what we say and they can count on us.

THREATS TO SAFETY

Threats to safety and to sense of safety will make kids feel unsafe. Then they will be focused on survival, self-protection, and worry about the bad things that might happen rather than on the work we want them to do, or on healing.

Adult Loss of Control

Kids' trust in adults is based on the foundation of adults being in charge, strong, and protective. If adults are not in charge, if adults lose control, the foundation crumbles. This is because if adults are not in charge of kids, the adult is not strong, not able to protect. Also, if adults lose control of themselves, they might lose more control and hurt the child. Adults can show loss of control in several ways:

- *Repeating a command.* "Put that down. I said put that down. I said put that down. I said put that down." An adult who is in charge only says it once, then gives a warning, then enforces the consequence. Only an adult who is not in charge resorts to whining, begging, or haranguing.
- *Arguing with a child.* "Yes." "No." "Yes." "No." "Yes." "No." An adult who is in charge may give a command, make a request, or give an explanation. An adult may be willing to discuss. When adults argue with children, they are on the child's level; they have lost their authority.
- *Yelling.* An adult who is in charge does not need to yell. An adult who is in charge can state feelings or expectations calmly, and this will be enough. People yell when they are feeling helpless and frustrated. Yelling may also be a danger signal for some children, that something even worse is coming.
- *Threatening.* When an adult threatens to hurt a child or reject a child, the adult is losing control, by being unable to manage the child using the established rules, and by being on the way to doing something very bad. When the adult says, "If you do that, the bogeyman will get you," or "One more time and I'll send you to foster care," the child will live in fear, focused on survival. Threat of an unrealistically severe punishment brings a similar problem. When the adult threatens, "If you do that again, I'll ground you for the next year," the child knows that the adult is feeling out of control and is threatening a consequence that will not happen; the adult is preparing to break a promise.
- *Hitting, throwing, breaking.* Sometimes an adult loses control to the point of physically attacking the child or making some other physically threatening gesture. When the adult hits the child, in some situations this can become a new trauma. Even with less severity, it can still become a sign of ongoing danger. Similarly, if an adult throws an object in anger, or breaks something, or even slams the door loudly in anger, this signals to the child that the adult is not in control, and that worse may be coming.

Broken Promises

Kids need to be able to count on us to do what we say we'll do. Promises can be broken in many ways, and some of them aren't so obvious:

- *Not coming through with a wanted consequence.* If you say, "If your room's clean in ten minutes, I'll give you a popsicle," and then, even though the room is cleaned within the time limit, you say, "Oh, the room looks good, but there's no popsicle for you," then you've broken a promise. Most of the time we don't do that. However, when the child "spoils" the anticipated reward by breaking some other rule, we may be tempted to say, "Well, you earned your popsicle but you can't have it because you hit your sister." No matter how we might justify this to ourselves, that's a broken promise.
- *Not coming through with an unwanted consequence.* If you say, "Stay out of the street or you'll have to go inside for half an hour," and then the child goes into the street again, but then says, "Oh, I forgot. Please give me another chance; I'll try," what will you do? If you give the child another chance, you've broken the promise! All the child can learn from this is (1) that you don't care what happens to him (you told him to stay out of the street for safety, right?) and (2) that you can't be counted on to keep your promises. Maybe you thought you were doing him a favor, but all you were really doing is making him feel insecure.
- *Not sticking to rules or routines.* Kids count on us to do what we say. When we say that you have to do your homework before playing, you have to do your homework before playing. When we say that dinner is at six, dinner is at six. Rules and routines allow kids to know

what is going to happen. This helps them to feel secure. Being loose with these rules and routines, even to do kids a favor, really does the opposite; it makes them feel insecure. Of course, occasionally rules or routines need to be changed, for example when someone is sick. In such situations, the adult should explain why the rule or routine has been changed, and explain that in normal circumstances, it will be the same as usual.

- *Allowing adults to be "split."* When one adult makes a rule or a promise and the child works with another adult to undo that or go around it, then the first adult's promise is broken. Splitting can be a serious problem when adults work as a team with a child, such as in a family, school, or treatment facility. When the child is able to split the adults, then the adults are not in charge and cannot keep their promises, and the child cannot feel safe or secure. An additional problem with splitting is that the adults become distracted by anger with each other and toward the child, which makes it harder to help the child the way they want to.

Allowing Attacks or Threats

When we allow kids to be attacked or threatened, they will not feel safe. Even if we are not doing this ourselves, or not doing it intentionally, the effect is the same. Here are some common types of attacks or threats that kids may experience:

- *Bullying.* Bullying used to be termed unfortunate but acceptable, "normal," and just part of life—along with drunk driving, sexual harassment, and racial discrimination. However, when we decide that such behavior is not acceptable, and we make rules to express this decision, things change. Drunk driving still occurs, but to a lesser degree. Our society is in a transitional stage regarding acceptance of bullying. In some schools and facilities, bullying is no longer tolerated, and thus much less occurs. In facilities where it is still tolerated, it occurs more often. If your facility chooses to tolerate bullying, many of your kids are living in fear because of that choice.
- *Threats and put-downs by peers.* The slightest comment or look from a peer can be a put-down or a threat. When this is allowed by the adults, then kids learn that no one will protect them and they have to protect themselves. This leads to fear and fighting.
- *Put-downs by adults.* For better or worse, adults who work with kids are as human and varied as everyone else. In some families and some facilities, the adults who are supposed to be helping kids are instead meeting their own needs in a twisted way, feeling important by putting kids down or making kids feel small or helpless. I know of one instance in which certain counselors in a residential facility engaged in a daily contest to see who could get more kids "off program" that day, by getting the kids so upset that they would misbehave. Although hopefully this is an unusual extreme, it is not so unusual to abuse power in smaller ways, even with kids that we care about. We are especially vulnerable to doing this when we are feeling helpless or frustrated ourselves, whether in our personal lives or in the work situation.
- *Aggressive physical restraint.* In some situations, physical restraint is necessary to keep kids safe. During a tantrum, while being restrained, many kids state that they are being mistreated or hurt, when in fact they are being carefully and lovingly handled. However, in some treatment facilities, an outmoded style of physical restraint is used. In one facility, the physical restraint method was described by kids and staff alike as an aggressive, fighting type of maneuver. In another facility, a staff member explained that the good thing about his restraint method was that "the more the kid wiggles and squirms, the more it hurts." Again, although this is an extreme (and the man was later fired for hitting a child), the

"fighting move" type of restraint is all too common. Kids know when they are being protected and when they are being assaulted, no matter what we say we are doing.

- *Continued exposure to an unwarranted trigger.* We cannot protect kids so well that they are never upset. Trauma-exposed kids tend to be extrasensitive to daily stressors, and to react to small challenges that would not affect another child. However, when kids are repeatedly exposed to situations that should not have occurred, they will become focused on their fear of that situation. Examples of unwarranted triggers include bullying, continued exposure to an abuser, and untreated learning disabilities or medical problems. When kids face such situations, their experience is of being constantly exposed to bad things happening to them.

EXERCISE: HOW SAFE IS YOUR HOME OR WORKPLACE?

Think about the place where you work with distressed kids—your home or your work setting. Answer the following questions:

- What procedures or situations are already in place that help kids to be safe and feel safe?
- What procedures or situations are in place that make kids be unsafe or feel unsafe?
- What ideas do you have about how to improve the safety of your setting?

THE SAFETY THEME APPROACH

The safety theme approach is a good way to tie all the safety strategies together. This approach is more than the sum of its parts—it is a philosophy, a way of seeing children and work-

ing with them. It requires coming from a place of love and understanding (not anger or fear). It requires an understanding that a child's "bad" behavior comes from fear, not malice. A cornered animal is the most dangerous, and people are no different. If we can see past the fangs to the fear, we can help the child feel safe and able to trust us. Safety is the foundation of learning and healing.

Words

Safe should be the most-used word in the day. Every intervention should be explained in terms of its safety value. For example, a child may be disciplined for calling another child a name, not because it's "not nice" or even that it "hurt his feelings," but because "he doesn't feel safe when you call him names; he feels attacked." Starting a fight is against the rules. This approach does take practice.

Rules

Rules should be relatively few and simple so they can be overlearned. Before certain activities (or every activity), rules should be recited by the children, as their "ticket" to participation. A rule should reflect safety concerns explicitly, or it should probably be dropped. Rules should be followed inflexibly so that children learn to take them seriously and to count on the adults to keep them safe. (Adults *must* enforce safety rules consistently. Otherwise, children will get the message that the adults don't care about their safety.)

It's helpful to frame rules in a positive manner: what to *do*. The following are examples of helpful rules:

- Follow directions (a catchall).
- Let teachers teach; let students learn (addresses potentially disruptive behavior).
- Respect others, yourself, and property (addresses threatening, aggressive, and destructive behavior).
- Additional rules can be made for specific activities.

Adult Vigilance

The adults should be highly vigilant to intervene in potentially unsafe situations before they get out of hand. Examples of unsafe activities include rock-throwing, play-fighting, insulting another child, taking another child's possession, or failing to follow directions. Early intervention has many benefits. When a problem is addressed quickly, unsafe situations will rarely progress to the point of actual physical damage to person or property. Also, early intervention tends to prevent adults from becoming frustrated or angry—thus they are more able to respond with appropriate concern. Finally, because kids do unsafe things to express their own insecurity, a quick response by adults is very reassuring and precludes the need for escalation. Adult vigilance, although it may seem too strict initially, will go a long way toward creating a safe place and helping the kids to feel more calm and secure.

Daily Routine

The daily schedule should be adhered to strictly and consistently. When we tell a child what to expect, we are making a promise. If we want kids to feel secure, we have to keep our promises to them. They also need to know that what they expect to happen at school will actually happen. Keeping to the daily routine is extremely important to children's sense of security.

If a child should lose control at any point in the day, becoming unsafe and/or disruptive, it is critical that he not be allowed to alter the routine. Even if he needs to be removed, the activity should continue. If he is very loud or disruptive, he should be moved far enough away so that his behavior does not disturb others. The other kids must be able to count on the routine and to count on the adults to be in charge. If acting-out kids are able to destroy the plans and promises of the adults, the adults are not as powerful as the children, a notion that frightens children.

The adults should be deployed so that sufficient staff is available to support kids in need of assistance with self-control (e.g., by monitoring time-out or implementing a physical restraint) while other staff are available to carry on the scheduled activity.

Physical Environment

The physical environment should also be carefully structured and defined such that each space has a specified function—schoolwork, cooling off/regaining control, recreation, etc. This should be carefully designed to avoid possible disruption of one activity by another. Ideally, a separate space will be available relatively nearby when a child is so disruptive that she must be removed from the group.

Positive Focus

Criticism, scolding, and punishments have already been tried with your kids. A focus on the negative only feeds it; this risks escalation, does not solve the problem, and teaches the child to live in fear of attack (criticism, punishment). Although some consequences for misbehavior are inevitable, a positive focus works better. This includes a focus on what the child is doing right, a focus on incentives/rewards, and a focus on the pleasure of participating in group activities and being successful.

Discipline

Discipline comes from love, not from anger. The purpose of discipline is to keep the kids safe so they are able to pursue their daily activities. There is no role here for punishment, which children may perceive as an angry attack on them. Since many children are accustomed to angry discipline, it may take them a while to learn the difference, but they will. Note that if the child can get the adult angry enough to yell or argue, the adult has lost control and the child is no longer safe. Adults must be in charge.

"Consequences" occur naturally as a result of the child's choices. The child constantly earns the opportunity to continue participation in the group activity, and also earns points toward some reward on a behavioral plan. These are seen as positive consequences. If a child is not behaving safely, he is removed until he is ready to return and behave safely. This may be seen as a negative consequence and he may be upset about missing an activity. However, it is also a positive consequence in that he—and others—are being kept safe.

Our job is to keep the kids safe until they learn to keep themselves safe. When a child loses control we provide it externally. Eventually the child will internalize control through this experience. A "bad" behavior is just the child's way of asking for our help. The child deserves help, not punishment.

The disciplinary rules should be well defined and adhered to consistently. This way the child will know what to expect, the adults will know what to do, and a safe, secure setting is provided.

The specific tools and methods that support the safety theme will be the focus of Chapters 21, 22, and 23.

Physical Restraint

Physical restraint is a good example of a safety theme tool. It is the safety theme "bottom line." In essence, we are saying to kids, "We will do whatever it takes to keep you safe. Even if you are out of control, I will hold you until you can control yourself again." This is not a punishment; it is a gift. We do this without a second thought for a two-year-old who is having a tantrum. If an older child needs to be held until she can regain self-control, then we do this for the older child too.

There are many "brand names" of physical restraint methods on the market. Competent practice of physical restraint requires special training. If you're not already trained but need to be, you might need to shop around for the method that meets your needs. If you are already trained, perhaps you can take a second look at your procedures. Here are some of the essential features of physical restraint, when it is done in support of the safety theme approach.

Kids (and Parents) Know What to Expect

If physical restraint is part of your repertoire, and any possibility exists that you might use it with, or near, a certain child, then you'd need to inform the child ahead of time. Then you can explain it the way you would like him to understand it, while he is calm. "Part of my job is to keep kids safe, no matter what happens. If someday you get out of control and your body starts doing something that's not safe, I will do my best to hold you and keep you safe until you get control of yourself again. I can show you now how I would hold you. Do you want me to show you with you, or with this doll here?" Then the therapist can demonstrate the hold, the child can ask questions, and it's no big deal. When (or if) the restraint occurs, the child already understands what will happen and why.

This preparation is also important for kids who will see or hear other kids being restrained. If they have not been prepared, they are likely to be frightened and may believe that the restrained child is being assaulted because restrained children often struggle, scream, cry, and claim that they are being hurt. When kids understand what they are seeing and hearing, then being exposed to a restraint only confirms their impression that here, the adults keep the kids safe.

It's also important to inform parents and other caregivers about physical restraint, if restraint is a possibility, and to discuss it with them. This makes them part of the treatment planning. Then when you do restrain the child and he threatens to tell his parents, you can say that his parents have agreed that you should do this to keep him safe. Also, if the child tells his parents that you "attacked" him, his parents can probably figure out what he's talking about.

Restraint Is Used Only to Enforce Safety

When you use physical restraint in support of the safety theme approach, you use it only to keep kids safe. Using it just to enforce rules or to get kids to do what you want is coercion. Use other consequences for that, and let kids make their own choices and learn from their experiences.

Restraint is the obvious choice when a child is actively harming or threatening herself or someone else and refuses to stop. For example, if a child refuses to stop hitting her head against the wall, or swinging a chair around with peers nearby, she clearly requires restraint.

With the safety theme approach, many problem behaviors can be viewed as a threat to safety, possibly requiring physical intervention. For example, if a child strays so far from the group that the adult cannot see her to supervise adequately, that is a safety issue. The adult might say, "I promised your mom that I would keep you safe. I have to be able to see you to keep you safe. If you leave my sight again, you will have to hold my hand after that to make sure you're close enough that I can keep you safe." For another example, if a child disrupts the classroom and refuses to leave on his own, the adult might say, "This classroom is a safe place, and the other kids need to feel safe here so they can concentrate on their schoolwork. For kids to feel safe here, they need to be able to count on doing their schoolwork, and they need to be able to count on the rules. When you make so much noise, you're keeping them from doing their work, so you have to go to your time-out for a few minutes. If you don't go on your own, I will help you." Of course, the adult would not make this whole speech in the moment, but the building blocks would all be in place from earlier discussions with the individual and with the group.

Note that neither of these examples will automatically result in a restraint. However, if the child does not maintain self-control by following the safety instruction, the adult will help, physically. Even then, often children will cooperate when they are given a helping hand. However, if the child resists at that point, a restraint may be required.

The Safety Words Are Used

When physical restraint is used in support of the safety theme approach, it's always clearly about safety. Safety words are used before, during, and after the restraint. First of all, physical restraint is introduced to the child as a last resort to keep kids safe. Then right before the restraint, the adult typically gives safety-related instructions (e.g., "You have to hold my hand so I can keep my eye on you. To keep you safe, I need to be able to see you." or "Put that chair down right now! That's not safe."), so the child knows that she is being restrained for continuing to be unsafe. During the restraint, the adult continues to repeat statements such as, "I've got you. I'm keeping you safe." Afterward, the restraint is discussed in the same vein—as something the adult did to keep the child (and/or others) safe.

The Holds Are Not Hurtful

The goal here is safety, not attack. If you learn the proper method of physical restraint, and if you keep yourself calm and in control, this won't be a problem. The physical restraint "holds" are designed to protect and contain children, not hurt them, no matter how much the child might struggle.

Adults Keep Themselves Calm

Restraining a child can be an intense experience, both physically and emotionally. With this intensity, we risk becoming overly emotional and squeezing too hard, hurting the child, or perhaps arguing with the child instead of comforting him. Special precautions should be taken during a restraint to remain calm. We use the safety words, because while we remind the child of the reason for holding him, we also remind ourselves. When we remember that we are helping the child and keeping him safe, we operate from a sense of love and protectiveness. Deep, slow breathing should be practiced during the restraint in order to stay calm and keep focus and control.

This Is Help, Not Punishment

A restraint is not used to punish, but to protect. Punishing may hurt the child and may occur because we feel angry at the child. Protecting the child involves feeling loving. If we are punishing, then when we have punished enough, we can let the child go; if we are protecting, then we don't let go until we are sure that the child is safe and able to self-control. If we are punishing, then restraint makes the child feel ashamed; if we are protecting, then we give needed support until the child grows enough to keep herself safe.

Hold Until the Child Can Self-Control

Because this is not punishment but help, we don't release the child just because the restraint has lasted "long enough already." The restraint ends when the child is calm and can keep herself safe, which she demonstrates by keeping control of her arms and her legs while still being held by the adult. If you end a restraint too soon, the child will let you know by quickly acting up again and requiring further restraint. It is better to end slowly and cautiously, so that you can be confident that the child is really in control and doesn't need your help anymore.

A Story About Physical Restraint

Here's a true story from my own experience that highlights the difference between good and not-so-good methods of physical restraint. Many years ago I worked as a part-time therapist in a fairly good residential facility for boys with severe behavior problems. Unfortunately, in this facility the physical restraint method was aggressive. I told the director of my concerns, and he actually agreed with me, but explained that because of all the staff retraining involved, he would not be able to make the change for a few months. I told the director that meanwhile, I would do restraints my own way. Since I was a therapist and not a direct care worker, my stance did not seem to be a problem because I was not expected to be involved in a restraint anyway.

One day I was meeting with a ten-year-old boy who seemed particularly distressed, though he did not tell me why (I did ask!). We had met several times previously and things had gone pretty well. But this time, he insisted on hitting his hand against a wooden table. I asked him not to do that, because I didn't want his hand to get hurt. He did it again. We went through the routine several times, until I finally told him that if he did it again, I would hold his hand to keep it safe. To make a long story short, he essentially forced a physical restraint, had a tantrum (while being held), and then eventually calmed down and regained his composure.

The next day I learned more about how that physical restraint had fit into the boy's day. He had known that following his meeting with me, he was to be interviewed by child protection investigators regarding his experience of having been physically abused in a foster placement. My understanding, with hindsight, is that he was anxious about this interview and made me hold him so that he could feel protected and reassured. Apparently, this worked for him. Not only did he handle the interview smoothly, but later that night, when everyone else on his unit acted out and got into trouble, he was the only one who did not misbehave. Since he was not typically better behaved than his peers, I am guessing that he had gained a sense of calmness from his experience of being held and contained.

I thought that was the end of the story, but I was wrong. A couple of weeks later, his mother came for a visit. The boy took his mother's hand and was showing her around the facility, introducing her to people (including me) and telling her stories about his experiences there. I had some opportunity to observe them together when he did not know I was nearby. By and by, he pointed to another staff member, who had apparently restrained him some days before, according to the aggressive method required by the facility. "There!" he said to his mother, "That's the one who attacked me!"

This boy was clearly able to distinguish between a loving, protective restraint and an aggressive one. He experienced reassurance from mine, and violence from the other. I am not saying I was a better person than the other staff member, only that my method of physical restraint better expressed my intentions than his did.

Physical restraint is a complex intervention that does require specialized training and supervision to do well. It's also an important intervention to have in your repertoire for those kids who may need it. If kids can't keep themselves safe, and you can't keep them safe, you can't do much to help them. If you are working with kids who need physical restraint, take the trouble to learn how to do it well.

EXERCISE: MAKE THE CHILD'S ENVIRONMENT SAFER

- Complete the Meaning of Behaviors form for each of the vignettes.
- Identify the main thing that is challenging the child's sense of safety.
- Decide what needs to be in place to reinforce safety and a sense of safety.
- Role-play getting this done; include all involved parties.

Jesse and Mischa

Jesse, eleven, and Mischa, seven, are siblings in foster placement because their biological father is long gone and their biological mother was neglectful. The children had been returned to their mother on several occasions, but although she tried to keep them, she was a drug addict and was not successful in making her kids a priority. The last time the judge sent them back to their biological mother, the judge said it was "against my better judgment" and described it as a last chance. The last chance lasted for five months. Now, parental rights are in the process of being terminated, the kids are back again in the same home where they had stayed for three years prior to the last stint with their biological mom, and the foster parents are in the process of adopting them. Although the foster parents have a good relationship with Jesse and Mischa, the kids are sensitive regarding their biological mom, and the foster parents don't really know what happened while the kids were with her.

The adoptive parents have a friendly, open home. Plenty of food is always available, and friends often show up to visit or share a meal. The parents are loving and permissive, letting the kids eat what they want and where they want; the kids often avoid vegetables, and sometimes eat while watching TV. Bedtime is the same; kids are allowed to go to bed when they are tired, and sometimes end up falling asleep in the living room or wherever they were when they got tired. The kids each have their own room, and although they are not allowed to leave messes in the rest of the house, are allowed to keep their own rooms as they wish.

The kids, though ambivalent about losing their biological mom again, seem relieved and happy to return to this home and family. Within a week they seem settled in, and they are trying hard and doing well in school. Their behavior at home varies. Sometimes they are okay, but often they fight with each other, throw and break objects, and on occasion run out of the house and stay away for half an hour or more.

Exercise: You are one of the adoptive parents, or you are their social worker/case manager. Choose one.

Lisa

Lisa is a sixteen-year-old girl currently living in a girls-only group home. She was molested for several years by her stepfather before disclosing to her school counselor at age thirteen. She has had a number of serious behavior problems including cutting classes, smoking cigarettes and marijuana, drinking, lying, stealing, fighting, running away, and going out (and having sex) with much older boys/men. Chances are good that she'll be in this home, or a similar placement, until she turns eighteen.

Although she gets along with many of the residents and staff members in the group home, she is also a disruptive influence. For example, she will make up a story about one of the girls and tell others that this girl said something mean about another one. She is particularly close to one of the staff members, who acknowledges that they have a special relationship. He feels that he has a chance of really reaching her and helping her. In general, Lisa gets in a lot of trouble in the group home because she breaks so many rules. However, when her favorite staff member is working, he often gives her a break and will talk to her instead of making her pay the set price for her rule violation.

Exercise: You are on the staff.

Discussion Questions

1. What were your solutions?
2. How did it feel to be in each part in the role-play?
3. What can we learn from that?

Meaning of Behavior Worksheet

1. Trauma/loss event (all events):

2. Negative beliefs (negative self-statements):

3. Piled-up feelings:

4. Trigger situation (what sets off the reactivity):

   Theme:

   Example:

5. Problem behavior(s):

Chapter 21

Discipline Is Love

Many caring adults are hesitant to discipline children. Why should this be? Many of us grew up learning to associate discipline with anger, yelling, and even revengeful punishment. If we believe that discipline is inherently hurtful, naturally we don't want to inflict it on kids we care about. The problem is that when we don't discipline kids, they keep misbehaving, and we become more angry and frustrated. When the discipline finally does occur, it's just as we feared: it's done with anger. No wonder so many adults try to avoid disciplining kids!

Because kids do need discipline, we might as well do it in a way that works, and in a way that also communicates our true intentions. Your approach to discipline depends on your answers to the following questions:

- Why do kids act out? Because they're bad and want to spread their badness around? Or because they have been "triggered"—something hit their sore spot—and they are feeling anxious and unsafe?
- Why do you have rules? To help kids to be safe, to heal, and to learn to do right? Or to get revenge when kids break the rules?

If you believe that kids break rules because they are bad, then you will probably want to use discipline to punish them and get revenge. Unfortunately, that approach to discipline does not really make kids feel safe, nor does it teach them to do right. It only adds more pain to the pile, and teaches them to fear the punishing adult.

If, on the other hand, you believe that kids break rules because they are trying to make themselves feel okay when they are feeling unsafe or insecure, then you will probably want to use discipline to help kids to feel safe, to heal, and to learn to do right. This approach to discipline takes considerable effort, especially at first. The good news is that this compassionate approach to discipline is also the effective one.

This positive, compassionate approach to discipline is based on several assumptions:

1. When kids act out, that means that they feel unsafe or insecure. They use their actions to let us know that they need our help.
2. We want to do what we can to reassure kids, so that they can feel safe and secure again. We can reassure them with discipline.
3. We want kids to learn good things from their experience of our discipline. We want them to learn:
   - They are safe.
   - They can count on us.
   - What they do matters. Good actions get rewarded; bad actions do not get rewarded, and may require discipline.

An effective discipline approach is best offered within the context of a safe, supportive environment (see Chapter 20), in which kids work toward goals they care about (see Chapter 22). We'll be focusing here on several components to the positive discipline approach: focusing on the positive, using a time-out system, and using natural consequences.

ACCENTUATE THE POSITIVE

The first principle in positive discipline is to focus on the positive. This is not just to be "nice," but because it works. Here are some keys to this approach.

Kids Will Try to Meet Your Expectations

A famous study was conducted in a public school system some years ago. Researchers came into a few classrooms and gave each child an assessment. After the assessments were completed, the researchers gave each teacher a list of several children in their class who, based on the test results, would be "late bloomers" and do especially well as the year progressed. The kids heard nothing about the lists; only the teachers knew. The tests turned out to be highly predictive, and the kids on the list did do better and better at school as the year progressed. The teachers were very impressed and wanted to be able to use the tests with their future classes.

Maybe you already know the punch line: the tests were phony and the kids were selected for the lists at random! So if the whole thing was a hoax, why did the kids all do so much better? We can only draw one conclusion. The only special thing about the kids on the list was that their teachers believed that they would do better over time. Somehow, the teachers' beliefs and expectations toward these kids were communicated, and the kids responded by coming through, by meeting the expectations they perceived.

Since kids do tend to respond to how people view them, why not use that to their benefit? When we find ways of communicating that we see kids positively and that we expect them to do good things, many kids will naturally respond by proving us right.

Attention Is Reinforcing

Kids learn from experience. When they have a repeated experience of being rewarded, or "reinforced," for doing a certain thing, they learn that doing that certain thing brings rewards. Then they're more likely to do that thing again. So you might as well focus your reinforcements on the behaviors that you hope kids will do again and again.

Give positive attention whenever you "catch" the child doing something right. Your noticing is itself reinforcing. And if the child is also working with a formal incentive system, your noticing will also serve as encouragement that she is on track toward her goals.

You can give positive attention not only for obviously good actions, but for neutral ones, as long as you can find some way to call it a positive action. For example, a boy who sometimes punched other children with no provocation was praised simply for walking down the hall: "I see you walking down the hall keeping your hands to yourself. This makes other kids feel safe around you, so they'll be more likely to want to play with you." Again, he is seen as practicing friendly behaviors, he is reinforced for these, and thus is more likely to continue them.

Reinforcement Builds Relationship

You may know of a family in which the new stepparent attempts to discipline a child before establishing much of a relationship. The child correctly says, "I don't have to listen to you! You're not my [mother/father]!" This highlights an important principle in discipline: we earn the authority to discipline a child by becoming someone he cares about. We become someone he cares about, in part, by providing for his needs and by helping him feel good.

When we focus on the positive aspects of a child, we are building the relationship. Whenever possible, we want to get to know a child in a way that makes her feel that she is seen in a positive light. We can accomplish this by engaging in enjoyable activities together, and by letting her know that we see the good things about her. When she feels that you like her and that you are noticing her positive behavior, she will feel safe and comfortable with you. When you develop a positive relationship with a child, the child is likely to try to please you. The more she cares about you, the more she will value your comments, and the more reinforcing they will be. Finally, if you do need to discipline the child later on, you will have earned the authority to do so.

ELIMINATE THE NEGATIVE

Ignore the Negative

When we ignore behavior that we don't like, we are not reinforcing it with our attention. If the goal of the bad behavior was to get our attention, this strategy will be discouraging. (Certain behaviors, such as when one child physically attacks another cannot be ignored. We are obliged to intervene to keep kids safe. Other times, we may have more leeway.)

Notice Someone Else's Positive

While we are ignoring one child's problem behavior, we can actively give our attention to another child's more appropriate behavior. Often, the first child will join the other child in an attempt to get a share of the reinforcing attention.

Distract or Rechannel

Another way to stop a child from doing something you don't want her to do is to engage her in something else instead. With this strategy, you are not reinforcing the bad behavior, and you are giving the child another option to earn your attention and reinforcement. As kids become involved in positive behaviors, we can reinforce them for doing something we approve of.

Explain Why the Behavior Is a Problem

Sometimes when we see a child doing something we don't want him to do, it makes sense to explain this to him. Kids may not know all of our rules or our reasons for them. Often, this kind of explanation can be enough to help a child do better next time.

Set a Consequence

It can be effective to tell kids what will happen if they continue the problem behavior, or if they do it one more time. For a consequence to be a meaningful deterrent, it must be something the child doesn't want, for example, removal of reinforcement, or a punishment of some kind. The latter parts of this chapter focus on this strategy in more detail.

Keep the Consequence

If the child continues doing the problem behavior after you've set a consequence, the next strategy is to keep the consequence. Then the child can learn from experience that when she behaves badly, an unpleasant consequence will occur.

DON'T MESS WITH MR. IN BETWEEN

It's very important for adults to be firm and consistent in their approach to discipline. Otherwise kids will not learn what you are hoping they will learn. Then they will continue to feel unsafe and insecure, and continue their problem behaviors. Of course, adults are not machines, and no human can be exactly the same all the time. But we can learn from machines, and use this understanding to help us to help kids. Specifically, let's learn from slot machines.

Imagine you are playing slot machines that cost a quarter for each play. Now answer this question: What will you do with a machine that gives four quarters each time you play it? Chances are, you'll put another quarter in, and another, and another. Each time, you are being reinforced with a small win. Play this machine enough times and you can buy yourself a new car.

You've been playing that machine for a while, and it's always worked for you the same way. Now what will you do when you put in a quarter, but the machine does not give the four quarters back? Chances are, you'll say to yourself, "I know that this machine works; it always works," and you'll put in another quarter, and another, and another. If you're still not getting the four quarters back, after a while you might try hitting or kicking the machine, perhaps out of frustration, or to try to get it to fix itself.

You've put in the quarters, you've kicked the machine, and still you're not getting any quarters back. Now what will you do next? Chances are, you've had enough. You're telling yourself that this machine doesn't work anymore, and you're not going to keep wasting your money on it.

So you've left that machine, and now you're playing a different one. With this machine, you put in a quarter and nothing comes back. You put in another quarter and nothing comes back. You put in another quarter and nothing comes back. You put in another quarter and nothing comes back. You put in another quarter and—*jackpot!* Many quarters come back. You put in another quarter and nothing comes back. You put in another quarter and nothing comes back. Now what will you do? Chances are, you'll put in another quarter, and another. Because each time, you're telling yourself, "The next one could be a jackpot."

Of course, you recognize that last machine as the way the slot machines work in gambling casinos. This exemplifies the principle of "random intermittent reinforcement," and it's the hardest kind of behavior to get rid of. Because the next try could win the jackpot!

So how does this apply to your discipline approach? Imagine a child who is always reinforced for a certain problem behavior. That's like getting four quarters from the machine every time you put in a quarter. It works, so you keep on doing it. This is why kids keep repeating their problem behaviors—because in some way, it's working for them.

Then one day the adults change the rules, and the problem behavior is not reinforced anymore. That's like when the quarters stop coming back from the machine. Remember, the behavior won't stop right away! First, the child may try many more times, perhaps even more than usual, so be prepared for a bit of a storm. But if you hang tough and keep from giving in, if you keep from reinforcing the problem behavior, after a while the child will finally realize that it just doesn't work anymore. Then, why waste more quarters? Better to try a different machine, find some new way of getting reinforcement.

The trick, when you are trying a new discipline approach, is to avoid the in between. What happens if the child is putting in those extra quarters, being frustrated over and over again, and then suddenly hits a jackpot? Then you have created a random intermittent reinforcement system, and the problem behavior will be much more difficult to get rid of, because no matter how many times you stick to your new rules, the child will keep hoping for a jackpot.

You have surely seen the following scene in the checkout line of a supermarket.

CHILD: Mommy, can I please have one of those?

MOTHER: No.

CHILD: Mommy, please?

MOTHER: No.

CHILD: Mommy, please?

MOTHER: No.

CHILD: Mommy, please?

MOTHER: No.

CHILD: Mommy, please?

MOTHER: No.

CHILD: Mommy, please?

MOTHER: No.

CHILD: Mommy, please?

MOTHER: Okay, here. Just be quiet!

I hope you are thinking, "Jackpot!" This mother is training her child to be obnoxious. She is reinforcing the child for asking over and over again, by teaching the child that if you ask enough times, there's a good chance of hitting the jackpot.

If you don't want your kids to be obnoxious, or to repeat their own preferred problem behaviors incessantly, then don't reinforce it. Stick to your rules every time; don't hand out jackpots.

PRINCIPLES FOR IMPLEMENTING DISCIPLINE USING A POSITIVE DISCIPLINE APPROACH

When you are responsible for kids, sometimes you must take actions that they complain about, such as enforce the rules, take away reinforcements, and give other consequences for their behaviors. The following principles and practices will help you to do this in a caring and effective way.

Problem Behavior Is a Way Children Ask for Reassurance

Reassurance calms kids down. When you can keep in mind that discipline is reassurance for kids, it will be easier for you to do this from a caring mind-set. Your goal is not to punish but to help kids to feel more safe and secure. When kids are out of control, they need the adult to take charge and get them back into control. You can do this with discipline. Then they feel protected and safe.

You Are the Adult

You are the child's rock of security. Kids need to be able to count on you to protect them, to keep things safe and under control, and to keep your own promises.

If You Are in Charge, You Are Strong and Can Protect

If you cannot take charge of a kid, then you aren't very strong and can't be counted on for much. You can show you are in charge by enforcing the rules without losing control yourself. Then kids can feel that someone strong and caring is protecting them and keeping them safe.

Keep Your Promises

Remember, routines, rules, and consequences are all promises. If you "give the kid a break" and don't enforce the rules, you are giving the kid a broken promise.

Only Make Promises You Can Keep

Don't offer treats or special activities that you won't be able to deliver; it will just teach the child that you can't be trusted. Also, don't threaten consequences that are unfair or overly severe. Later, when you are calmer, you will realize that you were wrong, and you will correct it. That also teaches the child that you can't be trusted, that you don't mean what you say. It's better to have small, reasonable consequences prepared ahead of time, so that when it's time to discipline, you already know what the consequence will be. If you find yourself disciplining while angry, you can tell the child that you will decide the consequence later.

Stop a Problem Quickly

Stop a problem before it gets too bad, and before you become too angry. This is the key to the whole thing. If you stop a problem behavior early, then

- You have offered reassurance at the first cry for help. You've come through for the child.
- The child has not had to escalate the problem behavior to get your attention. He did not have to act too "bad" to get reassurance from you. He is learning that he can get reassurance with small offenses and may not need big ones. This is not the final goal, but it's a good step.
- Because the problem behavior is still small, it only requires a small consequence. This will be easier for the child to tolerate, and easier for you to tolerate.
- Because you have not had a chance to become angry or frustrated yet, you can discipline calmly, from a caring mind-set. Then the child can learn more easily that discipline is love, and so can you.

TIME-OUT

The exact format of your discipline approach isn't the most important issue. What's really important is that you follow the principles and practices, and that you have a clear system that you stick to. If you don't like the following time-out system, change it to one that you like better; that's fine. But stick to your system, and use these principles.

Many parents have been taught a quickie version of the time-out approach, and have tried it but found that it didn't really work for them. That doesn't mean that time-out will not work in their household. What it does mean is that they were not taught carefully enough, or that they were left on their own to do it, and when problems came up, they didn't know what to do. Time-out does work, but it should be used within the context presented here (including a safe environment, focus on the positive, etc.). Also, don't expect it to work all at once. Kids find the loopholes, and it's our job to plug them up. This is an effective system, but it takes work to get results.

The main point of a time-out is that the child is being removed from the action, from the family or group. A time-out intervention should reflect the following principles:

- Time-out is nonreinforcing. That means that the other activity (from which the child is being removed) should be reinforcing. This is part of the context that makes time-out work.
- Time-out is nonpunitive. The goal is to keep kids safe and to remove reinforcement for bad behavior. There is nothing angry or punitive about giving a time-out.
- Time-out allows for learning. Kids have a chance to learn that certain behaviors lead to removal of reinforcement. They also have a chance to calm down and to think about what they did and how they want to act when they are able to rejoin the group or family.

The advantages of the time-out are closely related to the structure of the time-out, and include the following:

- The time-out keeps the child from hurting someone. This keeps the setting safe.
- The time-out keeps the child from disrupting, from preventing others from doing their own activities. When other kids can do what they expected to do, this means that adults are keeping their promises.
- The time-out removes reinforcement for bad behavior. No more quarters!

- The time-out allows the child time to regain self-control.
- The time-out gives the adult a chance to demonstrate control when the child was out of control. This is reassuring to the child, who has been contained and kept safe.

The time-out method includes the following components:

- Use this with previously established rules. The child should already know the deal before the time-out is given.
- Use with preestablished duration (e.g., one minute for each year of the child's age). Some people use thirty-second or one-minute time-outs, to allow the child to return to the family or group as quickly as possible. In general, shorter time-outs are better, because the goal is really to set a limit and remove reinforcement, not to drag things out. However, for some children, a very short time-out may not have the desired effect, so you'll have to figure out what works best for your kids, in your setting.
- Some actions (e.g., hitting) get automatic time-outs. If damage is already done, it's too late to start talking about it; the child is clearly a danger and must be removed immediately. Additional consequences could occur as well, depending on your rules and on the nature of the offense.
- Some actions (e.g., disobeying) get a warning. When the child still has a chance to correct her behavior, then give her the chance. If she can catch herself and get it together without needing a time-out, that's great.
- Warning: restate request, then count: one, two, three. Tell her what she's doing and what you want her to do instead. Count to three in a steady manner so that each count takes about one second. Do not fudge this or slow the count down, because that would be breaking your promise.
- If the child fails to initiate the action before the end of the count, then say, "Take a time-out." Sometimes the child will do what is asked just after the count has finished. He may say, "I'm doing it; I'm doing it!" but you should tell him, "You missed the chance; you can do it after the time-out is done." If you let him get away with it (if you let him do it without taking the time-out first), you have broken your promise and he will know that he can't count on you to do what you say.
- Time-out occurs in a designated space. This can be a certain chair, wall, or corner of the room, or it can be another place farther away. Your choice of a time-out spot will depend on your facilities, on your staffing, and on the nature of your kids. Make sure that the time-out spot will allow you to accomplish your goals to keep kids safe, to allow others to continue in the activity, and to remove reinforcement during the time-out. If you are traveling or not in your usual setting, you can invent new time-out spots wherever you are.
- Follow rules while in time-out. The child in time-out should not communicate with anyone during the time-out. He should not make faces or noises; he should not ask you if he's almost done. He should not play with toys or jump around. You will have to make your rules realistic for the children you work with; some kids can handle being still and silent, while others should be given something to do such as writing or drawing.
- During time-out, the child should receive no conversation or other attention. If the child in time-out makes faces and other kids laugh, then you haven't removed the reinforcement, and others are distracted and not doing their normal activity. You might control this by locating the time-out spot farther away, by starting the time-out over again whenever the child in time-out misbehaves, and/or by sending other kids to time-out as a consequence for interacting with kids in time-out. There's no one right way to manage this; you'll have to figure out what works for you. If possible, it's good to have the time-out spot in plain view of the rest of the group. Then the child in time-out can see what he's missing, and you

can keep an eye on him. However, with kids who are too disruptive, you will need to devise another plan.
- When the time-out is finished, the child is asked to explain what happened, then is welcomed to return to the group/activity. You can help the child learn from the experience by asking her to state what happened and how she would like to handle it next time. However, the "cognitive processing" component is not always appropriate. For example, if you are using thirty-second time-outs during a high-interest activity, it's probably enough just to name the behavior that caused the child to get the time-out.

Time-Out Problem Solving

Many problems will arise as you try to use these methods, because kids are all different. Here are some of the more common types of problems, along with some suggested strategies for handling them:

What if other kids try to interact with the kid in time-out?

- Have a rule against that. Enforce consequences for kids who try to communicate with someone in a time-out.

What if the child acts up in time-out?

- Then he is breaking the time-out rules. Start the time-out again when he starts following the rules again. After a while he will learn that he is just making his time-out longer.
- If the child in time-out is being too distracting, and this is keeping others from doing their activity, then consider having the time-out spot farther away from the others.

What if the adult can't resist interacting with the kid in time-out?

- If the adult is concerned for the child's health or safety, then it is appropriate to interact, even during a time-out. For example, if the child needs to go to the bathroom and really can't wait, let him go, and then pick up the time-out where it left off. Of course, if he tries this every time, then you'll know to ignore it.
- The adult must not get caught up in arguing or explaining to the child during the time-out. The intervention is negated by giving the child reinforcement instead of removing it. Do not reward the child for breaking the time-out rules.
- If the adult is unable to control his or her own reactions to the child during time-out, consider the situation:
  —If this is a staff member who is unable to achieve self-control, the first strategy is education and training. If it's still a problem, then he or she is probably in the wrong job. It takes a great deal of maturity and self-control to work with distressed kids.
  —If this is a parent, other options must be explored. The quick solution is to find a time-out spot that is far enough from the adult to prevent opportunity for interaction during the time-out. The parent does not interact until the child has completed the time-out properly, to say that the time-out is over. This saves the reinforcement for the positive behavior only (for more detail on this approach, see Chapter 10). In the long run, the parent might benefit from working with a therapist on self-control skills so that she or he can be more effective in handling the child face to face.

What if the child won't go to time-out, or won't stay there? Then some way must be found to enforce the rules, otherwise promises are not being kept and kids are not safe. Here are some ideas for enforcing rules in this situation:

- If the child does not go to time-out immediately, the adult can count to three to indicate the time the child has to start toward the time-out spot. If the child does not start before the count is done, then the time-out period is doubled (or add whatever amount of time was set).
- If the child does not go to time-out and this is an urgent threat to safety, then, depending on the degree of urgency, the adult must take him away, or let him know that he will be taken away if he doesn't go by himself. A typical statement is, "I'll count to three; if you are not on your way by then, then that means that you're asking me to help you get there. One, two, three." If he is not already on his way, then the adult should take his hand and walk him there.
- The same strategies can be used for the child who will not stay in time-out. Set up consequences for this, perhaps additional time-out minutes, or some other consequence such as loss of TV time.
- When safety is at stake, and when these other strategies don't work soon enough to keep safety, physical restraint must become an option. Otherwise, the situation does not keep kids safe.

What if the child likes to be in time-out? It's important to figure out why the child likes to be there. This can take some careful observation and questioning. Different reasons lead to different strategies:

- Some kids like time-out because of the attention that this brings them, from kids or adults. If this is happening, then time-out isn't being used properly. Figure out the weak link and fix it. This might mean moving the time-out spot farther away, enforcing consequences for other kids who encourage this child, or getting the adult under control.
- Some kids get themselves placed in time-out to avoid doing tasks they don't like, or to avoid situations they find uncomfortable. Kids should not be allowed to escape their obligations, so perhaps (for example) missed schoolwork can be made up during recess. However, adults can also learn from what the child is avoiding, and make extra efforts to help her to learn how to handle those challenges.
- Some kids find time-out calming. This is not such a bad thing. Work out a system in which they can take a voluntary time-out to calm themselves down. This can also involve prompting on the part of the adults. This is a good step toward helping kids to become better at self-management.

The real key to the time-out system is to catch the problem quickly. If you are new to using time-outs, try to make sure that you use time-outs at least three times per day in the first week of practice. Even if you must be very, very strict to do this, it's worth it to get the practice and get good at it. If you have allowed a problem to continue long enough to cause you frustration or anger, you probably should have used the time-out strategy previously. That's okay—just use the time-out right away, before the situation becomes worse.

Many parents and child care workers object to this suggestion for such active use of time-outs, stating that this seems overly strict. However, remember that "strict" and "harsh" are very different in the positive discipline approach. The sooner a problem is stopped, the smaller the problem will be, and the less chance you will have to get upset about it. If you use this strategy, and if you stick with it 100 percent for a few weeks, you will find that your kids are calmer and better behaved. At first they might complain that you're too strict, but they will notice in the long run that you don't yell at them so much anymore.

Discipline Is Love: A Story

This is a story of an unusual intervention made by a therapeutic aide (a paraprofessional) in an elementary school. The purpose here is not to suggest that the intervention be imitated, but to illustrate one way that a direct careworker tried to help a child.

"Tom" was a nine-year-old boy who had experienced significant violence and major losses in his family, including one family member murdering another. His behavior at school was extremely volatile. The aide's job was, in essence, to create a one-person day treatment program for the boy, within the context of a mainstream classroom in the public school setting. Because Tom's behavior could become so disruptive, his time-out spot was not in his own classroom, but in another smaller room down the hall.

By about three weeks after the aide had initiated the milieu treatment program, Tom had learned the system but still didn't quite get the point. One day he had to go to his time-out room for ten minutes. He sat at his desk in the time-out room, jabbing his drawing paper furiously with a marker and muttering to himself. After a few minutes, the aide came by and gave him a couple of cookies, then left again to avoid engaging in conversation during the time-out.

Afterward, the aide asked, "Are you wondering why I gave you cookies?" and they talked about it. The aide was able to explain that he had given the time-out and the cookies for the same reason: that he cared about Tom and wanted him to be safe and to feel good. Although the aide had been using the safety words all along, it wasn't until after this time-out that Tom began to realize that the aide actually cared about him. Someone who is angry at you and punishing you doesn't give you cookies!

Natural Consequences

The time-out system will cover many of the discipline issues that arise, but sometimes kids' behavior requires more of a consequence than a time-out can offer. Even so, angry, punitive revenge must be avoided. Set limits to help kids to feel safe and secure, and to help them learn that their actions do matter, and actions bring consequences. Good actions might bring rewards, bad actions might bring other consequences. We can help kids learn these important lessons by using the natural consequences approach. To make this work, it's important to use the following principles:

- Keep your promises—be willing to follow through on the consequences you select.
- Avoid retaliation or revenge—by definition, this represents adult loss of control.
- Avoid depriving the child of meals, sleep, school, and (if possible) other worthwhile activities. This is bad for the child and becomes a vengeful punishment.
- Use consequences that are fair, make sense, and offer opportunities for a positive outcome.

The natural consequences concept can help kids face the real consequences of their actions and learn from these experiences. Natural consequences are different from punishments in a very important way. A punishment makes you hurt. An example of a punishment would be that if you lie, you get a spanking. A natural consequence just naturally results from an action. An example of a natural consequence is that if you lose the dollar that you were going to use to buy ice cream, you won't be able to buy ice cream. No one is punishing you; it's just what happens. There are several advantages to using natural consequences rather than punishments:

- The child learns that actions have consequences.
- This relies on fairness, not revenge. The focus is not on the child's anger toward the punisher, because there is no punishment. This gives the child the chance to focus on himself and therefore he has a better chance to learn from the experience.

- The child has a chance to "make up" for the misdeed and rehabilitate herself. This is very important for kids who get down on themselves and dig themselves deeper and deeper into their problems and misdeeds and punishments. When a child can fix what she broke, she has a chance to dig herself out of the hole and start again from a better place. She can repair relationships, self-esteem, and perhaps her standing in her program or community. This restores resources and supports, and makes more room for hope.

For some problem behaviors, the natural consequences are very obvious, whereas to find the natural consequences for other problem behaviors can take some creativity. Here are some examples of common problem behaviors and the natural consequence that might be offered:

- You lost that dollar, now you don't have it for the ice cream you were going to buy.
- You were slow getting ready, so you'll miss the first part of the movie.
- You made a mess, so you can clean it up.
- You broke it; now fix it or pay for it.
- You didn't give it back on time. Now I know not to lend it to you again until you earn my trust back.
- You haven't been keeping your grades up, so now you have to finish your homework before you go out to play. (Of course, in another situation this could also just be a rule and not a consequence at all.)
- You made me wait for you and worry for half an hour after curfew. Now you owe me time. You can do half an hour of chores to pay me back.
- You hurt the group (or family or class or community). Now you can do something to help the group. Note that this strategy is extremely flexible and is the rationale behind community service penalties for minor legal offenses. Here are some examples:
  —You disrupted the art class and slowed down everyone's work. It will be hard for them to get their work done and still clean up afterward. Why don't you come in at lunchtime and clean the room up then?
  —When you stole the candy bar, it made everyone here feel unsafe, because now they have to worry about people stealing. What can you do to help people here to feel safe again? Maybe if you share your own candy for the next few days, they'll think that you're serious about not wanting to steal again.
  —When you broke that chair, you made this a worse place to be; it's not as nice here anymore. To make up for that, you can do something to make the place nicer. You can choose. Do you want to do some work in the garden, or some cleaning inside?

Response Cost

In most cases, as long as the primary focus is on positive behavior, the time-out system plus natural consequences will be enough to handle the discipline for the problem behaviors. However, occasionally it can be helpful to include another type of consequence in the mix. This is a special type of reinforcement remover called response cost. The basic method is to "charge" or "dock" the child every time a particular behavior occurs. It should be used carefully and according to the following principles:

- The problem behavior should be very specific and easy to identify. Examples: cursing, name-calling, failing to go to the time-out spot when told to, poking other children with a pencil.
- Use items or activities that are highly valued by the child. You can figure this out by observing the child. What does he covet? What does he spend his time doing?

- Do not use this method to harm the child. That means that you should not be thinking about taking away any object or activity that is important to the child's health, education, or welfare. For example:
  —Don't take away food (except perhaps dessert).
  —If a child is working on social development, don't take away time with peers. If he is spending hours every afternoon phoning or instant-messaging friends, then this is fair game. But if he has only an hour or less for that already, it's important to his social development. Leave it alone.
  —If a child needs exercise, don't take away time for playing sports.
- Find objects or activities that the child values, but you don't. Fortunately, many kids really like to play video games or watch TV, but as adults we don't really mind if the child gets to watch only ten minutes of TV tonight instead of the hour she was planning on.
- Money can also be used as a response cost, but it should be a relatively small amount, with opportunity to earn it back. Otherwise this becomes a real punishment rather than the modest irritant it is intended to be.
- Don't get into a hole! If you find that the child is losing and losing, and getting more and more discouraged, then you are on the wrong track. You should probably make the response costs smaller (for example, pennies instead of nickels) or abandon the response cost strategy altogether.

Response cost can work. However, it is a high-risk strategy because it opens kids to the risk of repeated failure. When kids feel bad and helpless, this hits their trauma-related sore spot and they are likely to overreact. Then it's difficult to pick up the pieces and do well. Also, when they are experiencing failure with you, they become worried about what will happen next, and they don't feel safe. In general, a positive focus is more effective. When the focus stays positive, you don't risk the failure trap. Most kids will work hard for incentives, and in most cases, remaining problem behaviors can be managed with time-out and natural consequences.

EXERCISE: WHEN WE DON'T COME THROUGH

Part 1: Challenge yourself!

1. Think of a time recently that you did not discipline according to the rules.
2. Be honest with yourself: why did you do what you did? Common reasons include the following:
   - Didn't know what else to do that might have helped
   - Too tired/didn't have the energy
   - Too angry or frustrated
   - Didn't want to be hard on the kid, because he or she has been through so much already
   - Wanted to give the kid a break/one more chance
   - The kid deserved it (he or she is bad, doesn't care)
   - Other (what?)
3. Keep notes, just enough to remind you of the situation, what you did, and why.

Part 2: Challenge One Another! (Ideally, in a Small Group)

1. Present the situation, your action, and your reason(s) to your small group.
2. Group members, be respectful! This is a person who cares and is making an effort.

3. Group members help the presenter to understand the child's needs in the situation, using the fairy tale model as a guide. Use the following worksheet for ideas.
4. Presenter suggests a more productive strategy for next time. Group members respond.

Worksheet: The Child's Needs in the Problem Situation

Here are some common reasons for not coming through for kids, for not keeping our promises, not enforcing the rules. Following each reason is at least one idea that can help us to find our way back to coming through for the kids:

1. Didn't know what else to do that might have helped
   - Try the methods presented in this book: safety theme, positive focus, time-out, natural consequences.
2. Too tired/didn't have the energy
   - Remember the slot machine? Do you want to train the kid to go for the jackpot? Then it will never stop. It's worth taking the energy now, even when you're tired. This will save energy in the long run.
3. Too angry or frustrated
   - She's acting that way because she's hurt/scared and asking for help. It's not just to hurt your feelings or make you mad; it's because she doesn't know any other way to ask yet.
   - Why not help her sooner, before you get so mad?
   - Is it okay to talk about what keeps you from coming through for this child the way you want to? Do you think this is hitting a sore spot of yours?
4. Didn't want to be hard on the kid, because he or she has been through so much already
   - Enforcing the rules makes him feel more secure. Then he knows what to expect, knows he can count on you.
   - You can enforce the rules without being harsh.
5. Wanted to give the kid a break/one more chance
   - How many "one more chances" has this kid already had? Did that work the other times? Did that stop the problem behavior?
   - When you don't enforce the rules, you are teaching the kid that you can't be trusted or counted on.
   - When you don't enforce the rules, the child learns that crime pays. He got some quick relief or satisfaction from doing the bad behavior, and no penalty. That's reinforcement for bad behavior. Is that what you want him to learn?
6. The kid deserved it (he or she is bad, doesn't care)
   - Have you completed a Meaning of Behavior form focused on this child? When you understand the meaning of the problem behavior, will you still view the kid in the same way?
   - It sounds as if this kid really got to you. Hit a sore spot? What can you do about that?

Discussion

Presenters, share your experiences. Group members, share your experiences.

HANDLING OUR OWN EMOTIONS

One of the consequences of working with kids is that we get involved. We can't do good work unless we care, and when we care, our emotions come into play. This exercise can highlight times that people often come across places where our own emotions can mess us up, keep us from doing our best. This happens partly because we really care about the kids and want them to do well. It also happens because when we work with kids, our own sore spots get hit, from our own histories of trauma and loss. This isn't automatically good or bad, but it is part of the territory.

There are five primary strategies for keeping our own emotions in check so that we can do our best work.

Use the Fairy Tale Model

When we understand kids' problem behaviors from a trauma perspective, we tend to see kids as sad, scared, or mad, rather than bad. When we see kids as hurt, we want to help them. When we can understand children's problem behaviors by using the Meaning of Behavior form, we see these behaviors as their way of showing their pain. Then we don't tend to take their problem behaviors personally; it's not about us. This way of understanding kids helps us to focus on kids and their needs.

Do Good Work

When we care about kids that we can't make any progress with, we are likely to feel helpless and frustrated. It's important to understand kids as thoroughly as possible and to help them as effectively as possible. That's why you're here. When we are able to help the kids, we feel better about ourselves, and we feel better toward them. Then our work is less stressful and it's easier to stay focused on kids and their needs.

Have Adequate Structures and Supports

You may have looked at your situation and figured out that it's really impossible. You may be right. This is a serious problem. If you are unable to keep kids safe, if you are unable to do the job, it may be that you need more help. For example, you may need access to another room so that the time-outs can be done without disrupting other kids. You may need an additional adult working with you, so that when one child is being physically restrained, the others are still being supervised. You may need respite so that you are not with kids too long during the day. It's wise to recognize limitations and try to do something about them.

Stop a Problem Quickly

The quicker you can stop a problem, the better everything goes. Kids get their reassurance before they have to escalate. The consequence can be small, which kids and adults can tolerate relatively easily. You don't have a chance to get frustrated or angry because you've taken control of the situation as soon as you noticed it. Kids feel safer when they feel that they are being carefully supervised and well protected. Everything stays calmer, and it's easier for you to focus on kids and their needs.

Monitor Yourself

There are going to be times when your own sore spots come into play. Then you'll have to figure out how to take care of this. Sometimes awareness is enough. Sometimes you'll want to do extra work with your own self-control skills, focusing on the challenging situation. Sometimes you'll want to work with a therapist on your own trauma/loss history, so you can take care of the sore spot at its source.

There is no shame in having emotional reactions while working with kids; it's part of the territory. However, as adults responsible for taking care of kids, for keeping them safe, and for helping them to heal and to achieve their potential, we have special responsibilities. We are responsible for handling our own emotions so that we can do our job, so that we can come through for the kids. The kids need this and they deserve it.

As many people have surely told you, this work is not for everyone. Part of our commitment in working with distressed kids is to take care of ourselves. This might mean stopping a problem more quickly, reducing our own stress level by exercising more, getting better at self-control skills, or even going to therapy for a while. Whatever it takes, this is our commitment to kids.

Chapter 22

Using Incentives for Success

In the fairy tale, the hope of marrying the princess motivated the guy to get himself ready to slay the dragon. In a child's life, long-term goals are important, but are not always enough to carry the child through daily challenges. Kids need all the encouragement and motivation they can find, to help them to overcome their challenges and learn new skills and habits. We can help them by identifying, and sometimes creating, sources of motivation, and then attaching these to the tasks and challenges they face.

Some people object, on philosophical grounds, to the idea of using motivators to get kids to do what we want them to do. "We shouldn't need to bribe kids," they say, "to do what they should be doing anyway. Kids should do it because they want to, because it's the right thing." Part of me feels the same way. I wish kids were already motivated and able to just do the right thing. However, this argument has a few flaws:

- There's a big difference between a motivator and a bribe. Motivators encourage us to do the right thing, whereas bribes encourage us to do the wrong thing. If you're paid to give someone an unfair advantage, that was a bribe. If you're paid to do your job, that was a paycheck, a motivator.
- We all need motivators to keep us going; there's nothing wrong with this. We are motivated by our interest in our work and other activities, by the money we can earn, by the chance to feel good, by the chance to be with and to help those we care about, and by the chance to make progress toward our long-term goals. Kids deserve to have these kinds of motivators, too.
- It takes great effort and determination to change a habit. We are asking kids to change long-standing habits. To help kids get "over the hump," some extra motivators may be needed. That doesn't mean that we'll always be throwing all kinds of big rewards at these kids. But while they are making a special effort to develop new habits, the extra motivators can make a big difference.

SOURCES OF MOTIVATION

We want to use as many sources of motivation as possible to provide a better chance that, at any given moment, at least one of these motivational forces are in play. Hopefully many will be in play at the same time; the more, the better. Here are the sources of motivation that we will be trying to tap.

High-Interest Activities

High-interest activities are an important, but sometimes overlooked, component of a treatment program. Think about the example of school curriculum. Even many "regular" kids have trouble staying focused on the classroom activity and on their assignments. Many (though not

all) distressed kids have particular trouble with this, as well. To give kids the best chance of being successful in school, the curriculum should be carefully designed to interest the student as much as possible. There are many ways to do this—depending on the subject and on the needs of the students—potentially including making the curriculum personally relevant to the students, adjusting the level so that it is both accessible and challenging (not too easy, not too hard), and including other learning modalities such as experiments, music, or performance. Outside the classroom, high interest activities are also important, so that kids are motivated to participate and to be successful.

Inclusion in the Family/Group and in the Activity

Many kids really want to be included in activities. Kids generally like to be near others, to feel that they belong. They also don't want to miss out on what the others are doing. When kids feel this way, they want to do whatever it takes to be allowed to keep participating. We can enhance this motivator by developing a positive family or group culture, and by providing high-interest activities.

Please the Parent or Caregiver

Many kids will make an effort to please the parent or caregiver, to win approval and attention and to deepen their sense of attachment or belonging with that adult. We can enhance this motivator by reinforcing positive behaviors, by not reinforcing negative behaviors, and by developing a positive relationship with the child.

Opportunities for Success

Kids like to feel good, and it feels good to be successful: to win, to do something well, to do something right, to make progress toward a goal. When kids have a reason to believe that there's a chance to be successful, they're more likely to make an effort. We can enhance this motivator by providing numerous opportunities for small, quick successes, to get kids used to having the success experience.

The Child's Personal "Princess"

It's important to find out what each child's personal goals are, what she cares about the most, how she wants her days to go, what she wants for her future. It doesn't work to tell kids what we think they should want; others have tried that already. When we know what she wants herself, then we can help her to work toward what she wants. Then we are on the same team—her team—and she's more likely to make the effort.

Formal Incentive Programs

Formal incentive programs can—and should—incorporate these principles in a systematic way. Formal incentive programs also use the science of learning and reinforcement to help kids overcome their challenges and develop better habits. Getting a regular paycheck for doing your job is an example of a formal incentive program—so is getting an allowance for doing your chores. This chapter will focus on two types of incentive programs: the point system and the individual behavior contract.

POINT SYSTEMS

Point systems are commonly used in group educational and treatment settings. The point system is a way of keeping track of specified behaviors and awarding points for each child, depending on which behaviors the child did or did not do within the specified period (e.g., the class, the day). Points are valuable because a certain number of points earns the child certain privileges or special activities. One variation of the point system is the "token economy" in which points count as a kind of in-house "money" that can be exchanged for the child's choice of prizes, perhaps from the in-house "store." Items of higher value cost more points.

Another variation is the level system in which the participant can achieve a higher level by earning a minimum number of points for a specific period. For example, if a maximum of 100 points can be earned in a day, the participant can move from the first level to the second level by earning at least seventy-five points in a day for five days in a row. Perhaps the participant can move from the second level to the third level by keeping this minimum daily point count for ten days in a row, or by earning at least ninety points in a day for five days in a row. The system can be designed to suit the needs and goals of the setting. The goal of advancing to a higher level is to allow the participant to enjoy a higher status and more privileges.

These types of point systems are used in many settings because they offer many benefits:

- This approach can be used systemwide, with all children. Staff can be trained to use the system, and staff can learn how to intervene in a consistent way. This makes it an efficient and organized way to manage behavior within a program. It can help a program to "make sense"—to be coherent and consistent.

- This is a flexible approach that can be tailored to suit the setting. The points (and levels, if any) can be awarded for whatever is most important in the program.
- Kids perceive it as fair if they are all in the same system. Even when kids are being treated differently because they have earned different levels of privileges, they can recognize that everyone has the same opportunities. When they are not able to be angry about playing favorites, they have a better chance of focusing on their own behavior.
- Peers can set the example for newcomers. A peer culture can develop around the value of working to advance oneself. Kids who are more advanced can become leaders and set the tone for others. When kids in a program value what good behavior can earn, the newer kids will probably learn to value it too.

Perhaps the bottom line is that these systems can work. When a point system is designed and run well, it can keep a facility under control and help kids improve their skills and habits.

A point system can't be bought at the store. It must be designed to fit the needs and circumstances of each setting. A system can be designed to express the values and accomplish the goals that are a priority in a program. Because not everyone is good at designing point systems, it can be very helpful to study point systems used in other programs or similar settings, which have already worked out some of the kinks and can provide a head start on a new program.

Even if you have borrowed a nice-looking point system from a similar setting, or if you are working in a setting that already has an operating point system, don't be so sure that it's achieving all of your goals. When you are using the fairy tale model of treatment, you need to make the most of kids' own sources of motivation, and you need to stay focused on the positives, on building kids' strength and competence. Not all point systems support this goal. Here are the two most common shortfalls of point systems, along with suggestions for correcting the problem:

Problem: Some point systems work by docking kids points for each offense they commit, or for each task they fail to complete. In this type of system, kids may start out with (for example) 100 points in the morning, and lose points throughout the day whenever they do something wrong or fail to do something right. Staff in this type of system may say, "I feel like I'm a prison guard. All I do is bust kids all the time for what they're doing wrong. I don't want to be always focused on the negative like that, but I have to. It's my job to keep the score." Kids may have similar complaints, for example, "All the staff here does is tell me what I'm doing wrong. No one ever gives me credit for all the things I do right. But do one little thing wrong, and you can bet I'm gonna hear about it!" When this is the atmosphere, the energy and attention is focused on the negative. Then kids know that negative behavior gets attention, and they also feel unsafe because they are put down all the time. This is not a good way to build relationships or to help kids to become stronger and more confident.

Solution: The solution is simple: flip the math; count up instead of down. Instead of (using the same example) starting at 100 and losing points for every flaw, start at zero and add points for every good action and completed task. That way, it's the staff's job to catch kids doing things right, and the whole focus becomes more positive. This change can take some creativity, but it's not too complicated. For example, instead of penalizing a kid ten points if he swears once or more during the day, you can award him ten points for keeping control of his mouth (an active, positive way to describe "not swearing") all day. Negative behavior can be restated as an opposite or incompatible positive behavior that can earn rewards.

Problem: Many point systems rely on the assumption that kids will want what the point system offers: status, privileges, toys, or whatever. Although the system was probably designed with popular incentives in mind, not every child cares about what's popular.

Some kids will really care about the chance to go to the movies, but others won't care. Some kids will want to work for the chance to "buy" a toy, and others won't. When you use a one-size-fits-all approach, you'll find that one size may fit many, but not all. You'll fail to engage some of the kids, you won't be motivating them as you hope to, and they risk falling through the cracks of your program.

Solution: Even when a point system is used throughout the setting, components of it can be individualized. Some ways to do this are simple, others are more complicated. The more complicated way is the individual behavior contract, discussed in detail later in this chapter. Here are some examples of simple ways to individualize:

- If you are using a token economy in which kids earn points to buy toys, ask each child in your program which toys she would like to be able to buy, and then you can stock those in your store.
- You can have a group discussion to find out what kinds of activities the kids are hoping for. Then you can offer these activities as motivators for good behavior. If different kids want different activities, and these can be done without involving the whole group, then kids can each work toward earning the activity of their choice.
- Suppose that a maximum of 100 points can be earned in a day. Most of the points, say ninety, are earned the same way for everyone, but the other ten points can be reserved for individualized behaviors and accomplishments. This way, one child might earn that final ten points by controlling his mouth (not swearing), another by showing friendliness toward peers (being helpful, inviting them to join in activities), and another by practicing penmanship for ten minutes during free time.

INDIVIDUAL BEHAVIOR CONTRACTS

Individual behavior contracts are formal, written agreements between an adult and a child, focused on specific child behaviors and consequences. The consequences, or incentives, are designed to encourage the child to develop new skills and habits. These contracts can be very effective in helping kids to make progress, but they have a much better chance of working when the rest of the important things are also in place. Kids first need to feel relatively safe and secure, to be involved in high-interest activities, to have positive relationships with adults, and to have opportunities to succeed. Then the individual behavior contract can help them with challenges they have not been able to master on their own.

Individual behavior contracts can be used in settings that also use point systems, or in settings that do not. If you are doing this in a setting that has an established point system, you'll want to figure out if, and how, to integrate the two kinds of incentive programs being offered. For example, in some settings kids are only allowed to work on their individual behavior contracts while they are on a higher level in their point system. In other settings, the individual contracts are in addition to the point system, and one does not depend on the other. You'll have to figure out what makes the most sense for your setting and for your kids.

What to Tell Other Kids

If you are using individual behavior contracts, and other kids are in your setting, then you should expect some questions or complaints from the other kids. "That's not fair! How come she gets all this cool stuff and I don't?" That's a fair question. Here are several possible ways to respond.

Special Needs Get Special Help

This strategy is most often used when a special-needs child is getting a contract while the more "normal" kids in the same setting are not. The point here is that children should not be treated all the same; they should each be treated as special, and each offered what they most need. You can explain to others that this child has a special problem or special need, and thus requires special help. You might point out that they are getting benefits that this child does not get, such as good grades, friends, and privileges, because they do not have these special needs. Of course, you do not want to disclose confidential information, but if kids are in the same setting, they already know plenty about one another, and it's okay to name these things. You might also be able to point out ways that they are getting special treatment, for example by being allowed to do independent projects, go someplace on their own, or whatever might apply.

Do You Want One, Too?

This strategy is most often used when the other kids in the setting might also benefit from a chance to focus on improving their own behaviors. Then you can explain that the first child has made a real commitment to improving himself in certain ways, and that the adults are trying to help him do this with the contract. "Is there something that you think you'd like to get better at? Maybe at getting your chores done? Or at being better at following directions the first time? If there's something you want to work on, maybe we can do one of these for you, too." There's no harm in offering a simple behavior contract to kids who might not really need one, if it will help them to feel fairly treated. Everyone's got something that can be improved!

Individual behavior contracts can range from simple to complex. One size does not fit all, but there are principles that can guide you, and strategies that work. Here are some of the basics.

Don't Get Too Ambitious

Target just one behavior, or at most two or three. The smaller your goal, the better chance of success. Remember, when you are starting a new child on a behavior contract, you are not trying to solve all her problems at once. You're trying to help her to build a track record of success, so that she will be more capable and confident when it comes to tackling other problems.

Be Specific

The behaviors you are targeting should describe a specific action. If you aren't able to visualize the child doing it, as clearly as if you are seeing it on TV, it's not specific enough. For example, "bad attitude" or "showing respect" are not specific enough. You need to come up with examples. Try specific behaviors such as "following directions without argument" or "saying please when asking for something." When the child does one of these, everyone will be able to agree that it happened.

Failure-Proof the Contract

The contract should be failure proof, especially at first. This means that there is no opportunity to fail, only to succeed either quickly or slowly. The reason for this is that many kids are easily discouraged, and if they keep on failing, they might be tempted to give up altogether. Failure-proof contracts provide fewer opportunities for frustration and discouragement. For example, suppose a child has a contract that requires him to wake up in a dry bed for five mornings in a row in order to win the prize. If he goes three mornings and then blows it, he's lost all his momentum and must start over. You can make this a failure-proof contract by saying that as soon as he has five dry mornings, he'll win the prize. Then if he has three dry mornings and then a wet one, he hasn't gained any ground today but at least he hasn't lost any. He still has only two more to go, and he's more likely to keep trying.

Visuals Can Help

When kids can see their contract, it's easier for them to keep it in mind. So it's worthwhile to make the contract visually striking, and to have it posted where the child will notice it. You might want a drawing of the prize(s) the child is working toward. If she can easily see her progress at a glance, so much the better.

Arrange for the Likelihood of a Quick Reward

Kids can't wait forever for their prize; if it takes too long to succeed, they'll lose hope. Keep in mind that your first goal is not to make them perfect this week. Your first goal is to help them to succeed at something, so they'll be willing to take the next step. Set up the contract in a way that, according to your best guess, they'll find success pretty quickly.

Consider Multiple Levels of Reward

This is especially useful in more complex contracts. If the "grand prize" is going to take too long to win, you might want to have other smaller rewards along the way. This will keep kids motivated, feeling successful with the more frequent achievements on their way to the larger goal. For example, a child might earn a cookie for each successful day, on the way to earning an ice cream sundae for five successful days. For some children, just the fact of getting check marks or stars on their "chart" can feel like a reward.

Build a Step at a Time

I've been encouraging you to start very small, with only one target behavior, and with opportunities for quick successes. Now think like a personal trainer. Once the child can handle the first challenge, add a few pounds, but not too many! The goal here is to build achievement and strength one step at a time, so that kids will continue to face the next challenge, and continue to succeed.

Individual behavior contracts are not for everyone. If the child is making good progress without a behavior contract, then why fix something that's not broken? For kids who do need extra incentives to make progress, a simple behavioral contract may be sufficient. For example, you might have a chore chart for kids to complete in order to receive their allowance. Or you might have a contract focused on a specific habit or behavior such as bed-wetting, cursing, or completing homework.

For many kids whose emotional distress and problem behaviors are severe enough to require day or residential treatment, a more complex behavior contract will probably be useful. This behavior contract becomes a centerpiece of the child's treatment, and targets the two or three most significant problem behaviors. If your kids do not fit this category, please read the rest of this chapter anyway! Many of the principles and techniques that are used to implement a complex individual behavior contract can also be used with the simpler ones.

DESIGNING A MORE COMPLEX CONTRACT

Here is an example of an approach to developing a complex individual behavior contract. This builds upon and extends what has already been presented on individual behavioral contracts. You might not use every component of this approach, or do it exactly the way it's presented here. This is just presented as a model. You will want to use as many of the principles and techniques as possible, since these will generally maximize the effectiveness of the contract. Typically, this contract is set up with the therapist's active participation.

Get the Child to Ask for the Contract

You can get the child to ask for the contract by explaining what it's about: a way to help the child develop better habits to achieve his goals, by earning items or activities that he wants. Most kids do want to achieve their goals, and will jump at the chance to earn incentives. However, if the child does not actively say that he is interested, do not go ahead with the contract. If it's yours, not his, it won't work. Just back off gracefully, acknowledge that he might not be ready for this yet, and when he decides that he's ready to work toward his goals, to let you know. Or perhaps you'll check back at another time to see if he's ready. If other kids are receiving rewards for their contracts, this one is more likely to want one too.

Use Specific Behaviors, Matched Positive to Negative, That Are Mutually Incompatible

Don't use "not [doing the problem behavior]" as a behavior, because you can't watch someone not doing something. Figure out what the child will be doing instead of the bad thing. To make this work, you might need to identify the situation in which the problem behavior would most likely occur. For example, if "hitting" usually happens when someone calls him a name, then "ignoring" would be a positive, and incompatible, alternative behavior. Typically you will have a list of two or three problem behaviors, with a matching list including an alternative, positive and incompatible, behavior for each.

Positive and Negative Symbols or Ego Ideals to Go with Each Behavior Cluster

Help your client to think of symbols that represent, on the one hand, the person she is trying to become, and on the other hand, the problem that she does not want to be anymore. The therapist should have a good idea of the child's goals and fears, and can provide help here. However, ideally the child will be the one to come up with the symbols, so that they have the most personal meaning. Examples of the positive symbol: Teacher, cop, or some celebrity or cartoon figure such as Batman, Michael Jordan, Ariel. Examples of the negative symbol: Volcano, rat, baby, broken record, loser. Do you want to be a teacher or a loser? These symbols can convey power and can help kids focus their energy.

Client-Generated Array of Incentives

It's also important for kids to suggest their own incentives, the things they want to try to earn. The more they care about the incentives, the more power the incentives will have. The adult can encourage the child to "brainstorm" everything she might wish for, whether big, small, or in between. Items on the list might include a trip to Disneyland, a trip to the local video arcade, a new CD, a chocolate chip cookie, getting to be the one to choose the movie that is rented for the group or family, getting to stay up later, getting to be the one who gets the mail from the mailbox, one-on-one time playing a game with a favored adult, ice cream, a peach, extra time playing video games, and on and on. The bigger the list, including a wide range of possible rewards, the better your chance of creating a contract that will work. This is a good chance to be creative, as many kids will work for privileges that are good for them, such as special time with an adult, or being allowed to help with younger kids.

Organize the Incentives by Size

When you are talking with the child about possible incentives, you should have a piece of paper with three columns labeled Small, Medium, and Large. As the child suggests each new item, you decide which column to place it in. A small incentive can be earned within a short period of time, perhaps several hours or a day. A medium incentive can be earned in a modest period of time, perhaps several days or a week. Typically, when four to seven small incentives have been earned, a medium incentive is earned as well. A large incentive is the grand prize that represents success in accomplishing the goals of the contract. Typically, when four to seven medium incentives have been earned, the large incentive is earned. The entire contract should take from one to three months, depending on the age of the child and the circumstances of the setting.

Organize the Incentives by Priority

Once you have completed the list, hopefully with at least a few items in each column (more than a few is great!), then you need to find out which of the items, in a given column, are most desired by the child. You can do this by showing the column to the child and asking what her first choice is in that column, what her second choice is, etc., all the way down the line. Then repeat this until you have a priority rating for each item in each column. If certain items are rated the same, that's okay. For example, supposing that in the Small list, apple and pear are both rated as the first choice. Later, when you set up the contract, the child can choose an apple or a pear whenever she earns that level of reward.

Select the Incentives

Now that you have the fantasy list of all possible incentives, you must select the incentives you'll actually be using in the contract. Check with all parties regarding the possibility of using the highest rated incentives on each of the lists. You will also need to use your own judgment in this regard. In general, you will select the highest-rated item that is likely to work, on each of the lists. To make sure the item will work, you should check for several things.

When parents are actively involved in the child's treatment, and in the child's life, they should be included as much as possible. When it comes to selecting incentives, parent-related concerns might include:

- *Child's health.* Some parents will object to their child being given sweets such as cookies or soda. If such an item was high on the list and the parent does not agree to it, you'll need to cross it off and try the next high-rated item. Sometimes parents will negotiate (for example, "It's okay as long as he brushes his teeth afterward"), but don't push too hard or they might end up agreeing when they don't really approve.
- *Values clash.* Some parents will object to an incentive because it is not consistent with their values or with what they want their child exposed to. For example, some parents do not allow their children to play certain video games or to own certain toys.
- *Interferes with family life.* Some incentives are already present, or anticipated, within the normal family life, and the parents may not want their hands tied by the terms of the con-

tract. For example, if they like to take their family out to a favored restaurant every Friday night, going out to this same restaurant should probably not be an incentive in the contract. Otherwise, the family will not be able to follow their normal routine unless the child has earned the reward. Or even worse, the family will follow their normal routine, and the incentive will lose its power because the child is getting it no matter what he does.

- *Resources, fairness, etc.* Make sure that parents can handle what is being asked of them, especially if they are being asked to contribute money and/or time for the incentives. Make sure that this contract does not become a way for this child to claim a disproportionate share of the family's resources at the expense of the other children in the family. Some families cannot afford even a few extra dollars in a week. On the other hand, even if a family can afford a trip to Disneyland, that is probably too big a prize for the child to earn.

Several issues should be considered within your setting, especially if other kids are also working with similar contracts:

- *Available money and other resources.* You can't offer items that you won't be able to deliver. Is enough money available to purchase the incentives you want to include in the contract? Is a refrigerator located near the place the child will be when it is time to receive his cold soda? Is the specified adult able to provide one-on-one playing time without compromising the supervision of other kids?
- *Fairness.* Individual behavior contracts are individualized, so we don't need to knock ourselves out trying to make sure that everyone gets the same thing. Insead, we try to make sure that everyone gets whatever's best for them. Even so, a rough consistency should exist across contracts, so that at every level, not too much discrepancy occurs in the monetary value of the prizes. If one child's grand prize costs $24 and another's costs $30, that's probably okay. But if one is $24 and another is $100, such a discrepancy will lead to problems in your setting, and the $24-prize may not seem as valuable to the child anymore.

Write the Contract

Once you have the list of matched positive/negative behaviors, the corresponding symbols that personify each cluster of behaviors, and the best workable incentives at each level, you're ready to put it all together. Try to make the contract as short, simple, and clear as you can, while still covering all the bases. A sample contract follows. The contract should easily fit on a single page, with plenty of room at the bottom for people to add signatures. The following elements should be included, in this order:

1. *First paragraph: Introducing the contract.* First person introduction. Then state the child's positive goal/metaphor, explaining this with the desired behaviors and the wanted consequences. Then state the child's negative metaphor, explaining this with the negative behaviors and the unwanted consequences. Finally, introduce the contract as the way to help the child achieve the goal.
2. *Second paragraph: How points are earned.* Explain in very clear detail how points are earned on the contract. This should be tied to specific behaviors as well as specific time periods and places.
3. *Third paragraph: How rewards are earned.* Explain in very clear detail how rewards are earned on the contract. This is usually a matter of converting accumulated points to Small rewards, converting accumulated Smalls to Mediums, and then converting the Mediums to the Large.

4. *List of metaphors and behaviors.* This is done in a column so that the positive metaphor is the column title for the positive behaviors, and so forth.
5. *Signatures.* List the name of each person who will be participating in the contract, with space next to his or her name for a signature. The child's name should be first.

Create the "Chart"

Contracts need to be kept track of and documented. Typically a daily chart lists the times, places, and behaviors to keep track of each point and when/how it was earned. This daily chart may be signed, turned in, or however you have arranged this. Also, an overview chart marks the child's progress in the contract as a whole. Make the charts as clear and visually appealing as possible. Highlight the behaviors and the incentives as much as possible. Think about where the charts will be kept, to help to remind the child and others of the contract.

Child Actively Obtains Agreement from All Participants

Once the contract is written, then the child signs it and asks others to sign. Of course, you have made sure that the others have already seen the contract, and already understand their roles. Even so, it's important for the child to explain it to each person and tell each person what is expected from each party. This increases the child's ownership of the contract and emphasizes that it is being done for her own goals.

EXERCISE: DEVELOP AN INDIVIDUAL BEHAVIOR CONTRACT

In groups of three, choose a child, a counselor, and a coach.

Part 1

If you are the child, role-play the child in the vignette. Don't do the counselor's job, but please be cooperative. *If you are the counselor,* use the script, verbatim. If you are asking a question, give the child a chance to answer before you continue. The words [in brackets] are not to say out loud, but to guide you on what to do, and in which order. *If you are the coach,* observe, and if necessary, help the counselor to get back on track.

Vignette: Frankie

Frankie is an eleven-year old boy or girl (same gender as the role-player) in a self-contained classroom at school; all twelve kids in this classroom have been identified as having significant behavior problems. Frankie was sent to this class because of poor work habits in addition to a habit of harassing other kids. Frankie's therapist has told you that Frankie wants to improve upon getting work done in school, so that he or she can go back to the regular class with the kids whom he or she has always gone to school with. Frankie also wants to get along better with other kids and have more friends. You have been observing in the classroom, and you have noticed that Frankie does seem to try to do the work, but upon getting confused or stuck, just gives up and finds something else to do instead. You have also noticed that the times that Frankie starts to bug other kids (calls them names and makes faces) are when they are talking to one another but Frankie is not included.

Sample Individual Behavior Contract

I, Johanna de Vries, want to be more like a teacher. When I'm like a teacher, I do my work and I respect others. Then I get good grades and have more friends. Sometimes, though, I act like a rat. Then I mess around instead of working, and I call other people names, and end up getting in trouble. To help me get better at being like a teacher, I agree to the following contract:

In each of the six class periods each day, I can earn one point for doing my work during that period, and one point for respecting others during that period. If I earn eleven points in a day, I get a two-point bonus; if I earn twelve points in a day, I get a five-point bonus.

For every ten points, I get a Small reward, either a cookie or a piece of fruit, at the end of the day. For every six Small rewards, I also get a Medium reward, a banana split sundae at Ice Cream Palace. When I have gotten six Medium rewards, I get the Large reward: a sundress from K-Mart.

Teacher	**Rat**
Doing my work	Messing around during work time
Respecting others	Calling people names

Signatures:

Johanna de Vries ______________________________

(Father) ______________________________

(Mother) ______________________________

(Teacher) ______________________________

(Aides) ______________________________

(Therapist) ______________________________

Script for Talking with the Child About Setting up the Contract

COUNSELOR: [Warm-up] Frankie, you've been in this classroom for over a month now. You've learned how things go here, you know what to do, and it's obvious that you're trying. You've said that you want to get better at getting your schoolwork done, so that you can go back to your regular class. You've also said that you want to get better at getting along with other kids, so that you can have more friends.

[Get the kid to ask for it.] You've probably noticed that other kids have behavior charts, so when they do the things they're trying to get better at, they get rewards. Kids are only allowed to have a chart if they really want to work on something, get better at something. Do you think you might want to do something like this, have a chance to earn rewards while you're trying to get better at doing your schoolwork and stuff?

[Identifying the first problem behavior and a positive alternative.] Okay, so what we'll be doing now is talking about the behaviors you want to get better at; then we'll talk about the things you'd like to be able to earn. Let's start with the schoolwork. I've noticed that sometimes when you're doing your assignment, if you get confused or stuck—you're not sure how to do it—you just start doing something else instead. Then you get in trouble and your work isn't done. When you're not sure how to do the schoolwork, when you're feeling stuck, what do you think you could do if you wanted to be able to get your schoolwork done? [If you get a good answer, accept it and move on. However, if the child does not respond with a useful idea, you can ask, "Do you have any other ideas?" If the child still does not come up with a useful suggestion, you can say, "Let me tell you what some other kids do in this situation, and you can tell me what you think would work for you." Then give two or three strategies and let the child choose.]

[Identifying the second problem behavior and a positive alternative.] You also said that you wanted to get along better with other kids. I've noticed that you kind of give kids trouble sometimes; you call them names and make faces. When you do that stuff, do you think that makes kids want to be with you more, or want to be with you less?

That's what I think, too. I've noticed that you do that when you see other kids talking or doing something and they're not doing it with you. I wondered if you are just wanting to be included, to be a part of things. When you see kids talking or doing something, if you decided not to call them names or make faces, what could you do so that kids would want to be with you more? [If you get a good answer, accept it and move on. However, if the child does not respond with a useful idea, you can ask, "Do you have any other ideas?" If the child still does not come up with a useful suggestion, you can say, "Let me tell you what some other kids do in this situation, and you can tell me what you think would work for you." Then give two or three strategies and let the child choose.]

[Generate the metaphors.] You've told me that you want to be able to [name the positive behaviors] so that you can go back to the regular class, and so that kids will like you more. What kind of person can you think of who can handle things the way you wish you could? [If you get a good metaphor here, great. But it can be tricky. You might need to ask it a few different ways, perhaps giving examples of different kinds of role models: occupations (e.g., teacher, cop, sports star), celebrities, etc.]

You also said that when you do it the bad old way, you're doing other things during schoolwork time, and you're calling kids names and making faces at them. The problem is, that means that you're not getting your work done, and kids don't like to be around you. What kind of person or thing do you think of, that's like that? [If you get a good metaphor here, great. But it can be tricky. You might have to ask it a few different ways, perhaps giving examples of different kinds of negative metaphors: baby, loser, chump, etc.]

[Make a list of possible incentives.] Okay, now it's time to make a list of all the things that you might want to be able to earn as a reward. You won't get everything on the list; I'll have to figure out which things will work. Right now, we're just having fun, and thinking of everything you might wish for, no matter how big or how small it is. So what kinds of things would you like to be able to earn? [This is brainstorming. Write down everything without judgment or critical comment. Put the item under Small if it could be earned in a day or two, Medium if it could be earned in a week or two, and Large if it could be earned in a month or two. If needed, encourage the child to think of a variety of possible incentives, including food items, privileges, activities, toys, etc. Keep going until you have at least five items on each list; more is okay too.]

Small	**Medium**	**Large**

[Rank order the items.] Okay, we have a lot of things on the list! Actually, I've made three lists, for rewards of different sizes. Now I'm going to ask you to tell me your first choice, and then your next choice, on each of the lists. So look over all the things on the Small list. Of all of these, which is your first choice? Which would you want the most? After that, what's your next choice? And after that? [Write down 1 next to the first choice item on the Small list, 2 next to the second choice item, and so on. Continue until each item on the Small list is rank ordered. Then do the same with each of the other lists. When you have finished, every item should have a number next to it.]

[Wrap it up.] Okay, that's enough for today. Now my job is to try and put this together into a contract, so you can get started on trying to earn the rewards. You won't be going for all the rewards on the list—only certain ones. So I'll talk to you tomorrow and show you what I've worked out. Now, before we end, tell me what you liked about this meeting, and what you didn't like.

Discussion

Give one another feedback about your experience in this exercise. After the child gives feedback, the coach can give feedback as well. The counselor may also have questions or observations.

Part 2

Once you have completed the list of incentives, give up your previous roles and become a working team. Using what you got from the first part of this exercise, figure out how to make a contract that will work. Do this by completing the Contract Form, starting at the top and completing each item before going to the next.

Discussion Question

1. What was it like to be in each of the roles?

Contract Form

I, ______________________, want to be more like a _________________________.
(child's name) (positive metaphor)

When I'm like a ____________________, I ________________________________
(positive metaphor) (positive behavior)

and ____.
(positive behaviors)

Then I ____.
(the good things that happen in life when I do these kinds of behaviors)

Sometimes, though, I act like a ______________________________________.
(negative metaphor)

Then I ____.
(negative behaviors)

To help me get better at being like a ______________________, I agree to the following contract: (positive metaphor)

I can earn points on my contract as follows: ______________________________
(Include time, place, and required behaviors, also the maximum number of points possible.)

I can earn rewards on my contract as follows: _____________________________
(Name the rewards, and explain how many points/Small reward; how many Smalls/Medium, and how many Mediums/Large.)

______________________________	______________________________
(Positive metaphor)	(Negative metaphor)
______________________________	______________________________
(Positive behavior #1)	(Matching/incompatible negative behavior)
______________________________	______________________________
(Positive behavior #2)	(Matching/incompatible negative behavior)
______________________________	______________________________
(Positive behavior #3, if any)	(Matching/incompatible negative behavior)

Signatures (include names of all parties, child first) __________________________

____

IMPLEMENTING THE CONTRACT

Once the contract is signed, you must do it! If the adults in the system don't follow through, the whole thing will fall apart. Here are some guidelines that will help you to carry the contract through to successful completion.

One Adult Should Be the Contract "Champion"

The contract champion is in charge of making sure that the contract is carefully monitored and followed, and that everyone is doing their part. Without one person who is clearly responsible, it's too easy for things to go wrong, to fall through the cracks.

All Parties Should Be Doing Their Part

The contract champion makes sure that each required action is accomplished. Is the teacher checking off which behaviors were done during the class period? Are the teacher and the aide using the right words (more on this later) to prompt the child? Are the right rewards being delivered at the right time? Is the parent being kept in the loop?

Keep Consistent Discipline and Structure

If the child's environment is falling apart, he will go back into survival mode, and the contract won't be a priority. The contract can't carry a child through an unsafe or nonsupportive environment. Only if the structure and support stay in place will the child be able to focus on earning incentives and achieving goals.

Keep a Positive Focus

The contract provides a structure for noticing the child's positive behaviors. Take advantage of this. Give attention for positive behavior so that this behavior is reinforced. The child who feels successful will be more likely to persevere.

Label the Child's Behavior Using the Contract Language

When you see the child engaging in the problem behavior, you can make a comment relating the behavior to the negative metaphor. When you see the child doing the positive behavior, you can make a comment relating the positive behavior to the positive metaphor and to the incentives. When you see the child on the edge, you can make a comment highlighting the choices between the negative behavior/metaphor on one hand, and the positive behavior/metaphor and incentives on the other. The contract, including the metaphors and the incentives, is designed to be emotionally significant for the child, to have power. Using the words and concepts in the contract invokes its power. This can help the child tap into that power and make the right choice.

PROBLEM SOLVING THE INDIVIDUAL BEHAVIOR CONTRACT

No matter how elegant a contract you put together, things can and do go wrong. That doesn't mean that you didn't do a beautiful job. It just means that kids are human, life is complicated, and things don't always go as planned. Part of the routine when you implement a behavior contract is to monitor it carefully. When you find that the contract is not working as planned, you need to figure out why it isn't working. Once you discover the problem, you can adjust the system accordingly. Most behavior contracts will require some tinkering. Here are some of the more common problem areas to look for:

- Is a problem behavior being inadvertently reinforced?
- Is the monitoring system failing? Why? Too demanding for the teacher? Parent does not understand?
- Is the reward system being undermined by failure to reward, or by premature reward?
- Is the child becoming too discouraged? Are there too many opportunities for failure? Are the rewards too difficult to obtain, too slow in coming?

Problem solving a contract can be very simple, or can require some ingenuity, depending on the situation. An exhaustive list of possible solutions cannot be provided, but here are a couple of examples, just to give you an idea of the range of possibilities.

Nina was an eight-year-old girl whose contract focused on getting better at asking an adult for help when she felt nervous, instead of running away. Although she sincerely wanted to improve her behavior, and the incentives seemed appropriate, she continued to run away as much as ever. When the adults studied the situation, they noticed that whenever Nina ran away, this led to a physical restraint (because otherwise she would just keep going farther and farther away). Of course, many children like to be held by an adult they trust. Based on a guess that the restraints might have been reinforcing the running-away behavior, the consequence was changed. Now, although an adult would still run after her to catch her and bring her back, Nina would then be put alone in a room with an adult who would not hold her or even talk with her until she calmed herself down. Once she learned that running away didn't pay off so well anymore, it was easier for her to try something new that would be rewarded.

Ryan was a thirteen-year-old boy whose parents were actively involved with his day treatment school program. Ryan was in this placement mainly because of his habit of being aggressive toward other kids. He would call them names, punch them, or hit them with objects. He was doing very well with his behavioral contract, which was focused on staying on task in school as well as controlling his aggression. Two months into the contract, when he appeared close to earning the reward within a few weeks, the whole thing seemed to collapse. He wasn't bothering much with his schoolwork anymore, was lashing out at kids and staff the way he used to do, and was not responding to the prompts that had motivated him with the contract only days earlier. It turned out that his parents had been so proud of him for doing so well in his program that they had purchased and given him the "grand prize" (Large) reward, a CD player, over the weekend. When the boy received the CD player, he thought that meant that his parents didn't want him to continue with the contract anymore (or to improve his behavior!), and he stopped working on it. This was actually a very difficult salvage job, involving several meetings with the family, and finally the creation of a new contract with a new grand prize. It's better if you can make sure, up front, that the parents are on board and understand how to show support.

Ned was a seven-year-old boy who was working with a simple contract: If he could stay in his chair during most of each class period, he would earn a treat at the end of the day. After earning a number of daily treats, he would earn a bigger treat. However, the contract wasn't working. Ned was immature and did not grasp the idea that the treat would come at the end of the day. He needed more immediate reinforcement. The adults started posting a gold star on his chart for every time period in which he earned his point. He was thrilled with the stars. These became another level of reinforcement (maybe "Very Small") and this helped him to stay motivated.

Clarissa was a twelve-year-old girl who was working with a contract focused on staying on task during classes. However, the chart was not being completed correctly by the teacher. The chart was set up to be marked after each class period, but the teacher only marked it once or twice on most days. It turned out that the teacher was willing to do her part, but she was so busy with her large classroom that she just didn't usually remember to mark the chart. The system was changed so that whenever the bell rang at the end of a period, it was Clarissa's job to take her chart to the teacher to have it marked. This worked, and the contract got back on track.

This chapter has focused on how to help kids achieve their goals by harnessing the things that motivate them. A number of principles and strategies were presented, with a focus on formal incentive systems. In general, these work by integrating trauma treatment principles and practices with the science of learning and reinforcement. The final example here shows another kind of incentive program and demonstrates the flexibility of the incentive approach.

POPCORN POINTS: ANOTHER STRATEGY USING INCENTIVES

Tom is the nine-year-old boy who was featured in the "cookies during time-out" story in Chapter 21. Although he was trying hard with his individual behavior contract, it just didn't seem to be making much of a dent in his volatile, aggressive behavior toward his peers. Too many times in a day he would throw a pencil at another child, grab someone's book and throw it, or take a random swing while walking down the hall. The treatment team did not want to disrupt his behavior contract because otherwise it was going well, so they decided to add something new to try to reduce the aggression.

Tom really wanted to have more friends, so this was used as a motivator. It was easy to get Tom to see that when his behavior frightened kids, they would try to stay away from him. If he did "friendly" things instead, kids would feel safer around him and he would have more chances to make friends. "Friendly things" was defined by the aide, loosely at first, as anything that Tom might do that would make other kids feel good around him.

Tom was offered a chance to develop his friendly behaviors, with incentives, as follows. The aide showed Tom an index card with the words "Popcorn Points" written in large bold letters on the top edge. The rest of the card was filled with a grid of lines making twenty-five empty boxes. Tom was told that when the boxes filled up, he would be able to invite a peer of his choice to make a big batch of popcorn together. Then they would give the popcorn to the whole class. (The rationale was that friendly behavior would earn rewards that would further improve his social status.)

He could get the boxes filled by doing friendly things. It was up to the aide to decide which behaviors "counted" as friendly, and on which occasions those behaviors would earn a check mark, filling a box on the card. This gave the aide the flexibility to modify the program along the way. Here's how it worked.

Early in the program, the aide made a point of noticing many behaviors as "friendly" and as earning a check mark. For example, the aide would say, "I see that you're walking past people without hitting anyone. That makes kids feel safe around you," and then conspicuously check off a box. Perhaps half a minute later, this would be repeated. Tom learned that it didn't take much to be successful at this game, and he could already smell the popcorn. Gradually, the aide would notice fewer of the more neutral behaviors (not doing something bad) and award more check marks for active prosocial behaviors, such as picking up an object that a peer had dropped, or encouraging a peer who had made a mistake during a game.

One of the initial strategies is called "shaping" because at first the reinforcement is for frequently occurring behaviors, but as the child gets used to making the effort to earn the reinforcement, the reinforcement is progressively given for behaviors closer and closer to the desired ones. When the desired behaviors are not very frequent initially, shaping can be a good way of getting things rolling while gradually moving the child closer to where you want him to be.

Another of the initial strategies is called "priming the pump" because the reinforcements are given so freely early on. This helps boost the child's confidence in the possibility of success and gets him used to looking for reinforcement for targeted behaviors. If you don't prime the pump, the desired behavior may never start to flow.

Tom started to look at the aide after doing a behavior that had previously been reinforced, to see if the aide noticed it this time and had marked the card. Sometimes the aide would comment that the behavior was friendly, and would make the mark. Sometimes the aide would make the mark with no comment. Sometimes the aide would make the comment, but no mark! At first, this confused Tom, but the aide explained again that it was up to the aide to decide which behaviors counted and when to make the marks. Tom learned to accept this, but he kept on checking with the aide to see if and when he was earning the check marks.

The "fading" strategy was used here, because at first, the aide reinforced every possible example of the friendly behavior, but later only reinforced some of the examples. Also, the strength of the reinforcement faded; whereas at first, the reinforcement included eye contact, a praising comment, and a check mark, later only one or two of those might be used at any one time. When fading is not introduced too quickly, it can help the child keep up the good habit even as the structured reinforcements are gradually withdrawn.

This is also an example of the "random intermittent reinforcement" strategy that is used by the gambling casinos. Kids—like the rest of us—will keep on doing something in the hope of an occasional jackpot. Tom learned to keep on trying to use friendly behaviors because he knew that sometimes, some form of reinforcement would come. When combined with fading, the random intermittent reinforcement can be very effective in helping the child to keep up the good habit.

The aide made sure that the first Popcorn Points card was filled in only three days. Tom invited a friend to make popcorn for the class. This made everyone happy with Tom, and Tom felt pleased with his success. Then the aide said, "You're getting so good at this, I think we should make it a little harder. How about thirty points this time?" Tom was proud of his success and glad to accept the greater challenge.

The whole routine was repeated several times. Each time five more points was added. It never took more than about a week to fill the card. When the aide felt that Tom was getting discouraged or at risk of becoming aggressive, a flurry of check marks would ensue; this usually helped Tom to get himself back on track. Otherwise, the fading and random intermittent reinforcement strategies were used more and more. After the third batch of popcorn, Tom asked if he could work toward making cookies for his class the next time. Yes.

Chapter 23

The Magic Words: Cognitive Interventions

Words have power. We can use words to help kids learn and heal.

Words get inside your head and take on a life of their own. See what happens inside your head when you read the following words.

- Easy come . . .
- If at first you don't succeed . . .
- Quitters never win, and . . .
- You never get a second chance to make . . .
- Winston tastes good . . .
- A day without orange juice is like . . .

When we choose our words with care and intention, these "cognitive" interventions can help kids to learn, to think in a different way. The strategy is to "label" kids' behaviors, by giving the behaviors a name that will make a difference. We have three overall goals in doing this:

- Getting our voice and our words inside the kids' heads—the way parents, and advertisers, have done with us. This is done by saying the same words over and over again in the same situations. Over time, the words take hold. They become the kids' own thoughts, even when we are not saying anything, even when we're not there.
- Reinforcing positive intentions and behaviors. We can use cognitive interventions to find and reinforce positive intentions even when we see negative behaviors. This is a "shaping" strategy to encourage more of the positive. We can also make comments that support and reinforce the positive behaviors that we observe.
- Help kids to gradually transform their acting out to talking out. This is done by labeling the intention behind kids' acting out behaviors. Over time, as kids learn that their intentions are accepted, they start to express their intentions more directly and effectively.

Here's one last Tom story to illustrate how words can help to transform behavior over time. In the first month or two of treatment, Tom required frequent physical restraint. Each time, the aide used the safety words during the restraint, and described Tom's prerestraint behaviors as Tom's way of asking for help, for external controls to help him feel safe and secure. This was done over and over again in simple, direct ways. For example, "If I see anything flying from that hand, I'll know that the hand is asking for help staying in control, and I'll hold it."

About two and a half months into treatment, one day Tom said, "Can we play that game where I run and you try to catch me?" He had figured out how to get what he needed without breaking rules or acting out. He had learned to ask for that physical reassurance with words.

Down the line, we hope kids will get even better at this, more sophisticated. Then they would say something like, "I'm feeling nervous. Can you hold my hand?" The way we label their behavior helps them to make progress, one step at a time, from acting it out to talking it out.

STANCE OF THE ADULT

The labeling methods are not very complicated. However, it takes a great deal practice to do this well and consistently. To paraphrase the old swing standard, "It ain't what you say, it's the way how you say it, that's what gets results." Saying the right words does matter. But even the right words won't get the job done, unless they come with the right attitude, intention, feeling, body language, and tone of voice.

For example, if the adult's words say, "The choice you make is up to you," while the body and the tone of voice is saying, "Do it my way or I'll go nuts," what do you think the child will "hear"? In other words, the delivery of the message should be consistent with the content of the message. This isn't always easy, because we really do want kids to do it our way. It makes life easier for us, and we believe that kids will be better off for it. Still, giving a mixed message doesn't get the job done.

It would be impossible to control our body language and tone of voice if we were always in conflict while talking with kids. The way to give kids clear and effective messages is to say the right words that come from the right place. You can use your caring for the child, your understanding of the child, and your understanding of what will be helpful, to keep yourself on track. Here are some additional guidelines to help you to direct your own attitude in a way that will help the words to come out right.

Keep an Attitude of Supportive Neutrality

Supportive neutrality means that you do care for the child and hope that she will do well, but you don't get emotional about it. Root for the home team, but don't let the outcome of the game affect your mood or your day. Root for the child, but don't worry about a particular behavior; that's just part of the overall process. Give the message: "I'll do my best to help you, but it's your choice. I have my life, you have yours. Your choices will affect only you." When you are able to convey the attitude of supportive neutrality the following occurs:

- Kids feel cared for, but they don't feel pressured or coerced.
- You are in charge of yourself, the child is not in charge of you. If you get too hung up on what the child does, then she is in charge of you, and she can use her behavior as a tool (a weapon) to get to you and control how you feel.
- When kids do take initiative and make choices, they feel that the choices are theirs. No one else is to blame when something goes wrong. No one else takes credit when something goes right. Kids can learn from their own choices and feel proud of their accomplishments.

Use the Power of the Incentive System

When you are working an incentive system, all of the child's actions can be labeled as the child making a choice for a particular consequence. When you are working the incentive system, the following happens:

- The child is not fighting with you, only with himself. What happens to him is up to him; it only depends on the choices he makes. When he can't focus on anger toward you, there's a better chance that he will focus on himself and learn something.
- When kids do try to insult or accuse you, you know that it's only a misplaced expression of their own frustration with themselves. You know it's not really about you. So you don't have to take it personally, you don't have to get sucked into an argument—you know what's really going on.
- Because you're working an effective system, you can feel confident that you are helping the child learn from her experiences. This is true whether she happens to be doing well or poorly at the moment.
- When you know the child is learning from every choice she makes, you don't need her to make any particular choice at the moment. When you know that her frustration and anger, even if directed toward you, is really about herself, you don't need to take it personally or be offended. When you do not become angry or frustrated, it's easier to stay focused on the child, and it's easier to stay calm and supportive.

THE LABELING METHODS

Here are the labels that tend to be more effective with kids:

- Name the intention
- Name the action
- Name the action as a choice for the consequence
- Pair the labeling with a specific suggestion

Name the Intention

Kids often don't even know why they're behaving in a certain way. Or maybe they do know, but for some reason they feel that it would not work to express it directly. Perhaps they are afraid to show their need for fear of being rejected. Maybe they just haven't learned how to recognize what they are thinking and feeling, and/or how to express it more directly.

When we name the intention behind the child's action, we try to do it in a simple and clear way that kids can easily understand. We also try to do it in a way that shows that we see them in a positive light and find them acceptable. When we name the intention behind the child's action, we are potentially helping kids to

- Understand what they were feeling or thinking;
- Learn that their intentions are acceptable and don't need to be hidden or disguised;
- Learn that they might have a better chance of having their needs met if they can express their intentions more clearly; and
- Learn how to express it in words.

Paul was a fourteen-year-old boy who belonged to a small group of at-risk teens who received a variety of special services and recreational opportunities at a local youth center. Several months into his participation, Paul was invested in the group and had formed positive relationships with the staff. One very popular activity was a six-week movie series in which, every Tuesday evening, the staff would prepare a dinner with one or two of the group members, then the rest of the kids would arrive to eat and then watch the movie. Sometimes kids got rides from staff; sometimes they found other ways to get to the center.

On the third Tuesday evening of this movie series, it was time for dinner but Paul had not arrived. This was unfortunate but not a huge surprise, because he had been promised a ride by an unreliable family member. After dinner and before the movie, when many people were standing around outside, Paul pulled up in a taxicab. This meant that he had spent perhaps the only few dollars that he had been able to earn all month, from a small job helping a neighbor to move some junk the week before, to make it to the movie event.

Paul strode up to the youth center, said a couple of quick hellos to his peers, lit a cigarette, and proceeded to blow smoke into the face of his favorite staff member—who he knew hated cigarette smoke. The staff person looked at Paul and asked, "You spent all that money on a taxicab to blow smoke in my face?" Paul's face broke into a big smile and he said, "Yeah!" There was no more smoke in the face after that, and Paul went on to tell the story of how his ride had fallen through and how much money he had spent to make sure he didn't miss the movie event.

Why is this story in the "name the intention" section of this chapter? Because that's what the adult did, in a friendly, joking way. Let's speculate a bit, and try to analyze this interaction.

Why did Paul go to all that trouble to show up and then, once he got there, act so stupidly? Here's a guess: He cared about being part of the group, but was afraid to show how much he cared. Many kids have learned that to expose your feelings means to risk being hurt. Since paying for a taxi showed how much he cared, he was trying to undo this, to make the caring seem less strong, and less frightening. So he acted casual with kids, and blew the smoke in the face of his favorite staff member.

When the adult said, "You spent all that money on a taxicab to blow smoke in my face?" the real message was, "Are you trying to tell me how important it was for you to make sure you made it here?" or more simply, "You really care about being here, don't you?" When Paul's intention—caring about being here—was accepted in a friendly and casual manner, he was not so afraid anymore, and was able to express himself more directly after that.

Fortunately, "name the intention" interventions work well even when they are not delivered so subtly. In fact, it's usually best to spell it out as explicitly as possible. Note that it's not okay to tell kids how they feel; that would be intrusive and offensive. So we try to make our point without being too pushy. Here are some examples of how the adult might name the intention behind a child's action:

- A sixteen-year-old girl is taking an extra helping of dessert, which is against the rules. The intervention: "Are you wondering if I'm paying attention?"
- A seventeen-year-old boy is alternately looking at a comic book and pretending to snooze during a group meeting. The intervention: "Are you trying to let us know that this is getting boring?"
- A seven-year-old girl is storming around during homework time, slamming her book down and crying, "I hate myself!" The intervention: "Are you trying to let me know that this might be too hard for you?"
- A ten-year-old boy sees two other boys playing with toy cars. He takes one of the cars and, making a loud engine sound, crashes it through their playing space, destroying their carefully laid roadways. The intervention: "It seems like you really want to be playing too."

Name the intention is perhaps the most powerful of the labeling interventions because it shows acceptance for the child's needs, even while implicitly acknowledging that the behavior is a problem. When the child feels recognized, understood, and accepted, this opens the door to finding other ways to get his needs met. This intervention also helps kids learn to understand themselves, and to express themselves.

Name the Action

Naming the action can help to make kids aware of their behavior. Many kids' bad habits have become automatic, and they may not even realize that they are doing "it" again. When the action is named, this serves as a prompt, and they can catch themselves and decide to do better.

When you name the action, you might also want to point out how that action relates to the child's goals. You can refer directly to the child's goals (e.g., if the child wants more friends, you can explain how her action might affect how peers relate to her) or to the child's incentive program (perhaps referring to the positive or negative metaphors from the individual behavior contract). Here are some examples of name the action interventions:

- You're looking away while I'm talking to you. That makes me wonder if you're listening or not.
- When you mutter under your breath like that, people think you're making a threat or saying something bad about them. That's how fights get started.
- You're making your voice loud, like how the "Volcano" acts.
- You're talking calm like how a teacher would do it.

Name the Action As a Choice for a Consequence

Naming the action as a choice for a consequence is a powerful way to help kids to catch themselves, make conscious choices, and take responsibility for their behavior. This intervention also clearly establishes the adult as the interested-but-hands-off helper and prompter, while the child is free to make decisions that will affect only herself. This intervention is frequently used within a formal incentive system, but it can apply more widely. Here are some examples of name the action as a choice for consequence interventions:

- You're moving too far away. Your body is asking for me to hold your hand.
- Looks like you're deciding to get a good grade, working hard like that.
- When you cheat at pool, you're choosing to play by yourself, because you know no one wants to play with a cheater.
- You can do your homework now or later. It's your choice: now during homework time or later instead of watching TV.

Pair the Label with a Positive Suggestion

Pairing the label with a positive suggestion is a slightly more involved intervention. It may not always be easy to just slip this in as a quick comment. If you are working with a formal incentive system, especially with an individual behavior contract, then the positive alternatives have already been spelled out. Then it's easier to make the suggestion briefly. Any kind of label—intention, action, consequences—can be combined with a suggestion. Here are some examples of pair the label with a positive suggestion interventions:

- When you act mean like that, it scares other kids away. If you want to make friends, why don't you ask if someone wants to do something with you?
- When you say, "I'm stupid," you're putting yourself down. That's against the rules. What could you say to show that you're frustrated, that would not lose you points?
- If you're looking for ways to earn back the points you lost, I think that Mr. P. could use some help moving those boxes.
- If you're having a hard time waiting for dinner, you're welcome to take a piece of fruit.
- It's not okay to talk about people behind their backs. That makes everyone here feel unsafe. If you want to know what she did, why don't you just ask her?

EXERCISE: FIND THE MAGIC WORDS

If you are on your own, you can do this just by filling in the responses in the exercise. However, this is best done in groups of four. For each vignette, have one person take the child's part, and the others take each of the adult parts, in order. Then for the next vignette, each person rotates one position.

The exercise does not involve two-way conversation, not until the discussion. However, each of the adult statements should be addressed directly to the child.

If you are the child, do not respond to the comments. Just notice what it's like to be you, for each of the comments in turn. If you are an adult, do your best to keep the "supportive neutral" adult stance. Don't worry too much about being clever; just do your best to be helpful while using the specified cognitive intervention. It is okay to infer details that are not included in the vignettes. For example, in your intervention you can refer to (what you imagine might be) the child's concerns, goals, or incentives.

For Each Vignette

Child: Say what would be a typical "quick relief" (but maybe not helpful) adult response. In other words, what do you expect to hear, even though maybe you don't hope for this?
Adult 1: Name the (child's) action and the positive intention. Address it to the child.
Adult 2: Name the action as a choice for a particular consequence. Address it to the child.
Adult 3: Name the intention and the action, and give a suggestion. Address it to the child.

Discussion After Each Round (Before Going to the Next Vignette)

1. What was it like to be the child for each of the comments (including the feared comment)?
2. What was it like to be the adult for each of the comments?
3. Also give one another feedback and suggestions regarding each of the adults' presentations of the cognitive interventions. Did it convey supportive neutrality? Was it effective? Tell each adult about one of his or her behaviors or statements that worked well, and one that could be improved.

Vignettes

1. April is a fourteen-year-old girl who has been home for only about a minute. Already, clothes and books are strewn all over the living room and kitchen.
2. Nathan is a nine-year-old boy who hates to lose. You have seen him dump game boards because he didn't like falling behind. Another child is about to surge ahead of Nathan on this next turn.
3. Crystal is a six-year-old girl who is arguing with another child about a toy that the other child was, in fact, playing with first. The other child is not backing down, but is clearly afraid, perhaps because of Crystal's reputation for hitting and biting her peers.
4. Jeremy is a sixteen-year-old boy who has just come in five minutes late to his job. This is the third day in a row that he has been late. Having the job is a high privilege, and one of the only opportunities to earn money in the setting.

SECTION VI BIBLIOGRAPHY

Long, N., Wood, M. M., & Fecser, F. A. (2001). *Life space crisis intervention* (2nd ed.). Austin, TX: Pro-Ed. The current authority on life space intervention.

Phelan, T. W. (2003). *1-2-3 magic: Effective discipline for children 2-12* (3rd ed.). Glen Ellyn, IL: Child Management. A popular parent training guide that works pretty well.

Redl, F. & Wineman, D. (1951). *Children who hate.* Glencoe, IL: Free Press. The classic on "life-space intervention" with acting-out children.

Appendix A

Trauma-Informed Psychological Assessment

Many psychologists may understand the value of trauma-informed evaluation and feedback, but do not quite know how to deliver this within the constraints of the psychological evaluations they are used to conducting and the reports they are used to writing. This appendix is not intended as an exhaustive treatment of this subject, but hopefully it will give you a few good ideas for ways that you can make your own assessments more trauma friendly. The focus here will be on evaluation methodology and especially on presentation style and content.

TRAUMA-SPECIFIC ASSESSMENT TOOLS

A number of trauma-specific assessment tools can easily be integrated into a psychological battery or even into clinical practice. Ideally, you will select the instruments that measure what you are most interested in and that are valid (they measure what they are supposed to measure), sensitive, and efficient. A selective review of child trauma-related measures is published on the Child Trauma Institute Web site (www.childtrauma.com) and periodically updated.

The following are several good reasons to use such instruments:

- You can find out about trauma-related symptoms that you might not have been able to detect so efficiently otherwise.
- By using standardized instruments, you can compare your client's responses to others, and see where your client's scores fall within the normative range.
- By using validated instruments, you enhance the credibility of your findings. This can make a big difference when you are giving explanations to the child, the family, the teacher, the judge, or others.

You may also wish to use other standardized instruments, as may be required in your setting, and/or to find out what you need to know. For example, if a child is having problems with schoolwork, you will also want to assess possible learning disability and any other angles that might help to explain the problems.

It's also important to remember that there is no substitute for a good clinical interview. This is the only way you can really learn about the current situation, the history of functioning, and how the history of exposure to adverse events may have impacted those. The type of interview described in Chapters 5 and 6 works well for a psychological evaluation. When you have conducted a good interview with the child, a caregiver, and maybe others (and perhaps some observation as well), then you can integrate the findings from standardized instruments and have a very strong basis for your conclusions.

WRITING A TRAUMA-INFORMED ASSESSMENT REPORT

This section focuses on general considerations in writing a report, and then on trauma-specific considerations. I want to start by asking a fundamental question: What is the purpose of an assessment report?

The answer will vary according to circumstances, but it generally comes down to this: Someone wants to have a better understanding of the child so that the right decisions can be made on the child's behalf. What this means is that the psychologist is serving as a consultant to the person or people who want to have the understanding so they can make the decision.

In most cases, the people to whom the report is addressed are parents, teachers, judges, case managers, and others. So why are assessment reports often written so that they can be understood only by other psychologists? In my opinion, delivering a nonunderstandable report represents a failure on the consultant's part. I believe that reports should be written for the clients of the consultation, using language and concepts they are likely to understand, and limiting the length of the report to what they are likely to actually read. If you can't imagine sitting down with those who want the report and giving them all this information face to face, you should not be writing it for them.

What would such a report look like? There's rarely any justification for listing all the specific findings or scale scores from each test used. The evaluator's job is to interpret the findings and provide the explanation, the bottom line. So spare your clients all the details and just tell them what they need to know. If a psychologist wants to see your data, you have it on file. No one else wants to see it. By cutting out all that garbage, you ought to be able to write a good explanation of a child in a couple of pages, more or less. It's easier to make it longer, but longer reports don't get read, so they're not as useful to your clients. It's worth learning how to edit; it helps you to be more clearly understood.

What about the format of the report? Some settings or situations require certain formats, or at least certain contents are required. For example, many evaluations must provide a formal diagnosis. If a diagnosis is required, you must find a way to include it, even if you don't like the requirement. Even with meeting various requirements, it is often possible, and worthwhile, to modify the format as needed to do the job well. It may feel risky to do something different than what has been expected, but if the new product is more user friendly, the response is likely to be positive. A less rash alternative is to write the standard huge report that may be expected, but then to tack on a briefer "summary"—the part that will actually be read—with a more useful approach.

My next suggestion will not be a surprise to you. I think that trauma-informed assessment reports are most helpful when they use the fairy tale model. This means that when it is time to give the case formulation, we start out with strengths and resources, then describe the dragon and other challenges, and how that has led to the symptoms and presenting problems. You can sneak the diagnosis in here somewhere, but you don't need to emphasize it; the case formulation is the real focus. The report can end with recommendations for the usual treatment plan, including specific details appropriate to the case.

SAMPLE REPORTS

Here are some examples of real (disguised) assessment reports that exemplify this approach to evaluation and report writing. The required information was included, in a way that allowed the psychologist to present a trauma-informed case formulation, with language and detail appropriate to the intended readers. The first evaluation was requested as part of a victim compensation case; the others were requested in a school setting, for kids who were having various school-related problems. These evaluations were selected to show how a wide range of presenting problems and diagnoses can be presented with a trauma perspective.

June 2, 2000

LIMITED PSYCHOLOGICAL EVALUATION
of Robert Johnson

Sources of Information

Interviews with:

Arnold Johnson (father)—5/21/00
Natalie Robins (Robert's girlfriend)—5/27/00
Robert Johnson—5/27/00

Impact of Events Scale; Child Report of Posttraumatic Symptoms—5/27/00

Reason for Referral

Robert Johnson is an eighteen-year-old man who was referred for evaluation and treatment by his father, who expressed strong concern regarding a number of symptoms he had observed, including apathy, irritability, aggression, and negative outlook. These symptoms reportedly developed following a brutal assault of Robert and another young man on July 5, 1999. This evaluation was requested for guidance regarding appropriate treatment or other recommendations, as well as for documentation in a pending civil suit.

History

Robert was born healthy, without complication, and was described as an "easy baby." No history of medical problems was reported. Developmental milestones were reportedly on the fast end of the normal range. Robert was described as a happy child who had many friends and enjoyed many activities, especially sports. He also showed talent; for example, in his early teens, Robert and his brother each played in the all-star game in the local baseball Little League. Robert was respected by peers and adults alike as a "good kid" who always tried to do the right thing.

Although Robert's parents are clearly devoted to their children, their divorce and related family dynamics apparently weighed heavily on Robert. When he reached puberty at age thirteen, he became argumentative with both parents, and depressed; at age fourteen he was hospitalized for a month. Robert apparently responded very well to this treatment, and did not become depressed again. On the contrary, he was very happy in his late teens, saying he "couldn't wait for the sun to come up; I looked forward to every day."

Robert reported no prior history of major trauma. He has been in two car accidents, but was not seriously injured and reported no posttraumatic reaction on either occasion. No criminal history was reported, with the exception of a single shoplifting incident at age twelve. No substance abuse problem was reported, although Robert acknowledged a history of occasional recreational use of marijuana.

Robert was an average student through grade school. In middle school, he ranged from near failing to honor student status, fluctuating while he wrestled with his family situation. In high school he continued to make passing grades, and graduated, but was more interested in socializing, sports, and work.

Robert has always been full of energy, not only for sports, but for work. Since he was old enough he generally held down a job, sometimes two. Whether he was in high school, college, or out of school, his work habits have been a strong point. Robert has worked many types of jobs, reportedly learning quickly and doing well wherever he applies himself. He has long had an ambition to run his own business. At the time of the assault, Robert had completed a year of community college, was playing basketball daily, and working in a local store.

After the Assault

On the evening of July 5, 1999, Robert went with a friend to the park, expecting to meet some other friends. Instead, Robert and his companion were attacked by a group of young men. They were robbed, threatened, tortured, and severely beaten. For example, Robert was threatened with a gun, and hit repeatedly on the shoulder with the gun. Finally, they were tied up with duct tape and left. Fortunately, Robert and his companion managed to get free and get to a telephone for help. Later, Robert spent the night in the hospital, and then several days in bed. The traumatic exposure apparently continued for some time as he went through the ordeals associated with medical treatment as well as the legal system.

In the weeks following the assault, Robert was unable to sleep, afraid to go out in public, and unable to get the thoughts and images of the assault out of his mind. He said, "I just couldn't be here," and on the spur of the moment he moved to Florida where a friend had offered both work and housing. Later, his girlfriend moved there to join him. He described this period as a big relief, since there were few reminders of the assault—"We didn't even have cable TV." However, they got homesick, and Robert needed to participate in the trials, so they returned home by the end of 1999.

Except for the partial, temporary relief Robert obtained by moving away, he has been so intensely haunted by his memories that his level of functioning has substantially declined in many ways. He sought help, but after several counseling sessions, he felt only slight relief and had no expectation of further progress, so he stopped going. According to Robert and to those close to him, the suffering continues, as described in the following.

Intrusive Symptoms

Intrusive images, memories, and thoughts of the assault persist, causing considerable distress. For example, he started a factory job involving twelve-hour shifts, and "I thought about it [the assault] for twelve straight hours—I couldn't stand it." He wanted to quit immediately, but forced himself to stay for a month before finally giving up. The intrusions also occur when any of a number of cues remind him of the assault. For example, if he sees a gun on TV, he says, "you can hear it hit your bone." Robert says that his memories "overpower any other thoughts—it's hard to think about anything else."

Sleep Problems

Robert has been consistently unable to get to sleep before about 3 a.m., and then only after using marijuana. Since Robert has never had trouble sleeping before, and has never been a regular drug user, he finds his current situation quite disturbing.

Avoidant Symptoms

Robert has taken to avoiding many formerly pleasurable activities, for example, he has not played basketball for over a year since the assault, although he used to play daily. His girlfriend reports that he consistently refuses to go out, although they used to enjoy restaurants as well as a variety of social and recreational activities. His explanation for this change varies from "I'm afraid of seeing anyone [I don't know], not knowing what can happen," to "I just don't feel like it." He makes a constant effort to avoid reminders of the assault, even though that restricts his range of activities to a seemingly absurd extent. For example, he can't watch the news or many other TV shows, because of the guns and the stories about interpersonal violence. And despite his ambitions and his strong work history, he has taken little initiative in either getting a new job or going back to school.

Overreacting

Those close to Robert certainly agree with his comment that "it doesn't take much to set me off [lately]." Since the assault, Robert has frequently found himself in a rage on small provocation—and sometimes when others don't see any provocation at all. "'I could have died at any second' keeps going through my mind." Robert's girlfriend reports that, although she "used to be able to talk to him about anything," now she is turned away with a shouted, "I almost died—I don't want to deal with your problems!" She also reports that their arguments used to lead to resolution, but now are cut short by Robert's yelling or telling her to leave. Robert's father has also observed that Robert now tends to "explode" when faced with minor conflict; and that Robert's usual roughhousing with his brother has recently turned vicious on occasion. Robert acknowledges that he is often angry, has a short fuse, and feels unable to deal with formerly comfortable levels of conflict, stress, or frustration.

Negative Outlook

Robert's girlfriend said that he "used to be so positive and optimistic—now he just looks at the down side." Robert's father is also concerned that Robert has lost his motivation, pointing out that he has only worked for one month in the past six. Robert insists that he still "love[s] life" and has ambitions. However, he acknowledges that he has been unable to overcome his posttrauma symptoms.

Two objectively scored self-report measures of posttraumatic symptomatology were administered for another perspective on Robert's symptoms over the previous week. The Impact of Events Scale is a widely used indicator of posttraumatic symptoms in adults, focusing on the hallmark avoidance and intrusion symptoms. Robert scored a 56, way above the cutoff of 30, indicating a "clinical disorder" level of symptomatology. The Child Report of Posttraumatic Symptoms is a recently validated measure for children and adolescents, which covers a wider range of posttraumatic symptoms. Robert scored a 34, also well above the "clinical concern" cutoff of 19.

Diagnosis and Recommendations

The data is overwhelmingly consistent with a diagnosis of post-traumatic stress disorder due to the July 5, 1999, assault. Robert was doing rather well prior to the assault and living what we would consider a normal and successful life. He has clearly been severely affected by his response to this traumatic event, in every facet of his life. The months following the assault have been characterized by haunting memories, fear, avoidance, temper, and inaction, and his functioning has been limited accordingly. Robert is apparently unable to work, play, go to school, sleep, or get along with those closest to him.

Intensive psychotherapy is strongly recommended as a means for Robert to face and work through the traumatic memory so that it plays a less damaging role in his daily life. Although treatment can be expected to help considerably, it is impossible to predict the degree to which it may be successful, and conversely, the degree to which Robert may be burdened with current symptoms indefinitely.

____

Ricky Greenwald, PsyD
Licensed Psychologist

CONFIDENTIAL

Psychological Evaluation

Date: June 14, 1999
Name of student: Martin Tuismen
DOB: 4/18/86
Age: 13 years 2 months

Sources of Information: Review of Records; State-Trait Anger Expression Inventory; Trauma Symptom Checklist for Children; Report of Posttraumatic Symptoms—Parent and Child forms; Revised Children's Manifest Anxiety Scale; Children's Depression Inventory; Child & Adolescent Functional Assessment Scale (CAFAS); Clinical interview with father and with Martin.

Reason for Evaluation

Martin Tuismen is a thirteen-year-old boy in the seventh grade at King Intermediate School. He has earned failing grades this year and seems to have a lot of trouble focusing on his work. This supplemental evaluation was requested as part of a comprehensive Chapter 36 evaluation for information and guidance regarding possible mental health-related needs.

History and Current Situation

According to father, pregnancy with Martin was normal with no exposure to toxins, and birth was normal as well, except that he had jaundice and was hospitalized for a week. No other serious injuries, head trauma, or illnesses were reported, nor current health concerns. Martin was described as an active, healthy baby with no special problems, who achieved developmental milestones on track. He did wet his bed on occasion until the age of eight. Martin was described as "rascal" and liked to do things like wrestle with his uncles, but in a playful (not malicious) way. He has always been good at making and keeping friends, and has several good friends at present.

Martin is the oldest of three siblings born to the same married parents who were separated when Martin was ten and divorced a couple of years later. Starting after the earthquake (Martin age seven) the children were exposed to a lot of parental conflict (no violence). Although the parents have made considerable efforts to be cooperative regarding the children, there is remaining conflict and bitterness, and they are currently in a legal dispute regarding custody-related issues. Martin and his siblings currently live about half time with father and half with mother.

Martin always did well in school through the fifth grade, getting mostly Bs and Cs and not getting into any trouble. However, in sixth grade he had a lot of trouble with his teacher and was frequently placed outside the classroom as punishment; he got Ds and Fs then. Then he was changed to a different classroom, and the new teacher gave him considerable attention, and he got excellent grades for the rest of the year. This year in a new school he did poorly again. His father has taken away PlayStation until the grades go up, and is allowing Martin to play on a sports team as long as he keeps his grades up. Martin has pulled his Fs up to Ds but seems stuck there. He shows a "don't care" attitude and often doesn't do his work, or starts but doesn't finish, and then doesn't turn it in.

His father believes that he is hurting inside and has too much on his mind. Father and Martin agree that he was "normal" until the parental conflict began. Martin is also still bothered by memories of times that mother's safety was in jeopardy, once with a medical problem and twice with car accidents.

Strengths

Martin is a likable boy who is close to family members. He has good friends who are involved in positive activities and don't get into trouble. He is a good athlete and participates in community football and basketball leagues. His involvement in sports helps him to release some energy and to stay out of trouble. He has positive and realistic long-term goals. He would like to stop getting into trouble and to do better in school. Martin believes that he is smart enough to do well, but he would have to work hard at it.

Challenges

The history of exposure to parental conflict and divorce, as well as the scares related to mother's safety, left Martin with a pileup of bad feelings such as sadness, hurt, anger, and even self-blame. The ongoing exposure to parental conflict continues to add stress. Finally, when he had trouble with his teacher last year, it all became "too much" hurt, and Martin just gave up in some way. Now the "don't care" feeling takes over much of the time because it feels safer than caring and then getting hurt again. Also, he is so preoccupied with the bad memories and current stresses and worries that it is difficult to keep his mind on school work. Then fooling around with peers becomes much more compelling than concentrating on school. Martin currently qualifies for the diagnosis of adjustment disorder 309.4 with features of dysthymia and ongoing stressors, CAFAS score of 40.

Recommendations

1. Parents can help Martin by getting better at keeping the conflict to the adults and not exposing the kids to it. This means that they can talk honestly and calmly to the kids but should not bad-mouth the other parent. Rather, they should encourage and support their children in having positive relationships with the other parent. That way Martin will not need to feel torn apart or like he has to choose one parent over the other.
2. The more parents can keep consistent rules and routines at home, the more Martin will start to feel that the bad times are over and things are okay now. It is also helpful for parents to keep their tempers under control when around the kids. Then Martin can feel more secure and less worried about what might happen.
3. Parents should keep very close track of Martin's school performance and use privileges or other incentives to help Martin to try harder and do better. Parents must keep to agreements they make, following through on both rewards and punishments. Any punishments should be limited to something small enough that parents will be willing to follow through.
4. Once the stress level is down and Martin is not put in the middle of the adults' conflict, he could use some special help in getting through the bad feelings that he has piled up inside. Talking with a therapist can help him to get through those feelings and start to feel better and more hopeful again. A therapist can also help Martin with self-control skills and self-discipline.

____

Ricky Greenwald, PsyD
Clinical Psychologist

CONFIDENTIAL

Psychological Evaluation

Date: March 10, 1999
Name of student: Charles Wong
DOB: 3/11/89
Age: 10 years

Sources of Information: Review of Records; Child Behavior Checklist—Parent and Teacher forms; State-Trait Anger Expression Inventory; Trauma Symptom Checklist for Children; Report of Posttraumatic Symptoms—Parent and Child forms; Revised Children's Manifest Anxiety Scale; Children's Depression Inventory; Child & Adolescent Functional Assessment Scale (CAFAS); Clinical interview with mother and with Charles.

Reason for Evaluation

Charles Wong is a ten-year-old boy attending regular education classes in the fourth grade at King Elementary School. This year his school attendance and performance have declined dramatically, and he is at risk of having to repeat the grade. This supplemental evaluation was requested as part of a comprehensive Chapter 36 evaluation to provide information and guidance regarding possible mental health-related needs.

History and Current Situation

Mother reported a normal pregnancy with no exposure to toxins. She said that Charles was a happy, healthy baby who achieved developmental milestones quickly. Although Charles has positive attachments in his family, mother said that he was "always a loner" and Charles said that he does have a couple of friends but wishes he had more. Charles has no history of head injury or other injuries; medical history includes surgery for a neck tumor (?) at age seven, and ear problems, which are ongoing. No other medical concerns were reported and he is using no medication.

In previous screening, Charles's intelligence and achievement scores have been in the average to high-average range. He has always done well in school, getting good grades and behaving well, all the way through the end of the last school year. The first quarter of fourth grade he got mostly As and Bs but then began missing school more and more often, as well as being very late many days, and he has also been doing much less of his homework, so now he is at real risk of failing the year. In school there have been no reports of problematic behavior.

Charles currently lives with his maternal grandmother, mother, stepfather, five siblings, and two cousins. Charles is the second-oldest of the siblings. Charles's mother and father have been married and divorced twice. When they were together, father regularly physically abused mother and children, and memories of this abuse continue to bother Charles. Mother reported that father has also let the children down by failing to follow through on various promises. Father is currently incarcerated in a distant location, and Charles claims to not care much about his lack of contact with father. Mother remarried three years ago and the two youngest children are fathered by her current husband. Charles gets along very well with some of his siblings, including the youngest, but fights a lot with his next-youngest brother, including physical aggression. Many of the children are beyond the parents' control and don't listen despite parents' various discipline attempts. The family has been evicted from various housing situations because of complaints about the children being unruly. There is a lot of arguing in the family and also a lot of love.

Around the time that Charles began to do worse in school and stay home more, his mother had threatened to kill herself by cutting her throat. The children were very worried at the time and hid all the kitchen knives from her. Charles described this as the most upsetting memory he has, and he admitted that he likes to stay home sometimes to keep his mother company and make her feel better. Mother described Charles as "Mommy's boy" and said that he does care for her and helps out sometimes.

Strengths

Charles is a bright boy who can do well in school if he tries. He can be helpful around the house "when he wants to be" and is good with his youngest siblings. He likes math and is good at getting around on the Internet. He associates with positive peers. He feels sad to do badly in school and wants to do better. He also wishes that he wouldn't get angry at home and fight with his siblings, and recognizes that this would come from "feeling different inside." He has positive and realistic goals for the future, including college and working with young children.

Challenges

Charles is faced with two major challenges. First, the long exposure to physical abuse has left him with angry feelings that he doesn't know how to handle, so he ends up fighting with his siblings and disobeying his mother and stepfather. The adults are not sure how to really be in charge, so the children (not just Charles) never can feel entirely secure, and that makes them nervous and they act up even more. The second challenge is that Charles is worried about his mother, so much that he is willing to miss school to take care of her. He is trying to keep her feeling happy so that she doesn't get so angry and overwhelmed that she might want to hurt herself again. Charles currently qualifies for the diagnosis of disruptive behavior disorder NOS (not otherwise specified) 312.9, CAFAS score of 60.

Recommendations

1. The first recommendation is to get Charles back to school on time and every day. He should have an enforced bedtime so that he is less tempted to oversleep, and then awakened on time every morning and sent (or taken) to school, with no exceptions. Mother can help Charles to feel willing to go to school by insisting that he go, and by demonstrating that she can take care of herself and be okay. If the parents are unable to get Charles to school on their own, they should get help, perhaps from a mental health professional and/or a law enforcement officer.
2. Charles's mother and stepfather could use some support and advice in getting their kids under control. When kids have been exposed to trauma such as physical abuse, they feel scared and insecure. When parents can take charge, the kids feel more secure and calm down. This would probably help Charles to calm down and not to fight so much with his siblings.
3. Therapy might help Charles learn to control his anger better and to get through some of the memories and bad feelings that make him so mad.

____

Ricky Greenwald, PsyD
Clinical Psychologist

CONFIDENTIAL
Psychological Evaluation

Date: January 18, 1999
Name of student: Tiffany Delano
DOB: 4/24/82
Age: 16 years 9 months

Sources of Information: Review of Records; State-Trait Anger Expression Inventory; Trauma Symptom Checklist for Children; Report of Posttraumatic Symptoms—Parent and Child forms; Revised Children's Manifest Anxiety Scale; Children's Depression Inventory; Child & Adolescent Functional Assessment Scale (CAFAS); Clinical interview with mother and with Tiffany.

Reason for Evaluation

Tiffany Delano is a sixteen-year-old girl who is attending ninth grade at King High School for the second time, having also repeated eighth grade. She is a regular education student who has a history of cutting classes and failing to complete assignments; she is also involved in peer conflict. This supplemental evaluation was requested as part of a comprehensive Chapter 36 evaluation to provide guidance regarding possible mental health-related needs.

History and Current Situation

Tiffany is the second of five girls born to the same still-married parents. According to mother, pregnancy was normal with no exposure to toxins, and birth was also normal although birth weight was under six pounds. Tiffany was described as a healthy baby who liked to be carried and to stay near her mother. Although she was smaller than average, her developmental milestones occurred on schedule. Normal social development was also reported. Medical history includes a couple of fever/seizure incidents at about age four that were never diagnosed or well understood. No other health problems or concerns were reported.

Tiffany has had a long history of school-related difficulty. In early elementary school she did fairly well, earning mostly Bs and Cs, but in grades four through seven she was getting some Ds as well. In grade school she often had to miss field trips due to incomplete assignments. It is unclear to what extent the work may have been too difficult for her, as her mother feels that it may have been over her head, whereas teacher comments indicate that they felt she was capable. In eighth grade she got involved in a negative peer group, and with them engaged in such activities as harassing others, substance abuse, and cutting classes. She failed to pass the year and had to repeat. In ninth grade she also failed and is currently repeating.

Partway through last year, Tiffany left the negative group of peers and now spends her time with a couple of good friends who appear to be more positive influences (although details of current activities are unknown). However, one of the girls from the prior group has apparently engaged in a harassment campaign against Tiffany, which she has found extremely upsetting. This problem continues despite various attempts at resolution, including mediation as well as calling the police.

Tiffany's history is significant for trauma, loss, and stress. Although her family is generally supportive, at times there can be a lot of yelling as well as occasional physical discipline (slap for disrespecting). When Tiffany was about ten she was exposed to two traumatic experiences, the earthquake and an auto accident. A year or two later her grandmother died. Over the past few years she has been very upset by involvement in a fight in school, by the harassment of the peer noted previously, and by her cousins' recent move out of state. The deterioration of Tiffany's behavior and school performance closely follows the increasing burden of upsetting experiences she has faced.

Strengths

Tiffany is able to form good relationships with family members as well as friends. Mother and teachers see her as being generally smart and capable. She helps her younger sisters with their homework and other tasks, and also helps out at home by cooking. She loves animals. She is image-conscious and takes care of her appearance. She has realistic and positive goals (to be a beautician) for the future.

Challenges

Tiffany has become overburdened over the years with a series of upsetting experiences. These have given her a "sore spot" that leads her to have a quick temper, to be angry at authority and peers, to feel picked on and isolated, to feel that something is wrong with her, to be preoccupied with upsetting memories, and to feel generally sad and anxious. It is no wonder that she becomes overwhelmed with a legitimately challenging situation such as being harassed, to the point where she can't concentrate on her schoolwork. She currently qualifies for the diagnosis of disruptive behavior disorder NOS (not otherwise specified) 312.9 with posttraumatic features, CAFAS score of 90.

Recommendations

1. Every effort should be made to curtail the peer harassment, through school, legal, or other means. Tiffany is already under constant pressure from her own feelings; it is unreasonable to expect her to function well while she is actually being threatened and attacked on a regular basis.
2. Therapy could help Tiffany to work through some of her upsetting memories so that she can move on instead of being so burdened by them. Additional therapy focus should include motivation as well as self-control skills.
3. Consistent rules and natural consequences will help Tiffany to learn that what she does matters. This way she has the best chance of making better choices.

____

Ricky Greenwald, PsyD
Clinical Psychologist

Appendix B

Child Trauma Resources Online

Online information changes so fast that I think that the best way to give you good information is to give you access to information as it develops. Here are a couple of good, reliable sites that can help you to find what you need, including up-to-date links to other sites.

CHILD TRAUMA INSTITUTE

<www.childtrauma.com>

This site is developed and maintained by Ricky Greenwald, PsyD, the founder and director of the Child Trauma Institute and the author of this book. This site won't overwhelm you with links, but the important ones are there. The site also offers the following:

- Information on training programs related to child and adolescent trauma treatment
- Information on child trauma assessment, including reviews of measures, samples of some instruments, updated data, and abstracts/reprints of published papers
- Information on child/adolescent trauma treatment
- Information on trauma and problem behaviors, including abstracts/reprints of published papers
- Information for parents, including understandable articles, an "advice column," and handouts you can use
- A list of publications that can be accessed on site or elsewhere online
- Links to selected sites that offer important information related to child and adolescent trauma

TRAUMA INFO PAGES

<www.trauma-pages.com>

This site is developed and maintained by David Baldwin, PhD. It is highly regarded as *the* trauma information site online. Although this site is not specifically focused on children, it is comprehensive in providing many types of information about trauma, trauma research, and trauma treatment. Here is a partial list of this site's offerings:

- About trauma
- Trauma articles
- Trauma resources
- General support
- Trauma bookstore
- Disaster handouts and links
- Trauma links: psychology, research, medical
- Search of this site and several other trauma sites

References

Ahrens, J. & Rexford, L. (2002). Cognitive processing therapy for incarcerated adolescents with PTSD. *Journal of Aggression, Maltreatment & Trauma, 6,* 201-216.

American Psychiatric Association (1980). *Diagnostic and statistical manual of mental disorders* (3rd ed.). Washington, DC: American Psychiatric Association.

Chemtob, C. M., Nakashima, J., Hamada, R., & Carlson, J. G. (2002). Brief treatment for elementary school children with disaster-related posttraumatic stress disorder: A field study. *Journal of Clinical Psychology, 58,* 99-112.

Chemtob, C. M., Novaco, R. W., Hamada, R. S., & Gross, D. M. (1997). Cognitive-behavioral treatment for severe anger in posttraumatic stress disorder. *Journal of Consulting and Clinical Psychology, 65,* 184-189.

Chemtob, C. M. & Taylor, T. L. (2002). The treatment of traumatized children. In Yehuda, R. (Ed.), *Trauma survivors: Bridging the gap between intervention research and practice* (pp. 75-126). Washington, DC: American Psychiatric Press.

Chemtob, C. M., Tolin, D. F., van der Kolk, B. A., & Pitman, R. K. (2000). Eye movement desensitization and reprocessing. In E. B. Foa, T. M. Keane, & M. J. Friedman (Eds.), *Effective treatments for PTSD: Practice guidelines from the International Society for Traumatic Stress Studies* (pp. 139-154). New York: Guilford Press.

Child Welfare League of America. (2004, February). *Creating parenting rich communities.* Available online at <http://www.cwla.org/programs/r2p/biblioparenting.pdf>.

Cohen, J. A., Berliner, L., & March, J. S. (2000). Treatment of children and adolescents. In E. B. Foa, T. M. Keane, & M. J. Friedman (Eds.), *Effective treatments for PTSD: Practice guidelines from the International Society for Traumatic Stress Studies* (pp. 106-138). New York: Guilford Press.

Cohen, J. A., Deblinger, E., & Mannarino, A. (2004, September). Trauma-focused cognitive-behavioral therapy for sexually abused children. *Psychiatric Times, 21*(10). Available online at <http://www.psychiatrictimes.com/p040952.html>.

de Roos, C., Greenwald, R., de Jongh, A., & Noorthoorn, E. (2005). *A controlled comparison of CBT and EMDR for disaster-exposed children.* Manuscript submitted for publication.

Deblinger, E. & Heflin, A. H. (1996). *Treating sexually abused children and their nonoffending parents: A cognitive behavioral approach.* Thousand Oaks, CA: Sage Publications.

Dodge, K. A. & Coie, J. D. (1987). Social information processing factors in reactive and proactive aggression in children's peer groups. *Journal of Personality and Social Psychology, 53,* 1146-1158.

Dutton, P. (2004). *Superkids: Practical child management* (2nd ed.). Dollar, Scotland: Psynapse.

Erikson, E. (1963). *Childhood and society* (2nd ed.). New York: W. W. Norton & Co.

Figley, C. R. (1995). *Compassion fatigue.* New York: Brunner/Mazel.

Fletcher, K. E. (1996). Childhood posttraumatic stress disorder. In E. Mash & R. Barkley (Eds.), *Child psychopathology* (pp. 242-276). New York: Guilford Press.

Foa, E. B. & Meadows, E. A. (1997). Psychosocial treatments for posttraumatic stress disorder: A critical review. *Annual Review of Psychology, 48,* 449-480.

Foa, E. B. & Rothbaum, B. O. (1997). *Treating the trauma of rape.* New York: Guilford Press.

Foa, E. B., Steketee, G., & Olasov, B.R. (1989). Behavioral/cognitive conceptualizations of posttraumatic stress disorder. *Behavior Therapy, 20,* 155-176.

Ford, J. D. (2002). Traumatic victimization in childhood and persistent problems with oppositional-defiance. *Journal of Aggression, Maltreatment, and Trauma, 6,* 25-58.

Gerbode, F. (1989). *Beyond psychology: An introduction to metapsychology* (3rd ed.). Menlo Park, CA: IRM.

Giaconia, R. M., Reinherz, H. Z., Silverman, A. B., Pakiz, B., Frost, A. K., & Cohen, E. (1995). Traumas and posttraumatic stress disorder in a community population of older adolescents. *Journal of the American Academy of Child and Adolescent Psychiatry, 34,* 1369-1380.

Gil, E. (1991). *The healing power of play: Working with abused children.* New York: Guilford Press.

Greenwald, R. (1996). The information gap in the EMDR controversy. *Professional Psychology: Research and Practice, 27,* 67-72.

Greenwald, R. (1997). Children's mental health care in the 21st century: Eliminating the trauma burden. *Child and Adolescent Psychiatry On-Line.* Available online at <http://www.Priory.com/psychild.htm>.

Greenwald, R. (1999). *Eye movement desensitization and reprocessing (EMDR) in child and adolescent psychotherapy.* Northvale, NJ: Jason Aronson.
Greenwald, R. (2000). A trauma-focused individual therapy approach for adolescents with conduct disorder. *International Journal of Offender Therapy and Comparative Criminology, 44,* 146-163.
Greenwald, R. (2002a). Motivation—Adaptive Skills—Trauma Resolution (MASTR) therapy for adolescents with conduct problems: An open trial. *Journal of Aggression, Maltreatment, and Trauma, 6,* 237-261.
Greenwald, R. (2002b). The role of trauma in conduct disorder. *Journal of Aggression, Maltreatment, and Trauma, 6,* 5-23.
Greenwald, R. (2003, spring). The power of a trauma-informed treatment approach. *Children's Group Therapy Association Newsletter, 24*(1), 1, 8-9.
Greenwald, R. (2004). MASTR treatment protocol for acting-out teens: A manual. Unpublished manuscript.
Greenwald, R., Greenwald, H., & Smyth, N. J. (2005). *Trauma-related insight improves therapist attitudes toward acting-out clients.* (Manuscript submitted for publication.)
Greenwald, R., Johnston, K. G., & Smyth, N. J. (2004, November). Trauma-related insight reduces worker reactivity to acting-out clients. Poster session presented at the annual meeting of the International Society for Traumatic Stress Studies, New Orleans.
Greenwald, R., Stamm, B. H., Larsen, D., & Griffel, K. (2003, October). The impact of child trauma therapy training on participants. Poster session presented at the annual meeting of the International Society for Traumatic Stress Studies, Chicago.
Herman, J. L. (1992). *Trauma and recovery.* New York: Basic Books.
Hyer, L. & Brandsma, J. M. (1997). EMDR minus eye movements equals good psychotherapy. *Journal of Traumatic Stress, 10,* 515-522.
Ironson, G., Freund, B., Strauss, J. L., & Williams, J. (2002). Comparison of two treatments for traumatic stress: A community-based study of EMDR and prolonged exposure. *Journal of Clinical Psychology, 58,* 113-128.
Jaberghaderi, N., Greenwald, R., Rubin, A., Zand, S. O., & Dolatabadi, S. (2004). A comparison of CBT and EMDR for sexually abused Iranian girls. *Clinical Psychology and Psychotherapy, 11,* 358-368.
James, B. (1989). *Treating traumatized children: New insights and creative interventions.* Lexington, MA: Lexington Books.
Jensen, J. A. (1994). An investigation of eye movement desensitization and reprocessing (EMD/R) as a treatment for posttraumatic stress disorder (PTSD) symptoms of Vietnam combat veterans. *Behavior Therapy, 25,* 311-325.
Kazdin, A. E. (1987). Treatment of antisocial behavior in children: Current status and future directions. *Psychological Bulletin, 102,* 187-203.
Kazdin, A. (1997). Practitioner review: Psychosocial treatments for conduct disorder in children. *Journal of Child Psychology and Psychiatry, 38,* 161-178.
Kendall-Tackett, K. A., Williams, L. M., & Finkelhor, D. (1993). Impact of sexual abuse on children: A review and synthesis of recent empirical studies. *Psychological Bulletin, 113,* 164-180.
Kübler-Ross, E. (1969). *On death and dying.* New York: Macmillan.
Lee, C., Gavriel, H., Drummond, P., Richards, J., & Greenwald, R. (2002). Treatment of PTSD: Stress Inoculation Training with Prolonged Exposure compared to EMDR. *Journal of Clinical Psychology, 58,* 1071-1089.
Lipke, H. (1994). Eye movement desensitization and reprocessing (EMDR): A quantitative study of clinician impressions of effects and training requirements. Reprinted in F. Shapiro (1995), *Eye movement desensitization and reprocessing: Basic principles, protocols and procedures* (pp. 376-386). New York: Guilford Press.
Marlatt, G. A. & Gordon, J. R. (1985). *Relapse prevention: Strategies in the treatment of addictive behaviors.* New York: Guilford Press.
Maxfield, L. & Hyer, L. A. (2002). The relationship between efficacy and methodology in studies investigating EMDR treatment of PTSD. *Journal of Clinical Psychology, 58,* 23-41.
Miller, W. R. & Rollnick, S. (2002). *Motivational interviewing: Preparing people for change* (2nd ed.). New York: Guilford Press.
Nader, K., Dubrow, N., Stamm, B., & Hudnall, B. (1999). *Honoring differences: Cultural issues in the treatment of trauma and loss.* Philadelphia: Brunner/Mazel.
Newcorn, J. H. & Strain, J. (1992). Adjustment disorder in children and adolescents. *Journal of the American Academy of Child and Adolescent Psychiatry, 31,* 318-327.
Pearlman, L. A. & Saakvitne, K. W. (1995). *Trauma and the therapist: Counter-transference and vicarious traumatization in psychotherapy with incest survivors.* New York: W. W. Norton & Co.
Perry, B. D., Pollard, R. A., Blakley, T. L., Baker, W. L., & Vigilante, D. (1995). Childhood trauma, the neurobiology of adaptation and use-dependent development of the brain: How states become traits. *Infant Mental Health Journal, 16,* 271-291.
Power, K. G., McGoldrick, T., Brown, K., Buchanan, R., Sharp, D., Swanson, V., & Karatzias, A. (2002). A controlled comparison of eye movement desensitisation and reprocessing versus exposure plus cognitive restructur-

ing, versus waiting list in the treatment of posttraumatic stress disorder. *Journal of Clinical Psychology and Psychotherapy, 9,* 299-318.

Puffer, M. K., Greenwald, R., & Elrod, D. E. (1998). A single session EMDR study with twenty traumatized children and adolescents. *Traumatology, 3*(2). Available online at <http://www.fsu.edu/~trauma/v3i2art6.html>.

Pynoos, R. S. (1990). Post-traumatic stress disorder in children and adolescents. In B. D. Garfinkel, G. A. Carlson, & E. B. Weller (Eds.), *Psychiatric disorders in children and adolescents* (pp. 48-63). Philadelphia: W. B. Saunders.

Pynoos, R. S., Frederick, C., Nader, K., Arroyo, W., Steinberg, A., Eth, S., Nunez, F., & Fairbanks, L. (1987). Life threat and posttraumatic stress in school-age children. *Archives of General Psychiatry, 44,* 1057-1063.

Resick, P. A. & Schnicke, M. K. (1993). *Cognitive processing therapy for rape victims: A treatment manual.* Newbury Park, CA: Sage Publications.

Rogers, S., & Silver, S. M. (2002). Is EMDR an exposure therapy?: A review of trauma protocols. *Journal of Clinical Psychology, 58,* 43-59.

Rogers, S. & Silver, S. M. (2003, September). CBT v. EMDR: A comparison of effect size and treatment time. Poster session presented at the annual meeting of the EMDR International Association, Denver.

Rubin, A., Bischofshausen, S., Conroy-Moore, K., Dennis, B., Hastie, M., Melnick, L., Reeves, D., & Smith, T. (2001). The effectiveness of EMDR in a child guidance center. *Research on Social Work Practice, 11,* 435-457.

Saakvitne, K. W., Gamble, S., Pearlman, L. A., & Lev, B. T. (2000). *Risking connection: A training curriculum for working with survivors of childhood abuse.* Baltimore: Sidran.

Scheck, M. M., Schaeffer, J. A., & Gillette, C. S. (1998). Brief psychological intervention with traumatized young women: The efficacy of eye movement desensitization and reprocessing. *Journal of Traumatic Stress, 11,* 25-44.

Shapiro, F. (1995). *Eye movement desensitization and reprocessing: Basic principles, protocols and procedures.* New York: Guilford Press.

Shapiro, F. (2001). *Eye movement desensitization and reprocessing: Basic principles, protocols and procedures* (2nd ed.). New York: Guilford Press.

Smyth, N. & Poole, D. (2002). EMDR and cognitive behavior therapy. In F. Shapiro (ed.), *EMDR as an integrative psychotherapy approach: Experts of diverse orientations explore the paradigm prism.* Washington, DC: American Psychological Association Books.

Soberman, G. B., Greenwald, R., & Rule, D. L. (2002). A controlled study of eye movement desensitization and reprocessing (EMDR) for boys with conduct problems. *Journal of Aggression, Maltreatment, and Trauma, 6,* 217-236.

Sommers-Flanagan, J. & Sommers-Flanagan, R. (1995). Psychotherapeutic techniques with treatment-resistant adolescents. *Psychotherapy, 32,* 131-140.

Stamm, B.H. (Ed.) (1995). *Secondary traumatic stress: Self-care issues for clinicians, researchers, and educators.* Lutherville, MD: Sidran.

Sue, S. (1998). In search of cultural competence in psychotherapy and counseling. *American Psychologist, 53,* 440-448.

Sweet, A. (1995). A theoretical perspective on the clinical use of EMDR. *The Behavior Therapist, 18,* 5-6.

Taylor, S., Thordarson, D. S., Maxfield, L., Fedoroff, I. C., Lovell, K., & Ogrodniczuk, J. (2003). Comparative efficacy, speed, and adverse effects of three PTSD treatments: Exposure therapy, EMDR, and relaxation training. *Journal of Consulting and Clinical Psychology, 71,* 330-338.

Terr, L. (1991). Childhood traumas: An outline and overview. *American Journal of Psychiatry, 148,* 10-20.

van den Hout, M., Muris, P., Salemink, E., & Kindt, M. (2001). Autobiographical memories become less vivid and emotional after eye movements. *British Journal of Clinical Psychology, 40,* 121-130.

van der Kolk, B. A., Pelcovitz, D., Roth, S., Mandel, F. S., McFarlane, A., & Herman, J. L. (1996). Dissociation, somatization, and affect dysregulation: The complexity of adaptation to trauma. *American Journal of Psychiatry, 153,* Festschrift Supplement, 83-93.

Vrana, S. & Lauterbach, D. (1994). Prevalence of traumatic events and post-traumatic psychological symptoms in a nonclinical sample of college students. *Journal of Traumatic Stress, 7,* 289-302.

Wallerstein, J., Corbin, S. B., & Lewis, J. M. (1988). Children of divorce: A ten-year study. In E. M. Heatherington and J. Arasteh (Eds.), *Impact of divorce, single-parenting, and stepparenting on children* (pp. 198-214). Hillsdale, NJ: Earlbaum.

Wierzbicki, M. & Pekarik, G. (1993). A metaanalysis of psychotherapy dropout. *Professional Psychology: Research and Practice, 24,* 190-195.

Winnicott, D.W. (1965). *The maturational processes and the facilitating environment.* New York: International Universities.

Index

Page numbers followed by the letter "b" indicate boxed material and those followed by the letter "f" indicate figures.

THE HAWORTH MALTREATMENT AND TRAUMA PRESS®
Robert A. Geffner, PhD
Senior Editor

THE SOCIALLY SKILLED CHILD MOLESTER: DIFFERENTIATING THE GUILTY FROM THE FALSELY ACCUSED by Carla van Dam. (2006).

A SAFE PLACE TO GROW: A GROUP TREATMENT MANUAL FOR CHILDREN IN CONFLICTED, VIOLENT, AND SEPARATING HOMES by Vivienne Roseby, Janet Johnston, Bettina Gentner, and Erin Moore. (2005). "This superb book captures the suffering, the bewilderment, and the hypervigilance of children who have witnessed parental fighting or have themselves been victims of violence, providing the clinician with new ways to restore the developmental processes that have been disrupted in these children and their families." *Judith Wallerstein, PhD, Divorce Researcher, Author of* The Unexpected Legacy of Divorce; *Founder of the Judith Wallerstein Center for the Family in Transition*

ON THE GROUND AFTER SEPTEMBER 11: MENTAL HEALTH RESPONSES AND PRACTICAL KNOWLEDGE GAINED edited by Yael Danieli and Robert L. Dingman. (2005). "A must-read for disaster planners as well as the many agencies that respond to large-scale mass fatality events. The variety of experiences shared prove the need for close collaboration and coordination before an event occurs in order to initiate and manage an effective response." *Dusty Bowenkamp, RN, CTS, Senior Associate (Ret.), American Red Cross, Disaster Mental Health Services*

CHILD TRAUMA HANDBOOK: A GUIDE FOR HELPING TRAUMA-EXPOSED CHILDREN AND ADOLESCENTS by Ricky Greenwald. (2005). "This is a fascinating book on how to respectfully approach and treat traumatized children. But it is so much more; it shows how to build on underlying health and strengths in both children and their caretakers. It is an empowering book and a well of clinical wisdom in a user-friendly step-by-step frame." *Atle Dyregrov, PhD, Founder, Center for Crisis Psychology, Bergen, Norway*

DEPRESSION IN NEW MOTHERS: CAUSES, CONSEQUENCES, AND TREATMENT ALTERNATIVES by Kathleen A. Kendall-Tackett. (2005). "Without a doubt, this book is a must-read for anyone working with childbearing women. The mothers we serve deserve nothing less than knowledgeable, prepared practitioners." *Karin Cadwell, PhD, RN, FAAN, IBCLC, Faculty, Healthy Children Project, East Sandwich, Massachusetts; Adjunct Faculty, The Union Institute & University, Cincinnati, Ohio*

EFFECTS OF AND INTERVENTIONS FOR CHILDHOOD TRAUMA FROM INFANCY THROUGH ADOLESCENCE: PAIN UNSPEAKABLE by Sandra B. Hutchison. (2005). "Insightful, provocative, informative, and resourceful. This book needs to be in the hands of all professionals working with children, preparting to work with children, or considering work with children. It illustrates the many faces of trauma and illuminates the many responses of children to trauma." *Osofo Calvin Banks, MDiv, Founder and Facilitator, Sesa Woruban Center for Spiritual Development; Certified Supervisor, Association for Clinical and Pastoral Education, Inc.*

MOTHER-DAUGHTER INCEST: A GUIDE FOR HELPING PROFESSIONALS by Beverly A. Ogilvie. (2004). "Beverly A. Ogilvie has succeeded in writing what will become the definitive resource for therapists working with mother-daughter incest....This book will be an invaluable tool for anyone working with this population." *Gina M. Pallotta, PhD, Licensed Psychologist; Associate Professor of Psychology and Clinical Graduate Director, California State University, Stanislaus*

MUNCHAUSEN BY PROXY: IDENTIFICATION, INTERVENTION, AND CASE MANAGEMENT by Louisa J. Lasher and Mary S. Sheridan. (2004). "This book is an excellent resource for professionals from all disciplines who may be confronted with this misunderstood disorder....This book is a must for every professional involved in MBP investigations." *Larry C. Brubaker, MA, FBI Special Agent (Retired)*

SCHIZOPHRENIA: INNOVATIONS IN DIAGNOSIS AND TREATMENT by Colin A. Ross. (2004). "Well-documented and clearly explained ... has hugely significant implications for our diagnostic system and for how severely disturbed people are understood and treated." *John Read, PhD, Editor,* Models of Madness: Psychological, Social, and Biological Approaches to Schizophrenia; *Director of Clinical Psychology, The University of Auckland, New Zealand*

REBUILDING ATTACHMENTS WITH TRAUMATIZED CHILDREN: HEALING FROM LOSSES, VIOLENCE, ABUSE, AND NEGLECT by Richard Kagan. (2004). "Dr. Richard Kagan, a recognized expert in working with traumatized children, has written a truly impressive book. Not only does the book contain a wealth of information for understanding the complex issues faced by traumatized youngsters, but it also offers specific interventions that can be used to help these children and their caregivers become more hopeful and resilient. . . . I am certain that this book will be read and reread by professionals engaged in improving the lives of at-risk youth." *Robert Brooks, PhD, Faculty, Harvard Medical School and author of* Raising Resilient Children *and* The Power of Resilience

PSYCHOLOGICAL TRAUMA AND THE DEVELOPING BRAIN: NEUROLOGICALLY BASED INTERVENTIONS FOR TROUBLED CHILDREN by Phyllis T. Stien and Joshua C. Kendall. (2003). "Stien and Kendall provide us with a great service. In this clearly written and important book, they synthesize a wealth of crucial information that links childhood trauma to brain abnormalities and subsequent mental illness. Equally important, they show us how the trauma also affects the child's social and intellectual development. I recommend this book to all clinicians and administrators." *Charles L. Whitfield, MD, Author of* The Truth About Depression *and* The Truth About Mental Illness

CHILD MALTREATMENT RISK ASSESSMENTS: AN EVALUATION GUIDE by Sue Righthand, Bruce Kerr, and Kerry Drach. (2003). "This book is essential reading for clinicians and forensic examiners who see cases involving issues related to child maltreatment. The authors have compiled an impressive critical survey of the relevant research on child maltreatment. Their material is well organized into sections on definitions, impact, risk assessment, and risk management. This book represents a giant step toward promoting evidence-based evaluations, treatment, and testimony." *Diane H. Schetky, MD, Professor of Psychiatry, University of Vermont College of Medicine*

SIMPLE AND COMPLEX POST-TRAUMATIC STRESS DISORDER: STRATEGIES FOR COMPREHENSIVE TREATMENT IN CLINICAL PRACTICE edited by Mary Beth Williams and John F. Sommer Jr. (2002). "A welcome addition to the literature on treating survivors of traumatic events, this volume possesses all the ingredients necessary for even the experienced clinician to master the management of patients with PTSD." *Terence M. Keane, PhD, Chief, Psychology Service, VA Boston Healthcare System; Professor and Vice Chair of Research in Psychiatry, Boston University School of Medicine*

FOR LOVE OF COUNTRY: CONFRONTING RAPE AND SEXUAL HARASSMENT IN THE U.S. MILITARY by T. S. Nelson. (2002). "Nelson brings an important message—that the absence of current media attention doesn't mean the problem has gone away; that only decisive action by military leadership at all levels can break the cycle of repeated traumatization; and that the failure to do so is, as Nelson puts it, a 'power failure'—a refusal to exert positive leadership at all levels to stop violent individuals from using the worst power imaginable." *Chris Lombardi, Correspondent, Women's E-News, New York City*

THE INSIDERS: A MAN'S RECOVERY FROM TRAUMATIC CHILDHOOD ABUSE by Robert Blackburn Knight. (2002). "An important book. . . . Fills a gap in the literature about healing from childhood sexual abuse by allowing us to hear, in undiluted terms, about one man's history and journey of recovery." *Amy Pine, MA, LMFT, psychotherapist and co-founder, Survivors Healing Center, Santa Cruz, California*

WE ARE NOT ALONE: A GUIDEBOOK FOR HELPING PROFESSIONALS AND PARENTS SUPPORTING ADOLESCENT VICTIMS OF SEXUAL ABUSE by Jade Christine Angelica. (2002). "Encourages victims and their families to participate in the system in an effort to heal from their victimization, seek justice, and hold offenders accountable for their crimes. An exceedingly vital training tool." *Janet Fine, MS, Director, Victim Witness Assistance Program and Children's Advocacy Center, Suffolk County District Attorney's Office, Boston*

WE ARE NOT ALONE: A TEENAGE GIRL'S PERSONAL ACCOUNT OF INCEST FROM DISCLOSURE THROUGH PROSECUTION AND TREATMENT by Jade Christine Angelica. (2002). "A valuable resource for teens who have been sexually abused and their parents. With compassion and eloquent prose, Angelica walks people through the criminal justice system—from disclosure to final outcome." *Kathleen Kendall-Tackett, PhD, Research Associate, Family Research Laboratory, University of New Hampshire, Durham*

WE ARE NOT ALONE: A TEENAGE BOY'S PERSONAL ACCOUNT OF CHILD SEXUAL ABUSE FROM DISCLOSURE THROUGH PROSECUTION AND TREATMENT by Jade Christine Angelica. (2002). "Inspires us to work harder to meet kids' needs, answer their questions, calm their fears, and protect them from their abusers and the system, which is often not designed to respond to them in a language they understand." *Kevin L. Ryle, JD, Assistant District Attorney, Middlesex, Massachusetts*

GROWING FREE: A MANUAL FOR SURVIVORS OF DOMESTIC VIOLENCE by Wendy Susan Deaton and Michael Hertica. (2001). "This is a necessary book for anyone who is scared and starting to think about what it would take to 'grow free.'. . . Very helpful for friends and relatives of a person in a domestic violence situation. I recommend it highly." *Colleen Friend, LCSW, Field Work Consultant, UCLA Department of Social Welfare, School of Public Policy & Social Research*

A THERAPIST'S GUIDE TO GROWING FREE: A MANUAL FOR SURVIVORS OF DOMESTIC VIOLENCE by Wendy Susan Deaton and Michael Hertica. (2001). "An excellent synopsis of the theories and research behind the manual." *Beatrice Crofts Yorker, RN, JD, Professor of Nursing, Georgia State University, Decatur*

PATTERNS OF CHILD ABUSE: HOW DYSFUNCTIONAL TRANSACTIONS ARE REPLICATED IN INDIVIDUALS, FAMILIES, AND THE CHILD WELFARE SYSTEM by Michael Karson. (2001). "No one interested in what may well be the major public health epidemic of our time in terms of its long-term consequences for our society can afford to pass up the opportunity to read this enlightening work." *Howard Wolowitz, PhD, Professor Emeritus, Psychology Department, University of Michigan, Ann Arbor*

IDENTIFYING CHILD MOLESTERS: PREVENTING CHILD SEXUAL ABUSE BY RECOGNIZING THE PATTERNS OF THE OFFENDERS by Carla van Dam. (2000). "The definitive work on the subject. . . . Provides parents and others with the tools to recognize when and how to intervene." *Roger W. Wolfe, MA, Co-Director, N. W. Treatment Associates, Seattle, Washington*

POLITICAL VIOLENCE AND THE PALESTINIAN FAMILY: IMPLICATIONS FOR MENTAL HEALTH AND WELL-BEING by Vivian Khamis. (2000). "A valuable book . . . a pioneering work that fills a glaring gap in the study of Palestinian society." *Elia Zureik, Professor of Sociology, Queens University, Kingston, Ontario, Canada*

STOPPING THE VIOLENCE: A GROUP MODEL TO CHANGE MEN'S ABUSIVE ATTITUDES AND BEHAVIORS by David J. Decker. (1999). "A concise and thorough manual to assist clinicians in learning the causes and dynamics of domestic violence." *Joanne Kittel, MSW, LICSW, Yachats, Oregon*

STOPPING THE VIOLENCE: A GROUP MODEL TO CHANGE MEN'S ABUSIVE ATTITUDES AND BEHAVIORS, THE CLIENT WORKBOOK by David J. Decker. (1999).

BREAKING THE SILENCE: GROUP THERAPY FOR CHILDHOOD SEXUAL ABUSE, A PRACTITIONER'S MANUAL by Judith A. Margolin. (1999). "This book is an extremely valuable and well-written resource for all therapists working with adult survivors of child sexual abuse." *Esther Deblinger, PhD, Associate Professor of Clinical Psychiatry, University of Medicine and Dentistry of New Jersey School of Osteopathic Medicine*

"I NEVER TOLD ANYONE THIS BEFORE": MANAGING THE INITIAL DISCLOSURE OF SEXUAL ABUSE RECOLLECTIONS by Janice A. Gasker. (1999). "Discusses the elements needed to create a safe, therapeutic environment and offers the practitioner a number of useful strategies for responding appropriately to client disclosure." *Roberta G. Sands, PhD, Associate Professor, University of Pennsylvania School of Social Work*

FROM SURVIVING TO THRIVING: A THERAPIST'S GUIDE TO STAGE II RECOVERY FOR SURVIVORS OF CHILDHOOD ABUSE by Mary Bratton. (1999). "A must read for all, including survivors. Bratton takes a lifelong debilitating disorder and unravels its intricacies in concise, succinct, and understandable language." *Phillip A. Whitner, PhD, Sr. Staff Counselor, University Counseling Center, The University of Toledo, Ohio*

SIBLING ABUSE TRAUMA: ASSESSMENT AND INTERVENTION STRATEGIES FOR CHILDREN, FAMILIES, AND ADULTS by John V. Caffaro and Allison Conn-Caffaro. (1998). "One area that has almost consistently been ignored in the research and writing on child maltreatment is the area of sibling abuse. This book is a welcome and required addition to the developing literature on abuse." *Judith L. Alpert, PhD, Professor of Applied Psychology, New York University*

BEARING WITNESS: VIOLENCE AND COLLECTIVE RESPONSIBILITY by Sandra L. Bloom and Michael Reichert. (1998). "A totally convincing argument. . . . Demands careful study by all elected representatives, the clergy, the mental health and medical professions, representatives of the media, and all those unwittingly involved in this repressive perpetuation and catastrophic global problem." *Harold I. Eist, MD, Past President, American Psychiatric Association*

TREATING CHILDREN WITH SEXUALLY ABUSIVE BEHAVIOR PROBLEMS: GUIDELINES FOR CHILD AND PARENT INTERVENTION by Jan Ellen Burton, Lucinda A. Rasmussen, Julie Bradshaw, Barbara J. Christopherson, and Steven C. Huke. (1998). "An extremely readable book that is well-documented and a mine of valuable 'hands on' information. . . . This is a book that all those who work with sexually abusive children or want to work with them must read." *Sharon K. Araji, PhD, Professor of Sociology, University of Alaska, Anchorage*

THE LEARNING ABOUT MYSELF (LAMS) PROGRAM FOR AT-RISK PARENTS: LEARNING FROM THE PAST—CHANGING THE FUTURE by Verna Rickard. (1998). "This program should be a part of the resource materials of every mental health professional trusted with the responsibility of working with 'at-risk' parents." *Terry King, PhD, Clinical Psychologist, Federal Bureau of Prisons, Catlettsburg, Kentucky*

THE LEARNING ABOUT MYSELF (LAMS) PROGRAM FOR AT-RISK PARENTS: HANDBOOK FOR GROUP PARTICIPANTS by Verna Rickard. (1998). "Not only is the LAMS program designed to be educational and build skills for future use, it is also fun!" *Martha Morrison Dore, PhD, Associate Professor of Social Work, Columbia University, New York*

BRIDGING WORLDS: UNDERSTANDING AND FACILITATING ADOLESCENT RECOVERY FROM THE TRAUMA OF ABUSE by Joycee Kennedy and Carol McCarthy. (1998). "An extraordinary survey of the history of child neglect and abuse in America. . . . A wonderful teaching tool at the university level, but should be required reading in high schools as well." *Florabel Kinsler, PhD, BCD, LCSW, Licensed Clinical Social Worker, Los Angeles, California*

CEDAR HOUSE: A MODEL CHILD ABUSE TREATMENT PROGRAM by Bobbi Kendig with Clara Lowry. (1998). "Kendig and Lowry truly . . . realize the saying that we are our brothers' keepers. Their spirit permeates this volume, and that spirit of caring is what always makes the difference for people in painful situations." *Hershel K. Swinger, PhD, Clinical Director, Children's Institute International, Los Angeles, California*

SEXUAL, PHYSICAL, AND EMOTIONAL ABUSE IN OUT-OF-HOME CARE: PREVENTION SKILLS FOR AT-RISK CHILDREN by Toni Cavanagh Johnson and Associates. (1997). "Professionals who make dispositional decisions or who are related to out-of-home care for children could benefit from reading and following the curriculum of this book with children in placements." *Issues in Child Abuse Accusations*